TWENTY-FIRST-CENTURY AMERICAN PLAYWRIGHTS

The early years of the twenty-first century saw several losses for the American theatre but also marked the emergence of a new generation of exciting playwrights. In this book, Christopher Bigsby explores the work of nine of these developing talents and the importance of issues including race, gender and politics for their writing. Increasingly, these new figures are gaining their reputations not on Broadway but in small theatres and towns or even abroad, bringing fresh and diverse perspectives to contemporary American drama. With a focus on female writers and on issues of personal and public identity in contemporary society, this volume investigates the styles and techniques these playwrights favour, the themes they embrace and their role in a changing America and a changing world.

CHRISTOPHER BIGSBY is Professor of American Studies at the University of East Anglia and a fellow of the Royal Society of Arts and the Royal Society of Literature. He has published more than fifty books, with his recent titles including *The Cambridge Companion to Modern American Culture* (Cambridge 2006), *The Cambridge Companion to August Wilson* (Cambridge 2007) and *Viewing America: Twenty-First-Century Television Drama* (Cambridge 2013).

T0384871

TWENTY-FIRST-CENTURY AMERICAN PLAYWRIGHTS

CHRISTOPHER BIGSBY

University of East Anglia

CAMBRIDGE
UNIVERSITY PRESS

CAMBRIDGE
UNIVERSITY PRESS

University Printing House, Cambridge CB2 8BS, United Kingdom

One Liberty Plaza, 20th Floor, New York, NY 10006, USA

477 Williamstown Road, Port Melbourne, VIC 3207, Australia

314–321, 3rd Floor, Plot 3, Splendor Forum, Jasola District Centre,
New Delhi – 110025, India

79 Anson Road, #06-04/06, Singapore 079906

Cambridge University Press is part of the University of Cambridge.

It furthers the University's mission by disseminating knowledge in the pursuit of
education, learning and research at the highest international levels of excellence.

www.cambridge.org
Information on this title: www.cambridge.org/9781108419581
DOI: 10.1017/9781108303620

First published 2018

Printed in the United Kingdom by Clays, St Ives plc

A catalogue record for this publication is available from the British Library.

ISBN 978-1-108-41958-1 Hardback
ISBN 978-1-108-41144-8 Paperback

Contents

Introduction   *page* 1

1   Annie Baker   6

2   Frances Ya-Chu Cowhig   29

3   Katori Hall   48

4   Amy Herzog   73

5   Tracy Letts   92

6   David Lindsay-Abaire   120

7   Lynn Nottage   142

8   Sarah Ruhl   167

9   Naomi Wallace   194

    Index   221

Introduction

As a Fulbright student in the Midwest in the early 1960s, I attended a student production of Edward Albee's *The Zoo Story*. I was so impressed that, with others, I drove 120 miles to see a road production of *Who's Afraid of Virginia Woolf?* That lit a touchpaper. A few years later, I would write a book about Albee, and, in the 1980s, *A Critical Introduction to Twentieth-Century American Drama* originally planned as a single volume but that rapidly, and somewhat to the alarm of Cambridge University Press, expanded to three. This, after all, was when the American theatre came into its own, and it merited extensive treatment. Later came *Modern American Drama*, first published in 1990 and revised in 2000, and then *Contemporary American Playwrights*, which celebrated the work of a selection of writers (John Guare, Tina Howe, Tony Kushner, Richard Nelson, Marsha Norman, David Rabe, Paula Vogel, Wendy Wasserstein and Lanford Wilson).

As is apparent, despite myself coming from a country with a powerful presence in world drama, I was drawn to the achievement of American playwrights. Why? There was something about their stylistic inventiveness, their sense that the private was invested in the public and the public in the private. There was often a sexual directness that had been absent from the British theatre, the latter subject to censorship by the delightfully named Lord Chamberlain until 1968. Its characters ranged across the social spectrum in a way that for long, and for the most part, had not been true of the English theatre and usually without the ideological pressure of a stratified society acutely attuned to class differentiations.

In a fluid society it registered shifts in the tectonic plates of the culture. For many years, indeed, theatregoers in Britain eagerly awaited new plays from America as Americans had once greeted the latest work of Charles Dickens.

Later I wrote a biography of Arthur Miller, a writer I had long admired and who had become a friend, though in truth he was unsure whether he wanted such a biography and I was unsure whether I could write it. He died in 2005, the year another powerful voice was stilled, that of August Wilson. Wendy Wasserstein died the following year, Lanford Wilson in 2011, Edward Albee in 2016 and Sam Shepard in 2017. Happily, other careers have continued, but in this book I want to examine the achievement of some of those who have emerged since the turn of the century.

Constraints of space (Cambridge University Press by now being wise to my tendency to write multi-volume works) mean that many significant writers have had to be omitted. Even to name some of them would invite complaints of further omissions. What follows, then, are considerations of just nine dramatists. These are all writers whose careers have substantially begun after the millennium, although one or two had started to write in the previous decade. I began with no agenda, and hence it came as something of a surprise when I realised that seven of the nine writers included here are women, two of whom are African-American and one Chinese – or more correctly Taiwanese – and Boston-Irish. This is not intended to reflect a theatrical demographic, although that has, indeed, been changing, as has the route to success, relying as it often does today, for better or worse, on staged readings, play development, a serendipitous journey from small venue to Off-Broadway and then – perhaps but only perhaps – Broadway, which still exerts its siren call, even as it is elsewhere that writers are born and theatres risk the new.

This was no less true of Lin-Manuel Miranda's musicals, which lie outside the scope of this book. *In the Heights*, which features characters whose origins lie in the Dominican Republic and Cuba, began at Wesleyan University before moving to the National Music Theatre Conference at the Eugene O'Neill Theatre Center in Waterford and then Off-Broadway, opening on Broadway in 2008. He followed it with the hugely successful hip-hop musical *Hamilton*, first staged at the Public Theatre in 2015 before transferring to Broadway that same year. Although born in New York, Miranda is of Puerto Rican heritage, and the musical itself retells history through actors, singers and performers drawn from various races and ethnicities. Revolution is not only a subject but also the substance of a work that celebrates diversity and has radically redefined the musical.

For Lin-Manuel Miranda, *Hamilton* has proved financially no less than critically rewarding, but this cannot be said for the generality of playwrights, however critically celebrated. Commissions are hard to find and not over-generous, and playwrights are lucky if they are paid for pre-production – lucky, too, if they have health care, if their plays run for more than a few months or are picked up for productions in subsequent years. There are theatres that make space for new plays, but second plays often fall outside the funding remit of the well-named not-for-profit theatres.

However central the arts are to a culture, to a nation's sense of itself and to its international reputation, those who work in art, music, the theatre and, indeed, the novel are often underpaid even as their visibility may lead people to assume otherwise. The theatre is particularly perilous, with most actors unemployed at any given time and most directors likewise. As to playwrights, the major names give a false picture. Committing to theatre is an act of courage or foolhardiness. The amazing thing is that there are those who do so, thereby enriching if not themselves then all those who enter a theatre to see the imagination made flesh, to engage with a living art.

The writers whose work I explore come from New York (Lynn Nottage), New Jersey (Amy Herzog) and Massachusetts (Annie Baker and David Lindsay-Abaire), from Pennsylvania (Frances Ya-Chu Cowhig), Illinois (Sarah Ruhl), Kentucky (Naomi Wallace), Tennessee (Katori Hall) and Oklahoma (Tracy Letts). Interestingly, for several of these playwrights (and others not featured in this book, such as Bruce Norris and Christopher Shinn), British productions have proved significant, although most began in small, sometimes very small, US theatres, with initial support from companies specifically dedicated to providing a stage for new writing. The Actors Theatre of Louisville in Kentucky is one example, but there are many more, often distant from New York. The very intimacy of these theatres has been used to effect by writers who have frequently invited audiences to become confederate, happy to make the mechanisms of theatre visible and confident that those who watch bring their own imaginations to the party.

For some, the transformations of theatre become a metaphor for psychological, social and even political change, although as Bruce Norris remarked, 'If you really want to change the world, and you go into theatre as a way to do that, I feel you've chosen the most inefficient means possible.' For him, theatre was remote from the experience of ordinary people:

> If you slice the audience for theatre, which is already 1% of the audience for all other entertainment, you take that 1% and slice it down to the audience that actually attends plays that are, first of all, new plays, and then cut it down to those who would actually be interested in so-called controversial new plays for whatever reason . . . It's almost like a tiny club . . . for a strange and useless obsolete art form . . . if the most important work of theatre goes unheard by hard-working citizens of the U.S., what does that say about how important theatre is?'[1]

It is true that many more visit the cinema than walk into a theatre (1.3 billion in 2016), but the top films from 2006 to 2016 were all awash with CGI, based on a theme park ride (*Pirates of the Caribbean*), products of the Marvel comics franchise, digital animation or *Star Wars* spin-offs, and nearly half were rated PG-13. At the same time, nearly twice as many people attended theatre as National Football League games (in 2015, 17.5 million), while those registered as 'very interested' in, presumably as opposed to attending, the National Hockey League in 2016 numbered 13.44 million. In the United Kingdom too, more people go to the theatre than Premier League soccer (22 million versus 13 million in 2012). Theatre, then, is not such a minority activity – evidently not *such* a useless and obsolete art form. It also has a life. In 2016, just over sixty years after it opened, *A View from the Bridge* remained the hottest ticket in town and even then was less popular worldwide than *The Crucible*,which always seemed relevant no matter when or where produced. Perhaps these are exceptions. Not many playwrights today can thrive on royalties as they once did. Instead they turn to film, television or universities where they can mentor the next generation while receiving a regular income and pension benefits.

Several of the writers in this book come from small towns with little on offer in the way of theatre, some finding inspiration at school or university where they experienced encouragement from playwrights working there, including Paula Vogel, John Guare, Richard Nelson and Tony Kushner. Some began as actors – in the case of Tracy Letts, continuing a double career. One or two are early in their careers, earlier than several I might have written about. Others are now fixtures in the American theatre, winning major prizes at home and abroad. They write in a variety of styles, ranging from farce, comedy and the absurd to realism, their prose lyrical or brutal, the America they summon varied.

This is not a period in which there are dominant voices, no O'Neill, Miller, Williams, who in a mere eleven years, from 1945 to 1956, produced a series of classics of the

American theatre that have not been equalled. Such periods are rare in the history of not only American but world theatre. What there are, are writers from a wide range of backgrounds who together are in the process of defining America in the twenty-first century, sometimes choosing to invoke the past as guide and warning, sometimes confronting present realities, all seeing in the theatre an art in which actor and audience inhabit the same time, breathe the same air, see on the stage and reflect in themselves a sense of community always under threat but always yearned for.

Today, and for nearly two decades now, drama has found a home on American television, the new freedoms of which – consequent in large part on the significance of changes in technology and the emergence of new platforms with business models that no longer depend on Nielsen ratings – have liberated show runners and writers from financial oversight and editorial interventions. The result has been a plethora of powerful and original works that have engaged with American realities and myths. Television, however, will always lack what the theatre can offer: a place where, on a nightly basis, disparate individuals come together to share experiences, in real time, and connect directly to actors attuned to their responses.

There is a ceremony to theatre, from the journey to the venue, the tickets required for entry, the attendant ushers, the programme notes, the audience members aware of their co-presence, lit as they assemble as though they are indeed part of what is to follow. The apparatus of theatre is on display – the curtain, the lights, the loudspeakers to channel sound effects. Even the most realistic of plays never eliminate our awareness of the artifice, but that, as Arthur Miller observed, is the paradox. This is not film or television in which we, the viewer, may respond but those we watch are insulated, even now filming on some exotic location or posed against a green screen in an anonymous space. In theatre, we are told we are in fair Verona and collude in that assertion, not even requiring scenery to prompt us. At the age of eighty, Glenda Jackson, after twenty-three years as a member of parliament, stepped back onto the stage, a woman playing the role of King Lear in a performance that audiences and critics alike had no difficulty embracing. We know that actors have another self, other selves, but for the moment, they are what they simulate, until simulation fades to transparency and they become those they inhabit, and we respond as to that person, empathy being what is required of actor and audience alike if also the subtext of drama. As Miller noted,

Theater does, indeed, lie, fabricating everything from the storm's roar to the fake lark's song, from the actor's calculated laughter to his nightly flood of tears. And the actor lies; but with all the spontaneity that careful calculation can lend him, he may nevertheless construct a vision of some important truth about the human condition that opens us to a new understanding of ourselves. In the end, we call a work of art trivial when it illuminates little beyond its own devices.[2]

For Miller, what distinguishes a culture is its art. Part of what survives of past societies, part of what we value, lies in 'a handful of plays, essays, carved stones, and some strokes of paint on paper or the rock cave wall'.[3] In a world, he suggests, in which performance has permeated many aspects of experience – most notably, he laments, the political realm – the playwright and the actor may forge an alliance to capture some essential truth about their society and those who constitute it.

Not every work of art, not every play, speaks an essential truth. Some are failed endeavours, some merely meretricious, and a bad play is less bearable than a bad film, perhaps because we have invested so much – and not merely financially – in the experience. The actor who walks onto a stage is vulnerable, but then so are those who do more than watch. Audiences at a play are not viewers. They are participants and hence sensitive when the contract is not observed. At their best, though, plays have the capacity not merely to move – a pop song can do as much – but to provoke a shock of recognition, to enter into a conversation with those who look for some insight into private and public concerns. Plays can register tremors in the individual psyche or a society whose contradictions, denials and illusions can be exposed or explored in the theatre as they are often not in the passing traffic of social affairs.

What follows in this book is an examination of the work of a series of playwrights who, of course, differ from one another in their objectives, their aesthetics and their approach to the theatre, its function and possibilities. They each, after all, stand on their own ground. What unites them, however, is the sense that theatre has a unique ability to engage with audiences in search of some insight into the way we live, move and have our being for the passage of an hour or two, coming together, moment by moment, to experience the transformations implicit in the form, to witness how words become manifest, how artifice can, at its best, be the midwife of truth.

Notes

1 Tim Sanford and Bruce Norris, 'Interview', *Playwrights Horizons*, n.d. www
  .playwrightshorizons.org/shows/trailers/tim-sanford-and-bruce-norris
2 Ibid.
3 Arthur Miller, *On Politics and the Art of Acting* (New York, 2001), pp. 83–4.

1

Annie Baker

I've seen people destroy their plays, their beautiful and mysterious plays, because they're worried the audience isn't going to get something, so then they make it really explicit and obnoxious. I really respect my audiences and I don't feel like they need to have things explained to them.[1]

– Annie Baker

Graham Greene once said of *A Burnt Out Case* that he hated it, finding it muddled and shapeless. Of *Our Man in Havana* he offered the opinion that 'it stinks'. Perhaps he was expecting disagreement. It is more likely that they seemed to him to fall short of some unacknowledged sense of perfection or that, like many writers, he was no longer sure what it was he had produced. Annie Baker is her own harshest critic with a tendency to distance herself from plays she later judges disappointing. Asked about an early work, she refused to answer because 'I hate *Body Awareness* and wrote it when I was 25 . . . I don't think it's a good play. I think it's pretty cheeseball'.[2] One of her best known, and best received, plays, *The Flick*, garnered similar treatment. Essentially, she wants to move on, try something new, sensing that she might have settled for less than she should have. Even after winning a Pulitzer Prize, her first response was that she could do better, like a runner breaking the tape first but regretting that her time fell short of a record.

For some audiences, she could be disappointing in a different sense, as her plays extended in length, including pauses that irritated those looking for plot momentum. Language, in Annie Baker's plays, is not fully transitive. It contains the lacunae, phatic communion, blank silences of ordinary speech even as it is carefully crafted. The British poet Lavinia Greenlaw has said that 'the most powerful experience of the real can be the most contrived'.[3]

The fact is that Baker can urge audiences out of their comfort zones as she takes herself into territory that comes into view as she is creating it.

I am slow and before I start writing a play I take notes for years. I have about a hundred pages of notes on my computer about every single play I have written. It is just details like, he went to this summer camp and this thing happened to him when he was a baby, crazy super specific details about their lives and once that document is long that is the template for the play. I then know everything about that person and I put them in a situation and see what they do. There is very little planning about what is going to happen in the play . . . My plays are very psychological but I try not to be overly psychological while writing them . . . My fear of therapy for so many years was that by talking about my childhood I [would think] that's why I couldn't commit to that thing but actually I would be further away from self knowledge because the moment you can pin something down like that it is probably wrong . . . I think a play is going well when a character does something I didn't know they'd do and I would never have predicted they would do.[4]

There can be something disturbing in her work as characters are revealed in their insecurities, their identities under pressure. What is denied, evaded, has a way of edging to the surface. Relationships are liable to offer comfort and threat in equal proportions, silences being charged with meanings not confronted. She deals in those never quite in command of themselves or the world they inhabit, often situated in places that fail to offer the security they seek. In *The Flick*, they are like Plato's philosophers responding to the flickering images cast not on a cave wall but a cinema screen in a building itself in a state of disrepair. Reality can be hard to grasp not least because her characters' needs, desires and anxieties shape their sense of it. In *John*, the world is mysterious because the everyday carries a threat difficult to define – not merely psychological but metaphysical as she dabbles with the gothic, itself a genre in which the repressed returns, internal fractures extending out into the world, the merely imagined taking concrete form. There is a tension in her work, her characters walking the edge, assured statements always seeming to contain a disturbing doubt. Looking for trust her characters are liable to find it denied or fragile, wishes seldom being granted as humour fills the spaces left open by a sense of alienation never quite grasped.

Annie Baker was raised in Amherst, Massachusetts, once home to Emily Dickinson, whose oblique poems for the most part stayed in a drawer (although not wholly by her choice), and also to Robert Frost, a poet who tried his hand at drama. The town is named for Jeffrey Amherst, who distinguished himself by proposing that smallpox-infused blankets should be used to eradicate Native Americans, whom he regarded as an execrable race. It is a college town, and Annie Baker's father worked as an administrator for the five colleges in the Connecticut River Pioneer Valley. Her mother was a therapist in a clinic in Northampton, working with abused children while studying for her PhD in psychology before becoming a teacher at Keene College in New Hampshire, until 2014. Annie Baker bears her mother's maiden name, while her older brother bears his father's last name.

Her parents, one Catholic, one Jewish, had met at a commune and divorced when Baker was six years old. She was raised by her mother and felt less disturbed by the divorce than by having to deal with those subsequently introduced to her as potential stepparents, even as, in turn, they disappeared. Her parents' multiple marriages later left her 'really depressed . . . immobilized by regret and self-hatred'.[5] With her psychologist mother, she has explained, she spent every evening dissecting their emotions; with her father, she read Oscar Wilde plays out loud.

Amherst, she has said, was a weird mix of people, including the pseudo-homeless. She was 'lonely and sad, and didn't have anything to do . . . I was crazy, angry and thought I was smarter than anybody else'. At ten she wanted to be a novelist, being an avid reader of Anne Tyler. At thirteen, she was an enthusiast for films, seeing the not very age-appropriate *Pulp Fiction* and covering her bedroom walls with film posters. She was also, though, fascinated by theatre, that same year being taken by her father to see a production of Richard Foreman's *Permanent Brain Damage*. Theatre, she has explained, became her religion in high school, the thing that got her up in the morning. She wrote her first play at sixteen. Titled *Taking Orders*, it was about the relationship between a daughter and her father. She submitted it to a play festival at her school, only to rush to take it back. In high school she acted, although with no ambition to become an actor. She appeared in *The Merchant of Venice* at twelve (they cut her only kiss, except once in rehearsals) and *Hamlet* at fifteen, playing the role of Horatio. She was, she confesses, 'a theatre nerd'. In her senior year, she was Adelaide in *Guys and Dolls*, choreographing her own dances and keeping a journal in character. She also wrote short stories without showing them to anybody. She has confessed to hating everything she wrote at that age, the beginning of that self-criticism that would characterise her career.

She was, she has said, 'raised by hippie feminists in a hippie town, with a lot of identity politics woven into education. As little girls, we were supposed to talk about a woman who inspired us and I wouldn't... I wouldn't name a woman and it was really important to me that I didn't have to'. It was a feeling that would later be reflected in *Body Awareness*, which she sees as in part 'investigating the hypocrisies of the modern-day feminist'.[6] She confessed to hanging around at age seventeen with thirty-year-olds who had drug problems and wrote their own music. She was 'nerdy with glasses'[7] and had no particular ambitions, reconciled to having a series of jobs. The word 'nerdy' recurs, itself suggesting an element of self-criticism or perhaps merely self-awareness.

Also at age seventeen, she recorded and transcribed people's conversations, even then seemingly fascinated by the language she overheard. Later, teaching at NYU, she would say, 'I can hear my students' voices through just the way they listen... I always tell them, if you lose track of your voice as a writer, go back, eavesdrop, write down everything you hear, and that's it. That's you listening to the world.'[8] She herself would read early drafts of plays aloud 'because it's so important to me that I capture the cadences of painful, ordinary speech, and it's hard to tell if it's believable when it's on the page... I record myself reading all the parts and sitting through all the pauses, and then I listen to it a bunch of times. If I can hear the writer writing, like if there's thinly-disguised exposition or a nudge to the audience or some kind of obvious point made, I go back and change it.'[9]

She loved reading and art and wanted to leave her small town to go to New York City where her father lived, see films and work in the theatre, having had an impressive drama teacher at school. In her freshman year at NYU she worked as stage manager at LaMaMa. At the Tisch School, she studied playwriting, although she later said, 'My plays got much, much worse after I started studying writing seriously at NYU... I became obsessed with Structure... which meant that we started plays that had clear PROTAGONISTS and QUESTS and TURNING POINTS and INSTIGATING EVENTS and THIRD ACT REVERSALS but not one believable or truthful line of dialogue.'

She was resistant to the idea that drama was about the intent of characters. Chekhov interested her because of the vulnerability of characters who were unclear as to their objectives. Indeed, in 2012 she would stage her own adaptation of *Uncle Vanya*. It was not until she was introduced to the plays of Maria Irene Fornes and Caryl Churchill, along with Thomas Mann's *The Magic Mountain*, that she realised there were other possible approaches, something underlined when she took courses at Brooklyn College with the playwright Mac Wellman: 'he had such an insidious and fantastic effect on my writing – he never told me what to do, but in his quiet, glass full way he encouraged me to be a little stranger.'[10]

She did not, however, see herself as a playwright, filling in time after graduation with a series of odd jobs as she was writing. She had, she explained, given up on the idea that anyone would read her work until she submitted an application to the Ensemble Studio Theatre's emerging playwrights group. She was accepted, and that was where she worked on her first play, *Body Awareness*, which found its way to the Off-Broadway Atlantic Theatre Company's Stage 2, a ninety-eight-seat black box theatre, on West 160th Street. The company was founded in 1985 by David Mamet and William H. Macy, an ensemble group dedicated to new writing.

For Henry James, character was action. So it is in the work of Annie Baker, whose plays have an oblique quality. There is something of O'Neill's figures talking past each other, contained within their own privacies yet conscious of the need to reach out. *Body Awareness* is like a seminar in which each of the characters has read a different book. They inhabit their own discrete linguistic worlds. The temptation is to condescend to them, trapped as they seem to be in their own limitations, and yet by degrees they make their demands on our attention. They are in thrall to ideas that have commandeered them, offering a frame to a disordered existence. It is easy to recognise ill-digested theories and fashionable cant, and yet there are moments when they sense the inadequacies of their own rhetoric or are challenged by those whose points of reference differ. It is their vulnerability that compels, although they seem assured of their own interpretation of experience. There is evidence of damage, a limited perspective.

The play, which opened on June 4, 2008, is set in 2005 and takes place in a kitchen and bedroom whose naturalism – 'There's a sink and a stove, a table with chairs, and a bookshelf with a multi-volume set of the OED'[11] – is balanced by instructions that the characters should 'wander freely in and out of the sets during the scene transitions, turning on lights, removing props, etc.' It is set in the small Vermont town of Shirley, the first, it transpired, in a series of plays that came to be known as her Vermont Plays. Shirley, she explained, was 'a combination of Amherst with a bunch of Vermont towns that fascinate me. Vermont fascinates me, period. The remoteness and the self-congratulation and the embracing of diversity and the fear of diversity and the beauty and the good intentions.'[12] The occasion is Body Awareness Week at the local college. The characters are Phyllis, a fierce feminist; her partner, Joyce, a school teacher whose son Jared may or may not have Asperger's; and a visiting artist, Frank, whose speciality is photographing nude women. *Body Awareness* does not advertise itself as a comedy, but in many ways it is, as its characters are caught in their contradictions, occasional bewilderments and confining languages.

It was a play, Baker has explained, that had both an immediate context and its roots in aspects of her family life, albeit transformed. She started writing the play

after this very scary period of self-hatred and crippling depression, and it . . . cheered me up. It was my first Vermont play, and coming up with this imaginary town and its confused residents was not only a real comfort and escape but also an opportunity to forgive – or at least laugh at – myself for being such a flawed human being. The issues in that play that my characters were grappling with were also all issues that I'd watched my mother grapple with while I was growing up . . . At some point during the rehearsals . . . I . . . realized that the play was about me and my mother – if we were a lesbian couple.[13]

The play begins as Phyllis marks the first day of the week on a blackboard and addresses her audience, and hence the play's, setting the agenda for subsequent discussions and the arrival of artists, including Frank, whose own artistic interests are not without a suspect dimension. As the week passes, tensions emerge – between the two women, between Phyllis and Frank and between Joyce and her son, Jared, whose lack of social awareness means that he has a tendency to an embarrassing frankness. It is not simply that his conversations are without grace notes but that he lacks an awareness of the impact of his remarks on others. In a house where body awareness is a point of discussion, he accesses pornographic websites while Frank tempts Joyce to pose for a nude photograph.

Although Joyce and Phyllis are partners, they view the world differently, and there is a tension between them: Joyce is sensitive about her status as a schoolteacher, which Phyllis insists does not make her an academic, lacking, as she does, a PhD. Phyllis may have body awareness but clearly lacks other kinds of awareness.

The same could be said of Jared, who obsesses over etymology (he believes that women will be impressed 'by how much etymology I know') (418), carries an electric toothbrush in his pocket, occasionally turning it on and off, and resists the notion that there is anything wrong with him, particularly that he might be suffering from Asperger's among other things, the evidence for which is his lack of empathy. On the other hand, this is a play in which empathy is something of a rarity. He makes threats of violence, which his mother is evidently used to and which seem never to be preludes to actual assaults. For him, language has its own fascination independent of its meaning and certainly of its effect.

This is a house in which no one drinks anything but milk and water. They eat organic soup. Phyllis is lactose intolerant and insists on getting away from the male gaze, while the words 'body awareness' substitute for eating disorder. Political correctness is enshrined here, although Joyce insists that she and Joyce pride themselves on being 'politically sensitive without being overly PC' (432). 'You're the one who's, like, the language police', (402) Phyllis accuses her partner of being, even though she is equally linguistically sensitive. Likewise, she is anxious to be in tune with politically correct policies, having, Joyce points out, brought an African-American woman to the event who is 'actually part Native American, too, I think', as if she were ticking the necessary social boxes (402). Jared's directness acts as an antidote, in a play in which language becomes subject as well as mechanism.

There is something of an isolato about Jared, but then much the same could be said of the other characters, trapped as they are in their own sensibilities. Indeed, for Joyce her son echoes something of the culture at large: 'America is very strange. We're so focused on independence. It's like, you can't need anybody. You have to be this totally autonomous . . . *person*' (380). With a meeting about self-image and body awareness under-way, there is the potential for a drift towards a degree of narcissism. Perhaps it is not irrelevant that Joyce is a teacher of cultural studies with 'an anthropological perspective' (389).

Joyce, whose father was guilty of some unspecified abuse, had once been married. Phyllis is her first female partner, although it is not a partnership without strains. Frank, the interloping stranger, is not entirely wrong when he observes that 'You really feel like you know each other after three years. But then one day the person says something really weird, and you're like: Do I actually know you? Or are you this total stranger?'(390–1). Joyce nods after the first sentence but fails to respond after the second, having just been taken by surprise by Phyllis's demeaning of her academic status. Frank, indeed, becomes a wedge between the two women. He, like Joyce, had been married to a Jew for ten years, and when he stages an impromptu Shabbat, albeit on the wrong day, Joyce (herself a non-practicing Jew) is enchanted and Phyllis alienated, not least because the ceremony brings tears to Joyce's eyes, reminding her of what was presumably her husband, whose pet name she invokes. Responding to Frank's singing, she says, 'Phyllis never sings. She's too self-conscious.' A stage direction observes that '*Phyllis stares at Joyce.*' (410). Indeed in the course of the play a tension between the two women develops. Phyllis accuses Joyce of flirting with Frank and not fully embracing what she takes to be her sexual identity.

For Phyllis, any man travelling the country taking nude pictures of young women should be eliminated 'from the face of the planet' and must be someone who 'chops women up and buries them in his backyard!' (414). Sensitive to other people's use of language, she has no restraint in her own while recycling jargon as if it were newly minted. When introducing a visiting psychiatrist who specialises in sexology and sex therapy, she begins a lecture of her own about women's identity being 'determined by her onlooker' and the fact that some women are prone to 'exposing and depersonalizing' themselves (420). While claiming to be 'anti-ideology', she is as prescriptive as Jared, even while laughing at his description of a fellow worker as a 'retard', her claimed sensitivity evidently having its boundaries. Her opposition to Frank derives not only from the fact that he photographs naked women and that Joyce wants to pose for him but from the fact that he is a white man and 'This is about POWER' (444).

Body Awareness stages a quartet of characters, none of whom seem to have a secure grasp of relationships or indeed the world they inhabit. Failed marriages, ambivalent sexuality and confused views of social roles combine often generating a humour of which they themselves remain unaware. Phyllis's earnestness, her second-hand language and fashionable stance, are satirised. Body Awareness Week includes puppets, a multiracial husband and wife singing duo who sing everything from klezmer (a musical tradition derived from Ashkenazi Jews) to gospel, along with an art exhibition that she feels obliged to encourage those attending to visit, although she feels equally obliged to warn against, caught up as she is in contradictory impulses. Her penultimate speech to those assembled for Body Awareness Week devolves into a barely coherent ramble.

Her own body awareness includes the conviction that she has a trembling eyelid, as her partner bleaches her moustache and shaves her legs and pubic hair in preparation for being photographed by Frank. This is the divorced Joyce who, in a lesbian relationship, is nonetheless drawn to a twice-married man whom she enlists to give her son advice on sex and relationships over cups of hot chocolate: 'try kissing them. If they kiss you back, you can touch their breasts', he suggests (453). This is a man who claims to see his dead mother 'everywhere'. Jared duly exposes himself to a girl, feeling this a legitimate path to a relationship, confessing as they sit eating frozen blintzes. Unsure what to do, they decide to celebrate Shabbat, improvising a prayer by reading from the book Phyllis has been reading. Unfortunately, the passage lacks a certain religious resonance as Joyce intones, 'Some menopausal women complain of vaginal dryness and thinning', (477) while Jared plays 'Jingle Bells' on a recorder he has stolen from Frank, who ends the play taking a flash photograph of them. A final stage direction indicates that Joyce, watching her son, 'is deeply sad' (480).

If *Body Awareness* is a comedy, there is an undertone of desperation. Jared is more than a figure of fun. Joyce wrestles with having a son whose future is bleak. She is uncertain of her own identity, while Phyllis, as Joyce suggests, is more at home with concepts than the messy reality of people and their lives. Frank drifts through the play, a naïf whose motives are not clear even to himself. If Annie Baker skewers the absurdities of feminist jargon, she is not invalidating concerns about how language itself operates or the emotional sensitivities involved in relationships and the manner in which they are negotiated. As she has said, 'My goal for the play is not to judge anyone, to get at that point where everyone is equally right and equally wrong, so the humor comes from that.' She wanted 'to write a play that wasn't an "issue play".'[14] It was the British television writer Paul Abbott who observed that 'Psychiatrists have known for years that neurosis is governed by the distance between what you think you are, and what others perceive you to be. Most good drama makes that gap visible, however small it may be . . . We should be able to have comedy and emotional truth in the same drama . . . Upsetting and funny in the same breath.'[15] This is something Annie Baker achieves.

Later, she was to be discontented with aspects of the play, confessing that '*Body Awareness* was written with very little thought about physical space and time and duration and design and all of the things that I think are integral to writing for the theatre – the first things I think about now when I sit down to write.'[16]

Her next play, *Circle Mirror Transformation*, opened on 13 October 2009 at the 42nd Street Playwrights Horizons, a theatre dedicated, in particular, to emerging talent. It was a play that came up against the theatre's subscriber base as the over sixty-five-year-olds in the audience shouted out their complaints. As Baker explained,

At one matinee we had a class of NYU students and also the entire population of some senior center. Most of the old people hated the play. They hated it so much and they were talking about how much they hated it while it was happening. Eventually the NYU students started yelling at them. A girl stood up and shrieked: 'If you don't like the play then just LEAVE!' I was cowering in the back row the whole time, humiliated... At first I was totally horrified. I felt disrespected, violated, etc. And then I kind of started loving it. It was a dialogue! It really was. Sometimes fights broke out.[17]

The play is set in a dance studio in Shirley with little more than a blue yoga ball and a mirror. Just as the days of the week had been spelled out on a blackboard in *Body Awareness*, so here the weeks are projected or displayed on stage. The play takes place over six weeks, the first four being divided into five scenes, separated by a blackout, the fifth into six and the sixth into three. The play begins after a designated fifteen seconds of silence, and silences are allowed to develop at key moments.

Gathered in this place is a group of people ostensibly brought together to try their hand at acting. Over the weeks, however, they are slowly exposed in their isolation, their failed relationships and thwarted ambitions, as acting exercises (of a kind Baker had experienced at the age of nine years) edge in the direction of therapy, Baker having read transcripts of therapy sessions at the Esalen Institute. These are people, Baker has said, who would never have signed up for a group therapy session, although in truth anyone who has attended rehearsals knows that therapy is in the air. They are not preparing for a production. There is no script to learn, no rehearsal for a final performance. They undertake exercises in empathy, seemingly not finding such in their own lives. By degrees a drama does develop both within the exercises and in the breaks between, as they are slowly stripped of their social performances. Here is theatre as evasion and as revelation, an interlacing of private pain and humour as we learn of adulterous affairs, alcoholic families, casual cruelties, betrayals, abandonments and fractured relationships in the context of exercises that, paradoxically, depend on trust and mutuality.

They begin with an exercise in which each person speaks a single number (all the exercises in the play are actual exercises used in the theatre, and Baker suggests that actors should use them in rehearsals). The point, Marty explains, is 'to be able to be totally present' (162). Following this prologue, James, a sixty-year-old man, addresses them in the guise of his fifty-six-year-old wife, Marty (a figure inspired by the leader of a tango class Baker took as a teenager), who, he explains, is 'into non-traditional healing', teaches pottery and jewellery-making (94) and now an adult creative drama class – perhaps not a guarantee of expertise. It is, in essence, an exercise in occupying someone else's sensibility and identity. Indeed the play consists of acting exercises (performing inanimate objects, speaking an invented language) interspersed with scenes in which we learn something of the background of those who are taking the class for a range of reasons, of which a career in theatre is perhaps not one. By degrees the privacies of the characters are exposed, the line between performance and being blurred.

Those taking the class range in age from sixteen to forty-eight years and are arranged in the circle of the title. The mirroring and transformation refer to the group reflecting a gesture or sound and then transforming it into a different gesture or sound. This is the only occasion in the play when there is genuine improvisation.

In the second scene we are introduced to Schultz, the sole character not referred to by a first name. Divorced, he has as a consequence been forced out his home and now lives alone in a condominium, although, as a fellow pupil, thirty-five-year-old Theresa, a deft hand, as it turns out, with the hula hoop, remarks, he is still wearing his wedding ring. In a situation in which they are going to be exploring stories, he plainly already has his own embodied in something as simple as a ring he has failed to remove. In a later scene sixteen-year-old Lauren speaks in the person of Schultz and, as he tries to attract her attention, reveals the truth he had evidently told her in confidence: 'We just Separated. Divorced. I'm in a lot of pain about it' (113). This may be a group of would-be amateur actors, but they discover the danger of exposed emotions.

When Schultz in turn plays the role of Theresa, he enacts what she has plainly told him, revealing that she has abandoned a potential career as an actress and is now studying for a certificate in acupressure and Rolfing (a way of maximising well-being in mind and body), having retreated from New York, a place where 'people didn't really care about each other' (126). She has broken up with her boyfriend after a toxic relationship, while her father has prostate cancer, and, for unspecified reasons, she is worried about her mother. Schultz and she are clearly drawn to one another, each bearing scars, and as the play progresses, their relationship ebbs and flows as they effectively mirror and transform one another and themselves. Acting exercises devolve into therapy sessions as they are severally exposed in their inadequacies, their repressed pain surfaces and their actual needs and desires begin to invade their performances. Set to enact a conflict, Schultz and Theresa play out their actual situation, Schultz insisting 'I need you to stay,' and she saying, 'I want to go' (166). In a subsequent scene, she steps forward less to prompt the actor playing her part than to intrude the truth. The scene is followed by a silence in which the implication of her intervention becomes obvious.

They are actors in more than a theatrical sense, their social performances being a strategy to evade what really troubles them. Acting is simultaneously an escape and a route to truth. Becoming someone else may be a means not to be oneself but equally to expose suppressed realities. As Baker has said, 'I wanted the audience to learn about the characters through formal theatre exercises. I knew I wanted there to be excruciating silences. I knew I wanted a doomed class romance that left one character embarrassed and the other heartbroken. I knew I wanted characters to deliver monologues as each other. I knew I wanted information about these people to come out in the strangest places, and I wanted us to know them all intimately by the end of the play . . . [I] also wanted to show how beautiful (and noble!) it is when people throw themselves earnestly and unconsciously into something, even if it is a therapeutic re-enactment.'[18]

When Theresa plays the part of James, we learn that his father had been in the military and that, implicitly, he had disappointed him by avoiding the draft, dropping out of a job and embracing Marxism, although that same father had been emotionally abusive, the whole family being alcoholics. His first marriage (to an alcoholic) had failed, and he is evidently alienated from his daughter, suppressing an unfocussed sense of anger. Beyond anything, he fears that he may become his father. As the details pile up, so James becomes an audience to his own life.

Lauren's life seems equally bleak as the parts of her parents are played by James and Marty. She is lonely with no connection to them. As the scene plays out, however, so James begins to cry, the role he is playing mirroring his own life, Lauren's situation reminding him of his relationship to his own daughter who, he later confesses, has refused to speak to him since an affair he had conducted during his marriage to her mother, a fact revealed to her by Marty, with what motive is unclear. When Marty plays the part of Lauren still more revelations spill out: 'my father has had some problems with the, um, law...My grandmother thinks my mother should leave my father. They fight about it' (164). The membrane between art and life proves permeable.

Stories, it turns out, can be disturbing as well as comforting. When Marty tells of meeting her husband-to-be, she is followed by Theresa, who recalls meeting someone she is sure must have been Jewish – 'he had this humongous nose and this long white beard with these big glasses' – and who had been regaling those on the subway with anti-Semitic remarks. Hers is a story followed by a long, embarrassed silence.

Circle Mirror Transformation begins innocently enough. Slowly, though, and by indirection, truths begin to surface. In some ways it is a parody of method acting, which invites actors to explore and expose aspects of their own lives, potentially at the price of psychological equanimity. It was the Belgian director Jacques Huisman who remarked of Lee Strasberg, co-founder of the Actors Studio, that he was a 'talmudic destroyer'. In an exercise, everyone is asked to write a secret on a piece of paper, these to be distributed randomly and read out to the group. What emerges is disturbing as one confesses to the fact that he or she may have been molested by his or her father, while another admits to a problem with Internet pornography. In one note, clearly written by George, he admits that he might be in love with Theresa, leaving Schultz looking traumatised. There is a ten-second silence. Marty reads out what is presumably her own secret: 'Sometimes I think that everything I do is propelled by my fear of being alone' (186).

By week six, Marty, who suffers from night terrors, and James are at odds, she having left home. A final exercise has all of them look forward ten years to where they will be then. Shultz says he will have remarried, although he is uncertain what his wife's name will be. Lauren claims she will have become a veterinarian and Theresa a massage therapist married to an actor. The lights then fade leaving only Lauren and Shultz in a spotlight. Now what seems to be the truth emerges as Lauren asks, 'How many times your life is gonna totally change and then, like, start all over again? And you'll feel like what happened before wasn't real' (208). Ten years on, Marty and James, Lauren explains, are no longer together, she being in New Mexico, he still in Shirley teaching economics. Lauren's own parents have divorced, while she and Shultz both now live in Burlington and the play ends as 'perhaps, very very faintly, we hear the sounds of a street in Burlington', (208) although quite what distinguishes the sounds of Burlington is hard to know.

Arthur Miller once observed that we begin to act the moment we walk out of the front door. Performance is not restricted to theatre. The face we see in the mirror is not that which we offer the world. We are Protean, a series of roles, transforming with circumstance and those we encounter. Communication is imperfect, truth alternately relative and hard to access. In the words of John Donne's 'Satire III', 'On a huge hill, / Cragged and steep,

Truth stands, and he that will / Reach her, about must and about must go.' What, then, is the status of truth in theatre? Edward Albee suggested that the lies of theatre may corrupt in the direction of truth.[19]

Circle Mirror Transformation, which won three Obie awards, explores the relationship between performance and being and is by turns funny and moving. None of its characters are in command of their lives. Failure is in the air. They have a history of broken relationships, which they enact in front of strangers as they show signs of replicating them. They are all in retreat, capable equally of evasion and confession. Power shifts from one to another as they perform their exercises in an anonymous room in a town of no particular significance. Lacking a past they can confront with equanimity, they lack too a real vision of the future. They have small ambitions and seem fated not to realise those they have. Yet there are moments when real emotions seep through the artifice, when it is clear that past wounds are not healed and that they are vulnerable in their guilt and anxieties.

Theatre, or its semblance, evidently has the power to tap into truths if not the truth. For the most part the exercises are trite. Designed to create an atmosphere of trust, they seem to achieve the opposite, as partnerships form and dissolve as they had before they stepped into the circle in which words were to be passed around, communication explored, stories told. As in a Pinter play, what initially seems secure slowly exposes an underlying sense if not of menace, then of barely suppressed pain.

In 2010, the Manhattan Theatre Club staged a reading of *Nocturama*, a play written in 2006 that she was originally convinced would never be produced. It takes place in 2007 in two overlapping houses, one once the home of a nineteenth-century woman poet called Elizabeth Collins, the other of the divorced Judy, her son Skaggs (both suffering from depression), and her new partner, Gary, who is addicted to food and video games (the one he watches being called *Nocturama*) and in therapy. Baker has explained that she wrote it when

I had just become interested in how, even if you're a really well-intentioned depressed person, you can really screw up the lives of everyone around you just through the things that being depressed can make you say. I was also interested in what we all mean when we say 'depressed'. I was also interested in historical house tours and depressed (or should I say melancholic) female 19th century poets (Emily Dickinson in particular), and at the peak of my own insane depression I was attending three historical house tours a week and became obsessed with the (always female) historical house tour guides and their fanatical interest in the minutiae of dead people's lives.[20]

Nocturama combines all those elements. Judy addresses her depression, following her now-divorced husband's infidelities, by attending seminars offered by a Buddhist nun who teaches techniques of forgiveness. She is a subscriber to *Psychotherapy Networker* (a real publication), is given to psycho platitudes, although also a theatrical mantra ('Live in the moment . . . stay in the moment'), while studying part-time for a certificate in Eye Movement Desensitization and Reprocessing (EMDR), a stress-reduction therapy that is, perhaps surprisingly, also real, a treatment aimed, according to the EMDR International Association, at discarding 'inappropriate emotions, beliefs, and body sensations' and that can begin with the question 'what event do you remember that made you feel worthless or useless?' Ironically, that last would be a good question directed at Skaggs, whose girlfriend has left him and who when Googling himself gets no hits, as the poet Elizabeth Collins had wanted someone to look at her, feeling that she had spent her life as no more than an observer. As the result of a theft, Skaggs is a drummer without drums, as his mother is a high school counsellor herself in need of counselling. Annie Baker's teenage discussions with her therapist mother plainly stayed with her.

Judy's solution to her problems is a partnership with a twice-married man who comes from a family of alcoholics and is himself guilty of serial infidelities, quite apart from his addictive attachment to video games and pornography. Skaggs, who claims he might commit suicide and who finds antidepressants depressing, turns to smoking cannabis from a bong and casually seducing Amanda, the tour guide, a young woman who otherwise spends her time repeating the same text as she narrates the story of a woman who was abandoned as she herself will be by Skaggs. Meanwhile we discover that the nineteenth-century poet, whose life she recites, had herself suffered from depression (then called melancholy) and had committed suicide when her husband left her for a woman who lived in the building now occupied by this trio. In a tour of the historic house, Amanda draws attention to some writing inscribed on the floor by the long dead writer: 'Cadere Animus . . . to lose heart' (223), and in a sense that is a subtext to the play. As a teenager, she had believed that household objects were alive, something that Annie Baker has confessed she also felt and that would later surface in her play *John*.

Like her other plays, *Nocturama* is laced through with a humour rooted in the self-deceits of her characters, oddly willing to confess to the very privacies that disturb them and with an unearned confidence easily exposed. Thus Gary, who confesses to multiple affairs, claims that 'I have a lot of trouble asserting my needs' (257). Relationships are broken, phone calls not returned, doors closed. Ostensibly the least troubled character is Amanda, the bespectacled, black, twenty-seven-year-old woman who divides her time between acting as guide and reading *Harry Potter*, although she confesses to obsessive thinking and being 'sort of sad' (301). She is also drawn into an unlikely, and possibly desperate, relationship with Skaggs, at his urging reading out pornographic emails he has sent. Unsurprisingly, he swiftly abandons her, calling her a 'weird little Vermont hobbit who's obsessed with dead white women' (334).

Betrayal is a step away, never an act without consequences, and there is perhaps a cruelty to Baker mirrored by her characters who she pins to their failings with all the precision of a lepidopterist, although she has insisted that she tries not to laugh too derisively at any of them. They have some redeeming characteristics even if that is only their vulnerability not unconnected with their capacity for self-concern. Her plays, she has said, are about inner conflict as well as the conflict between characters, and that conflict is as liable to generate comedy as moments of genuine feeling and insight.

Her next play, *The Aliens* (2010), was staged at the 104-seat Rattlestick Playwrights Theater in the West Village, which is dedicated to working with emerging playwrights. Once again it is set in an anonymous place, the 'desolate back patio of a coffee shop in

Vermont'. Baker has said that she was interested in locating the play in a closed space of a kind where people are forbidden to be. It has a single set and features three characters, KJ (Kevin Jano), with a beard, long hair and habit of adding magic mushrooms to his tea and, it seems, anything else (something Baker had seen people do in Amherst); Jasper (Jasper Kopatch), who 'simmers with quiet rage'; and Evan, a seventeen-year-old who works in the coffee shop, one of whose jobs is to throw rubbish into a large trash bin. Jasper has a barely suppressed anger that comes in part from the fact that his girlfriend has left him, not least because of his habit of calling her a cunt, a tendency he has perhaps picked up from his enthusiasm for Charles Bukowski.

KJ and Jasper, we learn, had once been in a band among whose many names was The Aliens (the title, Jasper explains, of a poem by Bukowski), although in truth they are alien in other respects, outsiders in more than their location. The Bukowski poem speaks of those who lead regular lives, with very little friction or distress, while insisting that he, the poet, is not even near to being one of them. Nor are KJ or Jasper who are the Vladimir and Estragon of the play, passing time, mutually protective, vaudevillians singing songs together. KG, who lives with his mother, is on medication, steered away from alcohol by his protective partner. Theirs is an alliance against a society whose rules and objectives they ignore. KJ dropped out college because, he claims, 'I'm not really interested in . . . Serious shit' (55), while later confessing to having had a breakdown. Jasper is a high school dropout from 'a shithole' in New Hampshire who describes himself as 'a living piece of trailer trash'. He is at work on a novel, part of which he reads out. It tips its hat to Bukowski – indeed its title, *Little Tigers Everywhere*, is named for a Bukowski poem. The surprise is that it is coherent even as it veers towards the narcissistic; but what else was Bukowski, a man who, like Jasper, felt anger and alienation?

At first, Evan, embarrassed to reveal that he is preparing to go to a Jewish music camp, seems no more than a naïve teenager somewhat in awe of the two men who, against the rules, hang out at the back of the coffee shop, except that he is prone to make surprising statements. As Fourth of July celebrations approach he says, 'I kind of hate America' (30). After an intermission that exists, according to Baker, 'for about ten different reasons' that she forebears to name, KJ is on his own. In the third scene he is found lying across plastic chairs with liquor bottles at his feet, Jasper no longer being around to stop him from drinking. Jasper is, KJ tells Evan, sick before confessing that he is, in fact, dead of an overdose, a fact that reduces Evan to tears at the loss of a man who he scarcely knows but whom he now declares to be one of his best friends. KJ is displaced not only by the threat of the coffee shop manager banishing him but because his alliance with a fellow quiet resister has been broken. He is Steinbeck's George after the death of Lennie. He prepares to move on to nowhere in particular, listing possible destinations as he had earlier listed the potential names of their band, bequeathing Jasper's guitar to Evan, who in the course of the play has transformed from insecure teenager. It is a laying on of hands, a potential passing of the baton. Evan reads Bukowski's semi-coming-of-age novel, *Ham on Rye*, coming of age himself, growing in confidence, although it is doubtful that his reading of Bukowski's misogynistic *Love Is a Dog from Hell* will bode well for the relationship with the girl he met at the Jewish music camp. As the play ends, it is unclear whether he is a Jasper in embryo or will be one of those who lead regular lives.

At least a third, if not half, of the play, a direction indicates, is silence, short silences lasting between five and ten seconds, other silences and pauses even longer, sometimes, in performance, several minutes. Stage silences are never empty. They have the power to disturb. When KJ tries implausibly to explain propositional calculus to Evan, finally stopping, caught up in his own confusion, there is a long pause in which the stage direction indicates that Evan 'is starting to feel uncomfortable,' understanding, for a moment, that there is something peculiar about this man who claimed to be a double major in mathematics and philosophy giving it up because he wanted to be 'the real thing'.

These are not the silences of a John Cage composition but, on occasion, spaces left by those who understand one another and have no need to fill them. More often they reflect sudden caesuras forced by conversations that run up against emotional limits. At times they allow room for interior worlds to become apparent. At one stage we are told that as KJ sits by himself, he 'thinks hard about something, and then, upon realizing something else, smiles. Then he goes back to thinking again' (57). About what? We are not told, yet it reveals something about his character, while it reflects the reality of a solitary individual.

Baker has said that 'one of the reasons I like putting really long silences into my plays [is because] crazy stuff happens during silences in the theatre. The audience suddenly becomes aware of itself, and [is] a little weirded out and uncomfortable . . . but if the silence goes on long enough eventually people adjust to it . . . and find their own way back into the reality of the play. And that moment – when an entire audience is relaxed and breathless together in a silence, when time slows down and then starts to speed up again – is very magical to me.'[21] 'I am interested in silence,' she has explained,

because I think it's a huge unacknowledged part of our daily lives . . . And by silence I don't mean portentous, Pinter-esque silence – although that can be great too – I just mean the absence of talk. It's not actually silence I'm after so much as the things that we do when we're not talking. Someone jiggling their knee. Someone staring into the sun for a full minute and humming . . . All this stuff is absent from most contemporary theatre because people are so freaked out about holding the attention of an audience who would rather be at home watching action movies and sitcoms . . . as an audience member, there's something really exciting to me about watching someone scratch their elbow on stage and not say anything . . . My plays are often about what happens when we're not talking . . . Movement. Silence. Stillness, then sudden movement. Interesting stage pictures. The living human organism in front of us doing strange things.[22]

In radio, unplanned silences are described as 'dead air' and are to be feared. They tend to induce panic in presenters and producers even if they last no more than a few seconds. Listeners are aware that something is wrong, even if they have no awareness of what it might be. There are such silences in daily life, silences that may provide space for contemplation or be an expression of anxiety or mutuality. What they are not is dead.

Baker has also said that she wished to explore boredom as an activity on stage and hers are, indeed, not characters caught up in the American rush towards the future. They are on pause, like the figures in O'Neill's *The Iceman Cometh*, except that they have no pipe dreams beyond abstracting themselves from an existence that seems to them irrelevant even as the small change of their conversations touches on larger issues to do with relationships, loss, abandonment. In other words, *The Aliens* is, in many ways, of a piece with her earlier plays. These are damaged individuals staring in on their lives from the outside. If there are overtones of Becket, it may be because she had found his novel *Watt* 'one of the funniest novels of all time,' having written a paper on it at school. What interested her was 'the gap between reality and language, or the simultaneous lack thereof ... the more you try to convey reality through language, the more it becomes clear that there is a reality that language cannot express. But at the same time, language is the only reality we have.'[23]

Language, indeed, is often an evasion, as much a shield against truth as a path to it. Silences, meanwhile, are spaces into which meaning can seep. The language of *The Aliens* has an authentic ring to it, but she is not simply transcribing, as she had at seventeen, aware that gesture is itself a form of language. As Henry James remarked, 'What is character but the determination of incident? What is incident but the illustration of character? ... It is an incident for a woman to stand up with her hand resting on a table and look at you in a certain way; or if it be not an incident I think it will be hard to say what it is. At the same time it is an expression of character ... If you say you don't see it ... this is exactly what the artist who has reasons of his own for thinking he *does* see it undertakes to show you.'[24]

To this point Annie Baker's reputation had been growing. *The Aliens* might have been staged in a ninety-nine-seat theatre far away from Broadway, but it attracted the attention of Charles Isherwood of the *New York Times*, for whom *Nocturama* was 'a gentle and extraordinarily beautiful' play, observing that 'the longer you look, the more you see and the more you feel'. Somewhat apologetically, he related her to Chekhov in that 'her writing accrues weight and meaning simply through compassionate, truthful observation',[25] apologetically because of what he acknowledged to be the risk of appearing hyperbolic. Baker was now clearly on the radar and indeed her next play, *The Flick*, commissioned and staged by Playwrights Horizons, with an audience capacity below 200, won the Pulitzer Prize, although that was no guarantee of a transfer. Indeed it was two years before it was revived and then not on Broadway but at the 199-seat Barrow Street Theatre in Greenwich Village. Ahead, however, in 2016, lay a production at Britain's Royal National Theatre.

The Flick is set in a 'falling-apart movie theatre' called The Flick in Worcester County, Massachusetts. The falling apart is literal as a piece of the ceiling has dropped next to a customer. There is seldom a full house. The carpets are dingy, the technology antiquated. As in her earlier plays, the characters are on the margin, here wearing 'the same degrading movie theatre uniform in every scene', employed to sell popcorn, clean the drinks machine and sweep out when the audience has left. The principal characters are Sam, thirty-five, a white man with a shaved head who wears a Red Sox cap; Avery, twenty, African-American and, we are told, a lover of movies; and Rose, twenty-four, 'sexually magnetic', who never wears makeup and has hair dyed forest green. As the projectionist, her status is higher than the two men by virtue of her role, which has an element of skill. As Baker has said, 'Most jobs in this country suck. We forget, when we achieve our dreams . . . that most people don't get to have the job they would really like to have.'[26] Sam, in particular, has always wanted to be a projectionist, but his boss, the absent Steve, has never responded, promoting Rose ahead of him.

Avery is new, inducted into his job by a man who has plainly never risen above his function as cleaner, which potentially represents the future of the man he now trains, except that we later learn more about him. On the screen are projected the bright images of Hollywood, while in the movie theatre are the by-products of consumption – abandoned popcorn and drink containers. In the restroom shit is liberally smeared around. Yet there is a camaraderie of sorts particularly because of their love of movies, whose qualities they discuss, Avery proving capable of memorising *Pulp Fiction* (the film that at age thirteen Baker had been taken to see), which in his view was the last great American movie. Indeed they play a game of six degrees of separation, linking the seemingly disparate names of film actors. 'For part of the time', Baker has said, 'they are just shooting the shit', but plainly shooting the shit is precisely what begins to build some kind of connection between these seemingly separate figures. One thing that does link them is that they are running a small scam to augment their wages, retaining some money from ticket sales, justifying it by their low wages and the fact that Steve, the owner, is 'a total douchebag',[27] a compulsive gambler whose ex-wife is taking him to court for child care.

When the play opens, the audience is confronted with rows of seats, the light from a projector shining out at them from the projection booth, its images impossible to decipher. A movie is finishing, after two minutes music fading away. There is a flash of green and white light, and then the movie theatre lights flicker on, Sam and Avery emerging with their brooms to begin cleaning.

Baker has said that she began with the idea that the fourth wall would be the movie screen. What interested her was the transition from 'the magic time machine of the movies into the crazy present tense with the fluorescent lights on . . . that to me seems so profound . . . I wanted it both to be a tribute to the movies . . . and a tribute to the theatre. It seemed super potent to me.'[28] It is a tribute to the movies in so far as all three characters are enthusiasts and a tribute to the theatre to the extent that seemingly inconsequential conversations between apparently inconsequential characters have the power to command the attention of an audience watching a form that eschews many of the powers of cinema. 'Eighty percent of theatre' Baker has observed, 'is the way it looks, the physical objects on stage and the bodies moving through space, like the way someone crosses their legs or gets up and walks across the room. That is so much of the play to me. I am really interested in movement and silence, movement happening during silence. To me that is just as important as the dialogue in the play. I am trying to orchestrate a whole event. The way you push up your glasses is as important as the thing you say. I feel that is true in real life. So I try to be super specific about that in my stage directions.'[29] She rejects the idea that 'theatre should be about people talking really loudly and debating issues in a really obvious, clear way and that there should be a really clear message you can take home with you . . . to me the thing theatre does is to slow time down and we can all be in the room together.'[30]

The audience is in a curious position, watching people who in turn are watching a film whose images we never see. Above is the soundproof projection booth through which we glimpse Rose, the projectionist, who can only communicate through gestures. Sarah Ruhl has written about watching her own plays from the sound booth with a pane of glass between her and the production. The effect, she observed, was to turn her into what she called 'an observer criminal'.[31]

Audience assumptions change in the course of the play as we learn more of characters who are not quite what they seem and who have a backstory outside this movie-house limbo. Avery is in fact a university student, the son of a teacher of semiotics at Clark University in Massachusetts, a private university (current fees $42,000 a year), although, as he explains to Rose, he has a free ride. He has taken a semester off, perhaps longer. Since he interrupts his therapist's holiday for a telephone consultation, something is plainly going on in his life. He confesses to being obsessed with movies: 'They're like my life' (89). Indeed his reason for being at The Flick is precisely that obsession because it is one of the only movie theatres that still show 35 millimetre films.

He lives at home, but so does Sam, a thirty-five-year-old man who never went to university and who 'lives in a shitty attic above his crazy parents' (156) with an older, learning-disabled brother, although he and the others prefer the word 'retard'. Rose, who never goes to the movies when not projecting them, went to a state university, Fitchburg State (which, incidentally, only gained university status in 2010) and is sexually ambivalent having 'been with girls a couple times' (87). Her mother is a secretary with a credit card overdraft and a $20,000 student loan to pay off.

Baker works by indirection. Small revelations seem almost inconsequential, buried in the small talk, the stories they tell one another, but a portrait is slowly built. Behind the daily banter, the jokes, there are thwarted hopes, anxiety and pain. The Sam who had dismissed Rose as a lesbian, later reveals that he has been in love with her for a year and a half, and that his disabled brother has been sent away. He is plainly in as much a state of disrepair as the movie theatre itself.

Much the same could be said of Avery. He has been angling to become a projectionist but Rose offers to teach Avery instead. What follows is an extended scene, with no dialogue, as they retreat to the projection booth where, through the glass, we see her teach him how to thread the projector. When they have finished they start a film. What follows is the six-minute opening credit music from *The Wild Bunch*, again with no dialogue. When they leave the booth and re-enter the auditorium Avery's eyes never leave the screen as Rose tries to seduce him. When, having switched the film off, she sits in the row across from him he 'covers his face in shame', before saying, 'I wanna kill myself' (91), confessing that 'there's something wrong with *me* . . . It's just. This has happened to me. Before.' (92). 'Today,' he adds, 'is the one-year anniversary of the day I tried to kill myself' by swallowing pins (96). Only later do we discover that his mother had abandoned his father for an old high school boyfriend, returning briefly a year later 'when a bunch of stuff happened in our family' (133). He has, he explains, refused to talk to her or look at her since.

He now admits to suffering from bulimia and depression, which explains his lateness on his second day of work at The Flick. Even his first day had been a strain: 'I had no idea how to hold a broom' (98). When Rose asks him why he is depressed, he says, 'Because everything is horrible? And sad.' (99). He is, he confesses, unsure who he is, unsure, indeed, who anyone is. He begins stories and then abandons them as Sam tells stories and then forgets their point. For all of them the movies, with their completed stories, are a relief, offering what their lives do not.

The movie theatre now comes under new management. Things fall further apart. They are required to wear new uniforms. Their scam is exposed, and the old projector is to be abandoned in favour of digital technology – a heresy to Avery and, in fact, to Baker, who recalled seeing Bergman's *Fanny and Alexander* and being disoriented by the fact that it was projected digitally, which seemed to her to change the experience. Such solidarity as they had dissolves when Sam and Rose suggest that Avery should take the fall for their thefts. In another wordless scene, the audience watches as Rose and Sam, in the projection booth, disassemble the old projector and install the new digital one. Once again light streams out, projecting images invisible to the audience. Eventually, after some minutes, they leave the booth and the movie theatre lights come on, different now with changed wattage or fluorescents. Avery has left, a new man being inducted.

In the final scene, Avery returns to collect the old projector along with films that Sam has saved for him. It seems a gesture of reconciliation. Avery plans to return to Clark, but this is a harder Avery who now believes that 'we were never really friends in the first place', that you cannot have faith in people and that you should 'not expect things to turn out well in the end' (173) as they do in the movies. Speaking to Sam, he envisages a time when 'I'll come back to Massachusetts and you'll still be here sweeping up popcorn' and 'I'll be living in Paris or something' (173), the 'or something', however, suggesting that he is no clearer about his future than he had been.

For his part, Sam insists that 'I know my life might seem kind of depressing to you, and you know, in a lot of ways it is. But there's some good stuff in it', despite his now resorting to the Internet to find a girlfriend. He is convinced that 'sometimes the people you fall in love with fall in love with you back . . . Sometimes they don't. But sometimes they do. And it's awesome' (175). They play a last game of six degrees of separation, which at first Avery fails to respond to, leaving, but after a 'very very long amount of time passes' (176), he returns to pick up the game until it is finished. The play ends as Sam sits smiling to himself and one of the orchestral themes from *Jules and Jim* plays before he rises, walks up the aisle, switches off the lights and leaves as the music swells.

Sam, it seems, is reconciled to his life, although he remains within the womb of the cinema, looking for love. Avery, meanwhile, has exchanged one performance for another, by turns confident about his future and embracing cynicism as though it were a carapace. Rose continues because hers is a job that puts food on the table. A university graduate, she has settled for what is on offer, no less looking for love than Sam but seemingly wary of commitment and confused in her sexuality. They have all betrayed one another, come from different classes with different necessities and yet at some level meet, sharing anxieties and occasionally visions of possibility. Speaking of the various characters in her plays who have failed to become what they wished, Baker has said that 'there's a kind of transcendence and nobility they embody through not having lived the lives they wanted to'.[32] 'If you write something small', she has remarked, 'like someone sweeping up popcorn or like a couple in a bed and breakfast [as in her next play, *John*] somehow if you do it the right way you achieve some higher spiritual meaning that you can't articulate or it wouldn't have that resonance . . . If you try to be profound, or if I'm too sure of what I'm doing, I feel that that can cripple the thing and make it mean nothing. You have to hope that that transcendent thing happens.'[33]

Like her other plays, *The Flick* is not short. The silences extend the play beyond the spoken words, which in the printed version are sometimes set out as though it were a poem, with end stopped lines a few words long. Her approach brought complaints from some attuned to more concise works and rapid-fire dialogue. Later, she confessed, 'I don't do that anymore because so many people told me that I was such an asshole.' Further, 'A lot of people complain to me about how long they are, which is really interesting because there are movies that are longer, other plays that are longer.'[34]

'I'm not that crazy about *The Flick* any more,' she has said, 'I'm not that crazy about any play I have written three years later. I started to realise my plays were a little too neat. I felt they were tying themselves up in a little bow at the end. With this new one I thought I want it to be a mess. I am going to make this play at the end kind of make no sense but at the same time make total sense. Half the people in the audience will think that added up to nothing and the other half will think that made perfect sense, that was completely cohesive.'[35]

That new play was *John* (2015) in which she stepped into the gothic (a character even reading from a copy of H. P. Lovecraft's 'The Call of Cthulhu'), a world reminiscent of the novels of David Mitchell in which life becomes a kind of theatre for an invisible audience. Perhaps, too, there are echoes of Edward Albee's metaphysical conundrum *Tiny Alice*. She has said that

I was a really weird, supernaturally obsessed kid. I really did feel that all my stuffed animals were alive watching me and that crazy stuff was happening that I didn't understand. My parents were atheists but I felt there was definitely someone up there, controlling us. My mother always said that I would have been a religious fanatic if we had let you. I built weird little shrines in my room and with this play I wanted to go back and investigate that. Before I had been writing plays with cool dingy sets. There was a witty coolness to what I was doing, plays with a kind of detachment and I thought I want a play where a woman is getting her period the whole time . . . and there are dolls everywhere and that lady might be an angel and people talk about God . . . I thought I am going to write something over the top. There's going to be magic, but maybe it's not real magic, but who knows . . . One of the things that inspired the play was this thing I read that dread is the first step in religious development. I was always scared and always creeped out and I never knew why. I feel that in a very secular household it was my way of accessing the divine, something bigger than myself.[36]

A young couple, Elias and Jenny, arrive at a bed-and-breakfast in Gettysburg, Pennsylvania, apparently on a whim having decided to visit the battlefield. Presided over by seventy-two-year-old Mertis, it abounds with glass menageries, porcelain angels and Parisian bric-a-brac, although we later learn that it had been a hospital in the Civil War where amputated limbs piled up.

Each act begins and closes as she draws a red velvet curtain as if this were, indeed, a play. It is she, also, who changes the hands on a grandfather clock to mark the time of the following scene. She is, it seems, a female magus directing events, a magus being half magician, half priest, a controlling force. She has an uncanny way of knowing the answers to abstruse questions, being, she says, 'a tiny bit of a mind reader'.[37] Her husband is apparently in another room, although we never see him and he may not exist in so far as people stay in the mind alive or dead. When Elias reads what appear to be nonsense words from Mertis's notebook aloud (although she denies it is hers) a player piano spontaneously begins to play as if this were a magic spell. And the play ends, or almost so, when she declares: 'The spell has ended' (154).

On the upstairs landing a large doll (an American Girl doll) sits, itself a kind of presiding presence, vaguely threatening to the woman visitor, Jenny, being the same model that had disturbed her as a child and thus seems to have pursued her, although the actual doll today remains advertised as 'kind, generous and always ready to make a new friend'. American Girl dolls are more than playthings. They are historical figures embedded in stories to be found in accompanying books. Samantha, the name of the doll in *John*, was and is the name of an American Doll that can today be purchased in stores.

When the play opens, Bach's *St. Matthew Passion* plays on a jukebox radio. For all the apparently reassuring homeliness of this house, it slowly emerges that it has its mysteries, rooms that are safe and those not, sounds not all can hear, or perhaps a sound like the beating of wings, a variable heat (Jenny is cold as, she is told by an elderly blind woman, will be the doll she abandoned in the family basement). The house is apparently haunted while itself having agency, as in David Mitchell's *Slade House*. The door of a room may, it seems, vanish. Mertis's first husband was electrocuted in the basement. Outside, lie the graves of the dead of the Battle of Gettysburg and a tour that takes in Devil's Den. There are ghosts, if only in the sense that the past is not securely buried being contained within these characters and, indeed, those who watch as the red curtains are pulled aside and the audience is welcomed in.

In the dramatis personae we are told that one of the characters is blind, one wears glasses and two do not. This is to be a play, then, in which not just sight but perhaps second sight, or perception, are to play a role. The blind character is Genevieve, eighty-five and herself not without a certain strangeness, having been clinically insane, convinced that her ex-husband, John, was trying to gain possession of her soul and destroy her. She still feels him watching her. As Baker explained, 'If you spend your time trying to figure out what other people are thinking, you will go crazy. That was a form of madness that I wanted to tackle with a character who had at one time in her life gone insane.'[38]

Genevieve recites lyrics from 'Gone', a song sung by country singer Roy Drusky: ('Since you're gone / the wheel that turns / the fire that burns'), a song about loss ('Love divine once was mine now you're gone / Since you've gone my heart my lips my tear dimmed eyes / A lonely soul within me cries). The voice within becomes regrets with as much power to shape a life as any mysterious force. She and Mertis join in the same song, this time invoking another country and western singer, Ferlin Husky, a song about abandonment: 'I acted smart / And broke your heart / But now you've gone.' A verse not quoted laments, 'Oh, what I'd give / For the lifetime wasted / The love I've tasted / I was wrong, now you've gone.' It is a song that seems to apply to all the characters

It is a play of echoes. The name 'John' recurs. It is the name of the man with whom Jenny betrayed Elias ('It felt like he cast a spell on me') (103). It is the name of the man who haunts Genevieve. Mertis quotes John Henry Newman as saying 'Numquam minus solus quam cum solus' (never less alone than when alone) (38) as Jenny later remarks that she had felt 'less alone being alone' (76) and Genevieve comes to feel that when she is no longer 'trying to get in anyone else's head' or worrying what others are thinking of her in their heads, she will be 'Alone in the universe! Standing in the center of my own life' (111). Mertis recalls a phrase – 'Deep Calling unto Deep' – but not where it comes from. In fact she is hearing an echo of the Bible, from Psalms ('Deep calleth unto deep at the noise of your waterspouts: all thy waves and thy billows are gone over me') in which one force echoes another.

The young couple, Jenny and Elias, two brittle people in a brittle relationship, have come close to breaking up. She already has a habit of grinding her teeth when asleep and objects to the sound of his eating. He suffers from depression and feels she is trapping him. What principally lies between them, though, is her affair with John, now assumed to lie in the past except that the play ends with her phone ringing and a text from that same John, unless, that is, Genevieve's ex-husband has found a way back into life.

John is in part a play about watching. 'I'm always thinking about how people see me', Jenny confesses as Elias admits to having been watched as a child, feeling an unseen presence. When Genevieve addresses the audience directly, calling on a member of it to time her speech, she thereby concedes their power to modify behaviour, accept or not the identity offered. Beyond that, perhaps, lies the question for which religion offers itself as an answer proposing, as it does, a God who in watching confers significance.

John is also a play about stories, the stories we tell ourselves and those other people tell of us. Jenny asks Elias to tell her a story as Mertis reads one out, both hinting at the gothic in this place familiar with death, the essence of the gothic lying in its suggestion of forces beyond the rational, the threat of unreason offering the thrill of menace and a sense of a hidden meaning threatening to spill into the present. It is also a play about loss, broken relationships, chances lost, obligations denied, regret, paths not taken. There are scenes in which we can barely hear the words, scenes in which music is played at some length and nobody speaks, where the characters are out of sight, placing obligations on an audience.

For Hilton Als, in the *New Yorker*, the play was 'so good on so many levels that it casts a unique and brilliant light' praising Baker's 'outstanding writing and empathy'.[39]

Alexis Soloski, in the *Guardian*, also highlighted Baker's empathy while acknowledging her 'almost superhuman flair for character and dialogue'.[40]

Baker herself has said, 'I have always written very sparse plays, with realistic settings, very neutral spaces, and I have also written plays much more about men than women. I wrote a play that had an all male cast, which was *The Aliens*, and I feel that *The Flick* is actually about the guys and I love writing for men. It's fun. But I was [thinking] why am I not writing for more women.' *John* was to be such a play. That it also turned out to be humorous was a surprise to her. As she has said, 'After every play goes up I realise it's funny. I'm really bad at being intentionally funny. I could never write for a sit-com. I have to be serious to be funny. With *John* [I was thinking] this is my not funny play. Laughter always surprises me.' At the same time she confessed, 'I want every laugh to come from humiliation and recognition.'

Baker has asked herself why she chose to work in a theatre world that is flawed, where she lacks control and so much can go wrong, being a perfectionist in a form where perfection is not possible, from forgotten lines to computer breakdowns. It is, she has suggested, vulnerable and humiliating yet with a compensating sense of elevation, a human interaction. In 2015, she had three or four plays on her computer including a two-person play with a lot of nudity. 'I'll never show that to anybody. That was a personal challenge. And I tried to write a play about myself and my mother. It didn't work out.'[41]

Notes

1 Hermione Hoby, 'From Pulitzer to Popcorn: Why Annie Baker Is Making the Theatre World Pause for Thought', *Guardian*, 1 April 2016.
2 April Ayers Lawson, 'If You're Going to Read Plays, Read Annie Baker's', *Vice Reader*, 6 June 2014. www.vice.com/en_uk/read/if-youre-going-to-read-plays-read-annie-bakers-plays
3 Lavinia Greenlaw, 'Author, Author: Audio Obscura: A Work for a Railway Station', *Guardian*, Review Section, 3S, 2 September 2011, p. 15.
4 Marc Maron, *WTF with Marc Maron*, WTF Podcast, Episode 645 – Annie Baker, 12 October 2015. www.wtfpod.com/podcast/episodes/episode_645_-_annie_baker
5 Nathan Heller, 'Just Saying: The Anti-Theatrical Theatre of Annie Baker', *New Yorker*, 25 February 2013. www.newyorker.com/magazine/2013/02/25/just-saying
6 Hermione Hoby, 'Pause for Thought', *Guardian*, Review Section, 2 April 2016, p. 16.
7 Maron, *WTF with Marc Maron*.
8 Heller, 'Just Saying'.
9 Adam Greenfield, 'Annie Baker Discusses *Circle Mirror Transformation* with Playwrights Horizons Literary Manager Adam Greenfield, Huntington Theatre Company'. www.huntingtontheatre.org/articles/Annie-Baker-discusses-iCircle-Mirror-Transformationi-with-Playwrights-Horizons-Literary-Manager-Adam-Greenfield
10 Ibid.
11 Annie Baker, *The Vermont Plays* (New York, 2013), p. 269.
12 Greenfield, 'Annie Baker Discusses *Circle Mirror Transformation*'.
13 Ibid.
14 Celia McGee, 'Childhood Is the Mother of the Play', *New York Times*, 25 May 2008. www.nytimes.com/2008/05/25/theater/25mcge.html?_r=0
15 Stuart Jeffries, 'The Monday Interview: Paul Abbott: Why I Write', *Guardian*, 7 February 2005. www.guardian.co.uk/media/2005/feb/07/broadcasting.arts
16 Heller, 'Just Saying'.

17 Carly Mensch, 'Annie Baker: Laughing at the Laugh', *Brooklyn Rail*, 4 May 2010. www
     .brooklynrail.org/2010/05/theater/in-dialogue-annie-baker-laughing-at-the-laugh
18 Adam Greenfield, 'Annie Baker Discusses *Circle Mirror Transformation*'.
19 Arthur Miller, 'On Politics and the Art of Acting', 30th Jefferson Lecture in the Humanities, 26
     March 2001.
20 Adam Greenfield, 'Annie Baker Discusses *Circle Mirror Transformation*'.
21 Carly Mensch, 'Annie Baker: Laughing at the Laugh'.
22 Laura Collins-Hughes, 'Fictional Town Sets Her Plays in Motion', *Boston.com*, 10 October
     2010. http://archive.boston.com/ae/theater_arts/articles/2010/10/10/fictional_town_sets_annie_
     bakers_plays_in_motion/
23 Carly Mensch, 'Annie Baker: Laughing at the Laugh'.
24 Marton Dauwen Zabel, *The Portable Henry James* (New York, 1977), pp. 400–1.
25 Charles Isherwood, 'Outsiders, Tender and Troubled', *New York Times*, 29 May 2010. www
     .nytimes.com/2010/04/23/theater/reviews/23aliens.html?_r=0
26 Maron, *WTF with Marc Maron*.
27 Annie Baker, *The Flick* (New York, 2014), pp. 34–5.
28 Maron, *WTF with Marc Maron*.
29 Ibid.
30 Ibid.
31 Sarah Ruhl, *100 Essays I Don't Have Time to Write* (New York, 2014), p. 110.
32 Heller, 'Just Saying'.
33 Maron, *WTF with Marc Maron*.
34 Ibid.
35 Ibid.
36 Maron, *WTF with Marc Maron*.
37 Annie Baker, *John* (New York, 2016), p. 57.
38 Maron, *WTF with Marc Maron*.
39 Hilton Als, 'The Way Station', *New Yorker*, 24 August 2015. www.newyorker.com/magazine/
     2015/08/24/the-way-station
40 Alexis Soloski, 'John Review – A Claustrophobic Drama That You Can't Take Your Eyes Off',
     Guardian, 12 August 2015. www.theguardian.com/stage/2015/aug/12/john-review-play-
     annie-baker-signature-theatre-new-york
41 Marron, *WTF with Marc Maron*.

2

Frances Ya-Chu Cowhig

I love that Japanese saying, 'A man is whatever room he's in.' I continue to experience that in terms of [a] double consciousness. It became so fluid to me.[1]

– Frances-Ya-Chu Cowhig

As her name suggests, Frances Ya-Chu Cowhig has a complex heritage. She was born in Philadelphia in 1983, of a Boston Irish Catholic father while her Taoist-raised mother came from rural Taiwan. They both worked for the US government – he as a diplomat, she with the Department of Defence. As a result they travelled, and consequently her schooling took place in different countries, although she lived in the United States for the first nine years of her life before spending two years in Taiwan. She attended a missionary school in Okinawa for another two years where she was told that the Japanese Buddhist holiday, Obon, on which families swept family graves and offered food, amounted to devil worship. Since her mother's village celebrated Chinese New Year, which involved honouring ancestors and sweeping the house, this left her confused.

In 1996 she went to high school at the International School of Beijing for five years, travelling to The Hague each year as part of the Model United Nations project, which involved delegates role-playing, simulating members of UN committees. At that time the family lived in the diplomatic compound, and she recalls the dead trees on the street being painted green when the Olympic committee arrived. Outside, members of Falun Gong, dedicated to truth, compassion and forbearance, were supposedly immolating themselves in Tiananmen Square, while school was cancelled when NATO bombed the Chinese Embassy in Belgrade, resulting in the US Embassy, where her father worked, being attacked with rocks and Molotov cocktails. Inside the gated compound, with its bars and nightclubs, life proceeded. She had diplomatic immunity because of her parents' jobs, but she had another kind of immunity living behind barbed wire and often witnessing events courtesy of CNN. Understandably, she has said that her teenage years were characterised by a sense of dislocation.

She returned to the United States in 2001, studying at Brown University, while her parents moved back to Chengdu in China. Unsurprisingly, she had a degree of confusion when it came to the question of identity. In Taiwan, Japan and China, she had been seen as an American, not least because she was tall; in America, she was seen as Asian and congratulated on her English. She recalls, 'I went through this whole period of racial crisis and paranoia in college', taking courses on ethnic studies and whiteness, attending a multiracial club and founding the college's Hapa club, 'Hapa' being a word originated from the Hawaiian Pidgin for a person of mixed heritage. In the end, she has explained, 'I think for me my interest in any affiliation to racial or ethnic identity ended by the time I was done with college...It became so fluid to me that I became uninterested in it. I think I reoriented myself towards just feeling a commonality with people who exist in the world in some kind of double-conscious existence or identity – people who don't identify with a singular -ist or –ism, but are...more interested in that gray area, or middle ground, or spaces between worlds. That's...where I ended up.'[2] Indeed she does not believe in placing constraints on who can tell a story, the idea of authenticity being defined by colour or a particular heritage. For her, 'there is no us/them, no "other".'[3] Even her first name, she notes, is androgynous, leading people to think she might be a man.

In later years she and her writer husband would spend time living in a Dodge Sprinter van, converting it into a camper van, moving from place to place, not, then, being defined by a particular location any more than a fixed identity. 'I'm not really of a place,' she has said, adding, 'A lot of the theatre-making process is similar to a nomadic childhood – a really intense finite period, and then dispersal. A wise friend once told me you can't make new old friends.'[4]

When she began to write, she was identified as a Chinese-American playwright, despite having no family ties to China, Taiwan not only being politically but also culturally distinct from the mainland (Chinese policy notwithstanding), her mother's family having been in Taiwan for centuries. After all, she objected, she was raised as much in a Boston Irish as a Taiwanese tradition. She thus felt that identification as a Chinese-American playwright was reductive; she would be happier if the words 'Taiwanese' or 'Irish' came before the hyphen or, indeed, to be identified as a former Texan since these had all fed into who she feels herself to be. There had anyway been a debate in the American theatre about the tendency to homogenise writers from a range of countries as constituting Asian drama while Henry David Hwang consciously played with the notion of being a Chinese-American playwright.

In some sense there is nothing more American than a concern with identity, a natural product of an immigrant society. There is a reason that more books have been published on American identity than on that of any other country. 'What then is the American?' asked Crèvecoeur.[5] It remains a good question. Cowhig, meanwhile, has confessed, 'I have grown weary of identity-politics conversations and questions of representation, not least because very often the works discussed in these regards aren't even very "good".'[6] Beyond that, plays that focused on marginalised groups were unlikely to be seen by those from such groups, more especially when her topic became Chinese migrant workers, although in fact, as her career advanced, China would become more central to her concerns.

She did not arrive at Brown meaning to be a playwright. There had been no writing courses at her Beijing high school, and, as a child of diplomats, she aimed to study public policy or international relations. She was a sociology major but enrolled in a playwriting class in her first semester, her professor later producing the play she wrote for that course, a work 'about foot-binding in ancient China and one woman's decision to defy tradition', an interesting choice given her comments about her own sense of confusion about her identity. 'I really found grounding and a kind of rootedness in the process of writing', she has said, 'and kept at it for many years not because it was enjoyable or I was any good at it, but because it was something to focus on and get better at'.[7] There is, indeed, a pragmatic dimension to Cowhig, who has said that while she is drawn to writing short stories, they fail to pay enough to justify her time.

There is, then, something almost casual about her initial commitment to drama: As she confessed, 'I wish I had some grandiose reason for focusing on the theatre as opposed to other genres – but it just happened to be the one I started in, the path I was encouraged along, so by the time I applied to graduate schools as a way of having something to do, a structure for life in my early twenties, the only work I had produced that could get me into anything was a play, so I applied to a playwriting program. And spent the next three years writing plays. It's not really the story of finding your passion and pursuing it. More like pursuing something until it becomes your passion.'[8]

After graduating she undertook an internship in the literary department of the Public Theatre but found the plays she saw in New York uninspiring, with the exception of a production by Ariane Mnouchkine's Théâtre du Sol and Yukio Mishima's Noh Plays – the common element being an emphasis on physicality. It was her interest in this that, four months after graduating, led her to apply to the Dell'Arte International School of Physical Theatre in Blue Lake, a former logging town on California's Redwood Coast.

Here, a year after a particularly traumatic incident, she found herself the only writer in a class consisting of actors, acrobats and dancers. The programme did indeed lay its emphasis on physicality and involved acrobatics, tai chi and the Alexander technique. In so far as they worked on plays, these were nonverbal. It was not a programme she found easy to adjust to, and she was tempted to return home to her parents' house in Virginia, except that that had been the site of the trauma to which she was still adjusting. In the end, however, she began to feel pleasure in the physicality: 'My year at Dell'Arte turned out to be a gateway to a new realm of existence: the capacity to feel joy, connection, and satisfaction through physical movement'. When, from 2006 to 2009, she studied for an MFA in Writing at the James A. Michener Center for Writers at the University of Texas in Austin, she began to feel that her new regimen of pre-dawn track workouts and group movement helped her evade 'the familiar tentacles of depression luring me toward emotional paralysis'.[9] In terms of her drama, though, that physicality had already been a mark of a play she had written back at Brown in 2004, which came directly out of personal experience.

She was twenty-one, and in her freshman year, when her seventeen-year-old brother Patrick attempted suicide; in her junior year, he succeeded. He had been struggling with depression for several years, and she had spent time with him in the adolescent psych ward or at the family home during vacations.[10]

I knew after his first few attempts that he was eventually going to kill himself, so a lot of my college experience felt like holding my breath, steeling myself for the moment. He was a cutter, and posted pictures of his scars and bloody cuts on the Internet at a support group for cutters, along with his thoughts about cutting and some poetry he had written ... I would go online and read what he had written as a way to feel some connection with him at times when he wasn't telling his family anything about what he was going through. He also spent a lot of time playing online games – so between this visual catalogue of his self-injury that he posted online to his support group and all the hours that he spent in chat-rooms and gaming, a huge part of his life was spent on the Internet, which is why in *410[Gone]* there is an exploration of technology and avatarization.[11]

Her own immediate response was to write an online blog, some of which took the form of letters to her dead brother along with a record of memories and dreams, some of which made their way into her play. Because she had been expecting him to kill himself for so long, she explains that it was more like the end of mourning than the beginning of it and that she felt liberated and free to follow her own ambitions. At the same time, trauma would echo through her plays.

Eurydice was the wife of Orpheus. When she stepped on a viper, she died, only for him to pursue her to the underworld to bring her back into the world of the living, the only condition being that he should lead her without a backward glance. He failed to obey the injunction, and she was forced to return to the underworld. This was a story at the heart of Sarah Ruhl's play *Eurydice*, but in the hands of Cowhig, in *410[Gone]*, originally titled *The Other Side of the Closet*, it is transposed to a Chinese context in a play that is clearly her way of addressing trauma without succumbing to it. Beyond what is obviously a deeply personal work, containing, as it does, at its heart, a sister's search for her dead brother, and still more for an understanding of his death, it is presented as a Chinese opera to a disco beat, a vaudeville double act, Becket colliding with the Cirque du Soleil, a television reality show, a video game crossed with farce. The use of a video game is in part a reference to her brother, and in part a metaphor for that blurring of reality and virtual reality that powers the play. In what is described as a possible pre-show speech, the audience is invited to the Land of Shade, to turn off their cell phones and 'recall the face of a loved one you are about to forget'.[12] Remembering and forgetting, indeed, become principal themes, as does a blend of darkness and humour.

For all her insistence on being Taiwanese-American rather than Chinese, *410[Gone]* features two Chinese-Americans and is a surreal blend of Chinese myth and modern technology. A woman, Twenty-One (Cowhig's age at the time of her brother's death), goes to the Chinese Land of the Dead in search of her brother, Seventeen (the age at which her brother Patrick died). The Land of the Dead is a mixture, her notes explain, of a disco, an arcade and a pachinko parlour. It has a dance-game console, a version of DanceDanceRevolution that requires players to step on particular places on a dance platform, and a set of seven telephones that light up. The Land of the Living is a closet.

The Land of the Dead is presided over by the Goddess of Mercy, who wears a white dress, black stiletto boots and Chinese Opera makeup and whose function it is to calm the suffering. She is joined by the Monkey King, described as a simian imbecile with the ability to transform himself into other beings. A third figure, Ox-Head, is the first person the dead encounter. He is the bearer of the Soup of Forgetting. The dead cross the bridge, drink from the proffered soup, and forget the life they have just departed, except that Patrick Seventeen takes so little that his memories survive; he is also not digitised and downloaded to the computer, much to the bewilderment of the Goddess of Mercy, unaccountably remaining three-dimensional, even remembering his name and that he is from America. Something has plainly gone wrong. The 401 of the title refers to the computer code for an unauthorised error, meaning that a page cannot be loaded without a valid log-in or that the page has gone.

Back in the world he has left, his sister buys the conventional paper money to be sent beyond the grave, each note having the word 'Patrick' on it. Immediately, it floats down into the Land of the Dead, evidence to the Goddess that someone is looking for him, that a door usually closed is still open, as Cowhig's own sense of loss had yet to be relieved. She follows this with food, including a giant pickle jar. When Patrick asks where he is, the Goddess of Mercy replies that he is in China, which, as he points out, is hardly commensurate with what he sees around him. She replies, 'Your ignorant stereotypes do not impress me' (17), insisting that his heritage is calling him back, a heritage that in his case is clearly ambiguous as, of course, it is for Cowhig, the scatter of cultural references never blending, merely co-existing.

There are moments when Twenty-One reveals that her search is not only for her brother, who she would wish to rescue from death, but for an understanding of what took him away, a process not without its psychological and physical pain. Speaking to the absent Patrick, she explains that she has discovered 'two unwound paper clips, one pair of scissors, and a razor blade rusted along one edge. Thorough inspection of each item revealed small quantities of your blood clinging to the razor blades in dry flakes. I transferred this specimen to a slide, sterilized the razor, and cut my wrists along your favourite vein' (21).

She struggles to discover a means of access, locked out by the 401 error, and in doing so revisits the significance of certain numbers, the seven minutes by which the paramedics were too late to rescue her brother, the four hundred and twenty-three miles away that she, like Cowhig, was when he was 'hanging in a closet' – a closet, in the play, being the place where the living move through to death. She contemplates multiplying 'by the difference in our blood samples, divided by the square root of the number of suicide attempts you made, subtract the angle of the pole you used to hang yourself', desperate to decode the mystery of his death. She is, she confesses, looking 'for the reason you left me, and the reason I wasn't enough to keep you alive' (24). She still has the clothes in which he died, while life-sized cardboard copies of her at different stages in her life penetrate into the underworld, memories made physical, each bearing Patrick's name, as she pounds on the walls of the closet trying to discover an access to the other world in which he still exists.

The set features a bathtub, this being where he cut himself, and Cowhig has confessed that she finds the sight of bathtubs and razors disturbing, summoning up, as they do, 'horrific visions'; Twenty-One insists, 'I hate you for hiding your razors in the stuffed animal I gave you for Christmas. For smashing my lightbulbs to cut up your wrists . . . For making our mother cry . . . For dying before me . . . For never loving me back' (27–8).

Patrick himself plays a number of games with the Goddess of Mercy and the Monkey King, each win gifting him more knowledge of his circumstances in a way perhaps reminiscent of Sam Shepard's duelling rock stars in *The Tooth of Crime*. *410[Gone]* is about the need to hold on and the equal necessity to let go. Memories are reminders of pain but equally consolations, a way of keeping someone alive, pulling them back for a moment into conscious awareness and hence into existence. As a portal opens and the siblings glimpse one another, Patrick's own memories are downloaded into the dance game console, memories of electroconvulsive treatment, of blood soaking through his shirt.

Although briefly together, momentarily outside the closet in the Land of the Living, they cannot communicate, and there is the sound of Seventeen breathing as he repeats the actions involved in his suicide in slow motion, struggling to resist. His breathing becomes faster as he hangs himself and his sister screams. Together, they enter the Land of the Dead and what seems to be a television show presided over by the Monkey King and the Goddess of Mercy. She confronts Twenty-One with the truth: 'He killed himself. He didn't leave a note. And now you're alone. Without answers, solutions, or any idea what comes next.' The truth she offers is that 'Life is suffering. Birth is suffering. Old age is suffering. Sickness, death, grief and despair – all suffering.' Yet her role is to offer compassion even if the sole consolation she can offer is the assertion that 'Only clear-eyed observation liberates you from the cycle of suffering.' What Twenty-One has to accept is that 'You don't want him back. You want your fantasy brother back. But it's been years since he's been that person . . . You want a little boy. Not this obnoxious, self-aggrandising mess' (34–5).

The principle truth Twenty-One now has to confront is that his death had allowed her to breathe. After waiting for him to die for so many years, she is now free, something that Cowhig has herself confessed to feeling. At this the Goddess of Mercy inhales her pain. Her brother drinks the soup of forgetting, his memory passing into the console, he becoming an avatar as they prepare to download him into 'the next available life form'(40). In future, she is told, objects will no longer be other than themselves, no longer recall pain, prompt guilt. She steps back into the Land of the Living where she begins to clear away the objects she had retained that had tormented her, reconciled at last not only to her brother's death and the need to move on but to a fundamental truth of human existence.

In one sense *410[Gone]* obviously functioned as therapy for Cowhig. It addressed her own sense of shock and bewilderment and reprises the process through which she came to reconcile herself not simply with her brother's death but her own response to it. Indeed the writing of it seems to have been part of that process. It is reminiscent of Paula Vogel's *The Baltimore Waltz*, Vogel being one of the people to whom Cowhig was exposed at Brown. Vogel's brother also died, although of AIDS, and the play she wrote to address that event was not a realistic one, although it came out of that same sense of distress and guilt. Not knowing of his medical condition, she had declined an invitation to join him on a trip to Europe, missing a chance for contact. He, meanwhile, had outlined details for his funeral or memorial service, which was to be in part a camp display and in part an invitation to remain friends after death, to breach a final boundary.

In the play Vogel deploys stereotypes, as does Cowhig when Twenty-One adopts a mock Mexican accent. She stages a cascade of images, again as does Cowhig. Both writers deal with death through fantasy and dream, telling a truth but telling it slant, pitching the imagination against the implacable fact of death. Both resurrect their brothers within a fiction as they cannot in reality but locate them in a comedy that is equally about reclaiming and relinquishing. Vogel uses her brother's real name, earthing her fantasy in the one irremediable fact that in both cases gave rise to their plays. It gave her the opportunity to use her brother's name in the context of the present tense. The same could be said of Cowhig; while both embrace the truth that, in the words of Anna in *The Baltimore Waltz*, 'There's nothing I can do. There's nothing you can do. There's nothing he, she or it can do.'[13] She has to learn to use the past tense, as does Twenty-One.

Tony Kushner's *Angels in America* also deals with AIDS and death, turning to fantasy, a dream world, to confront a sense of loss and, in his case – and to some degree in Vogel's – anger. Cowhig turned to a version of Chinese myth, while Kushner created his own involving an angel. In both plays there is a sense of desertion while both edge towards a resolution gifted by a fantasy figure. *410[Gone]*, however, lacks the political drive evident in Vogel and still more so in Kushner. She invokes Chinese myths, transposed into the world of computer games and television shows, in part ironically, mocking the tropes she deploys, and in part to embed the deeply personal in a broader debate about the way in which loss, grief and guilt are managed. Myths, their absurdities aside, are constructions designed to alleviate pain and sanction a continued existence through those who need to relinquish not only the dead but also the feelings that tie them to a past which obstructs the path to the future.

410[Gone] is itself a ceremony even as it plays with the idea of ceremony. An intensely personal play, it becomes a contemplation of the sometimes conflicting strategies we use to deal with death, and with which we are all familiar, from the laughter that oddly characterises funeral receptions to the moment when evidences of the dead, long clung to, are finally packed away, a process that simultaneously floods the mind with memories and marks a moment of release never entirely without guilt and regret.

410[Gone] was performed on the Brown campus and at the University of Texas at Austin, but it would be nine years before, in 2013, it was staged at the 80-seat Crowded Fire Theater in San Francisco's Potrero neighbourhood, by which time *Lidless* had had its premiere in 2010 in the unlikely venue of Halesworth, Suffolk, in England, Halesworth with a population of just 6,000.

Cowhig's motivation for writing the latter play was perhaps less political – although inevitably the events it references are such – than formal. As she has said:

I began writing the play that became *Lidless* with very simple constraints: I wanted to write a five-person ensemble play for three female and two male actors. I didn't want to write a ghost story, and I didn't want there to be any magical worlds that I would have to elaborate rules for. (The previous two plays I had written would both fall into the category of magical ghost-story.) I was pretty sick of my previous work and aesthetic and wanted to do something radically different. Each of my projects are in part a rejection of or violent departure from a previous project.[14]

The result was a play inspired by a low point in recent American history but one in which she was less interested in making an ideological point than continuing to explore her interest in trauma.

Under President George W. Bush, 'enhanced interrogation' was approved for use against those detained as terrorists. Notoriously, he and Vice President Cheney were both enthusiasts for waterboarding, but that was only part of the armoury deployed by the CIA. Sexual assaults were commonplace at Guantánamo Bay, as they were at Abu Ghraib prison in Iraq. In September 2005, Lynndie England, who had served in the latter, appeared at a court-martial on charges of conspiracy to maltreat prisoners and assault. Back home in West Virginia, where the family lived in a trailer, she had worked in a chicken factory in what was called spray down and evisceration, which involved washing the blood out of carcasses. As a member of the US Army Reserve, she was sent to Iraq in 2003. In 2004 a series of photographs were published showing her standing beside a pile of naked prisoners, leading one on a leash, pointing at the genitals of another and, according to Seymour Hersh in an article in the *New Yorker*,[15] watching still another required to masturbate in front of her. The shock was in part that a woman, indeed more than one woman (Sabrina Harman and Megan Ambuhl were similarly charged), was being used to humiliate defenceless detainees whose religious sensibilities, no less than bodies, were under assault by those who evidently took pleasure in their actions, willingly posing for trophy pictures.

Those pictures, however, were acquired by a military policeman outraged by what he had seen. The result was a worldwide scandal. The Bush government had done its best to suppress images of dead soldiers being returned to America. Efforts were now made to prevent further images entering the public domain, denial being both policy and strategy. Lynndie England served half of a three-year sentence. She did not regret her actions ('it's like saying sorry to the enemy'), although she was on antidepressants, paid for by the military.

In 2007, David Hare was asked to succeed Edward Albee as judge of the Yale Drama Series for a hitherto unpublished play in the English language. There were 650 submissions for the prize, nearly all from the United States. He and his fellow judges chose Cowhig's *Lidless*, a play set in part at Guantánamo Bay but essentially drawing on events at Abu Ghraib. What struck him was 'the vitality of the governing metaphor'. In Cowhig's play, he said, 'torture is quite literally a disease which has entered the American bloodstream. Nothing is as striking in *Lidless* as its basic conceit: by allowing Guantánamo, Americans have allowed something with which they will have to live for many years.' Himself a political playwright from his early days with Portable Theatre who had written about the Iraq War in *Stuff Happens*, Hare, together with the other judges, 'admired the play because, although it was stylishly written – although the governing metaphor and basic realism were held in fine balance – it also recalled the political urgency which had propelled a previous generation of writers into the theatre in the first place'.[16]

A fair number of plays have addressed the question of the Iraq War, torture and Guantánamo. In Britain, the Tricycle Theatre, which has specialised in political theatre, produced Victoria Brittain and Gillian Slovo's *Guantánamo Honor Bound to Defend Freedom* in 2004, a documentary drama that transferred to the West End. In 2007, Nigel Jamieson's *Honour Bound*, a collage of dance, image and sound prompted by the detaining of an

Australian at Guantánamo, opened at London's Barbican, a work already seen in Sydney and Melbourne.

Cowhig, however, who transposes events that occurred at Abu Ghraib to Guantánamo (although naked prostitutes had been paraded before detainees at the latter), focused less on the trauma of those suffering torture than that of those who inflicted it, and indeed her play is dedicated to 'the families of the men and women stationed or detained at Guantánamo Bay' almost as if there were an equivalency in the restricted sense that no one who emerged from that experience could be said to be unwounded.

This is not a play about the justification for torture. It is about the price to be paid for inflicting it and for suffering it, about the degree to which a role can transform the performer, the present be shaped by the past, how reconciliation, restitution or redemption is or is not possible. It is a play about remembering and forgetting and the extent to which either can be said to be a blessing. It is concerned to explore denial and repression, the fragility of the contract that connects us, the ease with which we betray not simply others but ourselves, the limits or otherwise of responsibility. It is set in two time scales, one some years in the future precisely because she was interested in consequences, the aftershocks of trauma. In a way, it is a family play, and not simply to the degree to which all in it are related, in one case surprisingly so, but because it is here that the consequences of public actions are later acted out in a context in which there is assumed to be no danger and trust is guaranteed, where it is presumed that everything and everyone is familiar and bonds are secure. Meanwhile, beyond this family is a wider one in which civilisation depends upon the cruelties of childhood being abandoned, society relying on the suppressions of certain instincts that can undo the self and society alike.

The *Washington Times* review attacked it as an anti-US diatribe about the real and alleged cruelties of war and a doctrinaire indictment of America that gave the enemy a pass, a response that could charitably be regarded as somewhat missing the point. It is true that the detainee featured claims his innocence, but it is another kind of innocence that interests Cowhig: how far can we wipe the slate clean, absolve ourselves of the consequences of our actions? Admittedly, it could be said that this is a play that, in exploring the life of the interrogator, shows a compassion towards her, which is surprising given the role she has played. The fact is, though, that she is at the end of a line of responsibility that stretches back up the military and political line to those who issue instructions but themselves never have to carry them out, who indeed subsequently continue to justify themselves and presumably never suffered trauma, never woke in the night, as does the central character in *Lidless* not even able to recall what it was that made her act out a past she could no longer fully recall.

It is set in 2004, the year of the aforementioned photographs, and then in Minnesota fifteen years later. It opens as an orange shaft of light falls on an interrogation room, while offstage Rhiannon, a girl of fourteen, is having an asthma attack, two time scales momentarily overlapping since she comes from the future. The play, Cowhig has said, is 'a work of speculative drama imagining the consequences of the United States government authorizing the use of the female body in the "War on Terror", specifically to make a Muslim man stop praying'.[17] Rhiannon's fight for breath, meanwhile, becomes a central motif in a play in which the right to breathe freely has a political, psychological and even metaphysical force.

Riva, a twenty-five-year-old US Army medic and a Texan of Iraqi-Assyrian heritage, enters and, facing the audience, dictates into a tape recorder details of what are obviously the wounds suffered by a detainee, including problems in respiration, although from a hood being placed on his head rather than from asthma. Guantánamo, we learn, is a place where men can be tortured but killing an iguana as it crosses the road can command a $10,000 fine because, this being American territory, the Endangered Species Act is enforced, even if habeas corpus is not. The iguana, though, has relevance beyond this irony, having, we are told, 'cells that, when activated by trauma, can regenerate a tail completely. It just lies on a warm rock and mends'.[18] The question is whether those in this play have a similar capacity to restore themselves.

She is then joined by her friend Alice, a white Texan, who addresses the audience, and Bashi, a middle-aged Pakistani-Canadian detainee. She taunts him with his daughter's photograph; later in the play, time having passed, the relationship between Alice and her own daughter becomes crucial. As Cowhig explained,

The protagonist was always a female interrogator, because the original idea for the piece came after reading a piece in *The Economist* about the sexual tactics being used by female interrogators in Guantánamo. In my work I am far less interested in the actual traumatic event than in its consequences over time, which is why I knew that Alice had to have a daughter, so that I could begin to examine how Alice's choices and behaviour in the past continue to affect her present life and specifically her daughter (her future). I also knew that I didn't want to write a political diatribe or anything that could be reduced to a simple 'Shame on you America' anti-war piece that could just as easily be expressed in an op-ed essay.[19]

For all that, there is room enough for shame as Alice dismisses the significance of waterboarding and, following what she declares is a memo from Washington, invoking Dick Cheney, prepares to taunt Bashi sexually, her assault not only being on his body but his soul as she seeks to force him to compromise his faith, the aim of torture, Sartre suggested, being to convince its victims of their impotence. Here, though, she tries to provoke him into sexual arousal, underscoring his ultimate impotence, being powerless to resist her. This is the weaponising of the woman's body. She daubs herself with lipstick to simulate menstruation, only for another voice to intrude, that of her daughter Rhiannon, ushering in a scene set fifteen years later, on Alice's fortieth birthday.

The action now moves to a family living room. Rhiannon's school project involves interviewing someone for an oral history paper. In this house, though, history has its secrets, and remembering is a dangerous occupation. Riva's family had fled Iraq when she was eight, and their curse is that they cannot forget, that they are 'trapped in their heads'. 'My mother only leaves the house at night', she explains. 'She never answers the phone or door because she thinks Saddam's men have followed her to South Texas' (15). As she says, 'I don't know a single Assyrian Iraqi who escaped as a child who is not crazy' (22). They are crippled by their memories.

In *Lidless*, the repressed returns in a literal form as, into Alice's flower shop comes Bashir, the man she had tortured and who himself has reason to forget. As he says, 'People should not be allowed to haunt other people. There should be an erase button in our brains that allows each person to begin again' (17), except that he himself still hears the voice of his wife who committed suicide in despair. It becomes evident that he has not come to forget or forgive. He brings with him a photograph of Guantánamo, in 2019 now closed and converted into a resort, and tells her that he had contracted hepatitis there during her watch and never been treated, being still on the transplant list. Knowing they share a blood group, he has come to give her the chance of redeeming herself by donating part of her liver to him; without a transplant, he has only a few months to live. The woman who had used her body is now being asked to sacrifice a part of that body; she tells him that, 'You think actions don't have consequences?' herself having suffered from them. When she declines to help him, he pulls a black plastic bag over his head, mimicking the infamous Abu Ghraib photographs, screaming as he does so.

Alice had also wished to 'start over', become 'a good mum', asking her sister and husband, Lucas, never to talk of their time in the camp; Lucas, too, has reasons to deny the past, having been a junkie, torturing himself as she did others but then covering his track marks with tattoos of sunflowers. 'They are still there', he admits, 'I haven't forgotten them. But they aren't going to define me, or us, or this family.' They have agreed to live in the present, as the past begins to press ever harder on them. The past, he insists, 'doesn't have to haunt us' (30). But it is not so easily rejected.

For her part, Alice had seen her father tormented by nightmares of his time in Vietnam and was determined not to repeat his experience, only to wake up one night and tear her daughter's pet chicken to pieces. Another night her husband discovers her screaming at an empty chair, breaking his nose when he suddenly wakes her, an incident she forgets. She has flashbacks that, as Lucas explains to Rhiannon, and not with irony, 'make you hurt the people you love' (31). Guantánamo has killed something in her. 'It's been a lifetime since something has moved you', he says to Alice, 'You went to war. You got back. You went to sleep. We're dust, Alice. Dead stars. We stopped giving off light lifetimes ago, but it's taken this long for anyone to notice' (48). He explains that Alice is suffering from post-traumatic stress disorder, although Cowhig has spoken of consulting a psychologist who worked with survivors of war and rejected the very idea of post-traumatic stress, preferring the term 'cognitive reframing' because the essence of what survivors experienced was a complete restructuring of a worldview. *Lidless* is a play not merely about remembering and forgetting but about transformed sensibility, two antithetical worlds in collision.

For Alice, power has disappeared. Her sexuality, once deployed as a weapon, has been compromised. Guantánamo had seemed a Manichean world, with torturers and victims, a collision of values, even a clash of races, yet in the play there is a hybridity. Even Alice's husband is described as 'racially ambiguous', while torturers and victims, as we discover, meet in something other than simple confrontation as Rhiannon encounters Bashir and enrols him in her project. For Lucas, Alice has been through 'some scary stuff' (32), although we know that she inflicted it.

The prisoners at Guantánamo were called orange fish, after the jump suits they were forced to wear. Rhiannon, who as noted earlier suffers from asthma, takes a goldfish from the water and, as she confesses to Bashir, watches as it 'kept flopping around, gasping for breath' (25). She admits to killing other animals inheriting, it seems, something of her mother's detachment.

Riva appeals to Bashir to leave her sister alone, explaining that her own father had been tortured in Abu Ghraib under Saddam, his hands cut off and put in a box for her mother. The circle of abuse, it seems, had continued, and there comes a moment when Rhiannon discovers her mother's role as an interrogator, telling her parents, 'there are people you've been around for ever . . . but you have no idea who they are. You pass each other every day, your feet touch the same ground, but the air you breathe is so different, you shouldn't be allowed to call yourselves human beings' (44).

It is finally revealed that Rhiannon is Bashir's daughter; Alice could not give him part of her liver because she, a hepatitis carrier, is the person who probably gave him the disease in the first place. In the end, it is his own daughter who saves him. As Bashir lies in the hospital, breathing carefully, Lucas practices tai chi, breathing in and out, while Alice holds the plastic childhood globe that pictured the countries she hoped to visit and lets the air out, herself breathing it in. Meanwhile Rhiannon has an asthma attack and dies for lack of breath. A metaphor becomes literal. The play ends as Alice and Bashir stare at one another: 'Electricity crackles between them. They stare at each other as the lights crescendo to full, blinding brightness, then fade to black' (61). They are, it seems, drawn together by a past neither can escape even as their child dies, an irony perhaps too great.

Lidless is not a realistic work. Scenes overlap. The roles of Riva and Zakiyah (Bashir's son), both of whose fathers had suffered, are played by the same actor. Stage objects, we are told, 'should be treated as if they are their own organisms'. An orange jumpsuit, black goggles, an army jacket resurface as physical reminders of the costuming of this national drama. There is a degree of contrivance about the plot and the almost melodramatic ending as if in acknowledgement that what is played out is as much myth, the playing out of a ritual, as plausible drama. Indeed, the theatricality of the piece is underscored by Bashir and Rhiannon's desire to perform the past in full costume as by Alice's sudden reversion to the role of interrogator, not a realistic gesture but a recapitulation of the staged drama of a camp in which the prisoners were indeed costumed and their movements prescribed. There was even a text, written many thousand of miles away, as there was an audience, their humiliations captured on film.

The force of *Lidless* lies in its portrait of characters, all of whom are trying to make sense of what has happened to them, to find a way forward as they are drawn back. Nor is it only these characters who wish to forget. America has moved on, even as Barack Obama's promise to close Guantánamo proved impossible to fulfil. The camp will never be the resort proposed in the play, a place in which the past is wiped away, even as denial has proved as much public policy as private necessity. It is not only interrogators and prisoners who have registered trauma. Apart from the camp itself, the photographs are still there, on the

Web. The play is still there, asking questions to which there are no final answers. Gatsby believed that it was possible to recover innocence, too late learning otherwise.

In Britain, *Lidless* moved from small theatre to small theatre, after its Suffolk premiere, travelling to Edinburgh and then London's Trafalgar Studio 2. Even so, it attracted the attention of the major daily newspapers, which responded positively. The *Guardian* reviewer found it 'fiercely intelligent', the *Times* called it 'intelligent and impassioned'. The *Telegraph* greeted an 'excellent new play,' while the *Independent* found it vital writing from a talented new voice. The play reached New York in 2011 with a production at Off-Broadway's Soho Rep. The *New York Times* review, however, was less enthusiastic than the British ones, commenting on its implausibilities and 'mannered introspection'.

Trauma of another kind featured in Cowhig's next play, *The World of Extreme Happiness* (2013), commissioned and developed by South Coast Repertory in Costa Mesa, California, given a developmental production by the Goodman Theatre in Chicago and staged in England by the National Theatre's 220-seat The Shed (created to fill the gap when the Cottesloe was being redeveloped), before reaching the Manhattan Theatre Club in 2015. Set in China in 1992 and 2011–12, it explores the plight of factory workers who are required to forget the past and serve the purposes of a country combining Party control with unforgiving capitalism. The 2013 published play carries an epigraph from the artist and political activist Ai Weiwei, whose own family had been exiled to Shihezi, Xinjiang, not returning to Beijing until after the Cultural Revolution.

In the same year that *The World of Extreme Happiness* opened in London, two other plays had already been seen, Howard Brenton's work about the arrest of Ai Weiwei and Lucy Kirkwood's *Chimerica*. For Cowhig, though, because of her time in Taiwan and China, her play was rooted firmly in issues that to her were both public and private.

She was drawn to the subject, she explained, because she had always been interested in internal migrations – in this case, migration in China from the country to the city – and in colliding belief systems. She had spent six months with her parents in Chengdu where her father was working at the American Consulate on a State Department Human Rights Report and met a number of dissident writers during that time. Her mother's family had had experience of rural life in Taiwan and later managed factories in China. *The World of Extreme Happiness* (originally to have been called *72 Transformations*) would draw on both. Interestingly, given *Lidless* and her comments on post-traumatic stress disorder, she recalls a conversation with the writer Liao Yiwu who suggested to her that China is full of people suffering from that condition because of the speed with which it has changed. From him she also learned of the prevalence of self-help books, which would also find their way into the play as they would into the Malaysian writer Tash Aw's *Five Star Billionaire*.

She has said, 'I wanted to write something about China . . . A lot of plays in the Western theatre tradition are [seen] through a Western lens and I wanted to write a play told completely through the lives of Chinese people. One thing I noticed while living in China is there are two completely different islands of existence . . . the older generation versus the younger generation, whose reality has been shaped by totally different contexts.'[20] Before writing, she read Leslie Chang's book *Factory Girl* and watched documentaries about immigrant workers. Once again she was interested in trauma and recovery but now, as she said, on a national scale.

If the play was provoked by her experience of China, it was also a result of her reading Arthur Miller's essay 'Tragedy and the Common Man', from which she derived the idea that a young peasant girl working in a factory in southern China could be a tragic hero. At its heart is the figure of Sunny, retrieved from the slop bucket into which she had been thrown as an unwanted girl child, her name prompted by her smile. Her father's affections are reserved for his pigeons. He is a miner whose hopes for the future depend on a male child, for which he has paid money to a woman who purports to be able to influence the gender of the child but who has failed now on five occasions. A girl is no more than a thing to be disposed of. They live in a dilapidated house from which, at fourteen, Sunny sets out for Shenzhen where she works at a menial task cleaning toilets and sending money home for her brother to have the education she could not have. It is a place where workers are disposable and where suicides are common as, indeed, they proved to be when actual deaths at the Foxconn factories, a Taiwanese company with factories in China where Apple products were assembled, made news around the world in 2010.

When a fellow worker introduces her to the vogue for self-help, she attends a meeting that fires her enthusiasm, although we later learn that Mr. Destiny, the man conducting the meeting, is a charlatan, failing to take his own advice and remaining a peasant living in a shanty. At home, her brother has ambitions to play the role of the Monkey King from the story told to him by his mother before she died, the Monkey King being able to transform himself seventy-two times (hence the original title).

The World of Extreme Happiness is about transformations – the transformation of China, transformations in the lives of those who believe they can change, transformations in political consciousness. The changes in China are epitomised by the two owners of the factory, James and Artemis, the former a Party member anxious not to prejudice his standing, the latter wearing a designer dress, a woman born in the countryside but who had gone on to attend Harvard. Their names and that of the factory are themselves indicative of cultural influence. The company is Price-Smart/Jade River Manufacturing. As James observes, 'Forty years ago this wasn't a Special Economic Zone. It was just dirt, rice and country people.'[21] Now it is an authorised bridgehead for foreign capital free of any of the limited rights available beyond its boundary. Their responsibility is to satisfy their customers and shareholders by keeping wages low but also to address the potential damage being done as news of the suicides leaks out, eleven in a month. The solution, they decide, is to commission a documentary showing how their company has transformed the life of a peasant for the better, initiating a competition that Sunny wins, having seduced her immediate superior and left her only rival suicidal.

The problem is that Artemis's family had all been executed, including her mother, shot through the head, and she, as a result, is the child of counter-revolutionaries. She is detained for a while and reminded that 'Subversives are sent to asylums for the politically insane . . . medicated and given electric treatments until their condition has stabilized.' The authorities see no purpose in public relations when 'everyone wants to sleep with us just the way we are' (65). As for her, 'There were only ever two choices. I can see the truth – and always be in pain. Or I can look away and be rich. And happy' (88). That is equally the choice for her country. As in *Lidless*, it is a question of remembering or forgetting.

Meanwhile, though, there is discontent, and not only in the factory. The son of Wang Hua, whose skills at ensuring the birth of boys had proved so ineffectual, loses her own son when he organises a strike. She insists that Sonny should marry him, although he is dead, and arranges a ceremony from which her father will receive money and Wang Hua a dutiful carer. She responds by serving a meal of her father's pigeons, their feathers being dumped in the same trashcan in which she had been abandoned as a baby. It is, she says, a question of the pigeons coming home to roost.

They come home to roost in another sense. Old Lao, Head of Sanitation at the Shenzhen factory, recalls life under Mao: 'Hitler killed eleven million and the world still feels bad. Mao killed five times that many – of his own people – and what do foreigners want when they come to China? His little red book, and a shirt with his face on it.' If people wish to kill themselves, he suggests, 'do it because you understand what has happened. Not because you missed some made up opportunity for success' (93). The new China embraces McDonald's and video games, but with blood on its hands hopes to erase memories. Old Lao jumps to his death holding a petition calling for strikes.

When Sonny makes her prepared speech for the cameras, in the Great Hall of the People, she abandons her text, instead calling for action: 'destiny is not something one person can change. We have to work together and make – demand – change. For all of us . . . I protest – and I ask you to protest with me. Demand you get the same rights as people born in the city. Go on strike. Stop working . . . Let city people try to live a single day without us' (102). She is duly seized by a security officer and declared a 'politically insane worker activist'. Her father now confesses that his own brother had died on a student demonstration, which he is told was actually 'a counter-revolutionary riot' in a 'period of political turmoil'. He relinquishes his daughter to the state, apologising for raising a 'Bad Element'. 'It's time to forget the past', he is told, 'and face a brighter future' and 'happiness'.

Sunny is now incarcerated in the Beijing Ankang Psychiatric Hospital where, after months of torture and medication, there is little of herself left. When her brother, Pete, contrives to enter the hospital as a janitor, he tells her that the workers have gone on strike, including the miners. The factories have closed, and the pollution has disappeared. Peasants have given up their city dreams, returning to the countryside to 'take care of each other'. She is now regarded as a peasant hero, and this the Sunshine Revolution. Corruption has ended. There has been an election for leader, and she has been chosen. She can, however, no longer move or speak beyond two repeated words: 'Change me.' Pete effects the only change he can: he smothers her, releasing her into the afterlife. 'When you open your eyes', he assures her, 'your life will be wide open with possibility . . . Let go of your past . . . Change, Sunny. Change. Change. Change'(108).

Is this, then, a political play and, if so, an echo of 1930s dramas calling for change, for the need to awake and sing? That would seem to be the essence of the Ai Weiwei epigraph that speaks of those who 'linger on in any steadily worsening situation, people who have been dulled and forsaken by the deceptions of culture, their personalities deprived and lost . . . people who have abandoned their rights and responsibilities, who walk like ghosts on the ever-widening streets, and whose true emotions, dreams and homes are long lost.' As Cowhig is aware, though, those here called upon to bring about change are the least likely ever to see her play, change itself being at risk of substituting one kind of control for another (reportedly some Chinese members of the audience in the London production refused to clap, unwilling to accept the version of China they were offered).

For all her concern to locate this drama against that curious blend of stasis and flux that characterises the contradictory politics of modern China, there are broader issues at play having to do with fractured identities (actors play several roles), complicity in systems of thought and behaviour. The self-help books embraced by the Chinese have always been a standby in an America that offers a dream of possibility out of reach for many, social mobility in the United States being on a par with that in the United Kingdom, which is to say unimpressive. Mr. Destiny is modelled on his American counterparts, hucksters for the future in a country dedicated to the pursuit of happiness, extreme or otherwise. Government surveillance, meanwhile, is scarcely foreign to contemporary America in which Homeland Security can breed domestic insecurity.

The dilemma of Cowhig's characters is that they are caught between different myths, none of which serve their human needs. Chinese traditions have their cruelties while communism has nothing to offer beyond lies and a suppression of all thought and freedom. The new myths of the modern world, to do with individual success, self-improvement and the trappings of wealth, represent a future void of any sense of community or transcendence. The arrival of McDonald's, Mercedes, designer clothes and violent video games signals nothing but a new promise of happiness found by possessing the world rather than inhabiting it, scarcely something limited to China.

These myths co-exist, and, like the Monkey God, cede territory to one another, transforming as the world about them is transformed. The Chinese myths are hermetic, sealed off against experience. So, too, are the Communist dicta, shutting people away. Yet they are not immune. They are all under threat. The irony is that, at the end, we are told that country dwellers are returning to their homes, a move against history that oddly echoes Mao's attempts to force city dwellers into the fields but here is reminiscent of American myths of the yeoman farmer as the backbone of democracy. When Arthur Miller visited China, he looked through the window at rows of factory workers. It reminded him of those he had seen in his father's company in the 1930s, the rhythm of their lives dictated by the cycle of production and consumption they served. Today, those jobs have been exported to China, as if in looking to American capitalism as a way out of the darkness, they are recapitulating its past.

The characters are at times, perhaps, rather too willing to conform to the roles they are given – new capitalists openly confessing to their strategies, a father too obviously committed to his pigeons in a dialogue intercut between his love for them and his open disregard for a new human life – but then, this is not a play dedicated to psychological realism.

It offers a mixture of styles and conventions. At moments there are comic set pieces, when, for example, efforts are made to marry Sunny to a dead man or his ghost. At other moments, serious accounts of past violence are offered, a national backstory quickly sketched. The play ends with a death, as did *Lidless*, much like Miller's, whose first four plays also ended with a death, he evidently believing this necessary to his sense of the tragic form. This death, though, functions differently, its stylised form suggesting that in a play about myths, Cowhig is concerned to create her own.

In truth, death has haunted all three of her plays to date. In *The World of Extreme Happiness*, a brother is responsible for the death of his sister as Cowhig has blamed herself to some degree for not being able to prevent the death of her own brother, an event that crops up even in her unpublished short story 'Monkeys of the Sea', in which a boy's brother apparently kills himself in a closet, a story that ends with the death of all the characters in a tidal wave. Cowhig paints with darkness and light, not always clear as to which will have supremacy.

Lyn Gardner, reviewing the National Theatre production in 2013, while thinking it a little overemphatic, observed, 'The beauty of Cowhig's play is that it offers a window on a hidden world',[22] its epic scope told through the lives of individuals. For Charles Spencer, in the *Telegraph*, it was an 'ambitious and often harrowing play' with 'an almost Dickensian indignation' and writing that was 'often raw and uncomfortable' but 'with many shafts of dark comedy'.[23] For Holly Williams, in the *Independent*, it was an 'ambitious, wide-reaching, politically biting' play, 'fearless, zippily-paced, and satirical'.[24] As with *Lidless*, it fared less well in the United States. Chris Jones, reviewing the Goodman Theatre production in 2014, while acknowledging that it was 'a smart piece' with 'great promise', insisted that its 'feelings and moral issues do not yet feel sufficiently deep or true'.[25] A year later, Charles Isherwood, reviewing the Manhattan Theatre Club production in the *New York Times*, found it coming close to being a dramatised lecture making 'its points with no great delicacy' while 'even the primary characters are drawn with minimal depth'.[26]

Cowhig is at the beginning of her career with, to date, only three plays produced, although she presented a reading in 2013 of *Go On Living*, an adaptation of Chinese dissident poet Liao Yiwu's *For a Song and a Hundred Songs* about his year as a political prisoner, detained as a result of his poem 'Massacre', a response to the 1989 protest in Tiananmen Square. It also draws on material from *Corpse Walker*, a collection of interviews Yiwu conducted. Cowhig was attracted to it, she explained, because 'it's unlike any prison story I've read. It's extremely theatrical and funny at the same time. [Yiwu] focuses on the ways in which prisoners try to create meaning for themselves through rituals and performances inside prison, which I think gives real levity to all of their struggles'.[27] She has also developed a play, set in rural China in the early '90s, about the use of infected blood that gave peasants HIV/AIDS. It was based on Dr. Wang Shuping, who revealed the scandal and whom Cowhig met in Salt Lake City. She was interested, she said, in characters who resisted and in challenging the idea that China is a wholly conformist society.

Frances Ya-Chu Cowhig has said that she is on a journey, even as, in her theatre work, 'the journey has to be the destination'. She has won the Wasserstein Prize (for young female writers), the Yale Drama Series Award, the David Callichio Award (for emerging playwrights), the Keene Prize for Literature (awarded by the University of Texas, Austin, and worth $50,000) and an Edinburgh Fringe First Award. As journeys go, it is impressive. The writer of Taiwanese and Irish heritage who had once declared that identification of her as a Chinese-American playwright was reductive has now confessed that effectively she became a Chinese-American playwright when she was produced in London; her attention seems to have moved in the direction of a country she first experienced from inside a diplomatic compound where her knowledge of what was happening outside came from watching CNN.

Notes

1 Diep Tran, 'The China Connection: A Conversation with Frances Ya-Chu Cowhig and Christopher Chen', *American Theatre*, 22 January 2015. http://francesyachucowhig.com/ images/amtheatre.pdf
2 Ibid.
3 Ibid.
4 Adam Syzymkowicz, 'I Interview Playwrights Part 379: Frances Ya-Chu Cowhig', 22 August 2011. http://aszym.blogspot.co.uk/2011/08/i-interview-playwrights-part-379.html
5 J. Hector St. John de Crevecoeur, *Letters from an American Farmer and Sketches of 18th-Century America* (Harmondsworth, 1981), p. 70.
6 Caridad Svich, 'Recovering Trauma: An Interview with Frances Ya-Chu Cowhig', *hotreview .org*, September 2011. www.hotreview.org/articles/recoveringtrauma.htm
7 Ibid.
8 Ibid.
9 Frances Ya-Chu Cowhig, 'A Playwright's Journey through a Year of Physical Theatre Training at Dell'Arte', *American Theatre*, 16 December 2015. www.americantheatre.org/2015/12/16/ a-playwrights-journey-through-a-year-of-physical-theatre-training-at-dellarte
10 Laura Brueckner, 'Interview with the Playwright: Frances Ya-Chu Cowhig', *Crowded Fire*, 5 July 2013. www.crowdedfire.dreamhosters.com/2013/06/interview-with-the-playwright-frances-ya-chu-cowhig
11 Ibid.
12 Frances Ya-Chu Cowhig, *410[Gone]* (New York, 2014), p. 6.
13 Paula Vogel, *The Baltimore Waltz and Other Plays* (New York, 1996), p. 14.
14 Caridad Svich, 'Recovering Trauma'.
15 Seymour M. Hersh, 'Torture at Abu Ghraib', *New Yorker*, 10 May 2004. www.newyorker.com/ magazine/2004/05/10/torture-at-abu-ghraib
16 David Hare, 'Forward' to Frances Ya-Chu Cowhig, *Lidless* (2011), pp. xii–xiii.
17 Adam Szymkowics, 'I Interview Playwrights Part 379: Frances Ya-Chu Cowhig'.
18 Frances Ya-Chu Cowhig, *Lidless* (London, 2011), p. 40.
19 Caridad Svich, 'Recovering Trauma'.
20 Alyssa Abkowitz, 'Turning the World's Largest Migration into a Play: Q&A with Frances Cowhig', *Wall Street Journal*, 29 January 2015. http://blogs.wsj.com/chinarealtime/2015/01/29/ turning-the-worlds-largest-human-migration-into-a-play-qa-with-frances-cowhig
21 Frances Ya-Chu Cowhig, *The World of Extreme Happiness*, typescript dated 22 February 2015, supplied by the author.
22 Lyn Gardner, '"The World of Extreme Happiness" – Review', *Guardian*, 1 October 2013. www .theguardian.com/stage/2013/oct/01/the-world-of-extreme-happiness-review
23 Charles Spencer, '"The World of Extreme Happiness", National Theatre Shed', *Telegraph*, 1 October 2013. www.telegraph.co.uk/culture/theatre/10347705/The-World-of-Extreme-Happiness-National-Theatre-Shed-review.html

24 Holly Williams, '"The World of Extreme Happiness" – Katrie Leung stars in Exposé of Migrant Chinese Workers', *Independent*, 3 October 2013. www.independent.co.uk/arts-entertainment/theatre-dance/reviews/the-world-of-extreme-happiness-katie-leung-stars-in-expos-of-migrant-chinese-workers-8856248.html

25 Chris Jones, '"The World of Extreme Happiness", in the Goodman's Owen Theatre', *Chicago Tribune*, 30 September 2014. www.chicagotribune.com/entertainment/theater/reviews/ct-world-extreme-happiness-review-column.html

26 Charles Isherwood, '"The World of Extreme Happiness", about China and Gender', *New York Times*, 24 February 2015. www.nytimes.com/2015/02/25/theater/review-the-world-of-extreme-happiness-about-china-and-gender.html?_r=0

27 Tanya Palmer, 'Filling the Gap', *Theatre Forum*, 45, Summer/Fall 2014. http://francesyachucowhig.com/images/TheatreForumWorldOfExtremeHappiness.pdf

3

Katori Hall

> ... being a woman of color ... those two parts of my identity are so inextricably linked that they inform one another ... I feel ... if I was a white woman I probably wouldn't write the stories that I do. And then I'm a black woman from the South and so I have been made to think about race just by virtue of growing up in [that] region ... but also my region affects me in terms of what I am writing about.[1]
>
> *– Katori Hall*

One of those mentored by fellow playwright Lynn Nottage was a young woman from Memphis who declared herself 'as Memphis as can be', complete with an accent that those training her at the American Repertory Theater/Moscow Art Theater Institute for Advanced Theater Training at Harvard did their best to eradicate. As she explained to Alexis Soloski in an interview in *American Theatre*, her early experience of theatre consisted of an elementary school visit to *The Lion, the Witch and the Wardrobe*, which 'just made ... a huge, huge impression on me'. In a city that was not 'a huge theatre town', it was church and sports that provided whatever drama was on offer.[2] On the other hand, she told the *Guardian* that she had seen 'plenty of theatre my parents weren't necessarily up on'.[3]

Hall grew up in a politically conscious household in a largely white neighbourhood, Allen Street, near Beale Street. Here, where there were just three African-American families, she learned how to perform a 'good' version of herself. After the family left, she has explained, it became a crack house and today is wasteland. Her maternal grandmother had been a sharecropper. Her father worked for Kraft before being laid off. Her mother, who grew up a block from the Lorraine Motel where Martin Luther King would be assassinated, was a phlebotomist and union worker who had the first of her children while young. When she voted for Barack Obama, her employer suggested that she should not revel in his victory because her fellow workers were upset. In Hall's grandmother's house, there were two pictures on the wall, Jesus and Martin Luther King, and growing up in the South, she experienced racism.

Hall is one of five sisters, she being the youngest, and recalls her mother's skill as a storyteller, also remembering herself inventing an array of invisible friends with whom she used to talk. She staged plays in her living room. At elementary school, she was part of a gifted children programme and in 1999 graduated from high school as valedictorian, the first African-American to do so since it had been desegregated twenty-six years earlier. She subsequently won a scholarship to Columbia University.

At Columbia she was a student of African-American studies, but with a concentration on creative writing, originally looking for a career in journalism. Indeed, she had been publishing articles in newspapers since she was fourteen and credits her attempts at journalism as honing her storytelling skills. She later came to think that in being a student of African-American studies, she had in effect been studying the social and cultural context of the characters she would later create.

As she explained, 'Growing up in Memphis, I didn't know who the hell Strindberg was', but it was exposure to his work and that of Suzan-Lori Parks, along with an acting class she took in her junior year, that steered her in another direction. As she told Alexis Soloski,[4] asked to research a scene appropriate to her and a fellow African-American student at Barnard College (a women's college affiliated with Columbia), she discovered that there were none in the library that seemed suitable (rejecting *A Raisin in the Sun* because neither of them was old enough to play Mama) so that writing one seemed a logical solution, although she had already started what would become *Hoodoo Love*, later produced at the Cherry Lane Theatre in 2007. It is a story she tells frequently, not least because she is asked the same question, but the library must have lacked the plays of Alice Childress, Ntozake Shange, Adrienne Kennedy, Anna Deavere Smith, Suzan Lori-Smith and, indeed, Lynn Nottage. She did play a part in a Barnard production of *The Three Sisters* but, despite arguing with the director, not that of twenty-year-old Irina but the old doorkeeper, Ferapont.

From Columbia, she moved on to take an MFA at the American Repertory Theatre, auditioning with speeches from *As You Like It* and August Wilson's *The Piano Lesson*. Her course involved study both in Cambridge and Moscow where she appeared in a number of productions, including Tony Kushner's *A Bright Room Called Day*, affecting a Czech accent (in 2012, with a play called *WHATDABLOODCLOT!!!*, she would write a satire about race and class in which an Upper East Side woman contracts 'foreign accent syndrome', which makes her speak with a Jamaican accent).

On leaving she picked up roles in *Law and Order* and worked for a while at XM radio while sketching out plays at her desk so that for a while it seemed unclear whether she would leave or be fired. It was then she learned that, on the basis of *Hoodoo Love*, she had been accepted by Julliard's playwriting programme. It was at Juilliard that she wrote *Saturday Night/Sunday Morning* and *Hurt Village* and began *The Mountaintop*.

When she started work on *Hoodoo Love*, she was unsure whether she was up to the task, and the play itself in part concerns a character who has a similar level of self-doubt and is looking to understand who she is through her art. She wrote the first act, she explained to Dan Piepenbring in a *Paris Review* interview,[5] in the course of a semester, planning to complete it the next, although in fact this play, which she began in 2002, would not be finished until 2007.

She knew she wished to incorporate blues music into *Hoodoo Love*. This, after all, was a play to be set in Memphis. Indeed, that was in part the inspiration for a play in which two of the central characters are singers and blues musicians. Knowing little about the technicalities of music, she was reassured because that was equally true of many blues musicians themselves. She graduated in 2005, and as she was looking for acting agents, also began entering the play to contests, finally ending up submitting it to the Cherry Lane mentor project, where Lynn Nottage selected it.

She has recalled standing up in the audience of a presentation by August Wilson and, to her embarrassment, telling him that she was going to be a playwright. He was not, though, a particular model, she being less inspired by writers, whose plays for the most part she had not read, than by those in the visual arts, naming Henri Cartier-Bresson, or that form of journalism exemplified by Tom Wolfe, both, of course, white and one of them not American. She was concerned to stage the lives of black women while not wishing to embrace any particular model. Confessing that people expected her 'to conform to this black box, quite literally when it comes to writing',[6] she wished to tell different stories in different voices. Feminism seemed to her to have left little space for black women, and that was a gap she wished to fill. Indeed, in *The Blood Quilt*, she would write a play with a cast comprised of black women and has said that her mission statement is to see more African-American women on stage and herself 'in the mirror that is the American stage'. Beyond that, she wished 'to write myself into existence'.[7]

While Nottage spoke approvingly of Arthur Miller, Hall felt uncomfortable with the figure of Tituba in *The Crucible* precisely because it failed, in her view, to present her as a complicated human being. She was, it seemed to her, a plot device rather than a flesh-and-blood black woman. Her own challenge was to offer that complexity, to locate black women in a different context and let them speak their own lives rather than see them as part of someone else's narrative. Her plays were not to lie outside the American canon but to broaden it.

Hoodoo Love is set in a cluster of shacks on a cul-de-sac, literal and metaphorical, during the Depression. At its heart is the relationship between Toulou, a young woman who has escaped the cotton fields of Mississippi for the possibilities of Memphis, and Ace of Spades, a blues singer and player, always on the move and with women ready to submit to his charms. It is a play suffused with blues music that speaks of abandonment lamented, emotions given shape, a rhythm to fractured experiences, consolation in the face of suffering. In the words of a Toulou song:

> My man got bowlegs
> Like the Mississippi
> No matter what I say
> He won't come back to me.[8]

The blues are about private experiences that also carry a history. The breaking of relationships, after all, was implicit in slavery, leaving a cultural marker but here is music about such relationships that paradoxically has the power to bring together. In writing about his television series *Treme*, set in New Orleans, another city in some sense built around music, David Simon said that anyone fast-forwarding their DVDs to bypass the music would be bypassing the point of the show, so central was music it. In *Hoodoo Love*, it is equally part of who these characters are as of those to whom they offer their art.

Toulou and Ace are both musicians of talent, she only just beginning but coming into her own and potentially surpassing her lover. He has been 'workin' the Cotton Belt for ten years' but now has an offer to make a recording in Chicago, although her talent means that together they could be more appealing to the white man, who has reasons of his own for taking them up. Indeed, when they come together in song, there is a harmony otherwise threatened by their conflicting needs.

But this is a blues song/play, and fate steps in to destroy not just Toulou's dream but also Ace's, as he loses his song in a game of cards, his 'song', as in August Wilson's work, being an expression of his life. Hope was the last object taken out of Pandora's box, the essence of Beckett's absurdist view, but hope denied is equally at the heart of Toulou's life as it is of the blues, the reiterated lines offering echoes and repetitions rather than escape. 'I got a lot of hope in my tummy,' she says, 'carrying a child in this shack off Beale Street' (64), to which Ace replies, 'We need a heap more than some fuckin' hope! I wanna kick yo' in your stomach so bad' (69). The blues moved from the South via Memphis to Chicago as many of those who sang them did, boarding the train they assumed would carry them from the past to the future only to discover that the future could seem very like the past.

What does a woman do who fears she will lose the man she loves here on this cul-de-sac of a southern city? She consults a former slave and now Hoodoo mistress, Candylady, who will give her a mojo bag and instruct her in the magical ways of ensuring that he stays by her side, as the sound of a train's whistle is a reminder that he is drawn in another direction. Sex brings them together but it equally pushes them apart – indeed has the power to destroy as Toulou's brother, Jib, a born-again missionary with a taste for alcohol, crosses a boundary that should not be crossed as an act of incest destroys her future as it taints her past.

Nor is hoodoo treated as fantasy. Hall was aware of it as she grew up. Her own mother, at the request of her grandmother, had carried a mojo (an aluminium packet filled with black-eyed peas) for a year, and it seemed to bring her luck. It is believed in by those, like the characters in *Hoodoo Love*, who live and breathe within the myths and stories of the South, although it is actual poison that is finally the agent of death, a tragic irony. After the death of her man, Toulou is left with a child, her music and a need to continue in the face of loss and what looks like defeat. As she remarks, 'They say, "When a woman heart broke, she break down and cries. When a man heart broke, he take a train and rides." I'ma catch that train' (85). It is Candylady who sings:

> And that's the way the story go
> On the bluff where blue grass grow
> That's the way this hoodoo tale end
> Where broken wings don't try to mend (86)

Hoodoo Love is a folk play, a morality tale, a celebration of creativity and a lament. Its characters act out a familiar story of love betrayed, bruised lives, broken connections reshaped into story and song. Religion and magic offer consolation, although both are suspect. Melancholy is balanced by resilience as the characters struggle to find a purchase on life, to discover who they are in a world that offers little back to those pressed to the edge of a society itself carrying the stain of slavery. Ace's father had worked in the cotton fields, dying there in an accident as he drove himself for a five-cent raise, but 'Daddy was a bluesman, too. Was the best man on slide Coldwater ever seen't. Nobody could pull a bottleneck over them strangs like my daddy. His hands was so worn, every crack held a memory that would stream into that guitar' (47).

Candylady had lost a child born on the fourth of July, 1865, Independence Day. It is a date that means nothing to her beyond the death of a child. She already carried the marks of her beatings as a slave and by her husband, paying the price for his humiliations, so that she accidentally smothers her daughter when he objects to her crying. Babies can be a future denied as well as a future desired. At the end of the play, Toulou abandons her own child and walks away to catch the train. She is going to sing the blues and 'Name myself for once' (85).

Hall wrote her own music and lyrics, although she notes that she had turned to Zora Neale Hurston's *Mules and Men* for the hoodoo recipe she invokes. The music is central, embedded in the lives of those who shape it from their own experiences. They seek a stage on which they will be acknowledged, a name beyond that which they inherited. Hall's characters carry the language of the South along with its history. Yet this is a play that, like the blues, hints at transcendence.

For her next play, she moved from the 1930s to the last days of the Second World War and from blues to comedy – albeit with a dark underpainting. In *Saturday Night/Sunday Morning*, the music is not that of the guitar and the doleful song but 'the roaring, heightened music of black beauty-shop banter', while the 'women's voices are often buoyed by an orchestra of beauty-shop sounds – sizzling irons, buzzing dryer, humming coke machines'. The set, she instructs, 'lives and breathes, groans and moans – a character unto itself' (89). We are still in Memphis, but this time in a beauty shop/boarding house for women.

The play was developed in October 2008 as part of the Classical Theatre of Harlem's Future Classics series, in partnership with the Frederick Douglas Creative Arts Center and the Schomburg Center for Research in Black Culture. It reached back, she explained, to her own memories of Miss Mary's Press and Curl shop where the cut hair was always flushed down the toilet (hair having potential use for hoodoo). Her memories, which feed into the play, were of submitting to the hot comb as her hair was tamed at the expense of the occasional burn and of Miss Mary in a shotgun house that functioned, much as it does in *Saturday Night/Sunday Morning*, as a place for gossip while being half party and half therapy session. As she has said, 'It was just as therapeutic (if not more) than the Sunday morning services we would spend all day Saturday preparing ourselves for.' The play was designedly a celebration of a place that offered 'solace and sisterhood, growth, and spirit' (xi). Thus in the play, Miss Mary says of the beauty parlour that it is 'Half fixin' hair, half fixin' poor souls' (103).

In a cast of ten, only two are men. The war is on and most of the men have disappeared, except Buzz, a postman/salesman with a damaged leg. The other man, Bobby, exists for much of the play only as the depressive Leanne invokes him, a man who had gone to war and promised to write to her but from whom she has heard nothing. A subplot of the play indeed consists of the enrolment of Gladys, a new boarder and would-be writer from Alabama, to fake letters from the absent Bobby only to be asked by the illiterate Leanne to write replies so that she ends up on both ends of the correspondence (an echo of Lynn Nottage's 2003 play, *Intimate Apparel*). The irony is that Gladys's letters are an expression of her own desire not for the absent Bobby but for Leanne, only one of the suppressed truths in a play whose rush of language and social action conceals what are often unexpressed emotions.

Gathered in the parlour are the teenage Taffy, socially inept, vaguely rebellious; her sister Mabel, out for a good time on the streets of Memphis; along with customers whose loyalty is tested when a magic hair treatment turns out to be lye, burning most of Mabel's hair off, thus playing into the hands of the owner of a rival establishment, Curlin' Curlin,' on the other side of the street. The rule of the boarding house is 'Boarders shall not bitch', yet bitching is what gives them energy. All are at their most fluent when delivering insults, pitch perfect arias, language a weapon of choice. Thus Mary says of Mabel, 'Her fast tail runnin' round out there all night wit' God knows who do what and when, and where they put it in. I done told her 'bout stayin' out late at night. Especially after ten. The only thing open after ten is legs' (92).

Gladys, meanwhile, dictates letters of lyrical beauty as the figure of Bobby appears 'in a pool of beautiful light', the embodiment of Leanne's dreams, alternative stories of irreproachable love amidst the chatter and rush of a place in which men are an absent force as Miss Mary insists that there is something special about women gathered together. Like Hall herself, Gladys's function is to spin stories that gain their authenticity because 'writin' is all about the necessary details . . . if I ain't got the right details it ain't gonna have the ring of truth.' Like Hall, she looks for poetry, for 'some kinda style' (118).

Beneath the humour, however, beyond the daily routine of work and verbal sparing, there is a darker undercurrent as Gladys explains to Leanne why she wears gloves even to bed: 'Couple years back . . . Daddy was a deacon . . . He preached a sermon one day the white folk in 'Bama didn't like . . . (*She Smiles*) One night the Klansmen came by the house . . . Threw a kerosene lamp in the house . . . Lucky I got out . . . Nobody else did' (126). She had burned her hands trying to go back into the house to rescue the dying. Why does the stage direction indicate that 'She smiles'? Presumably because she recalls with pleasure her father's act of resistance, even as it marked his death. This is a story, she confesses, she has not been able to write. The scars caused by racism are concealed. As Leanne remarks, 'I look this way. On the inside' (126).

Inside and outside are equally significant, not least because the action takes place in a beauty parlour in which women submit to pain to straighten their hair or contrive to have it turn into a cascade of ring curls, while on the radio we hear advertisements for skin whiteners: 'Tired of those dark spots? A complexion that leaves you feeling in the dirt? Try Cleopatra skin creams. Wash your way to a perfect, smooth, *brighter* complexion' (127). These are characters who have internalised the very racism from which they suffer. Taffy boasts of her long hair while insisting that she 'been told many a' time I look pretty for a dark-skinned woman'; Leanne replies, 'Long hair don't do nothing for a girl who's the color of *yellah-wasted!* All that high-yellah gone to waste on you' (128) – this, from a woman, who carries a parasol so as not to get 'dark'.

When the postman calls, with a postbag full of letters and postcards from all over Europe, he observes, 'They say they treat Negro men real right over there in Europe . . . it's be somethin' to be treated like a man. For once. Not have to be walkin' down the street and have to cross it when you see a white woman comin' your way . . . Just didn't make sense to go fightin' for freedom over there, when it a lota fightin' for freedom over here to do. Just ain't make no kinda sense' (131). And indeed, as the men begin to come home, they encounter the very racism they had in part been battling overseas. As one of the beauty parlour's customers explains, when her father returned,

He came in his uniform. The boys were so proud to see they daddy lookin' so good and proud. Ain't never seen him walk the way he walked in that uniform. This white man come up to him and say, 'Bwoy, what you got on that uniform for? Over there you might be a soldier, but here. Here . . . you just . . . a nigger.' We all walked home so quiet. Like it ain't happen. Ya know, Gerald had those smilin' kind of eyes . . . They used to twinkle. Be all full of light. Now. They empty now. He ain't put on that uniform since.

(135)

News of lynching penetrates even this place dedicated to appearance.

The play ends as Bobby returns from the war – not the warrior imagined by Leanne but limping and with an arm missing. He brings a letter, but it is not for her. He brings news of the death of Mabel's husband, Joe, a man she had affected not to miss as Gladys hands Leanne a letter expressing love that comes not from Joe but herself. Leanne has lost Joe, Gladys has lost Leanne and Mabel has lost her husband. Miss Mary, who has long since lost her own man, has even lost her trade to her rival, who is offering 'a free "conk" style', so that women can get 'fine for yo' man' (185). The war has ended, but so have the hopes of those gathered in Miss Mary's. Together, Taffy and Mary wash Gladys's hair as she clutches the letter that had brought news of her final abandonment. Some things cannot be washed away. The chatter is silenced, but this is a ritual, a ceremony of sorts, the only consolation on offer. What had been an exuberant comedy is stilled.

Writing for the *Wall Street Journal* in 2015, Terry Teachout greeted a Boston production of the play at the Lyric Theatre as confirming Hall's talent, having by then seen both *Our Lady of Kibeho* and *The Blood Quilt*. 'Each scene', he declared, 'trembles with tenderness and pain, and each character will lodge in the memory long after the lights go up at evening's end'.[9] The *Boston Globe* review of the same production, while accusing her of 'hastily cramming together several plot developments' and indulging in 'an ill-advised fantasy sequence that spells out too literally an aspect of the play (involving one female character's unrequited love for another),' praised her distinctive 'if a bit self-conscious dialogue'.[10] Critics looked for possible influences including Herbert Ross's *Steel Magnolias*, which also features a beauty parlour in the South and the bonding of a group of women. Beyond the setting, it is hard to see the connection. Ross's play goes in a wholly different direction. Hall creates her own world drawing on her own experiences, and the result is a play in which individual voices meld together even as they sustain their own individuality.

In these early plays, Hall draws on her past, her memories of growing up in Memphis, a language at one moment lyrical, at another caustic, her sense of a community both vulnerable and with a tensile strength. She hears music that is sometimes literal and sometimes simply embedded in the lives of those who negotiate a territory between hope and despair, and whose voices she orchestrates. She celebrates ordinary lives become extraordinary by virtue of the attention she pays them but also by their innate qualities. She stages the daily fluctuations of emotions, the small change of life that in some sense is what life consists of, contained as her characters are within social limits not of their making. There is sometimes a profundity in the quotidian, the surface, in chatter, verbal sparring, a language that expresses more than it seems. From the 1930s and 1940s, though, she now moved on to a time of change in which a new vision was glimpsed, not just the view from a shack on a cul-de-sac or a beauty parlour, in which women are abandoned as they turn to each other for consolation, but from the mountaintop.

On the third of April, 1968, Martin Luther King delivered a speech in Mason Temple, the Church of God in Christ headquarters in Memphis. He was there to support sanitation workers, in doing so recalling past battles in Alabama while insisting that there was no need to 'curse' and utter 'bad words, throw bricks or bottles'. They had, he insisted, economic power. He opened by thanking people for attending despite a storm warning. He was referring to the weather, but his speech suggested something else. In some ways it began curiously, as he asked himself in which age he would like to have lived – proceeding to invoke the Jewish exodus from Egypt; the Greece of Plato, Aristotle, Socrates, Euripides and Aristophanes; Imperial Rome; the Renaissance; Martin Luther at Wittenberg; the signing of the Emancipation decree by Lincoln; the era of Franklin Roosevelt who announced that there was nothing to fear but fear itself – only to conclude that the period he would wish to inhabit was his present, despite the fact that there was 'trouble is in the land, confusion all around'.

What he saw was a people battling to be free. It was, he said, not a struggle between violence and nonviolence but between nonviolence and nonexistence. He recalled that he himself had been stabbed. He spoke of the threats he had received but insisted on their irrelevance because he had 'been to the mountaintop'. Like anybody, he said, 'I would like to live a long life . . . But I am not concerned with that now . . . I've seen the Promised Land. I may not get there with you. But I want you to know tonight that we, as a people, will get to the Promised Land! . . . I'm not worried about anything. I am not fearing any man! Mine eyes have seen the glory of the coming of the Lord!'[11]

On the following day, at 6:01 PM, Martin Luther King was shot dead on the balcony of the Lorraine Motel by a single bullet fired from a Remington Model 760. He died just over an hour later. In Indianapolis, Robert Kennedy gave an impromptu speech, himself invoking the Greeks, quoting a line from Aeschylus's *Agamemnon*: 'Tame the savageness of man and make gentle the life of this world'.

At age fifteen, Hall's mother had wanted to attend King's speech at Mason Temple, only for her own mother to tell her, 'You know they're gon' bomb that church, girl . . . so you need to sit your butt down and you ain't going to that church.'[12] King was someone admired in her family. But it was not to be as a saviour, a public figure promising not the fire next time but a dream of possibility, that Hall decided to present him when she set out to write a play about him. What interested her was the man.

As she has said, what she wanted to create was 'a warts-and-all portrayal of Dr. King . . . because there's this extraordinary human being who is actually quite ordinary . . . with his flaws and foibles'.[13] She began writing the play in 2007, inspired in part by the approaching fortieth anniversary of King's death and in part by the emerging figure of Barack Obama who began his campaign for the presidency that year. For all his iconic status, she has confessed that she knew little about King's efforts on behalf of the poor or his involvement in the anti-war movement. He was 'just a statue to me'.[14] 'This is the uber-American hero. A Christlike figure to some',[15] but it was not the pubic figure that interested her. She was concerned with the private one whose anxieties and flaws made him more humanly understandable. She decided she would use nothing from his speeches. This was not to be the 'I have a dream' man but someone whose health had deteriorated, who smoked, who was depressed and fearful, and had an eye for a pretty woman.

She wanted to lift him out of the public arena, bring him down from the pulpit, and to do so she narrowed her focus. Where before she had choreographed a community, she now wished to concentrate on one man the night before his death by placing him in his motel room not with the man with whom he actually shared the room, Ralph Abernathy, but with a young woman who appears to be a maid. This mechanism allowed her to establish a dialogue involving two people of different genders, generations and perspectives, a Socratic dialogue, and it was Socrates who observed that the unexamined life is not worth living. Hall sets out to dramatise a life that was, from the point of view of most people, unexamined because it was lived on television screens or in demonstrations. Asked once what she had found important about August Wilson's work, she replied that it was his ability to stage spirituality in a naturalistic world. That might be said of *The Mountaintop*, which takes place in a down-at-heel motel room where water stains pockmark the walls, carpet is the colour of bile and the décor is fading, but in which a conversation ensues that engages with life, death and the hereafter, in which the naturalistic cedes territory to the fantastic.

It was not an approach that appealed to some directors, who did not warm to the idea of a play that demythologised a national hero – but that, of course, was precisely the point. On one level, it was a gift to her mother, a fact she underlined by giving the maid a contraction of her mother's name, Carrie May, something she only discovered when attending the London premiere at the National Theatre.

The play begins with King entering his motel room, having stepped out of the rain. The red and yellow glow of the motel sign shines on a man who is described as tired, overwrought and wet, calling out to an invisible Ralph Abernathy for him to bring him a pack of cigarettes before closing the door, locking the deadbolt, attaching the chain and pulling the curtain. We hear him urinating. He then checks his telephone for a bug.

His comment the previous night about not living to see the Promised Land is obviously more than rhetoric. When thunder sounds, he is visibly agitated, evidently waiting for a gunshot. When he takes his shoes off, his feet smell. This is not a man on the mountaintop.

When he calls down for coffee, it is delivered by a beautiful young maid who seems to be playing a game, although what it might be is not clear. She is more familiar with him than would be expected. At one moment she mockingly presents herself as a working-class black girl: 'They say folks was all cryin'. Sangin'. Mmph. Mmph. Mmph. I would like to have seen that. Something to tell my chiren. "When I wun't nuthin' but a chick-a-dee, I seen't Dr. Martin Luther King, Jr. cuttin' up in the pulpit." Mmmhmm.' (194). At another, she is probing into his life so that he observes: 'most maids don't sound like professors' (213). They share a cigarette and an intimacy that seems both strange and disturbing. When he explains that he used to be wild, she replies, 'How you knows what you ain't supposed to do if you ain't done it, yaself . . . That's what I call "work experience"' (202). She pours whisky in his coffee. He hints at a possible tryst in a room previously occupied by a prostitute, only for his wife to call. He lies to her saying that he is drinking tea rather than coffee, a small lie but revealing nonetheless.

Camae presents herself as a radical. Non-violence, she suggests, is getting King nowhere. She borrows his jacket and shoes, jumping on the bed and, in a parody of King's voice, calls upon an invisible audience to kill the white man not with guns but with their minds, building a separate world of their own declaring, 'Fuck the white man!' (210). 'Fuck 'em!' replies the man who in his speech at Mason Temple had rejected cursing and 'bad words'. 'Maybe the voice of violence is the only voice white folks'll listen to . . . They hate so easily, and we love too much' (211), says the man who only hours before had insisted that the real battle was between non-violence and non-existence and whose message was a New Testament call for people to love one another.

In the world conjured up by Katori Hall, it is not just a question of humanising King but offering a different version of a man whom she presumed must have internalised the battles he had with others. The arguments with Camae, meanwhile, turn out not to be with a maid but an angel sent by God – the God whom she calls 'a fuuuuhnny-ass muthafucka' and who, she assures him 'like dirty jokes'– to prepare him for his imminent death and to take him to the other side. When he touches her, he is sent reeling, as she uses his childhood name to him. She, it seems, knows things about him that others do not having, she confesses, read his file, while the God she invokes is a woman. Minor miracles appear. She speaks in the voice of 'Bunny', King's daughter Bernice; flowers bloom at her feet; the door burns bright red and begins to bulge 'as fingers begin to push and poke' through it as the snow that falls also fell in reality. It was a cold night in Tennessee.

He begs for more time to bring a message to America that it is going to hell, a 'country that sends its boys to bathe little-bitty babies in the blood of our greed' while 'Our young are flown back home in star-spangled coffins' (226). He wants time to plan a poor peoples' march on Washington. Finally, he persuades Camae to put in a call to God to see if he can be granted extra time. Although she uses a rotary phone, she explains that God is on her cell, something yet to be invented. She answers and King realises that not only is God a woman, she is also black. He pleads for time because he wants to see his people to the Promised Land, only for her to point out that this was not what he had said in his sermon. She discontinues the call and King and his 'death angel' engage in a pillow fight until the air is full of feathers. Death has become a game until King dissolves in tears, reconciled to his fate, as Camae explains her own death, a death that is more than literal, standing, as it does, for the fate of black women through time who had suffered at the hands of the white and black world alike, black men having suffered a sense of powerlessness. Her task before being accepted into heaven is not only to abjure her hatred but to bring with her a man who chose to counter hate with love.

A play that was to focus on the private now opens up, as King asks to be granted a vision of the future from the mountaintop, to glimpse of what lies ahead. There follows a pageant of images, a mosaic beginning with the burning cities of 1968 and proceeding with a cascade of pictures projected as the motel seems to float away ending, for the moment, in a black president. Here are those who followed in his footsteps fighting for justice, but here, too, are deployed a kaleidoscope of historical moments, national and international, triumphs and disasters, including the falling wall in Berlin and the falling towers in New York. As Hall explains in a note, 'The good, the bad and the ugly of America continue to proceed like a fluid mental freeway into the very edge of now and perhaps beyond. It's like a river with no levee and the images flood our senses, our minds, and our hearts.' The sound and the fury of it all rise to a frenetic peak until the images stop and a flash of lightning reveals King who is now seen 'in the dark blue of the blackness . . . floating above us in the silence' (247) before he speaks of a future that can only be gained if the baton is passed. The goal is in sight, but there is an ebb and flow to history and the struggle not yet over. In the London production, although not in the published text, the play ended with Obama's cry, 'Yes, we can!'

At the end of his life, King had broadened his perspective. His concern with civil rights had expanded to include the rights of the poor and, beyond that, to an engagement with foreign affairs, the Vietnam War then coming to a critical point. Indeed, exactly a year before his death, he had delivered a speech titled 'Beyond Vietnam: A Time to Break Silence'. America, he declared, was on the wrong side of a world revolution. There were those who criticised him accordingly, and he lost support, including from some in his own movement. The end of *The Mountaintop* reflects that broader perspective. Having deconstructed the image of a man seen as an icon, Hall reinvests him with that status, a status ironically reinforced at 6:01 PM on the fourth of April when James Earl Ray, a career criminal and supporter of the racist governor of Alabama, George Wallace, on the run from the law, shot him dead, although, ironically, the King family would come to believe he had not been involved.

The Mountaintop opened not in America but London. Hall sent the script to a British director, James Dacre, who gave it its world premiere at Theatre 503, a sixty-seat pub theatre in an unfashionable location, before it was transferred to the Trafalgar Studios in White-hall. At the annual Olivier Awards, it beat the two favourites, Jezz Butterworth's *Jerusalem* and Lucy Prebble's *Enron*, for Best New Play. Hall was the first female black writer to win it. The *Telegraph* review welcomed not only the play but the fact that it attracted a multi-racial audience. The *Independent* found it 'breathtaking, hilarious and heart stopping . . . an imaginative portrayal' of King.[16] For the *Guardian*, it was 'a well-made and enjoyable fantasy' with 'a light feminist touch' marking Hall as 'a playwright ascending the mountain if not yet reaching its peaks'.[17] Although the reviews were positive if not overwhelming, a quite different fate awaited her when the play opened on the other side of the Atlantic.

It took two years before it was staged in New York, where it opened at the Bernard B. Jacob's Theatre on West 45th Street with Samuel L. Jackson and Angela Bassett. It was critically savaged. Ben Brantley, in his *New York Times* review, dismissed it as 'at heart a comfort play, a nursery room fable for grown-ups' that 'never provides the organic details and insights that would make Martin Luther King live anew'. More than once, he suggested, it 'detours into that realm where spiritual uplift meets cuteness that I associate with some greetings cards and television Christmas specials'.[18] John Lahr, in the *New Yorker*, found that her dialogue 'meant to play as street-smart sass' instead 'plays as pandering' and the characters as a reversion to that stereotype identified by Zora Neale Hurston as the 'exceptional Negro' and the 'quaint Negro'. While granting that London audiences had embraced it and that the New York audience had responded positively, he declared that the play 'makes no sense; it's a mess disguised as meaning'. Camae's joke about her breasts being her wings may get a laugh but 'is preposterous', while King behaves 'nonsensically'. In the end the play offers 'pablum'. Rather than offering new light on King, 'it sheds no light'.[19]

Chris Jones, in reviewing a later production for the *Chicago Tribune*, found it 'a tad glib', its anachronisms 'forced', feeling that Hall had overreached in an 'overwritten' play, while acknowledging the 'sheer theatrical audacity' of her writing'. In trying to account for the difference between American and British responses, he suggested that 'Europeans are far more receptive to American culture painted with broad theatrical strokes' and that once the play had crossed the Atlantic, 'where King's life and death are known in more detail, and where the events of that night remain raw, painful and specific, Hall's writing seemed more forced and overly emblematic'.[20] It is a curious interpretation that manages to be patronising simultaneously to both British and Americans. Also, it is hard to follow the logic whereby the circumstances and fact of King's death could make a play seem overly emblematic while the British are hardly ignorant of King's achievements. Indeed, there is a statue of him in Westminster Abbey.

The discrepancy, though, might have something to do with the fact that a play featuring an intimate relationship was first staged in London in the intimacy of a sixty-seat theatre, with actors who were not major stars, but now found itself in an eleven-hundred-seat theatre with a Hollywood celebrity as King, a theatre that would later be home to a lavish musical, *The Color Purple*. Beyond that, it is not uncommon for responses to differ in the two countries. For the last thirty years of his life, Arthur Miller's new plays were dismissed in America and celebrated in Britain, where plays with a social concern were embraced. *Broken Glass*, his 1994 play about Kristallnacht, did poorly in America but won the Olivier Award as Best Play of the Year in England.

In fact, Hall's rival for the Olivier, *Enron*, was also dismissed by the *New York Times*, Ben Brantley noting his surprise that the British embraced something he regarded as simple-minded and of little substance. When it closed early, the *Guardian*'s reviewer, Michael Billington, attacked Brantley's 'obtuse and hostile review', along with what he saw as the conservative aesthetic of an American theatre that showed a preference for realism. The play had fared no better in the *Daily News*, but no play, he pointed out, can survive an attack by the *Times*. As far as he was concerned, its fate showed the irrelevance of Broadway to serious theatre,[21] although Butterworth's *Jerusalem* fared better, even with Brantley.

The Mountaintop is a witty, engaged, inventive work that de-sanctifies King without diminishing him. Himself a master of dramatic rhetoric, King is here presented as a dramatic character, a construct, into whom life is nonetheless breathed. This is a reverse Faust, as he is to be dragged, complaining, into heaven, or presented as an exhausted and fearful Jacob wrestling with an angel, except that a pillow fight offers a satisfyingly reductive version. In the end, his battle with Camae is a battle with himself, her warning of his fate an expression of his own apprehension, her attraction to direct action and even violence a temptation he feels as he resists it. The glimpse of the future at the end locates him in time, even as time is running out on a life to be stopped by a bullet but justified by his shifting of the moral compass of a nation.

Ben Brantley was no more enamoured of Hall's next play, *Hurt Village*, the world premiere of which was staged in 2012 at Signature Theatre's new 42nd Street building on Pershing Square where she was a Registry Five playwright, a scheme that guaranteed playwrights three world-premiere productions over a five-year period, along with health benefits and a stipend. Heart Village was a Memphis housing project dating back to the 1950s and named for the white philanthropist Dr. William Hurt. It was originally designed, Hall explained, to attract white people to an area that had been predominantly black but the King assassination, followed in Memphis by riots with some 4,000 National Guard troops ordered in and a curfew, led to a white flight, with a consequent erosion of the tax base and the decline of the area. As a child, Hall herself had been bussed from her suburb into the neighbourhood and played with some of the children from the projects. With the arrival of drugs, the area deteriorated still further until a government grant was received to redevelop the downtown area.

The Hurt residents were moved out and the project demolished in 2003, although, as Hall points out, only 15 percent of those residents returned to the new mixed-income housing. For her, this was a story repeated across the country, an attempt to deal with poverty, whose marker was so often race, but that was no more than a band-aid. Her play, which features a family about to leave for the new promised land, along with those who make up a community materially and spiritually depleted if resilient, was to 'give those who lived there in crumbling buildings on the corner of Auction Street a voice, a song'.[22] Hurt becomes not only the name of the project but also a description of the condition of those who inhabit it.

The word 'song' is doubly relevant. There has always been a lyrical aspect to Hall's work, which comes in part from her southern origins, her sensitivity to the language of the communities in which she sets her plays, as well as the particular idiolects of her characters, but that also reflects her own sensibility. The play begins with a literal song sung by children and a rap by Cookie, a thirteen-year-old girl carving out her own linguistic and emotional space, but this is preceded by a stage direction for which the designer has to find an equivalent: 'Dusk. Somewhere the sky is falling into the ground. Bits and pieces of magenta, peach and coral hues make the broken bits of beer bottles and crack vials glow with a stardust twinkle. No grass. No one. Dust rolls across this beautiful land like wisps of cotton candy blowing in the country wind.' The stardust, then, contains a 'constellation of garbage and debris', while the beautiful land consists of a 'two-tiered housing project served up Southern-style' with shattered windows, burned-out cars, 'tattered shirts and socks' that 'hang on for dear life to sagging clotheslines'. Meanwhile, it 'looks as if a wrecking ball has already slammed through the sides, exposing the units, as in the merging darkness a chorus of children sweetly sings'.[23] Ugliness and beauty, illiteracy and fluency, blunt prose and poetry co-exist. As Hall has said, these are people for whom 'words have to become armour. Your words have to fight for you. Words are the only currency you have, when you don't have anything in your stomach, when you have to go to bed hungry every night'.[24]

Cookie, like many women in the project, has had to grow up quicker than she would have wished, although she takes her schooling seriously, her eyes set on being a flight attendant. Meanwhile, she is an accomplished rapper, shaping her experiences into some kind of form. It is she who introduces the play:

> You can't see the stars no more /
> Just the bling from the dreams of souls searching for
> the same thing /
> For a lift of light from cavin' ceilings /
> This is my ode to project people strugglin'

She spins 'ghetto tales that will make you weep' (254). This is effectively Katori Hall, and the play her ode, her ghetto tale. Although gunfire sounds in the distance, battles in this place are, indeed, fought out in words, insults exchanged in language battles. Scatology is a lingua franca. Cookie's father, Buggy, is back from Iraq with a bad conduct discharge and nightmares of being eviscerated by a roadside bomb. He pops pills to control his post-traumatic stress in a place that Cookie, in her rap, declares to 'be the war'. Without his pills he loses command of words as well as his grasp on the real. In the past, he had been on drugs. Now, with no money, he is wooed by the local drug king who had raped his wife and already has eyes on his daughter, in a world in which generation echoes generation. He begins to cook crack in the kitchen – to become what he had hoped to escape.

Hall says she began to write *Hurt Village* around 2005–6 but that it had been 'scraping in her belly' for longer than that. It takes place during the 'Second Bush dynasty', with a war abroad and social dislocation at home. At its heart is a family, headed by Big Mama, preparing to leave for their new house, an echo of Lorraine Hansberry's *A Raisin in the Sun* but, as in that play, there is a problem. In the latter, it has to do both with the hostility of the white community they plan to join and an act of treachery within the family. In *Hurt*

Village, it is a system whose rules are inflexible as Big Mama's earnings belatedly preclude them from taking advantage of their opportunity. 'America ain't shit', she declares before going to the welfare office, pleading on her knees, a scene that even moved John Lahr in a *New Yorker* review, which otherwise accused Hall of a 'sprawling story' with a 'stew of street clichés' in which 'the indigestible gristle of poverty is tenderized with juicy slang, a dollop of violence, a sprinkling of drugs, and a slug of rap'.[25] And the challenge Hall sets herself is indeed to turn familiar stereotypes – the dominating matriarchal figure, the drug king, abandoned black women, drug and sex-obsessed black men – into a work that turns such figures into more than the products of a naturalistic drama, a Darwinian braiding of inherited characteristics with a coercive social environment, Theodore Dreiser in the hood.

Cookie, as part of her schoolwork, even conducts a Darwinian experiment, keeping nine fleas in a jar (the play has nine characters) to see if over time they will cease to jump only to strike the lid that encloses them, learning to accept the conditions in which they find themselves. And, indeed, all do, except one. The play ends with Big Mama succeeding in getting back on the list that will take them away from Hurt Village, the only person who can claim the future being Cookie, those lost to drugs, those walking away to nowhere being preserved only in her rap: 'I got 'em in my rhyme and in my heart and in my mind' (352).

Ben Brantley, while regarding the play as having 'an air of old-fashioned contrivance', thought it more persuasive and organic than 'The Mountaintop' while suffering from 'the same penchant for artificial dialogue that seems to be pasted onto the characters'. He conceded, however, that it was 'as lucid as any work I know in identifying rap (and dissing) as both a weapon and a release, a brandishing of arms and of affection'.[26]

There is an artifice to the characters because they themselves are constructions forced into roles at odds with their instincts, performers in a drama in which language is alternately denatured or refashioned. Beneath the traded insults is a tacit connection, the essence of 'signifying' being that it is a linguistic system which itself is indicative of a community. On the surface there are winners and losers, but they come together within the game which can be a form of the very respect it seems to abjure.

With *Hurt Village*, Hall concluded her Memphis plays and stepped into a wider world. In 2009, she travelled to Rwanda with fellow playwright Erik Ehn. She went to learn about the genocide that took place in 1994 in which between half a million and a million Rwandans, nearly all Tutsis, were killed by the Hutu majority. For two weeks, she joined a group that visited memorial sites and interviewed survivors and some of those responsible for the violence. She also went to the Shrine of Our Lady of Sorrows in Kibeho, a cathedral in the unlikely setting of a rural village, a place where girls had had a vision of the Virgin Mary and where they had seemingly referred obliquely to the forthcoming genocide. She returned the following year to find one of the girls, speaking to her about her visions, which dated to 1984, and her experience in surviving subsequent events.

Out of her visits to Africa two plays emerged, *Children of Killers* and *Our Lady of Kibeho*. The plays, she explained, 'are an exploration on the theme of forgiveness', not only in the context of Rwanda but in terms of herself, as she had found forgiveness difficult in terms of her own life, the plays becoming 'a kind of therapy for me'.[27] Forgiveness, though, would not be too apparent in *Children of Killers* commissioned by Britain's National Theatre and first produced there in 2011, before being staged the following year at the Castillo Theatre in New York, the latter originally established by a collective of political activists and artists and designed, among other things, as a home for black theatre.

There have been many books and films about the genocide, including the chilling *Machete Season*, in which the French journalist Jean Watzfeld interviewed ten unrepentant Hutu killers who came from an area in which five out of every six Tutsis were killed. The Hutus used to gather together on a soccer field, hence Hall's use of soccer in *Children of Killers*. Philip Gourevitch's film *We Wish to Inform You That Tomorrow We Will Be Killed* was based on his *New Yorker* dispatches. In 2010, Immaculée Ilibagiza, a survivor of the genocide, published *Our Lady of Kibeho: Mary Speaks to the World from the Heart of Africa*, having already published another book on the genocide in 2006. That same year saw the production of J. T. Rogers's play, *The Overwhelming*.

Children of Killers features a group of teenagers and a character called the Guhahamuka, the latter to be played by between three and ten actors. A note explains that Guhahamuka is 'the point of speaking where words cease to exist. It is where breath refuses to make syllables, amounting to silence and emotion instead'.[28] The boys, who are first seen playing football, are too young to have experienced the genocide themselves but are the children of killers who are about to be released and as such boast of the number their fathers killed, one claiming seven hundred and fifty-two, another forty in a single night. They compete in announcing atrocities with apparent pride, a man hacked to pieces with a machete, a woman beheaded and her children made to play football with her head. Eighteen-year-old Vincent is known as the son of 'The Butcher', a fact that his fellows announce with admiration, although he himself plainly feels shame. Fifteen-year-old Emmanuel, a child of rape who is now dying of AIDS, had been told by his now-dead mother that he has no father and is a child of God.

In a seemingly naturalistic play, Guhahamuka appears to Vincent, haunting his dreams, two young girls caked with blood play football until it turns into a skull, a boy carries a machete and is about to strike when he wakes. Later, when the boys play again, Bosco, described as carrying 'the seed of extremist hatred in his heart', finds the ball is covered with blood before disappearing. He hears the voices of the Guhahamuka. When a Tutsi girl, Esperance, sister to Emmanuel, passes, her body marked with scars, Bosco calls her cockroach, the contemptuous word used during the war. She is defended by Vincent. Later, she laments the death of her mother and her fear of the returning man as the singing of the Guhahamuka drowns out the sound of the machete song. The play ends with an act of resistance by Esperance, a repeat of the violence by Bosco and an ambivalent response by Vincent, drawn to Esperance but sitting with his father, a withered man of whom he is a mirror image.

For Charles Isherwood, for the *New York Times*, 'The play's brevity and lack of strong narrative probably explain why "Children of Killers" is having its United States premiere at a comparatively small theatre [the Castillo Theater].' Nonetheless, he felt that 'Hall's impressionistic approach feels right for the material; her subject is not so much the stories of this particular group of boys but the haunted atmosphere of the country itself, torn between the need to put the past behind it and move forward into a more stable future, and the equally strong imperative to remain attentive to the seeds of hatred that may still lie dormant in the soil.' While finding the writing 'uneven' and some of the 'more stylized passages straining for lyricism', he was impressed by the 'simplicity and specificity' of a play that contained disturbing and powerful passages.[29]

There is something blunt about *Children of Killers*. Perhaps it could hardly be otherwise. It is an unflinching portrait of those whose lives have been warped by violence. Dramatically, she sets out to establish the individuality of her characters even as that individuality is subject to forces that subvert it. Here, public myths are inherited and eagerly embraced. It is in some degree a morality tale whose implications reach out into a world in which tribal loyalties trump human necessities, an atavistic impulse finds justification. The conflict is not just between those who revel in cruelties and those who begin to doubt, between oppressors and victims, but between aspects of the human sensibility. Her characters are real and substantial but also required to play archetypal roles, and that tension is difficult to sustain, which is perhaps why the play itself has elements of myth.

In his book *Real Presences* George Steiner observes, 'One of the radical spirits in current thought has defined the task of this sombre age as "learning anew to be human". On a more restricted scale, we must, I think, learn anew what is compromised within a full experience of created sense, of the enigma of creation as it is made sensible in the poem, in the painting, in the musical statement.'[30] Katori Hall is 'not very religious' but does, she has said, 'believe in the Spirit',[31] and her plays frequently express this sense of real presences, of the desire to learn anew what it is to be human. Imminent meaning tends to take actual form: ghosts, visions, angels. An actor, as Steiner observes, is an interpreter of texts but a writer is an interpreter of experience discovering meanings but also forging them. As he observes, 'Each performance of a dramatic text . . . is a critique in the most vital sense of the term: it is an act of penetrative response which makes sense sensible' (8). Performance, as he suggests, is an enactment of meaning. The risk is that the more literal, the less transcendent. This is where language meets a challenge in that it has to express the inexpressible, which is perhaps why Hall approaches genocide at an angle.

A poet relies on the reader inhabiting the spaces in language, feeling a rhythm lacking in daily life. A novelist pitches words into the mind of a reader who tests those words against experience. The playwright predicates his or her work on the existence of a living community, an audience conscious of those who surround them breathing the same air as the actors, inhabiting the same moment. Hall's play is about a fractured society but in itself makes a claim for society as for the possibility of a meaning that can escape the logic of moral anarchy, a black hole into which all humanity, all compassion, seems to have been sucked, no light emerging.

Katori Hall has the ability to discover the differing rhythms of her characters, combine distinctive voices into a chorus. Language in her plays may seem naturalistic but is carefully orchestrated. Her characters, whether playing out the rituals of hoodoo, exchanging words in a beauty parlour, deploying a political rhetoric, fighting linguistic battles, or reaching for a way of expressing mystical experiences are all self-conscious performers, staging themselves in an attempt to define who they are and what the meaning of their existence might be. Frequently, she seeks to extend the action beyond the immediate, the physical, to embrace a sense of something beyond their comprehension. Meanwhile, music – blues, jazz, popular songs, rap – constitutes another character in her dramas of communities, another source of transcendence, containing a history, expressing a yearning, lamenting failure, celebrating possibility. Here is Schopenhauer as quoted by Steiner: music 'exhibits itself as the metaphysical to everything physical in the world' (19). Yet music has another power – a destructive one. For Steiner, Wagner's music already contained elements that would lead it to be embraced by the Nazis. In Rwanda, music would prove an agency of power, stirring the spirit against itself with its capacity to heal the wounds it causes.

In 2008, the Rwandan singer Simon Bikindi was found guilty of using his songs to incite genocide by the International Criminal Law Bureau. In *Children of Killers*, the villagers sing the Machete Song to welcome back those released from prison. The play is brief. If it is an exploration of forgiveness, there is little evidence of it. These are characters who for the most part revel in stories of the violence perpetrated by their fathers as doubt begins to intrude and hesitant gestures of reconciliation are made.

Many of Hall's plays begin in her own memories, while others are concerned to consolidate memories. These are not neutral acts. As Steiner has insisted, 'A cultivation of trained, shared remembrance sets a society in touch with its own past. What matters even more, it safeguards the core of individuality.' It is 'the ballast of the self'. Such issues 'are political and social in the strongest sense' (10). That is how they often function in Hall's work. But she is not concerned with offering a slice of life, a social freeze-frame. There is always an implicit critique, another dimension beyond offering a sepia print version of a long-lost Memphis. There can seem an inevitability to the past, as if those summoned from it for our present gaze were simply fixed figures in a social tapestry. Yet there was a reason they were as they were that hovers above them, sometimes articulated but more often implicit. There can be a tendency to patronise the past as if those who inhabited it lacked the will, the imagination, to do other than they did. Her portraits of the past, however, are more complex. Her characters are not contained by their own shortcomings, although they have such or they would not be human, but by constraints that are historically specific. As in most of August Wilson's work, the white world does not intrude but it does impact, and it is in this sense that Hall's work can be seen as political and social.

In 2004, she returned to Rwanda with *Our Lady of Kibeho*, a play for fifteen characters, staged at the Signature Theater. This was set before the genocide, although it focused on coming events. When it came to language, she explained that having visited Rwanda four times and Uganda nine times, 'My ear is finely-tuned to the East African rhythm, a softness, a closeness, a sparseness. A more succinct poetry than I'm used to. I felt that I had to learn a whole new language. A more subtle way of communicating. In Rwanda, silence is so loud.'[32] In her play, though, it is not so much silence that compels as moments when language defers to enacted visions. If there is a presumed sanctity to silence, which provokes an inwardness that may open the door to perception, there is also the coerced silence in which certain truths cannot be pronounced because they are presumed to be subversive of power. In *Our Lady of Kibeho*, some words are to be suppressed as dangerous to the institutions of Church and government alike.

Literature can be an inventor of worlds or a witness. Katori Hall feels the pressure to do both. In 1981, at Kibeho College, a school for girls run by nuns, one of the girls had a vision of the Virgin Mary. Soon other girls had similar experiences. One of them, Marie Claire Mukangango, would later be killed in the massacre of 1995, which took place at the same place with 5,000 people being shot. Although Hall does not reach forward to that time, the girls did make a series of prophecies that they claimed they had derived from the Virgin Mary and that are central to the play whose action, we are told, in a single word, takes place 'Before'. This is the before to which *Children of Killers* was the after. The pressure that would lead the one to the other is evident here. Some of those in this place are Tutsis, some Hutus, and hostility is in the air, contained by a religion with its bureaucracies and discipline. On the wall, a picture of Jesus is of a white man. When the Virgin appears she is neither white nor black but simply 'beautiful'.

The visions first appear to Alphonsine Mumureke, a sixteen-year-old girl whose name translates as 'leave her alone, she speaks the truth'. Together with two other girls, Anathalie and Marie-Claire, she forms The Trinity. Where in Miller's *The Crucible* the girls were precipitated into hysteria by the fraudulent Abigail, here the visions are presented as real. Indeed, Hall includes stage directions surely as impossible to realise as Eugene O'Neill's in *Lazarus Laughed*, but then that has been a marker of her work as the spiritual has been given substance. Here stars are described as streaming from Alphonsine's eyes. 'The noon sun, hanging high in the sky, begins to dance across the aqua blue of the day. Alphonsine raises her hands to the sun. It splits in half and starts dancing around her fingertips. Rainbows stream from her fingertip . . . Another sun pops out from behind the first, and it too splits in half. It is a sky with four suns spinning round and round. A sun with four suns has the light of four universes . . . A cloud parts and there is a face. A slight face. Something. Lips moving.'[33] A ball thrown through the air 'becomes frozen in air as if caught by an invisible hand' (79). Flowers bloom out of cracks in the wall.

The visions, then, are not illusions. There appears to be no ambiguity. Alphonsine holds her hand over the flame of a candle and is not burnt. The three girls rise into the air, as do three beds, which break in half. Father Flavia, who has flown in from Rome to test the girls, thrusts a needle into Alphonsine's eye and then deep into her sternum. Anathalie begins to speak in fluent Italian, a language of which she knows nothing. The church, meanwhile, suspends its doubts, Bishop Gahany who, outside of Hall's play, would later be charged in relation to the genocide, seeing advantage in an event that will attract pilgrims.

Although she confesses to compressing time and assigning ethnic categories arbitrarily, Hall remains faithful to the known facts. What interested her was capturing 'the essence, the emotion of the events',[34] and the prophecies of The Trinity are essentially accurate: 'Sorrow will sink Rwanda and the passion fruit that grows from our trees will bleed with the blood of the fallen . . . THE HILLS OF RWANDA WILL RUN RED WITH BLOOD' (90).

The power of the play lies in large part in the threat laced through what might otherwise be a familiar drama of holy visions in which we are asked to mediate between adolescent fantasies and genuine experiences. The embers of genocide merely await a political wind as Tutsis and Hutus express a mutual distrust. The girls do, indeed, seem to trigger one another, here in the name of religion but a few years later as neighbour would turn on neighbour in a spasm of violence. The prophecy itself seems authenticated by those later events that feed back into the play.

As in her earlier plays, this work embraces mystery – proposes an extension of experience beyond the immediately tangible. It is precisely in those moments when language exhausts itself in its own circularities of meaning that some other dimension to experience is realised. Hall writes about magic, about religious ecstasy, in a form that proposes a level of communication not earthed in words freighted with their own history. As George Steiner observed, 'We cannot, save metaphorically, ask in words of that which may lie beyond words' (55).

At the same time the different languages deployed in the play – the French of the former Belgian colonial masters, the Italian of papal authority, the native language – suggest differing interpretations of experience, a competition for primacy, divisions beyond those delineated by the two tribes who hold one another in contempt, and that extends the action beyond this small school in a remote village. To that degree the play offers echoes of other times and other places where divisions of language, faith, local and national antagonisms could breed.

Words can offer consolation or be forged into weapons, and in her two plays about Rwanda, she shows both at work. Those who killed could return home to loving wives, produce children who themselves flirt with a girl or attack her. Those with a love of God in their hearts could revel in the punishment they inflicted on those yet inducted into His mysteries as if there were only one truth to be embraced. What lies beyond words may be the swing of the machete or a moment of religious epiphany.

Arthur Miller declared that he did not write plays but metaphors, and there is a sense in which this is true of *Our Lady of Kibeho*. Despite its particularities, the fact that it can be sourced to a particular time and place, the idea of the potential for friends to become enemies, not enacted here save in the petty rivalries of the pupils, has a more general application. So, too, does the use for which myths may be deployed, serving power as they do here for the Church, as they would later for those who would unleash genocide. What is true may be of second-order significance. In faraway Rome, a miracle may affirm faith and thus underpin religious authority, as in Rwanda an assertion of difference, aligned with good or evil, may precipitate anarchy.

Hall received an enthusiastic response from the *New York Times*, with Charles Isherwood welcoming 'a transfixing play' with 'the gripping intensity of a thriller' and 'an assured sense of dramatic pacing'.[35] For *Time Out*, it was a thrilling new play, although *Variety*'s reviewer was impatient with her lingering on the miracles, her preoccupation with theatrical effects. It was Terry Teachout in the *Wall Street Journal*, however, who responded most positively, describing it as 'a tightly written play that places a chokehold on your attention right from the opening line . . . What makes "Our Lady of Kibeho" so impressive is that Ms. Hall circumvents all kinds of possible dramaturgical pitfalls along the way'.[36]

Our Lady of Kibeho is a play that addresses the nature of religious experience along with the differing motives and strategies of those who calculate the social and political advantages to apparent epiphanies. She looks for a theatrical means of projecting subjectivity, giving form to visions whether born out of emotions suddenly granted free rein or a glimpse of transcendent meaning. At the same time, there is a tremor in this world of Kibeho as the future infiltrates the present, as the first seeds of later horrors begin to thrust their way through the soil.

In 2008, the British novelist Zadie Smith gave a lecture at the New York Public Library titled 'Speaking in Tongues'. In it she explained that the concept of a unified black voice is a potent one. It has, she suggested,

filtered down, these past forty years, into the black community at all levels, settling itself in that impossible injunction 'keep it real', the original intention of which was unification. We were going to unify the concept of Blackness in order to strengthen it. Instead we confined and restricted it. To me the instruction to 'keep it real' is a sort of prison cell, two feet by five. The fact is, it's too narrow. I just can't live comfortably in there. 'Keep it real' replaced the blessed and solid genetic fact of Blackness with a flimsy imperative. It made Blackness a quality each individual black person was constantly in danger of losing. And almost anything could trigger the loss of one's Blackness: attending certain universities, an impressive variety of jobs, a fondness for opera, a white girlfriend, an interest in golf. And, of course, any change in the voice. There was a popular school of thought that maintained the voice was at the very heart of the thing, fail to keep it real there and you'd never see your Blackness again. How absurd that all seems now. And not because we live in a post-racial world – we don't – but because the reality of race has diversified. Black reality has diversified.[37]

Katori Hall writes about that diversified reality and is a product of it, while remaining committed to exploring what is shared by her characters although they embrace different ambitions, fates, possibilities and have radically different experiences. 'Everybody', she has said, 'is influenced by who they are and unfortunately how other people perceive them to be. And race is a perception . . . It is truly a mental construct but because it is this idea that is made very real due to other people's actions and reactions toward you, it's obviously going to inspire your work . . . it's just part of living as a female artist of color'.[38]

What interests Hall in particular is communities, and in her next plays, *Pussy Valley* and *The Blood Quilt*, she staged very different groups of people, themselves drawn from different backgrounds as they come together as women. *Pussy Valley* was originally workshopped in 2011 but opened in April 2015 at the 200-seat Minneapolis Mixed Blood Theatre, a multiracial company. *Pussy Valley* is the nickname of a housing project near Memphis, but the play takes place in a pole-dance club. It had its origin in Hall's own experience taking pole-dancing classes to get fit but, of course, as she has noted, it has other connotations to do with the commodification of women's bodies.

At its heart are four women who work at the Pink Pony, a club in the Mississippi delta. They are watched over by Uncle Clifford, a preoperative transsexual who bears his own psychological scars, exerting control over the women but himself vulnerable. It is a play that invites audiences to respond to the sheer athleticism of the actors, the aesthetics of their performances, Hall comparing them to artists using their bodies instead of brushes, and in monologues we discover what brought them to the Pink Pony. One, with four young children, is escaping from an abusive relationship while being urged to appear in porno-graphic films. Another, the only white woman, is looking for marriage to a drug dealer, whose interest, however, lies in one of her fellow performers. Still another is the daughter of a pastor who looks to benefit from her money. The cast, however, extends beyond these four to others with illusions of their own.

To prepare for writing the play, Hall visited strip clubs. She wanted to change the way people responded to those who worked there seeing them as artists, rather than those whose voices were never heard. The stories of her characters are full of pain and mis-directions. The language is brutally direct, but they are survivors who have to believe that there is something beyond their present circumstances while their language is partly shaped into poetry. As in her earlier work, this is a play about solidarity forged in the face of adversity.

The Blood Quilt, which had its premiere in May 2015, had its origins in a project at the Royal Court Theatre in England. Hall and a group of other writers were asked to explore Yoruba culture. It set her on a false trail as, having heard of the Gullah-Geechee people, she visited Sapelo Island off the coast of Georgia, once the site of settlements of former slaves. In fact their origins lay in Angola rather than, as she had assumed, Nigeria, but it sparked an interest in her own family history.

The play, produced by Arena Stage, is set on what Hall calls Kwamera Island (somewhat confusingly, if irrelevantly, Kwamera is a language spoken in Vanuatu), also off the Georgia coast. It is what she has called a 'neo-folktale' that focuses on four sisters of the Jernigan family, who get together every year for a quilting bee, as family members have since the time of slavery. This is the first time they have done this, though, since the death of their mother and the reading of her will, which creates what Hall calls a troubling inheritance. It takes place in the present but carries with it a sense of the emotional scars they carry with them, suppressed stories that have an impact on them. One sister asks another whether she herself wishes to leave a legacy of poverty or possibility. The personal issues that break surface also have political implications. Men are absent from the stage but not from the conversations or the memories they invoke.

The sisters all have different fathers and have had different trajectories. One is a midwife, one a police officer, another a nurse and one an entertainment lawyer. They are accompa-nied by the nurse's seventeen-year-old daughter. A storm is heading towards them, but there is storm enough in the house even as comedy and pain are interspersed. There are moments when they come together in a cappella singing, and other moments when they are in con-tention. Their differences are as significant as their similarities. As Hall has said, 'Others assume the African-American experience is monolithic . . . That we think the same things, have the same political views. But with these sisters, one is a Republican, one a Demo-crat; one is light-skinned, one dark-skinned. They have different experiences because they look different. For me, the fact that none of these sisters look alike . . . shows that how

African-Americans look can actually change how they experience the world.' One is 'agnostic, one believes in ghosts, another believes in God. They're all different, but they're all sisters. They're family. Part of the African-American experience is how you can be so diverse and yet be so supportive of one another'.[39]

Hall learned something of quilting from her grandmother and took quilting classes as well. The creation of the quilt not only brings the sisters together even in contention, but can stand as a metaphor, its beauty deriving from the assembled parts. She herself sees a parallel with her own writing in another sense because 'quilts can be about structure . . . about standing away and looking at something from afar when you're trying to figure out the overall design'.[40] As with her earlier work, she has suggested that this play is about the need for forgiveness to move forward, a reconciliation after the past carries evidence of unresolved tensions into the present.

Terry Teachout, for the *Wall Street Journal*, found it 'raucously funny and electrically intense', praising Hall's 'magical ability to sift poetry from everyday speech' concluding that 'this play belongs on Broadway'.[41] By 2017, it had not reached Broadway but a television series based on it was under development for the cable and satellite network, Starz.

From a Memphis slum, to a beauty parlour, from a near-derelict project to an African church, a pole-dancing club and an off-shore island, Katori Hall has explored aspects of black women's lives, articulating their anxieties, voicing their fears and hopes, the forces that have pressed upon them and the resilience they have frequently found in what they share. She has reached back into the 1930s and forward to the present, often combining a naturalistic presentation with evidence of a spirituality that takes literal form. Stylistically various, with casts that range from two people in a single room to more than a dozen, she has pieced together a history made from small moments, individual experiences, as what might have seemed disregarded figures are retrieved, their significance now acknowledged.

Notes

1 Paulette Beete, 'Art Talks with Playwright Katori Hall', *National Endowment for the Arts*, 28 May 2015. www.arts.gov/art-works/2015/art-talk-playwright-katori-hall

2 Alexis Soloski, 'The Ascent of Katori Hall', *American Theatre*, October 2012. www.tcg.org/publications/at/october12/katori.cfm

3 Nosheen Iqbal, 'Katori Hall: 'I've Had Two Hours Sleep', *Guardian*, 23 March 2010. www.theguardian.com/stage/2010/mar/23/katori-hall-the-mountaintop-review

4 Soloski, 'The Ascent of Katori Hall'.

5 John Piepenbring, 'Katori Hall on Hoodoo Love', *Paris Review*, 18 November 2015. www.theparisreview.org/blog/2015/11/18/katori-hall-on-hoodoo-love

6 Nosheen Iqbal, 'Katori Hall: 'I've Had Two Hours Sleep'.

7 Haley Levitt, 'Katori Hall Patches Together a Family History in *The Blood Quilt*', *TheaterMania.com*, 30 April 2015. www.theatermania.com/washington-dc-theater/news/katori-hall-the-blood-quilt-interview_72734.html

8 Katori Hall, *Plays: 1* (London, 2011), p. 12.

9 Terry Teachout, '*Saturday Night/Sunday Morning* Review: Finding Brilliance in a Beauty Parlor', *Wall Street Journal*, 2 November 2015. www.wsj.com/articles/saturday-night-sunday-morning-review-finding-brilliance-in-a-beauty-parlor-1446501711

10 Don Aucoin, 'Waiting and wondering in Lyric Stage's *Saturday Night/Sunday Morning*', 27 October 2015. www.bostonglobe.com/arts/theater-dance/2015/10/27/waiting-and-wondering-homefront-lyric-stage-saturday-night-sunday-morning/MnI6RASRyGm11tjFM6fnJO/story.html

11 Martin Luther King. 'I've been to the mountaintop' speech, 3 April 1968, Memphis, Tennessee. www.americanrhetoric.com/speeches/mlkivebeentothemountaintop.htm

12 'Broadway to Get a View from MLK's "Mountain Top"', *All Things Considered*, NPR, 31 March 2011. www.npr.org/2011/04/01/135019146/broadway-to-get-a-view-from-mlks-mountaintop

13 Ibid.

14 DoNeen L. Brown, 'Playwright Katori Hall: Young, Gifted and Fearlessly Redefining Theater', *Washington Post*, 3 March 2013. www.washingtonpost.com/entertainment/theater_dance/playwright-katori-hall-young-gifted-and-fearlessly-redefining-theater/2013/03/07/ac9db83a-85e0-11e2-999e-5f8e0410cb9d_story.html

15 'Interview with Katori Hall', *Playwrights Foundation*, 18 April 2008. http://playwrightsfoundation.blogspot.co.uk/2008/04/interview-with-katori-hall.html

16 Nicola Christie, '*The Mountaintop*, 503, London: The Strange Last Night of Dr. King', *Independent*, 15 June 2009. www.independent.co.uk/arts-entertainment/theatre-dance/reviews/the-mountaintop-theatre-503-london-1705910.html

17 Lyn Gardner, '*The Mountaintop*', *Guardian*, 18 June 2009. www.theguardian.com/stage/2009/jun/17/mountaintop-theatre-review-london

18 Ben Brantley, 'April 3, 1968. Lorraine Motel. Evening', *New York Times*, 13 October 2014, p. C 1. www.nytimes.com/2011/10/14/theater/reviews/the-mountaintop-with-samuel-l-jackson-angela-bassett.html

19 John Lahr, 'Ticket to Paradise', *New Yorker*, 24 October 2011. www.newyorker.com/magazine/2011/10/24/ticket-to-paradise

20 Chris Jones, 'Theatre Review: "The Mountaintop" at Court Theatre', *Chicago Tribune*, 16 September 2013. http://articles.chicagotribune.com/2013–09–16/entertainment/ct-ent-0916-mountaintop-review-2-20130916-27_1_camae-katori-hall-martin-luther-king-jr

21 Michael Billington, '*Enron*'s Failure Shows Broadway's Flaws', 5 May 2010. www.theguardian.com/stage/theatreblog/2010/may/05/enron-broadway-close-early

22 Katori Hall, *Plays: 1* (London, 2011), p. xiv.

23 Ibid, p. 253.

24 Barbara Chai, 'Katori Hall on Her New Play Hurt Village', *Wall Street Journal*, 28 February 2012. www.youtube.com/watch?v=x5FOJOrYnPI

25 John Lahr, 'Minority Reports: Nina Raine and Katori Hall on the Seen but Not Heard', *New Yorker*, 12 March 2012. www.newyorker.com/magazine/2012/03/12/minority-reports-john-lahr

26 Ben Brantley, 'A Family on the Cusp of Hope and Homelessness', *New York Times*, 27 February 2012. www.nytimes.com/2012/02/28/theater/reviews/hurt-village-by-katori-hall.html?_r=0

27 Lynn Nottage, 'Katori Hall's Raptures of the Spirit in "Our Lady of Kibeho"', *American Theatre*, 16 January 2015, p. 66. www.americantheatre.org/2015/01/16/katori-halls-raptures-of-the-spirit-in-our-lady-of-kibeho

28 Katori Hall, *Children of Killers* (New York, 2016), p. 7.

29 Charles Isherwood, 'The Genocide Is Past, the Lessons Are Not', *New York Times*, 2 October 2012. www.nytimes.com/2012/10/03/theater/reviews/children-of-killers-by-katori-hall-at-the-castillo-theater.html

30 George Steiner, *Real Presences* (London, 1989), p. 4.

31 Lynn Nottage, 'Where the Spirit Is: An Interview with the Playwright', *American Theatre*, 16 January 2015, p. 67. www.americantheatre.org/2015/01/16/katori-halls-raptures-of-the-spirit-in-our-lady-of-kibeho

32 Ibid.

33 Katori Hall, 'Our Lady of Kibeho', *American Theatre*, February 2015, p. 78.

34 Lynn Nottage, 'Where the Spirit Is', p. 67.
35 Charles Isherwood, 'Mysteries of Heaven and Earth: Our Lady of Kibeho', *New York Times*, November 16, 2014. www.nytimes.com/2014/11/17/theater/our-lady-of-kibeho-a-katori-hall-drama-set-in-the-1980s.html?_r=0
36 Terry Teachout, 'Visit from a Missing Person', *Wall Street Journal*, 17 November 2014. www.wsj.com/articles/visit-from-a-missing-person-theater-review-of-our-lady-of-kibeho-1416265905
37 Zadie Smith, *Changing My Mind* (London, 2011), p. 143.
38 Paulette Beete, 'Art Talks with Playwright Katori Hall'.
39 Ibid.
40 Mervyn Rothstein, 'Learn How Katori Hall Pieces Together the African-American Experience in The Blood Quilt', *Playbill*, 4 April 2015. www.playbill.com/article/learn-how-katori-hall-pieces-together-the-african-american-experience-in-the-blood-quilt-com-345665
41 Terry Teachout, '"The Blood Quilt" Review: A Richly Crafted Tale', *Wall Street Journal*, 21 May 2015. www.wsj.com/articles/the-blood-quilt-review-a-richly-crafted-tale-1432234465

4

Amy Herzog

I spent ten years learning how to write a play. It took me a long time. It's a hard thing to do . . . Every time I start to write a play, I think, I have no idea how to do this! But then, somehow, toward the middle of the play, I know how to get to the end.[1]

– Amy Herzog

In 2008, the playwright Christopher Shinn wrote an article about the relative absence of political theatre in America.[2] He was stung, in particular, by a reluctance three years earlier to produce *My Name Is Rachel Corrie*, a play based on the diaries and emails of the Evergreen State College student who was killed by an armoured bulldozer operated by the Israel Defence Forces in the Gaza Strip. It had played successfully at the Royal Court Theatre in London, but the transfer to the New York Theatre Workshop was postponed, citing the wider political context and the opposition of some Jewish groups. Harold Pinter, Gillian Slovo and Stephen Fry, among others – all Jewish – wrote to the *New York Times* complaining that the play had not been produced. It was, however, subsequently staged in Greenwich Village at the Minetta Lane Theatre in 2006, just a year later, and thereafter elsewhere in the country.

Shinn's wider point was that there was no hunger for oppositional political art. Non-profit theatres were, he suggested, cowed by the assumed politics of their funders, while playwrights were lured to Hollywood and television, which reinforced the ideology of a capitalist system. The last comment was somewhat strange given that American television had undergone a revolution, producing series such as *The Sopranos*, *Homicide: Life on the Street*, *The Corner*, *The Wire*, *Battlestar Galactica*, *Treme*, and, in that same year, *Generation Kill* – all works that engaged directly with the state of America, either at home or abroad. National and local politics, race, gender and, in the case of *Battlestar Galactica*, the impact of 9/11, were all engaged. This was not the theatre, but it was drama. What he may have been implicitly comparing the contemporary theatre with was perhaps that of the 1930s or 1960s, which had been very consciously seen as attempting to intervene in the national conversation, theatre groups even joining protest marches.

New York Times theatre critic Alexis Soloski begged to differ. While acknowledging that the British theatre regularly found space – even in its major subsidised theatres let alone its equivalent to Off-Broadway – for issues of the day (although in 2010 Athol Fugard would claim that the British theatre was failing to engage with political issues), he found ample evidence of it in America, invoking Naomi Wallace (admittedly initially embraced in Britain), Rajiv Joseph and Michael Weller. To this he added that there were revivals of Henrik Ibsen's *An Enemy of the People*, Irwin Shaw's *Bury the Dead*, David Rabe's *Streamers* and Arthur Miller's *All My Sons*. They were, perhaps, talking past each other, as his listing of these revivals suggests. To him, the contemporary could be addressed by works from the past, nor did they have to announce their ideological position. Shinn wanted a theatre that could be partisan, politically committed and challenging the status quo. Soloski seems to hint at a broader definition of the political, invoking works that explored the relationship between the individual and society, the nature of responsibility and the impact of past events on present behaviour.

It is true that this has not been a great period of committed drama in the United States. In the 1930s and 1960s, plays were often designed to be used up in their presentation, to intervene in the moment with no aim at a residual existence. Staged today they can seem of little more than archeological interest, the iconic *Waiting for Lefty* being a case in point. In 1935, the audience walked out of the theatre still chanting 'Strike! Strike! Strike!' Today they are liable to feel that for a moment they have breathed the air of an alien world. They do not feel that way when they see *All My Sons* or *The Crucible*, initially prompted by immediate events but in which the aftershocks of the past are registered within the works as they speak to current concerns. Amy Herzog, too, would be fascinated by the way in which past commitments echo forward – not by embracing an ideology but by inspecting it for its legitimacy and, as with Miller, exploring the private and public ramifications of past actions, aware, as she is, of her own equivocal response to a family history intimately connected to that of her society.

In 1995, details of the Venona project were released, followed four years later by the first book on the subject. The Venona project was a counter-intelligence programme run by the United States Signal Intelligence Service and consisted of decrypted messages sent by various intelligence agencies of the Soviet Union, a fact in turn revealed to the Soviet Union by a mole. One of the more striking aspects of the revelations was that a number of US citizens had been working as agents of the Soviet Union, among them Alger Hiss, one of at least six such people in the State Department, and Julius Rosenberg, whose execution was marked by the audience members of *The Crucible* as they rose to their feet in solidarity in 1953 on news of his death. There was also one former officer of the OSS, predecessor of the CIA. Although there were those who contested this, it was a blow to those who for decades had been insisting on their innocence.

The political battles of the 1930s and '40s had never been laid to rest. Not only were those on the left pursued in the McCarthyite 1950s, but the divisions within the left continued through the decades, the Stalinists and Trotskyites waging internecine war. Who kept the radical flame alight in a society that tended to regard radicalism as deeply suspect? In the 1930s, not only was the Communist Party legal, it seemed to many to have answers to the Crash of 1929 that capitalism did not. This was a time when at universities it was said to be easier to join the Party than a fraternity. Intellectuals, more particularly Jewish intellectuals, were drawn to it in part because the Soviet Union claimed to have outlawed anti-Semitism and in part because it seemed to represent the only bulwark against fascism, most obviously in Spain, which became the moral cause of the time. What followed, for convinced Marxists, however, was a series of events that challenged what paradoxically appeared an almost religious faith. The Moscow Trials of supposed Trotskyites had to be swallowed whole, as, more challengingly, had the Hitler-Stalin Pact. Some left the Party; others were in denial. Ahead, in 1952–3, lay the supposed doctors' plot in which a group of largely Jewish doctors were accused of planning to assassinate Soviet leaders, the anti-Semitism of the Soviet state standing exposed. For committed Marxists, denial was served at all meals. When they were called before investigating committees, many found themselves defending commitments in which they no longer believed, invited to purge themselves by offering the names of others.

In the 1960s, there was a resurgence as the Civil Rights movement and Vietnam re-energised those suspicious of the capitalist enterprise. Che Guevara and Mao had a certain fashion but, for all the excesses of the 1980s, the fall of the Berlin Wall seemed to settle the debate over contending values. The battle was won, though some still clung to an old faith or claimed a radical tradition with a certain pride. Then came Venona, a challenge especially to those who had lived through the ideological battles of the Cold War and to those who had inherited a radical tradition seeing the struggle for social justice on many fronts as unfinished business. Hiss turned out to have been guilty, as was Rosenberg. They were spies, and their names became public property. Did this, though, invalidate the ideology itself or those who had claimed it for their heritage? One who had inherited a tradition now challenged, a past suddenly more problematic, was a young playwright from Highland Park, New Jersey, Amy Herzog, for whom the Venona revelations would have a personal significance.

Asked when she began writing plays, she referred back to an experience in third grade when she discovered that in a school play, there was to be only one character who was human. The others were animals. Not only was she not cast as the solitary human being but she would be required to create her own costume out of paper. She offered to write the play herself and, in doing so, wrote herself a decent part. At school, though, she was more interested in novels than plays.

She went on to earn a bachelor's degree from Yale, where she was an actor rather than a playwright, appearing in Tom Stoppard's *Arcadia*. It was only after graduating that she began to write. She had been on tour with a Theatreworks production of a Len Jenkin adaptation, *Ramona Quimby*, when she felt increasingly uncomfortable. With a small group of people from her class at Yale, she founded a company and in 2001 wrote a brief play, *Granted*, about a young woman who had suffered a breakdown. Only ten minutes long, it nonetheless nerved her to take a playwriting course at Columbia before studying for an MFA at the Yale School of Drama (where she was taught by Richard Nelson and John Guare), having been accepted on the basis of what she has called a 'horrible play' titled *In Translation*, which she has described as being about a nineteen-year-old Kafka scholar and her professor set in New York in 2001 and Prague in 1910.

She wrote more plays while at Yale, *Willing*, again operating in two different time frames, involving 'a young female art historian studying a conceptual artist and the artist himself back when he was alive', and *Hungry*, 'about three teenage girls in New Jersey', which she regards as a breakthrough work: 'It was just three people on stage dealing with each other, and it had none of these weird structural conceits.'[3] In her third year, she wrote *The Wendy Play* with a cast of sixteen based on her teaching at a creative writing summer camp where she had found herself in contention with a conservative leadership.

She also wrote an autobiographical work about herself and her mother titled *Love Song for Two* Voices, a solo piece she herself performed and an anticipation of the autobiographical strain in her first successful works. It was performed at the Yale Cabaret. Her mother knew nothing of it but attended the second performance so that 'I really had to tell her and my real feeling about it was that the piece was . . . a great tribute to her and was very loving toward her. But it also is not unequivocally so and there are certain things in it that I knew she would take exception to . . . It was hard for her . . . and makes her sad. But . . . I feel like, in an amazing way, it's opened up communication between us further . . . there are things I didn't say to her until I wrote this play, and then I effectively said them to her, and now she wants to make it clear she heard them'.[4]

That inevitably raises questions about the use of personal material, not least because it contained revelations about her mother's eating disorders and the breakdown of a relationship. Although she showed her mother the script, it was plainly harrowing for her. 'She had to confront these things in a very direct way. She came almost every time I performed it and she would always weep. But what she kept saying is that she was proud of me'.[5] It is hard to read those words without a sense of disquiet, more especially when asked about this Herzog replied that it was 'kind of okay'. However, when her grandmother saw *4000 Miles*, in which she is clearly a character, and received considerable attention as a result, the playwright observed, 'I think she thought even more attention should have been paid . . . she has enjoyed the limelight. She's not shy about it'.[6]

Her grandmother features in both *After the Revolution* and *4000 Miles*, and Herzog has confessed to being 'terrified because it's so much about her aging and losing her faculties – dying, in a way. But she read it three times in advance – because she can't hear that well – and she came and she loved it, and has surprised me by not being tougher on me about it.'[7] At the same time, those closest to her would offer material for works that touched on broader issues in the culture, while she was dedicated to understanding their lives by writing about them, combining a dispassionate presentation with an essential compassion. She is clearly still in search of an understanding of her family members and, inevitably, of herself, but these are works in which the intensely personal co-exists with a sense of a wider context to do with generational differences, conflicting values and needs. Beyond that, there is a sense in these plays that her family offer a kind of authenticity (although she denied reaching for that through this mechanism), a grounding in the actual, as they come to stand for shared passions, hopes denied, ideals compromised, a redemptive persistence as the generations communicate or not across a gap of experience.

She would be thirty before she was fully satisfied with what she had written. That was with *After the Revolution*, staged by Playwrights Horizons in 2010, and which, in 2012, won the *New York Times* Outstanding Playwright Award. The judges were Edward Albee, Lynn Nottage (who had also taught her at Yale), Richard Greenberg and James Lapine. It was that comparative rarity in recent American theatre, not primarily a political play but a play in part about politics. Perhaps with some irony, a work that featured Marxists won a $50,000 Whiting Award.

She came from a family that had always been involved in radical politics. Her own parents were liberal but her grandmother's first husband, Arthur Herzog Jr, a composer and lyricist, in one of whose productions that grandmother claimed to have appeared, had come from a conservative moneyed Jewish family but was himself almost certainly a communist. A philanderer, he married three times after divorcing her grandmother, who remembered it as being five times.

Lee Joseph, Arthur Herzog's first wife, had worked for the New York Drama Department, changing her name to protect her parents who might otherwise have lost their relief payments. She took acting classes with John Garfield, who refused to name names before the House Un-American Activities Committee while rejecting Communism. He was blacklisted and died of a heart attack. Lee, who according to Amy Herzog had had an affair with him, claimed to have spoken to him the night before his death. Although not by nature a joiner, she was first arrested for picketing at age twelve and claimed to have attended 'zillions' of demonstrations. In her nineties, she handed out leaflets in Union Square, dying in April 2013.

The real radical, however, was Amy Herzog's step-grandfather Julius, who had been blacklisted for refusing to name names but who, in 1999,[8] was revealed almost certainly to have supplied information to the Soviet Union in the 1940s. During the war, he had worked for the Office of Emergency Management and the Labour War Manpower Commission before joining the Far East section (Japanese intelligence) of OSS and becoming its Deputy Chief. A Venona decrypt of 8 June 1943 discussed five agents, one being Julius Joseph and another his then wife Bella, who worked in OSS's Motion Picture Division. His codename was 'Cautious', and hers was 'Colleague'.

It was a blow to the family who had thought of him as a socialist, not a distinction that many Americans anyway found easy to make. Herzog has said, 'I always had more of an observer kind of role, but I also grew up proud that my grandparents were communists and that my step-grandfather had been blacklisted. I think that was partly why, in my late 20s, I always felt eager to claim that tradition as my own . . . I felt a really strong connection to it, and I began to examine it more as I got older.'[9] The claim, though, was not one she really embraced. Indeed she has said,

I was really proud of having this strain in my family, but I don't think that I felt guilty. I think that descended on me later in my 20s when I started wondering why I was not picking up this mantle and why my generation in general seemed much less interested in fighting for social change than my grandparents and aunts and uncles. I also ran into funny contradictions even in the older generations. Though my grandparents were committed Communists, my grandfather, after he was blacklisted, was not able to work in government again and ended up getting a high-level job at a pharmaceutical company, earning quite a bit of money and getting to travel the world. And my grandmother loved travelling with him and staying in four-star hotels. So I saw enough contradictions in those generations that I felt less guilty about having them in my life.[10]

It was that story that would lead to *After the Revolution*, in which a radical family, proud of its tradition, has to come to terms with the news that their grandfather had been a Soviet spy. It is a play that explores, among other things, the ideas of loyalty, guilt, responsibility, denial, rationalisation, the nature and definition of truth and the stories we tell ourselves to justify our actions. It is a political play in that it explores the fate of past commitments and their impact on present actions. It is a private play in that it stages the tensions within a family, but as Arthur Miller was fond of saying about the connection between the private and the public, 'the fish is in the sea and the sea inside the fish'.

At the heart of the play is a family that has lived and breathed politics, seeing itself as having a historical role, albeit not with the same sharpness of definition they had inherited from Joe, the family patriarch. There are genuine convictions behind their actions but also a touch of hubris, the sense of being part of an evolving history only to discover that history is not a secure foundation. In one way, it is reminiscent of Arnold Wesker's 1956 play *Chicken Soup with Barley* about a Jewish family experiencing the challenge to old ideals. In another, inevitably, it recalls *The Crucible* except that the man who stands up for his values and challenges the state is here discovered to have been wanting.

The Joseph family is socially conscious, supporters of the bussing of black children to school in a white suburb, fighting in the courts to defend a black man accused of shooting a policeman. Ben, Joe's son, is head of the teachers' union. Emma, Ben's daughter and a new law graduate, heads a foundation in the name of her grandfather, a man who had worked for the Office of Strategic Services during the war before, in 1949, being appointed special assistant to Trygve Lie, the first Secretary General of the United Nations, only to be called before an investigating committee, his refusal to co-operate resulting in his blacklisting. Now, however, news of his spying is about to be revealed in a new book. A hero of the left is to be exposed as no more than a traitor, unless he could be thought to be loyal to something other than his country. The question is what impact will this news have on his widow, on the foundation that carries his name, on Emma who heads it and, in one way or another, on all of them?

Emma, a self-declared Marxist, almost by virtue of her inheritance, not only heads the foundation but makes key speeches. Her boy friend is a Latino, the second such she has had, perhaps itself a gesture of her social as well as private commitments, but she now moves away from him as if her grandfather's actions had in some way invalidated her own passions. It is not just the embarrassment of heading a foundation named for a man revealed to be a spy or even the degree of self-doubt that now seems to paralyse her and the realisation that she has herself been deceived by her family, which disturbs her, but the fact that betrayal and denial may be her true inheritance. When her father congratulates her on a speech she has made, insisting that she was not only speaking up for the accused man – Mumia Abu-Jamal, a former Black Panther charged with killing a Philadelphia police officer – but for revolution, she does not yet know that the word 'revolution' has been compromised. When she does learn the truth, she begins to doubt the justice of the cause she has signed up to, wondering if the accused man was perhaps not guilty after all even as she, in turn, fails to inform a potential donor of what she has learned. 'You are a young person with the courage of your convictions' (35), the donor says, yet both her courage and convictions are in doubt.

For the eighty-two-year-old Vera, Joe Joseph's second wife, he had been a symbol of resistance, an essential part of a myth which she had accepted and continues to perpetuate, not least because it confers on her a significance beyond her role in the family. Her response to the news of his treachery is denial. Challenged by Emma, she insists, 'A lot of what you hear about Stalin in this country is propaganda . . . There were a lot of wonderful things about the Soviet Union! The papers would never report that because they didn't want the American people to know the truth . . . it was really Stalin and the Russians who were stopping Hitler from killing all the Jews.' When Emma reminds her that 'Stalin was slaughtering Jews in his own country, and homosexuals, and dissidents', she replies, 'I still don't know how much of that is true . . . the question is which side are you on.'[11] It is not, though, just a question of who was on the right side of an intellectual, moral, political debate, which until this point had seemed no more than an historical footnote, but of the price to be paid for wilful denial as the past is suddenly re-invented and what has been repressed surfaces? Why, long after the revolution, after a history of radicalism and repression, does it matter at the end of the millennium?

Joe's espionage, although news to Emma, turns out not to be to her father, sister or, Emma presumes, Vera and not, it seems in retrospect, to his first wife, whom she had been taught to regard as abandoning him at his time of need for a rich man but now feels must have felt abandoned, seven months pregnant and with no money to support her children. In other words, there was an abandonment, but it was by Joe, the price of his idealism being paid by others then as it is again now, the rest of the family having known for four years, during which time they have allowed Emma to run campaigns for justice in his name, the foundation being established precisely at that time. They had remained silent, taking their own Fifth Amendment, because otherwise they would have incriminated themselves. Nor will this be the only abandonment in the play as Emma's drug-addicted sister is cut off from the kind of contact that might have helped her in her need, as public commitment takes precedence over individual distress.

Vera had suppressed the truth because it justified her life, the surviving wife of a radical hero, as the truth about Stalin was denied although common currency at the time of the hearings. Ben has suppressed the truth because he has convinced himself that there is a higher truth but also because it is embarrassing to compromise or even invalidate his own lifetime of commitment. For that reason, he swears Emma's sister, Jess, to silence. In a message Ben leaves on Emma's answer phone, in what he pointedly mentions is her privileged Upper West Side apartment, he reminds her why people had been drawn to the Party in the 1930s. In a time of desperation it had stood up for the poor and for racial equality. It had been at war with fascism while America wrapped itself in isolationist rhetoric and policy. More than half a century on, people have forgotten why it seemed not only a political party but a moral cause. By the 1950s, the wheel had turned. By the 1990s, it was no more than a minor aspect of history – but not for this family. He offers an impassioned plea for understanding while himself being dishonest both about the past and the present.

As a member of the OSS, Joe had been in the business of secrets (while America was keeping secrets from its ally, the Soviet Union). He moved in a world of ambiguity and deception as he clung to a Manichean vision himself. Summoned before a committee, he took the Fifth Amendment, scarcely a rarity at the time, but crucially he denied his involvement in espionage. Denial has passed down the line to his descendants.

Politics are in the foreground for them. It is part of their daily conversation and motivates their actions. Their compassion reaches out into the world, yet they are myopic about problems closer to hand, with Jess, in and out of rehab, trying their patience. They break off any real communication. As she says, 'it can be a challenge to have an addict in the family' (45). Her parents had not sought help, Emma observes, because 'individual suffering has no place in Marxist philosophy' (84). Jess's rehab fails, but that in itself raises a basic question for this family connected to their political dilemma: what happens when you have to deal with imperfection, betrayal, hope denied?

Emma, too, retreats from the public world into her private anguish, cutting herself off from her father and her lover. When she learns the truth, she seemingly forgets that she was supposed to be dedicating herself to the cause of a man on death row instead of debating ethical questions and her own moral state. As her assistant in the foundation remarks of her loss of focus on Mumia, whom they are dedicated to defend in court, 'I think making our work more about Mumia and less about 1953 is not the worst idea' (58). Those who had imagined themselves the inheritors of a history are at risk of being imprisoned by it. What debt, after all, do they owe to it? Taught to disobey authority, they have chosen to obey the authority of the past as they had understood it. When Emma confronts her father, she accuses him of telling her that the revolution was coming when he knew it was not. If the past was compromised then so was the future that was supposed to see a transformation in human values.

Jess momentarily wins her way back into favour when she declares she is in a lesbian relationship, much as Emma has garnered approval by dating Latinos, although Jess's relationship has only lasted a week and a half. The suggestion is that their father is happy to embrace any liberal cause that burnishes his credentials – that yesterday's radicalism has devolved into an embrace of fashionable causes. For their grandfather, the stakes were high. He faced imprisonment and worse. He impoverished his family for a principle, thus sacrificing them. For succeeding generations in the 1990s, there is less at stake except that secrets are still corrosive, lying regarded as a rational tactic (as children Emma and Jess had once lied to their father when sneaking out of the house, and just as they all now lie to one another and perhaps even to themselves), general principles trumping private relationships.

This is a play set in America and with a special significance for Herzog, but a similar and more widespread problem confronted those in eastern and central Europe in the years following the fall of communism; internal spies were revealed, and children of those who had betrayed their friends, neighbours and family members had to rewrite their own lives in the context of new information. Nothing was as it had appeared. Peter Esterhazy, Hungary's best-known writer, discovered that his father, Count Matyas Esterhazy, who came from a family that had lost everything to the Communists, informed on his own family. As his son remarked, 'He was a good father to us, and we learned a lot from him, especially with regard to ethics, my relationship to history and the family's history. He was a shining example in all of this. Anyone who knew him could only talk about him with love and respect. But all the time I was seeing a parallel story . . . after this moment, I felt like I was watching an educational film about what life is really like.'[12]

The references to being taught ethics, a relationship to history and a family's history carries an irony that is equally caught by Herzog's play, which is ultimately not about a Soviet spy and the justification for a radical view of the world but about those forced to a reinterpretation of the past and still more about the shifting dynamics of a family caught up in conflicting loyalties.

It turns out that the wealthy donor and friend to Joe had himself known of his spying back in the 1940s: 'Take a walk in the East Village, throw a stone you hit a spy.' The essence is 'we move on . . . You're disappointed in your family. It's terrible . . . this is not an uncommon predicament . . . it's not a reason to let down . . . all the people you have promised to help' (73–4). Although she is to resign, the foundation will continue. The final word is given to Vera, who poses a central problem in understanding what it was to live in a different age, to embrace different values, to be confronted with different challenges and to feel that a certain energy and commitment has drained away: 'You can look back and say we did this wrong, or we did that wrong, but the point is that it was *for* something. I look at most people your age . . . and I don't know what they're for. I don't know how they're going to feel when they get my age. When they look back and see how they spent their time' (90).

When Christopher Shinn lamented what seemed to him a lack of political drama, it is tempting to feel that he was really regretting the lack of political passion in society, perhaps not untouched with a sense of nostalgia. The battles of the 1930s were long over, as were the repressions of the 1950s, the Civil Rights movement of the 1960s, the anti-Vietnam drive, the rise of the women's movement and the battle for gay rights. There were, to be sure, causes – resistance to aspects of the Patriot Act, the Iraq War, Guantánamo, the financial crisis of 2008 – but there was no coherent mass resistance, no real sense of an alternative world order. The Cold War was over, replaced by a resurgent nationalism and international terrorism. Politically, there was a drift towards the centre by the Left (although in 2016 Bernie Sanders seemed to belie that) and away from it by the Right. *After the Revolution* reflects something of that. It is neither an indictment of past commitments nor an embracing of them. It is a portrait of a generation unsure of its attitude to the past and uncertain of its current role. A vocabulary has exhausted itself. Beyond the political, however, lies the dynamic of the family with its compromises, conflicting needs, evasions, tensions.

The play's achievement lies in the way in which the political invades the private and the private dictates responses to the political within the lives of characters struggling to negotiate their relationship with one another and the world beyond.

This is not a play that sets out to condemn the political commitments of the past. For all Joe's betrayals, and the wider betrayals of its own principles by the Communist Party, the conditions that made it seem such a plausible solution in the 1930s were real enough. Nor is it an invitation to recoil from commitments in the present. A speech made by Ben may be self-serving, but it is not without an essential truth. 'Emma', he says, 'it's 1999. In this decade we saw the Soviet Union collapse and my dad die. Clinton is a big-business president, the poor are getting poorer, racial divides are deepening, we're dropping bombs in the Balkans and people are complacent' (16–17). In a *New York Times* review, Charles Isherwood noted that the speech prompted 'a hearty chuckle from the audience', although whether that was a laugh of recognition or, a handful of years on, a sense that this was a lesson from the past, is not clear. For him, and surely correctly, this response was ignoring the fact that it was 'not merely a mordant jab at the trials of the decade just passed' but a concern with 'the way history shapes people's lives, their politics, their personalities, and how deep misunderstandings may arise between generations who fail to take into account how the brute heel of hard experience can bare down upon the honourable individual'.[13]

The play received positive reviews not only from the *New York Times* but also the *Wall Street Journal*, in which Terry Teachout praised dialogue that 'glitters with the knowing wit of a sharp-eyes observer' in a play that was 'a searching study of the power of dishonesty to corrode the ties of sympathy that blind even the closest of families'.[14]

When Herzog's own grandmother saw the play, she said, 'Amy is very creative, but ultimately she's a conservative.'[15] The remark says something about a play in which politics is less subject than context. Nor had she finished with her grandmother, who became a character in her next play, *4000 Miles*, which she had already written and was due for production. Indeed the play is dedicated to her.

After graduating from college, she had lived with her grandmother, whose hearing was imperfect and who suffered from the normal problems of aging; thus, for a while she was roommates with someone many decades older than herself, acknowledging that the gap in age led to conflicts and misunderstandings. Despite being affectionate, she was 'a contender in the room . . . tough on people whether or not they're related to her, more especially if they're related to her. And she doesn't assume that grandmotherly posture of sweetness and deference and distance from younger people. She just gets in the ring and engages with you, which can be wonderful and hard'. What she came to admire was her 'fight to remain present and relevant'.[16]

This was one stimulus for the play, a desire to write about an older character with understanding, aware that in society such can become invisible, existing on the margin of other people's lives. Another source was news that came to her when she was doing a workshop in Williamstow of *After the Revolution* in 2009. One of her cousin's friends had died in a rafting accident. As she has explained, 'I guess when I heard this horrible news about this very young man dying, there was some connection for me to how my grandmother deals with death at her age constantly. She's just losing people it seems several times a month. And, of course, she's confronting the fact that she's now 95.'[17]

The play is set in Vera's rent-controlled apartment in Greenwich Village, an apartment itself showing signs of age but still full of books. There is a rotary telephone. We learn that she owns a computer, forced on her by her family, but that it remains a mystery to her. The past, in other words, surrounds her, the present less so. The name on her buzzer is that of her long-dead husband. The action takes place in 'September of a recent year – maybe 2007'. She wears a hearing aid, has false teeth, is occasionally unsure of her balance and is forgetful, words slipping away from her. Some days, she admits, her 'head really isn't right' (109). She is ninety-one, 'tiny and frail but not without fortitude' (99), the fortitude being as important as the frailty. She has an arrangement with an old woman across the corridor whom she never meets but with whom she exchanges brief telephone messages to check whether they are still alive rather than quietly rotting. They share a radical politics, although this is now more a memory than present commitment as she invokes a 'pro-peace whaddayacallit' (107), 'whaddayacallit' being a stand-by word for that which she can no longer summon to mind.

Into this world, at three in the morning, intrudes Leo Joseph-Connell, her grandson, twenty-one, fit, dirty and with a laden bicycle that he has just ridden across the country from Seattle (the actual bicycle, as it happens, that Herzog had ridden from New Haven to San Francisco on a Habitat for Humanity fundraiser to mark her graduation). He is alternately described as New Age or a hippy, relying on cash from his parents despite their estrangement, as well as from the grandmother on whom he descends even as he claims he has come to keep her company. They represent two different times, have different values and inhabit two different languages, his being disturbingly denatured. Communication is difficult, and not only because she needs but does not always wear a hearing aid. Offered a banana, he recoils in horror at the thought of the jet fuel expended in flying it to America while, asked to call his mother who is worried about him, he insists, 'that's not something I can take responsibility for' (101). Indeed, he takes no responsibility for anything or anyone, beyond making arrangements when Vera's neighbour collapses. When he breaks a faucet, he insists that it 'came right off in my hand'. He breaks relationships in the same way, while insisting he believes in 'love and trust' (110) prompting a like response, and regards Marxism as 'cool' suggesting 'it was like . . . recycling, or whatever' (146) without actually embracing it or indeed anything that could be thought to be a coherent position.

He is the mirror opposite to Vera's commitment, even if that had involved self-deceit and is fading into a vague liberal progressivism that she is no longer in a position to act upon. He is ostensibly tolerant of everything because he wants to believe there is no moral structure beyond a vague antinomianism or the rhetoric of a fashionable social concern, mere gesture politics. Vera, though, preaches a tolerance that can seem too close to resignation when she speaks of her previous husband's multiple affairs. For his part, Leo believes that people should be left to their own devices, while she insists that 'The point is you help people, it's about the community, it's not about I do what's best for me and you do what's best for you' (120).

Something has happened on his trip, although what it was is not immediately clear; something has also happened at home, which had alienated his parents and sent his adopted Chinese sister into therapy. The something on his journey was the death of his friend in a bizarre accident, crushed to death under crates of chickens while, high on peyote, he had kissed his sister, already in a fragile state having taken three years off from college, 'not really sure what she's doing' (145). He objects that while it has sent her 'reeling into identity confusion', there was 'totally minimal tongue' suggesting that 'it's hard to think of something more emblematic of our society, that a kiss expressing mutual love between two people is considered destructive' (122). He had not attended his friend's funeral and now pursues a one-night stand with a Chinese young woman as if she were a handy substitute for his sister. When that sister, in a Skype call, pleads for him to come home, he breaks the contact.

Bizarrely, Vera confides that his grandfather 'never did anything for me in bed' only for Leo to attempt to return the intimacy by observing that his girl friend 'has kind of a weird pussy' (138). When he tries at length to describe his friend's accident, Vera is not wearing her hearing aid and misses much of it, two people inhabiting different social and linguistic worlds, seemingly deaf to one another's needs and vulnerabilities. The play ends, though, with a gesture from Leo that suggests he has a capacity for empathy for which there had previously been little evidence as he prepares a speech to make at the funeral of Vera's neighbour, being the only one of them to have met her. It turns out that she had been an actress, if not a successful one, and had lost her husband in the Korean War. Admittedly, his knowledge comes courtesy of Google. He is also about to leave for a job in Colorado where he is to be a leader for 'a bunch of rich kids,' which he characterises as 'a pretty cool program' for which, on no particular grounds, he regards himself as 'very qualified' (157).

Yet this is a play in which an elderly woman, drifting towards the end, seldom visited, with a neighbour she only hears on the telephone, does find contact of a kind and in which a twenty-one-year-old, plainly adrift and in retreat, seemingly unaware of the needs of others, briefly edges out of his isolation. This odd couple, often in a contention that sparks humour as well as misunderstanding, negotiates a way of co-existing, although they barely share a vocabulary. He is careless, for much of the time as disconnected from those around them as is she, content to skate over the surface of life while convinced he is spiritually in touch with the world. She is aware that she has lived on into a moment she no longer fully understands, the sharpness of her convictions dulled by time, history not unfolding as she had once believed it might, yet is still resilient.

There are moments when Leo can seem a stereotype, unaware of the fatuousness of his views and of the damage he does, but when he recounts the story of his friend's death, in a scene played out in silhouette, he and a silent Vera sitting together, it is not hard to see that there is more to him than appears. Nothing is resolved. He will go off, still convincing himself that drifting is a direction. She will be alone in her apartment to face the fading of the light, her contemporaries now dead, her physical and mental powers declining. For the moment, though, they come together to think of how to compose a fitting tribute to a woman they never knew, one more funeral whose implications must be ignored.

4000 Miles is laced with humour and human understanding that brings together two characters adrift for different reasons, who see the world differently. Both experience an essential loneliness, Vera because friends and acquaintances have disappeared, he because he severs himself from his family, self-obsessed and with no clear idea how to connect to the world.

The play was written for the SoHo Rep Writer/Director Lab in New York City. It opened at Lincoln Center's LCT3, designed for work by new playwrights in a new space with 112 seats and ticket prices considerably below those usually charged. It prompted positive reviews including, most crucially, from Charles Isherwood in the *New York Times*, who found it a 'funny, moving play', an 'altogether wonderful drama'.[18] It transferred to the Mitzi E. Newhouse Theater at Lincoln Center, which boasts 299 seats, but this is a play that benefits from a sense of intimacy as two principal characters, in a small room, discover both the distance between them and how, briefly, it can narrow.

Her next work, *Belleville* (2011), originally called *The Doctor's Wife*, very different from her family plays, was inspired in part by news stories she had read, in particular the case of Jean-Claude Romand who had dropped out of medical school but claimed to be a doctor working for the World Health Organisation. Living in France, he would leave for work every day, only to spend his time reading medical journals. In 1993, he murdered his wife and children as well as his parents before attempting to murder his mistress. He was sentenced to life imprisonment in 1996. A book about the events was published in 2000, which led to a number of films, including Nicole Garcia's *L'Adversaire* (2002) and a television documentary, *The Man Who Faked His Life* (2005).

Herzog had started writing *Belleville* earlier, in 2007, as a commission from Yale Rep. As such, it preceded the other plays. The first draft, written as a farce, called *The Doctor's Wife*, differed radically from the final version. She abandoned it and started again, only to abandon it once more. The process took five years. It opened at the Yale Repertory Theatre Workshop in 2011 and reached New York's Theatre Workshop in 2013. It is set in the Belleville area of Paris, a place she had visited, and features a young married American couple, their Senegalese-French landlord and his wife. It is, as she has said, a play about a marriage with a lie at its heart – indeed more than one lie. Twenty-eight-year-old Zack ostensibly has a job working, for Doctors Without Borders, on paediatric AIDS research. His wife, Abby, in emotional recoil from the death of her mother, sees Paris as a place to recover and has a sentimental attachment to it, or so it appears, but it is not quite what they imagined, and neither are they. They seem happy except that we slowly learn neither has told the truth. Indeed, we enter the play with evidence of a gulf between them as she catches him watching pornography on his laptop. From that moment, things begin to fall apart. The ending is both a shock and, in some sense, inevitable.

He goes to work every day while she is teaching yoga to college students. They are affectionate towards one another, and yet are both withholding not only crucial truths but also some final commitment for which they apparently yearn even as their deceits compromise their relationship and, it becomes clear, have done from the beginning. Indeed they have not been able or willing to examine their own motivations, confront their own missteps. In contrast, the landlord and his wife, Alioune and Amina, are grounded, happy and content in themselves, although their suspicions of their American tenants grow as evidence of their increasing instability introduces a level of threat that surprises them, as it does the audience.

It turns out that Abby is off the antidepression medication she has been taking for five years following her mother's death. She is constantly on edge, suffering from 'epic' migraines and looks older than she is, her hair going gray. Having been told, as she grew up, that she should do what she wished so long as she was happy, she is aware that she has neither done anything, nor is she happy. A desire for an acting career has come to nothing. Marriage had seemed a solution to her problems. In France, however, she has ceased to learn the language and relies obsessively on calls to and from her father. Her students have failed to turn up. Meanwhile, a visa problem apparently prevents their return to America to celebrate Christmas following a problem with her sister's baby. It is not, though, as if Christmases at home are relaxed occasions. For reasons not yet apparent, they involve 'hours of meaningful eye contact',[19] her sister and father themselves seemingly disturbed. Little by little her fragility becomes apparent.

For his part, Zack has not only been lying about his job, which he does not have, but also about his degree, having dropped out after two years. He did not, as he claims, sacrifice a residency job on behalf of Abby. He is neither a doctor nor is he working on a way to prevent infant AIDS, a claim that is not only false but morally offensive. It follows that, despite his claims, they did not come to Paris for his job, which is non-existent. They are four months behind on their rent, a fact he keeps from her. He spends his time smoking marijuana, evidently treading water against the moment his deceptions will become apparent.

They go out to dinner together, and on their return she is too drunk to function, while he breaks into his landlord's apartment in search of marijuana. Confronted by Amina, he is told that they are aware of his lies and insist that he and Abby must leave. The following morning, sensing that things are finally falling apart, she slashes her wrists – evidently not for the first time. As the truth begins to spill out, she is increasingly terrified of a man she realises she does not know. Trust, if it existed, now disintegrates. When he finally allows her to speak to her father on the phone, he goes into the bathroom and slashes his own wrists. The play ends as Alioune and Amina clean the apartment, Amina picking up a wedding album and dropping it into a garbage bag. It is not, she observes, a catastrophe, merely '*En fait*', a matter of fact.

The source material was about lies that led to murder. Here they lead in the direction of suicide. This is not a crime story, although the evidence accumulates. It is about the nature of relationships, the level on which people, even those assumed to be close, remain mysteries to one another, differ in their memories or what they choose to construct as their past. If Abby seems the more vulnerable, Zack is equally brittle. He is the one who has built an elaborate fiction. They are both failures, seeing in one another an escape that only serves to lead them back to themselves and their insecurities, but it is he who is the suspect figure. Herzog has said, 'It tends to be men who are the liars in these situations.' Who are these partners, she asks, only to answer, 'They might not be equally to blame. But there are situations, surely, where you have a feeling that something is not right, where there ought to be some kind of guarding against something, whatever it is; where you should be asking questions.' She further confesses: 'I had . . . this primal fear that people are so unknowable'.[20] It is that primal fear that drives *Belleville* and lifts it out of the particularities of an American couple in a Parisian arrondissement in 'the recent past'.

This is, in a sense, a crime thriller without a crime, a psychological drama in which layers of deceit are slowly pealed off. Herzog, like her characters, has perfected the art of misdirection. As in *4000 Miles* we are in an enclosed space, but in that no man's land the characters reached out for one another; here they are in retreat – from themselves no less than from anything approaching real intimacy. A knife flourished by Zach seems simply that. He cuts bread with it, except that it is more than that, and indeed turns out to foreshadow the later cutting of wrists. Here is Chekhov's gun, which he advised should not be introduced unless it is to be fired.

Again, the play was well received by Isherwood in the *New York Times*, as it was by Richard Zoglin in *Time*. 'No one', the latter asserted, currently writing for the theatre, 'has a sharper grasp of character, or more sheer storytelling technique'.[21] Herzog, he suggested, was in a class by herself. There were, though, dissenters. Andrea Simakis review in the *Plain Dealer*, was headed, 'Amy Herzog's Whiny, Self Indulgent Play about Whiny Self-Indulgence'. She found it 'one of the most pretentious plays I've seen in years, with the final scene delivered entirely in French',[22] and this by French characters, in France.

In 1860, Elizabeth Barrett Browning published a poem called, 'A Musical Instrument'. It begins:

> What was he doing, the great God Pan,
>   Down in the reeds by the river?
> Spreading ruin and Scattering ban,
> Splashing and paddling with hoofs of a goat,
> And breaking the golden lilies afloat
>   With the dragon-fly on the river.
>
> He tore out a reed, the great god Pan,
>   From the deep cool bed of the river;
> The limpid water turbidly ran,
> And the broken lilies a-dying lay,
> And the dragon-fly had fled away,
>   Ere he brought it out of the river.

Pan is creating the pipe on which he will play from a reed snatched from the river, disregarding the damage he does. The living reed is the sacrifice necessary for the creation of art but perhaps beyond that for the forging of a life.

> Yet half a beast is the great god Pan,
>   To laugh as he sits by the river,
> Making a poet out of a man:
> The true gods sigh at the cost and pain –
> For the reed which grows nevermore again
>   As a reed with the reeds of the river.

As Herzog herself explained in responding to a critic, where certain impulses are of necessity contained or suppressed in life, for the poet they must be released. For the artist, truths must be spoken 'at all risks', even if they are inconvenient to a peaceful life, even if privacies are invaded, as are the reeds in the river, even if the price is pain. Passions must be intensified for the music to stir a response. But Pan, she recalled, was a beast up to the waist and not a true god.

In 2012, *The Great God Pan*, commissioned by Steppenwolf Theatre Company, opened at Playwrights Horizons. She wrote it in three days, with relatively few revisions. In one way, it is a play in which suppressed truths are recovered by those whose own lives are as they are because, in the words of Browning's poem, they have been 'hack'd and hew'd', as Pan 'drew the pith, like the heart of a man'. In another way, perhaps, it reflects Herzog's justification for her own art, which has been created from the lives of others or from shaping suffering into form since '"This is the way," laugh'd the great god Pan / (Laugh'd while he sat by the river), / "The only way, since gods began / To make sweet music, they could succeed"', for once the music plays it has a transforming power: 'The sun on the hill forgot to die, / And the lilies revived and the dragon-fly / Came back to dream on the river'. Here is the playwright who commandeered the lives of her step-grandfather, her grandmother, her mother to create her drama, acknowledging the pain this caused but seeing this appropriation as justified in so far as it served her art. These are the reeds taken from the river to make the pipe on which she could play.

The Great God Pan is about damaged people torn from whatever comfort they may have expected. Marriages, partnerships, are strained, ambitions thwarted, bodies dysfunctional, while the past carries a menace whether true or not, since memory is imperfect. At the heart of the play is Jamie, a good-looking 'fairly clean-cut Brooklynite', who has a job as a journalist, albeit not an impressive one. He is one step up from a copyeditor but it is a job that includes health insurance. His partner is Paige. They are both in their early thirties, and things are not good between them. He has had sexual difficulties and is unable to commit. She has lost her career as a dancer through injury and now works as a nutritionist while studying part-time for her master's degree in social work, to be followed by a few more years of training. Neither of their careers is really advancing, and she has suffered from depression, perhaps an echo of *Belleville* with its depressive failed actress.

She is working with a girl who has anorexia and reveals a compassion hard to detect in her own relationship, but the treatment seems not to be working, so this is a client she may be losing. She, herself, is at crisis point, afraid that their relationship is leading nowhere and that her biological clock is running down. When she confronts Jamie, he replies, 'I'm hearing what you are saying' (15), a sure sign that he is not, and his request for a week to decide on their future would seem to be an indication that they have none. There is tension between her and Jamie's mother, also a social worker. Things are not well, and there comes a moment when Paige decides to abort a foetus, her pregnancy, he suspects, though she denies, being a deliberate attempt to force his hand.

Into this situation intrudes Frank, a childhood friend, described as 'a multiple-pierced, somewhat effeminate, wounded soul'.[23] Frank is a massage therapist who has been in and out of prison, an addict for nearly nine years. He and Jamie have not seen each other for many years, but Frank now explains that he intends to take legal action against his father for the sexual abuse he suffered as a child, abuse to which his father has admitted, precipitating a divorce after thirty-six years. He is anxious for Jamie to confirm that he, too, had been assaulted, something of which he has no memory, although when he visits his parents they tell him that he had spent a week at Frank's house, farmed out because their own marriage had been going through difficulties at the time.

Herzog had originally intended to make a woman the subject of sexual abuse. It was fellow-playwright Amy Baker who persuaded her otherwise, the decision giving her a sense of perspective: 'I was writing about someone in their early thirties dealing with these very common questions about making life choices and I thought writing a male character would help me find distance.' Not that it was entirely a play that moved away from her own background: 'I've been writing all these plays about my extended family and this is the play that had more to do with aspects of my immediate family. Not directly, but I set it in the town that I grew up in and it has some of the geography of that town – a creek that used to be there became really important in this play . . . It wasn't a wholesale borrowing as was the case with some half the characters in *After the Revolution.*'[24]

The assault remains problematic. When Jamie goes to see a former paid child-minder, Polly, who had looked after them during the day when this event was supposed to have happened, she knows nothing of it but does recall that Frank had a habit of lying, so memories of the past may be problematic. On the other hand, her memory, too, is suspect. What she does remember is taking them, as children, to a nearby creek into which she fell, reciting the Browning poem to them, as she does again now, the phrase 'spreading ruin' having a new and different resonance.

Was Jamie abused? Was Frank, since he acknowledges that his father's memories may be suspect? As in many of the recovered memory cases of the 1980s, there is a tendency to read back from present difficulties in search of an explanation for them. How far is that true here? None of the others approached recalled anything, because, he explains, they had been 'asleep'.

At first sight, it would seem that Herzog has here moved away from rooting her work in her experience, but in fact she has explained something of its origins. She recalls, in particular, the sense that, while having a happy childhood, most of her memories have a tinge of fear, remembering, among other things, an occasion when, during a sleepover at a friend's house, that friend's father had come into the dark bedroom after bedtime and been startled to find her awake. There is no suggestion of abuse, just a trace memory of fear. By the same token, Polly's fall into the creek was based on her grandmother's similar fall. Herzog had recited the Browning poem as she grew up and also recalled, at the age of twelve or thirteen, becoming interested in the stories of recovered memory then current.

More fundamentally, she has said that, 'my own mythology of my childhood . . . is a . . . foundation of the play'. At age four she suffered a trauma when a friend died suddenly. Memories of that stayed with her, and she was taken to a child psychiatrist, where she was encouraged to paint and write as a way of coming to terms with it. The family myth was that this had led her to become who she is today. In other words, the present is to be explained by past trauma. It is not an explanation Herzog is prone to embrace, but Jamie's parents have accepted a similar mythology about him, in the face of evidence to the contrary.

This is not, though, a play about recovered memories so much as the ambiguous nature of memory, particularly as adults try to re-process childhood events. Beyond that it is concerned with how these characters look for explanations for current problems yet fail to address them. There are traumas to spare in the play. All marriages and partnerships seem to have suffered tensions, although Jamie's parents have, perhaps, recovered from theirs.

Like most of her plays, *The Great God Pan* ends ambiguously. It is not clear whether or not Jamie had been abused or, indeed, that the events to which Frank refers ever happened. That is not where the play lives. It is equally not clear whether his relationship with Paige is irretrievably broken, although it seems to be as he finally comes to some kind of understanding of where he has failed. In the *New Yorker*, Hilton Als complained that the ending remained open, comparing the play to Lillian Hellman's *The Children's Hour* in which the truth is finally told. For Herzog, though, truth is altogether more elusive. Certainties, in her plays, are always subject to revision in a way that can breed guilt and confusion but that, perhaps, is the common currency of human affairs.

Where the great god Pan cut a reed to make a pipe, Herzog uses a scalpel to dissect conflicting human emotions, to expose ambivalent relationships. Illusions are stripped away, though, without any certainty that there is an inner core or even validity to feelings that seem assured but are so easily subject to spreading ruin. Her characters pay a price, often struggle to rebuild what they have broken much as the lilies revived in Browning's poem. In reaching into her family past, she has acknowledged causing some pain, but the result is the plays themselves, which become Browning's musical instrument sounding out beside the river. There has always been a price to be paid for art.

Notes

1 Carolyn Cantor, 'Amy Herzog', *Bomb*, Fall 2012, www.bombmagazine.org/article/6768/amy-herzog
2 Christopher Shinn, 'Bush Legacy: Market Rules', *Index on Censorship*, 37(4), 2008, pp. 88–93.
3 Alexis Soloski, 'The Political and the Personal Are in Dialogue in Amy Herzog's Plays', *American Theatre*, 1 March 2012. www.americantheatre.org/2012/03/01/the-political-and-the-personal-are-in-dialogue-in-amy-herzogs-plays/
4 Steve Levinson and Amy Herzog, 'Collaborator in Conversation: Amy Herzog and Steven Levinson', Huntington *Theatre*, n.d. www.huntingtontheatre.org/articles/Collaborators-in-Conversation-Amy-Herzog-and-Steven-Levenson
5 Ibid.
6 Chad Jones, 'Amy Herzog Gets Mileage Out of Grandma', 13 January 2013. www.sfgate.com/performance/article/Amy-Herzog-gets-mileage-out-of-grandma-4184621.php
7 Ibid.
8 John Earl Haynes and Harvey Klehr, *Venona: Decoding Soviet Espionage in America* (New Haven, 1999).

9 Gerard Raymond, 'Family Ties: An Interview with Playwright Amy Herzog', *Slant:* <ins>The official</ins> <ins>blog</ins> of *The House Next Door*, 9 April 2012. www.slantmagazine.com/house/article/family-ties-an-interview-with-playwright-amy-herzog

10 'Q&A: Playwright Amy Herzog on Family History, Political Activism, and the Culture of Capitalism', *Huffpost Arts and Culture*, 16 June 2012. www.huffingtonpost.com/artinfo/qa-playwright-amy-herzog_b_1429019.html

11 Amy Herzog, *After the Revolution*. In *'4000 Miles' and 'After the Revolution': Two Plays by Amy Herzog* (New York, 2013), p. 42.

12 'Son Reveals Count Esterhazy Was Communist Spy', *The Scotsman*, 5 October 2002. www.scotsman.com/news/world/son-reveals-count-esterhazy-was-communist-spy-1-623564

13 Charles Isherwood, 'A Stain on Her Marxist Mantle', *New York Times*, 10 November 2010. www.nytimes.com/2010/11/11/theater/reviews/11after.html

14 Terry Teachout, 'Review of "After the Revolution": Amy Herzog's Second Coming', *Wall Street Journal*, 26 March 2015. www.wsj.com/articles/review-of-after-the-revolution-amy-herzogs-second-coming-1427401512

15 Gerard Raymond, 'Family Ties'.

16 Ibid.

17 Ibid.

18 Charles Isherwood, 'Young and Old with No Particular Place to Go', *New York Times*, 20 June 2011. www.nytimes.com/2011/06/21/theater/reviews/4000-miles-with-mary-louise-wilson-review.html?scp=2&sq=Isherwood%25204000%2520Miles%2520Herzog&st=cse

19 Amy Herzog, *Belleville* (New York, 2014), p. 13.

20 Chris Jones, 'Herzog in "Belleville": How Well Do We Know each Other?' *Chicago Tribune*, 26 June, 2013.

21 Richard Zoglin, 'Down and Out in Paris', *Time*, 6 March 2013. http://entertainment.time.com/2013/03/06/down-and-out-in-paris-amy-herzogs-belleville/

22 Andrea Simakis, '"Bellville", Amy Herzog's Whiny, Self-Indulgent Play about Whiny Self-Indulgence, Is Just That at Dobama, Despite a Great Cast', *Cleveland Plain Dealer*, 22 September 2014. www.cleveland.com/onstage/index.ssf/2014/09/belleville_amy_herzogs_whiny_s.html

23 Amy Herzog, *The Great God Pan* (New York, 2014), p. 5.

24 Carolyn Cantor, 'Amy Herzog'.

5

Tracy Letts

Get rid of the censor.

– Tracy Letts[1]

Actors and writers are not so different from one another. They are both interpreters of life required to project themselves into the minds and passions of others. The actor literally embodies words written by another, makes physical the imagined, animates the inanimate, breathes into the lungs of figures no more than so many marks on a page. Yet writers, in their isolation, frequently speak aloud as they write, hear voices summoned into being as characters slowly form, already yearning for company – for a conversation that will serve to sharpen their own outline, gift them a past and present, a depth that defies a seemingly inert language. Sometimes actors become writers out of frustration, a sense of their second-order status, while writers become actors to protect their own sense of the forms they will inhabit, the rhythms of a language that will otherwise become the possession of others, bringing as they do their own gifts to the occasion.

Everyone who reads a novel stages the world summoned on the pages differently. Often writers forbear to offer too detailed a physical description to allow the reader to become a collaborator, infusing the text with an authenticity brought to the table and not already laid out for the feast. In the theatre, casting is an interpretation, as are all elements of the production. A change of cast is a change of the play. The brilliant cast of the film version of *August: Osage County* was not the same as that in the Steppenwolf production, the play itself, therefore, different beyond the changes necessitated by the medium.

Tracy Letts is an actor as well as a playwright, and the two careers do more than run in tandem. It is his experience as an actor that feeds into his writing. Such a symbiosis is, of course, scarcely rare. Shakespeare was an actor, as was Molière. In America the list would include Clifford Odets, Eugene O'Neill (briefly and disastrously), Tennessee Williams, David Mamet, Woody Allen, Sam Shepard, Anna Deavere Smith, Wallace Shawn, Bruce Norris, Jesse Eisenberg, Zach Braff and Tyler Perry, among others. He has said, 'my experience as an actor helps me to write anything. It certainly helped me to write *August: Osage County*... because I think one of the things I do well is write good roles for actors. And I wrote some nice meaty things for actors to do. I try to write fun – though difficult and challenging – things for actors to do because I know that if they're having fun, they're going to give it everything they got'.[2] Acting in *Who's Afraid of Virginia Woolf?*, in which he played the part of George, 'I learned a lot about playwriting...How can you not? There's something about being on the inside of it and seeing how it works from night to night, the arc of it and how you, the actor, have to piece it together.[3]

Tracy Letts was born in Tulsa and raised in Durant, Oklahoma, his parents working at Southeastern Oklahoma State University (his father was the first in his family to graduate high school and thanks to the G.I. Bill went on to receive a PhD). At the time he lived there its population was some 12,000. It was the final destination of the Choctaw Nation at the end of the Trail of Tears, hence today's two casinos. Home to the annual Magnolia Festival and the world's largest peanut monument, it had little to offer to someone growing up there. It was a conservative town, where people, at that time, were casually racist. The Letts family got into trouble when they were seen on their front porch drinking tea with a black man.

Unsurprisingly, Durant lacked a theatre. News of plays reached this Midwestern out-post in the form of movies, and it was in a movie theatre that he saw *Who's Afraid of Virginia Woolf?* His was not, though, a house lacking in literature. It was, he has explained, a household that valued the arts and free-thinking even though he insisted that they were Oklahomans rather than Parisians who had moved to Durant. Nor was it only books that shaped his imagination. His father took him to see the Rolling Stones when he was four and bought him jazz records at age six. His grandfather took him and his brother to see a double feature at the local drive-in. They were showing *Frankenstein Must Be Destroyed* and *Dracula Has Risen from the Grave*, which he has described as 'one of the cultural high points of my life'.[4] At six, his parents accompanied him to see *Serpico*.

His mother, Billie Letts, would go on to be a best-selling novelist (her novel, *Where the Heart Is* becoming an Oprah Book Club selection and being made into a film), while his father, Dennis, was an actor, first at university and then at community theatres (including Tishomingo Community Theatre) – community theatre, the playwright Sarah Ruhl observing, often seen as 'the most detested compound words in the annals of professional theatre'[5] though it was also where she had her own enthusiasm for theatre fired. Later he appeared in films and the stage version of *August: Osage County*. A generation earlier, Letts's grandmother, whom his mother would characterise as a monster, was married at fifteen and became a mother the following year. Her marriage was not a peaceful one. As Billie recalled, 'The atmosphere in my house growing up was very tense...I was the peacemaker. If I sensed an argument, a fight, I mean a physical fight, coming on, I was the one who tried to settle everything down.'[6] Billie's father committed suicide (Tracy was ten at the time) and her mother became an addict. A young Tracy was asked to film her in the psychiatric ward. She had smuggled pills into hospital using her vagina (an action ascribed to Violet in *August: Osage County*). Billie herself would later struggle with alcoholism. Interestingly, given her son's plays, she remarked, 'I think the beast was just in there waiting'.[7]

It was Alan Bennett who observed, 'for a writer nothing is ever quite as bad as it is for other people because, however dreadful, it may be of use', his mother once remarking 'By, you've had some script out of me'[8]; this would prove equally true for Letts. It is not hard to see where the playwright derived his view of the American family or why, as a teenager, he too turned to drink and drugs, like the characters in *Bug* freebasing cocaine, the drinking lasting into his adult life, indeed until August 1993, twenty-four days after the premiere of his first play, *Killer Joe*. He was, he has said, angry as a young man, while unsure where that came from beyond being bullied at school and feeling alienated from everything that Durant, with its focus on farming and football, seemed to represent. Asked about the darkness in his work he replied,

some of it comes from Grandpa's suicide and Grandma's addiction, but some of it came from within. They say you're much more likely to kill yourself if you have a family member who's killed themselves... The manner of my grandfather's killing himself was haunting to me. It was such a lonely way ... to jump in the water off a boat and intentionally drown yourself in the night ... seemed to me a particularly lonely way to go.[9]

Asked by his father why he wrote the kind of plays he did, particularly *August: Osage County*, he replied, 'Well, Dad, these events haunted me my whole life.' 'I think', he explained in an interview with the *New York Times*, that 'there comes a point in your life where you own your damage. You don't necessarily get over it, you don't necessarily have it all figured out, you just say this is mine, these are things I have to be aware of, take care of, work around.'[10] His was an anger that would fade but still persist. Later in life he would undergo years of therapy, confessing that there had always been what he called a dark streak in him

He began writing early, at age six. The story, tellingly, was called 'The Psychopath', and it won him an A-plus at school. The story was about a man who hanged himself while shooting himself in the head. At fourteen he got into trouble when he was found to have a copy of *A Clockwork Orange* in his desk. There is a reason that Jeff Still, an actor friend, has referred to Letts's acting style as 'Jimmy Stewart with an axe',[11] which is perhaps also an accurate description of much of his drama.

High school marked the end of his formal education, and he never took courses in writing or acting, although he did act out his own plays in his bedroom and at fifteen had his first acting part in *The Solid Gold Cadillac* at a nearby community theatre, which really wanted his father and saw Letts as a way of netting him. He had, however, laid down experience that would later feed into plays in which the family is a source of violence, addiction and paranoia even if there is also a desperate need for connection. Nonetheless, he has remarked that 'people are just as mean wherever you go'.[12]

The family, according to Ronald Reagan (until 2017 the country's only divorced president and scion of a dysfunctional family himself) lies at the heart of the American experience. In a Christmas radio address, he insisted that it was 'the nucleus of civilisation'. Perversely, America's playwrights have lined up to cast their contrary votes. For Reagan, the family reunion brings warmth, comfort, strength and joy. Not for him, then, were works such as *A Streetcar Named Desire*, *All My Sons*, *Long Day's Journey into Night*, *Who's Afraid of Virginia Woolf?* or *Buried Child*. Who, after all, knows someone's vulnerabilities better than those who have lived under the same roof, those linked by blood, though sometimes, it seems, by little more? Who else knows where the bodies are buried so that they can be resurrected when it serves their purpose? Social masks tend to be laid aside when the front door closes. It is harder to walk away, while betrayal in a family has an added edge, playing against the presumed commitment that is supposedly a product of kinship.

Playwrights from Sophocles to Pinter have found in the family unit the conflict that is the motor of drama. *The Homecoming* and *Killer Joe* are distant cousins. Perhaps the family is the natural place to explore human hopes and failures, the different generations not only at odds with each other but also underscoring the ironies of time. For the fact of those generations is a reminder of entropy, that what lies at the end for most is not a bang but a whimper – the lines, incidentally, with which *August: Osage County* nearly ends.

For the playwright, the family home, supposedly a place of security, is more often the site of conflict, a place where anxieties and fears take a concrete form; 'the last apparent refuge, the safe shelter, / That is where one meets them. That is the way of spectres',[13] T. S. Eliot's Harry observes in *The Family Reunion*, a play Edward Albee would turn to in writing *A Delicate Balance*, and Eliot surely hovers over some of Letts's plays.

At seventeen Letts moved to Dallas to become an actor, close enough to home to have his mother do his laundry but scarcely a major theatre city. From there, after two years, he moved to Chicago in the summer of 1985. 'I wasn't a playwright', he explained, 'I had written my whole life and had grown up in this literate household, so I came here to act in the theatre – and I had a hard time', but he finally found a home at Steppenwolf Theatre Company, by far the most exciting of the city's non-profit theatres. Founded in 1974, its members eventually including Gary Sinise (one of three founders), John Malkovich and Laurie Metcalf. The essence of Steppenwolf was its ensemble ethos. Actors would play parts small and large and share directorial responsibilities. As Austin Pendleton, a director unusually brought in to direct Ralph Pape's *Say Goodnight Gracie*, remarked, 'you came in a room and there were John Malkovich, Joan Allen, Glenne Headly, Laurie Metcalf . . . and Terry Kinney and Gary Sinise . . . It was like opening a broom closet and there stood the future of the American Theatre.'[14]

Letts began by acting in children's plays at $25 a show, appearing in *The Glass Menagerie* as part of the young audience series: 'I didn't have an audition scheduled and I wasn't going to go, but a friend of mine convinced me . . . I was the last person in line . . . I read for them and the casting director said, "Where are you from?" I said, "I'm from Oklahoma." He said, "Where the hell were you when we were casting *The Grapes of Wrath* when we needed all the Okies we could get."'[15]

Finally, he secured his 'first Equity job' on Steve Martin's *Picasso at the Lapin Agile*. As he has explained,

I was twenty-eight and newly sober by maybe a month or two . . . A lot of changes were happening in my life at that point. I had just opened my first play at the Next [Theatre] Lab in Evanston, *Killer Joe*, a play I had written and had spent a couple of years trying to get done – trying to find a theatre that would do it. Steppenwolf wouldn't do it, and I was bitter about that because I had tried to write something in the kind of rock-n-roll mode that I thought they operated in, but they were in a new space and they were a little less rock-n-roll . . . At the same time, my phone rang and it was Randy

[Arney] calling me to offer me the job in *Picasso*. No audition – just an offer at Steppenwolf ... I ended up doing 468 performances.[16]

The play was not his introduction to the company but it was

a solidification of the relationship between the company and me. Steve Martin had written *Picasso* and was in town to work on the play ... We were trying to raise money to take *Killer Joe* to the Edinburgh Festival. We had to raise about $16,000, which was an astronomical amount of money for us. We did bake sales, kissing booths, and everything else to raise that $16,000, but Steve gave us a cheque for $5,000 to take the show. He was largely responsible for us being able to take the show, which was not only successful at Edinburgh, but so successful that from there it went to the Bush Theatre in London.[17]

Later, at age thirty-two, he left for Los Angeles with his partner of many years, the actress Holly Wantuch, although she died of a stroke shortly after they arrived. He returned to Chicago four years later. In 2001, he played John Williamson in David Mamet's *Glengarry Glen Ross* and formally joined Steppenwolf in 2002. Later, with *Man from Nebraska* and *August: Osage County*, he would write specifically for them. Having, he explained, never felt accepted before he now discovered those with whom he shared a language and experience.

In 1991 he wrote his first play, *Killer Joe*. It was not a work that was easy to place. It eventually opened in 1993 at the Next Theatre Lab, boasting forty seats. It subsequently moved to an Off-Off-Broadway theatre and then to Edinburgh and London. He has said that 'when I wrote *Killer* Joe ... it was quite successful in Chicago, but it wasn't until it came to London at the Bush, and then the West End, that I really felt like a playwright for the first time in my life'.[18] Perhaps surprisingly, that initial production was seen by the *Chicago Tribune* reviewer Richard Christiansen, whose review could scarcely have been better. 'If you can stomach its ugly nudity, flagrant violence, foul language and blatant sleaze', he suggested, 'you're in for one tense, gut-twisting thriller ride in the theatre ... it's an astonishing piece of work, not only for the skill of its craftsmanship but for the kinks and depths of characterization.' It was 'strong pulp fiction ... vividly imagined'.[19] It ran for five weeks. In some ways, *Killer Joe* set the tone for Letts's future plays.

For many Americans, the country's values have a location – the business of becoming is urban, a world of constant striving and re-invention, a dream of social mobility, green lights across the bay, happiness pursued – but there is another version. This is the myth of high school Friday night football, in which the route to success, as the coach in *Friday Night Lights* insists, lies through clear eyes and full hearts. It is a place of *Our Town* neighbourliness where doors are left unlocked and God is still worshipped in His own country. It is a place of self-reliance where guns are for hunting rather than random slaughter, where a man's word is still his bond and people know who they are. Here is where families say grace before meals, bake cakes for the sick and read newspapers that tell stories of local affairs rather than national or international events because these are people insulated by distance and inclination from the anxieties that pass as news for those in the city.

Time is different here, as is space. Both are more expansive. This is heartland America, and it lies out to the midwest and west in states that are an idea and an ideal that has nothing to do with suspecting the stranger, seeking advantage, treble-locking the door, inhabiting a world of high-rise living to match high-rise expectations. Yet as F. Scott Fitzgerald knew, having come from the heartland himself, the careless people he created, and who he located on the East Coast, had all come from the west where innocence was as liable to be compromised as anywhere else. Sam Shepard knew as much, as does Tracy Letts, who sets his plays in Oklahoma or Texas.

Letts's plays feature motel rooms, trailers, passing strangers, fractured families and the threat and reality of violence. These are the left-behind Okies, Midwesterners whose yellow brick road leads neither to the past nor the future. They inhabit an anxious present, the same space as their fellow isolatos, but little else. They are often related less by blood than a shared incomprehension. There are no loyalties not readily abandoned, no civilities not ignored, no values not abrogated, no emotions not betrayed, no connections not broken. They are emotionally and psychologically wounded without understanding how they received such wounds or how they might be healed. The land may stretch out beyond the rooms in which they are trapped, the houses that are not homes, but that merely underlines their sense of dislocation and abandonment. As far as they can see, there is nothing beyond their present circumstances. They acknowledge the need for action but not the consequences of such. They feel the need for connection but sabotage their efforts to effect it. What they lack is a sense of transcendence. Religion offered that, but what happens when that faith is abandoned, as in *Man from Nebraska*? If they look for explanation, they are liable to discover it, as in *Bug*, in conspiracies that grant them the centrality they otherwise so obviously lack. They may not be seen by an absent God, but they suspect they are by others. Nor, in that play, are they altogether wrong. The most paranoid of his characters in *Bug* is well-versed in actual conspiracies conducted against members of the American military, while this, of course, predated revelations about the extent of the surveillance currently being deployed against ordinary citizens and make *Bug* disturbingly relevant.

There is a gothic dimension to Letts's imagination. He has a fascination with passions that bubble to the surface as if some internal regulating system was in disarray, but it seems to go farther than that. Characters in moral free fall abound. Psychological collapse seems to echo a wider social dislocation. There is a bleakness whose edge is not blunted by humour because that humour has a corrosive quality, never quite concealing the vulnerability that generates it and on which it depends. His characters deal in excess as if that is the only way they can function. Violet, in *August: Osage County*, has cancer of the mouth and therefore insists on an irresistible articulateness, spitting words out, challenging anyone to respond. She does so as evidence that she is still alive, swallowing pills not to relieve her pain but to justify a recklessness that is the source of her power, although that power is threatened not by her family but by her own sense of mortality denied. She revels in the human wreckage that swirls around her and seems the source of her febrile energy.

Often his characters lack an inner coherence, a moral touchstone, particularly in his first plays in which the threat of violence is not only in the air but brutally present. They have unfocused needs and inhabit largely anonymous places where nothing – certainly not human relationships – seems permanent. *Killer Joe* is set in a trailer home on the outskirts of Dallas. There are two rooms, with no separation between them. The ceiling is low. Everything about it is cheap and ugly. Such furniture as there is, is dirty and stained. There is a clutter of fast-food debris, empty cans and filled ashtrays. A television evidently only receives pictures by virtue of a tangle of coat hangers and tin foil. It is a television whose programmes will flicker in the background: karate movies, lottery draws, auto racing, the *Wheel of Fortune*, an episode of *Mannix*, a random scatter of images from an outside world that seems to offer an echo of a family lacking anything as definite as a human connection. The grimy refrigerator, we discover, is mostly filled with beer. This is the 'detritus of the poor'. At first the only sound is static from the television before we hear the barking of a nearby pit bull. Light comes from that television or outside streetlights. Sound and light indeed derive from specific sources rather than spotlights. The detail, in other words, is naturalistic if the action is not. These are imagined characters in a real environment even as that real environment leans in the direction of metaphor in a play that is a western Grand Guignol.

The action begins as twenty-two-year-old Chris Smith beats on the door, to be greeted by his stepmother, Sharla, dressed only in a man's sweat-stained T-shirt. It is almost three in the morning. We hear him urinate in the bathroom, the door propped open, as Sharla takes a soda from the fridge. Chris has a history of beating his mother, and she has finally thrown him out. He rolls a joint as he explains that he needs $6,000 or he will be killed but has a plan: his mother, who he is convinced sold his stash of cocaine, should be killed for her life insurance policy, the beneficiary ostensibly being his sister Dottie. Ansel, his mother's ex-husband, readily agrees, interested only in how much it will cost to hire a local cop, Joe, with a side line in contract murders, and how the proceeds will be divided. Dottie, of limited mental capacity with a tendency to sleepwalk, and whose unlikely ambition is to become a model, likewise sees no problem. 'Are you gonna kill my mamma?' she asks casually, perhaps because her mother had supposedly tried to kill her when she was a baby, something she improbably claims to remember.

Astonishingly, the story is based on an actual family in Florida in which a mother and son decided to kill their father until father and son discovered that the mother had been stealing their cocaine and so decided to kill her instead. For Letts it was 'the ease with which they changed their minds about which family member was going to die that sparked my feeling about how you gotta get pretty far down when family ties mean so little to you'.[20] More astonishing is the fact that such scenarios are not uncommon. In 2004, also in Florida, a son hired a hit man to kill his parents. In 2013, in Michigan, Julia Merfeld hired a hit man to kill her husband. He would be paid out of the insurance money. Unfortunately, the hit man turned out to be a policeman, and her discussion with him was recorded on video as she requested that her husband should be killed outside the family home because it would be messy if it were inside.

Beyond an unlikely source in reality, Letts has explained that he had been reading what he called 'very hardcore *noir* at the time; dirty, southern *noir*',[21] including novels by fellow Oklahoman Jim Thompson (born in Anadarko, Oklahoma Territory), one of which was called *The Killer Inside Me*. In Thompson he would have found not only a bleak view of human nature but also that willingness to push the boundaries of reality and taste that would characterise both *Killer Joe* and *Bug*. As Stephen King remarked of Thompson, 'The guy was over the top.' He 'didn't know the meaning of the word *stop* . . . he let himself see everything, he let himself write it down, then he let himself publish it'.[22] In Thompson's semi-autobiographical *Now and on Earth*, the protagonist has a breakdown, believing that spiders and centipedes are crawling over him and his bed, a foreshadowing of Tracy's *Bug*. As Letts remarked, 'I think one of the principal aspects of noir are people who want things really badly, who want and feel things really strongly, and yet who make some terrible decisions in their attempts to get them. I think something about that is very human . . . There's something about that we can all identify with. Those moments in our lives when we have wanted something and done absolutely the wrong thing to get it.'[23]

Sharla, a Pizza Hut waitress, is having an affair and has pornographic photographs of her lover – or at least part of him. Chris and Ansel are auto mechanics, pleased to overcharge the gullible. It seems probable that Chris raped his sister when she was twelve. The trailer has supplies of drugs and alcohol. Their exchanges with one another are characteristically limited to a few words, so that when they do speak at length, it is the more notable. For Letts, they are not simply trailer trash, but people who lack spiritual food, living in a moral vacuum. He saw, he said, 'something sad at the core of them'[24] insisting that he found them touching. Ironically, the only character with any moral code is the hit man, Killer Joe, who believes a contract must be observed. When the family fails to come up with the $25,000 down payment he requires, he suggests that Dottie can act as a retainer – as it turns out, to be retained by him. It is a bargain they readily embrace. As Chris remarks, 'which do you think would be better for Dottie, havin' ten thousand dollars . . . or havin' a beat-up, old, ugly, naggy alcoholic mother for another twenty years or so?'[25] When he says, 'we can . . . give him Dottie' her father replies, 'it might do her some good'.[26] She is, accordingly, dressed up to make her more attractive to the hired killer, gift-wrapped as Chris remarks, insisting that 'This whole thing makes me sick' (33), even as he presses forward with the plan. Later, he tries to call off the hit largely because Joe will not be 'a good influence' (47) because 'you kill people' despite the fact that he had hired him to do precisely that.

Chris, like Lenny in *Of Mice and Men*, dreams of keeping rabbits, although his bucolic dream differs from Lennie's. He wants to 'live in the country, smoke dope, watch tv' (48). He even starts a rabbit farm, only for the animals to become rabid, tearing themselves apart, an echo of the family. He turns to selling drugs on the grounds that that is a business he understands. His contradictions are in a sense what define him. Thus, while planning his mother's death and the prostitution of his sister, he insists that 'Nobody can accuse me of not havin' people's best interests in mind. People do the best they can. Anybody says he doesn't's lyin'. I didn't want to hurt anybody. Ever' (50), even as he praises the killer's proficiency in staging the killing as a traffic accident in which an autopsy is impossible because 'there wasn't much left to speak of' (50).

Joe himself, socially polite but morally corrupt, combines upholding the law with break-ing it, sometimes investigating his own crimes, which he describes as 'a convenience', and not arresting a fellow murderer on the grounds that he likes him. He sees himself as a businessman (Chris describes himself as a customer), wearing a double-breasted suit, looking for a rate for the job and taking pride in his professionalism. He treats Dottie as though he were a suitor, arriving with a bunch of flowers, complimenting her and offering to serve her dinner, even while observing that 'women are deceitful, and lying, and manipulative, and vicious, and vituperative, and black-hearted, and evil, and old'.[27] Over dinner, small talk consists of a discussion of the planned murder before he requires her to strip off her clothes and reach her hand inside his pants, subsequently moving in with her.

Joe is lawman/murderer, gentleman-caller/seducer, businessman/criminal, a believer in order and the source of anarchy, the irony being that audiences are likely to be drawn to him rather than a self-consuming family. When Chris is beaten, his father steps over him to reach the television. Emotional empathy is not strong in the Smith family. They feel no need to repress feelings and have no filter when it comes to speaking. The exception is Dottie, emotionally stunted, incapable of understanding love yet yearning for it, or what she takes it to be. She is the currency in which the rest of the family deal, but she clings to naïve trust and still more naïve hope.

Joe keeps his end of the bargain, obligingly committing the murder and packaging his victim in a garbage bag, too late for Chris's intervention who convinces himself that he is about to turn his life around. In the next scene as Chris tries to select mourning clothes, Dottie watches a Road Runner cartoon on the television. Their plot quickly falls apart, however, as it turns out that the scheme had been hatched by Sharla and her lover, Rex, and that the supposed $50,000 policy was in fact $100,000. The rest of the family have been cut out but more ominously so has Killer Joe, not a man to be crossed. Chris proposes to Dottie that they should leave for South America together, not something that Killer Joe is likely to accept, she being the collateral offered for a fee that will now not be forthcoming.

The play comes to its conclusion when Joe confronts Sharla, Rex having absconded with all the money. In a scene that was the cause of some controversy, he forces Sharla to simulate a blowjob with a chicken leg he holds in front of his crotch. Letts has said that if he writes an autobiography, it is likely to be titled, *Defending the Chicken Leg*. He has confessed that when the scene was being rehearsed in its initial production, he had to leave the room, finding it too upsetting to watch. It is, he has confessed, 'brutal, it's shocking, its horrible, and its horrifying',[28] but he wanted people to be shocked. It was, he insisted, intended precisely to be horrifying and the violence against women a reflection of society at large. When Matthew McConaughey was offered the role of Killer Joe for the film version, he threw the script across the room, finding it 'disgusting' (he later accepted the role). Letts himself has said that, having lived in Chicago for some years before writing it, he wanted to 'write something that was just as rock and roll as Steppenwolf or anybody else. Just something that was really in your face. Hopefully, you don't do that just to shock people – not that that doesn't have any value in and of itself. The truth is, you do it in the hopes that people are going to sit up and watch your story . . . As long as I am true to my characters, there's nothing I won't do to keep people's interest.'[29]

Joe forces them all to sit at the dining table with Dottie saying grace: 'Thank you that we're all here, together and safe' (68). The very last thing they are, of course, is safe. Joe announces that he and Dottie are to marry. Chris produces a gun, only for Sharla to stab him with a kitchen knife and potato peeler. When Chris has a momentary advantage over Joe, his father and stepmother attack him, but Dottie, who has picked up the gun, shoots Chris in the chest and Ansel in the stomach. The play ends as Dottie announces her pregnancy and points the gun at Joe.

Ironically, Joe, the contract killer, offers something the others do not. As Letts observed, 'The truth is that coming to this trailer, Joe represents a certain order in the chaos. There are some rules of behaviour that he clearly establishes. He's a man of order, and these people aren't.' The question is whether having a moral code, no matter how distorted, is a value. 'I always wanted the material to ask those questions', he added, 'and engage in that conversation without supplying easy answers . . . who made the right or wrong decisions, who's in power, who's not.'[30] It is hard to see that there are any right decisions. This is a world in which there are no moral axes, the ends justifying the means. Looking back, it seemed to Letts that the characters in *Killer Joe* see money as filling the void in their lives. They were

willing to make some terrible compromises in order to get it. The fact that they live in a kind of moral vacuum is frightening but in both play and the film we never step back and point our fingers at them and say, 'Look at these people.' We felt like they are us; they're a manifestation of us; the fringe of our society making some very bad decisions . . . I actually find them kind of touching in their own way . . . I have always liked the characters – as bad as they get, at their absolute worst. I still see something sad at the core of them.[31]

For Letts, the play 'operates in that place of moral ambiguity, where people really have to question themselves', although twenty years later he was inclined to say that it felt 'like a fever dream'[32] and that he was 'carrying over some childhood shit, some family shit, some shit from my past that had to express itself in some way. So I found the forum of the very hard core noir story – a good container for the expression of that stuff'. On the other hand, he was inclined to think that his work as a whole might perhaps be an antidote to a prevailing optimism. 'My pessimism', he declared, 'is my own kind of patriotism. My dissent.'[33] Beyond that, he confessed that he was 'hot blooded' and that he liked 'stuff that has heat and fire and passion to it', finding theatre more amenable to such an approach than film, although this play, *Bug* and *August: Osage County*, have been made into successful movies.

Killer Joe and *Bug* were both directed for the cinema by William Friedkin, who, fittingly, had also directed Harold Pinter's *The Birthday Party*, another play in which a room is invaded by an outside force and in which power is a central issue. As Friedkin explained, 'Most of the films I am most a fan of that I have made over the years deal with people in claustrophobic situations, like . . . *The Birthday Party*.' He was also drawn to Letts's concern with 'paranoia and obsession . . . played out in tight places, not open country'.[34] To his mind, though, *Killer Joe* was a love story, both Dottie and Joe looking for something beyond the moment. It was also a comedy whose humour was generated out of the outrageousness of the characters and their values. Something of the same could be said of his next play, *Bug*.

In 1964, Richard Hofstadter published an essay in *Harper's Magazine* titled 'The Paranoid Style in American Politics', defining this as the heated exaggeration, suspiciousness and conspiratorial fantasy he saw as characterising the left and right alike and stretching back through American history from the McCarthyite 1950s to the Populists of the 1890s, the anti-Catholicism of the 1850s and even the concern with the Illuminati at the end of the seventeenth century. Sometimes, though, conspiracies are real enough, from the CIA's two-decade-long infiltration of American cultural life to the covert surveillance of the country's citizens in the twenty-first century. In Letts's 1996 play, *Bug*, paranoia predominates, but although he has disavowed any wider implications, it is hard not to register them, not least because he has said, 'I'm just mistrustful of institutions – I don't think they have people's best interests at heart'.[35]

It is a play, once again, in which an apparent naturalism devolves into a nightmare vision, truth and fantasy intertwined. It is about loss and need, misdirected love and disorienting passion acted out in a dislocating society in which the idea of conspiracy offers the only kind of coherence. As in *Killer Joe*, these are characters trapped in their own myths, cornered by circumstance and inhabiting a compromised space. They interpret the world differently. There is a lost child and a child regained, a lost order and a substitute reality. Marginal characters in a marginal setting, they reach for some explanation or settle for the smallest gesture. They are damaged and look for explanation or respite. Drugs lift them out of time, deaden their sense of abandonment, turning need into terror, an absence of meaning into its excess. There is a dark humour but little in the way of self-awareness. For them, for much of the time, an unexamined life is precisely the only thing worth living when such an examination can only summon up an ominous past. Safety is sought but never assured. A telephone call can disturb, a knock on the door threaten. At its end we are left with a momentary doubt about what seemed their absurdity, knowing, as we do, that beyond this motel, on the edge of a city, fictions have been outpaced by reality and paranoia has been an agent of power.

The trailer of *Killer Joe* now becomes a cheap motel room on the edge of Oklahoma City. Outside is the drone of traffic, the sound of a garbage truck, music from a nearby room, the sound of a Latina couple; inside, an air-conditioner cuts in and out. There are dirty dishes, a dirty ashtray, an empty bottle and drug paraphernalia. Like Sharla, forty-four-year-old Agnes is a waitress who describes hers as a 'lousy life' consisting of 'laundromats and grocery stores, dumb marriages and lost kids'.[36] She explains that 'everyone I ever knew's married, or dead, or in prison' (9), each fate seemingly equivalent. Her friend, R.C., who is a lesbian, accuses her of having 'hermetized yourself', a reference to more than this room significantly on the outskirts of a place less chosen than fated. When she suggests that 'you could probably pick better places than Oklahoma to be a home', she replies, 'Like anybody ever picked it' (9).

If Agnes lives in a motel room, Peter, a stranger she takes in, is 'between addresses', while Jerry Goss, her brutal husband, has been in prison and is looking to join Agnes, having ratted out a friend he suspected of being attracted to her. They are all isolated, looking for a connection. Agnes had not only lost her husband, who offers her nothing beyond violence, but also, and literally, her son in a grocery store nine years earlier. She has lived with a sense of loss. When Peter offers a relationship, she begins to cry. Even as he slides towards insanity, detecting bugs invisible to her, she clings to him, declaring, 'I'd rather talk about bugs to you than talk about nothin' with nobody' (40). Accordingly, she enters his world, detecting bugs previously invisible to her, a circling helicopter increasingly more evident, drawn, he supposes, by another kind of bug, a device implanted in his body.

Gathered here, then, besides Agnes, are R.C., whose lesbian partner she describes as 'a big dyke' (11), the two of them fighting a custody battle, Peter, whose behaviour gets ever more extreme, and Goss, Agnes's violent husband, fresh out of prison. Peter prefers freebasing because snorting cocaine, as Agnes does, he regards as unhealthy. This is a play not without its dark humour. These are all characters who, like Peter, are trying to make a connection, although he believes that relationships, 'cloud me . . . make it difficult to be just me' (26), while she confesses that 'it's been quite a while since I had anyone to get . . . close to . . . I get damn lonely sometimes' (28).

Peter is the son of a preacher without a congregation, who home-schooled him and is mentally unstable. Peter had been in the army, serving in the Syrian desert where he was given pills and injections that he has convinced himself were experimental. He is now on the run, having gone AWOL. There was a time, he declares, when 'people were safe, but that's all over' because of 'all the technology, and the chemicals, and the information . . . people working their machines' (21). He looks for hidden messages in paintings, sees threats in all directions, although his account of the effect of his treatment recalls the Gulf War syndrome from which many soldiers genuinely suffered. He warns against smoke detectors because they have 'americium-241 in them', which he insists is more radioactive than plutonium.

Disturbingly, this is half true. Smoke detectors do indeed use americium-214, the synthesising of which involves plutonium, which is to be found in the sites of weapons tests and nuclear disasters such as Chernobyl. It is radioactive and harmful to life, although in smoke detectors largely emits alpha rather than gamma particles and is used in very small amounts. In 1994, a seventeen-year-old, who had earned a Boy Scout merit badge in Atomic Energy when he was fourteen, extracted americium from a hundred smoke detectors in an effort to build a nuclear reactor. He persuaded a company to sell him the one hundred detectors for a dollar a piece, claiming they were for a school project. The result was that radioactivity could be detected five houses away from his own. The material is now buried in thirty-nine sealed barrels in the Great Salt Lake Desert. In 2007, at age thirty-one, he allegedly wanted to give it another try and was charged with stealing sixteen smoke detectors.

The madness within this motel room, then, is an echo of the madness without. As Peter's paranoia deepens, it turns out that a number of the conspiracies he invokes were real, providing the foundation for his own sense of being pursued; further evidence of this is the helicopter that circles overhead. Convinced that the military has seeded his body with bugs, he recalls that that the government had conducted experiments that involved 'feeding LSD to enlisted men at Edgewood Arsenal' and giving syphilis to 'those poor fuckers in Tuskegee' (41). Both cases are real.

The Edgewood project involved testing a range of chemical agents, including LSD, on large numbers of soldiers. It was brought to an end in 1975. The CIA had conducted similar experiments under the name Project MKUltra, which ended in 1973. Among other objectives was the development of substances that would promote illogical thinking; cause the victim to age faster; suffer temporary or permanent brain damage; create amnesia, paralysis or dependency; and distort eyesight. At the end of the project, the CIA director ordered that all files should be destroyed, although 20,000 documents survived. Meanwhile Project 112, conducted by the US Department of Defense from 1962 to 1973, tested biological weapons, one involving release of an anthrax simulant in the Greyhound Bus Depot in Washington, DC, and the New York subway system (the substance was contained in light bulbs that were dropped in random places). The existence of this programme was denied until 2000. The Tuskegee experiments, conducted between 1932 and 1972 by the U.S. Public Health Service, involved studying the result of withholding treatment for syphilis from African-American men in Alabama under the guise of receiving free health care.

Equally real are other references Peter makes: the consortium of bankers, industrialists, corporate CEOs and politicians who met at Bilderberg in 1954 (48); the smuggling of Nazi scientists into the States at Calspan; the Peoples Temple, where more than nine hundred people died at the instigation of the Reverend Jim Jones. Peter also mentions Timothy McVeigh, a Gulf War veteran who was responsible for the worst act of domestic terrorism in US history at Oklahoma City who had served at Calspan. This was the McVeigh who believed federal agents had left him with a scar when they implanted a microchip. When Peter refers to the Intelligence Manned Interface biochip, a subcutaneous transponder he believes was inserted into him during the Gulf War, he invokes just such a microchip tested in the Iraq War by Dr. Carl Sanders. *Bug*, in other words, bizarre as it is, is outdone by reality. Letts was in Oklahoma City at the time of the bombing, which led him to become interested in people who had 'slipped out of the matrix' and desired to make sense of the event by locating it within a larger story.

In an essay published in *Commentary* magazine in 1961, Philip Roth famously complained about the challenge faced by the writer: 'the American writer in the middle of the 20th century has his hands full in trying to understand, and then describe, and then make credible much of the American reality. It stupefies, it sickens, it infuriates, and finally it is even a kind of embarrassment to one's own meagre imagination. The actuality is continually outdoing our talents.'[37]

Peter now plunges deeper into psychosis. As Act II begins, the motel room is full of an array of anti-bug equipment. R.C. is deeply sceptical, having taken Agnes to a doctor who finds no evidence of bugs but sees only self-inflicted injuries. She invokes a Dr. Sweet, who is looking for Peter, a man who Peter suggests comes from Groom Lake, a real Air Force base close to Area 51, itself renowned as the focus for conspiracy theories related to aliens. Agnes, though, rejects R.C.'s suggestion that she should move out because 'You come in here and try to take away the only thing in the world I have, that's mine' (39). Peter now pulls a tooth out with pliers, convinced that the bugs harboured there contain transmitters. When Dr. Sweet arrives, he claims that Peter is a delusional paranoiac with schizophrenic tendencies who has been in an army hospital for four years, although he also claims that 'I made a mistake . . . I didn't know what they were using it for. What they're doing . . . it's dangerous. It's wrong' (46). By now, though, Peter is beyond being convinced or deceived. He stabs Sweet, believing him to be a robot.

The plays ends in a paroxysm of violence the sound of a helicopter reverberating as Agnes shoots staples into Goss's hand and Peter and Agnes pour petrol on themselves. She strikes a match. In the blackout that follows, we see fire and hear buzzing, perhaps the buzzing of bugs.

Bug is a dark comedy in which characters are pushed to the extreme as their internal and external worlds implode, their paranoid visions no longer so aberrant, its 2016 revival in London being seen against a background of the gathering controversy about covert surveillance, the truth of national and international conspiracies revealed by Edward Snowden and Julian Assange.

Bug's premiere was in 1999 at London's seventy-five-seat Gate Theatre, before its first American production in Ithaca, New York. In revised form, it was then produced in Washington, DC, by the Woolly Mammoth Theatre. When it reached Off-Broadway in 2004, Ben Brantly, in the *New York Times*, called it an 'obscenely exciting play'.

His next play, *Man from Nebraska* (2003), represented a change of direction in terms of language, style, form and subject. Granting that his first two had found a limited audience, even in their film versions, he looked to expand that audience. Those early plays had been deliberately intimidating. This was to be disturbing in a different sense as a man suddenly finds himself in a state of crisis that threatens more than his marriage. The hermetic, single set of those earlier works makes way for multiple locations. The action moves out into the world, being partly located in London. Frenetic activity gives way to moments of silence, random violence to internal tensions. There is, it seems, a redemptive ending, although everything that has happened to that point colors that ending with irony. Letts has said that it is softer in tone than his earlier work, but that that softness is misleading. Devoid of physical brutality, it remains emotionally disturbing.

Once again the play is initially set on the outskirts of a city – in this case Lincoln, Nebraska – although not in a materially impoverished world. This is a rich suburb, and these characters churchgoers, saying grace before cafeteria meals and prayers before going to bed. There is a routine to their existence that passes for a life. The opening scene is set in a luxury sedan as Nancy and Ken look out of the window. They speak to each other, but there is something intransitive about their conversations. This is followed by a scene set in the local church where they sing a hymn celebrating their submission to God, their determination to live for Him and not themselves, although Ken later confesses that in church he had fantasised about being free; free of what, he is not clear. His mother, meanwhile, is suffering, it seems, from Alzheimer's. Death clearly beckons but without the grace of a coherent meaning.

There is a hint of an underside to the bland surface of this suburb. Religion represents less a search for meaning than a shared etiquette. The pastor, who suggests that Nancy seek consolation in shopping, playing bingo and watching a movie when she is abandoned by her husband, recalls that his own father, as a prisoner of war, had eaten a dead fellow prisoner. For her part, though, Nancy remains committed to a Cheeryble vision of life. 'That's awful', she says, 'Can I get you some more coffee?' (27).

For his part, Ken finds himself in a state of collapse, experiencing a moment of existential crisis. He suffers what Edward in Eliot's *The Cocktail Party* describes as the death of the spirit. The only excuse he can offer is that he has ceased to believe in God, though he realises that this is 'tied up with . . . everything . . . My life, *way* of life . . . routines. My routine with your mother . . . And the job, and the . . . town.'[38] Everything, he suggests, seems alien, the food people eat, the way they walk, as if obeying some edict. There is, he comes to feel, no will involved. People are not in possession of their own lives.

He has all the trappings of success, but it serves no purpose. Even the desire for transcendence is formulaic, and the lack of transcendence seems a common theme in Letts's work. In *August: Osage County*, he would quote from T. S. Eliot's *The Hollow Men*, and there is a sense in which, for Ken, that is what he and those around him are, theirs an existence which has shape without form as they utter prayers 'to broken stone'. Ken, like Edward in *The Cocktail Party*, is a man who has 'lost touch with the person'[39] he thought he was, a fact that sets him, as it does Edward, 'To finding out / What you really are. What you really feel. / What you really are among other people' because 'Most of the time we take ourselves for granted, / As we have to, and live on a little knowledge / About ourselves as we were.'[40] As in Eliot's play, it is a stranger who will set him on a new path, although already in church he had had 'a secret world in my mind' (55), as Lucasta, in Eliot's *The Confidential Clerk*, speaks of the secret garden into which it is possible to retire

Ken's sudden sense of alienation is not unfamiliar from *Ecclesiastes*: 'Vanity of vanities, saith the Preacher . . . all is vanity . . . What profit hath a man of all his labour which he taketh under the sun? . . . the thing that hath been, it is that which shall be . . . all is vanity and vexation of spirit.' Ken suffers precisely from a vexation of the spirit, no longer seeing any meaning in his faith, his marriage or his work.

There is in this family an echo of *The Cocktail Party* as we are introduced to those who 'maintain themselves by the common routine, learn to avoid excessive expectation . . . Two people who know they do not understand each other / breeding children whom they do not understand / And who will never understand them.'[41] As in Eliot's play there is a sense of lost desires, a failure of communication, of awareness. In *The Family Reunion*, Eliot pictures a family that goes through life as though half asleep, to whom nothing has happened, who have 'never woken to the nightmare'.[42] Only one character in Eliot's play, Harry, has a sudden insight, abandoning his wife (pushing her overboard). As a consequence, he is pursued by the Furies others cannot see.

Advised by his pastor to take a break, Ken leaves for England, abandoning his wife and with Furies of his own. On his way, travelling first class, he encounters Pat, a woman who makes a play for him, confessing that her husband had divorced her, but he is largely oblivious, caught up, as he is, in his own anxieties. When the plane experiences turbulence, he offers the far-from-consoling observation that 'I don't know if this helps you at all, but I don't think it matters . . . If the plane crashes' (38).

His real journey, though, is one towards self-knowledge, and he has two teachers. The first is Tamyra, a young woman who serves in the bar of his luxury hotel at the heart of London, a city he had visited decades earlier when serving in the military, itself an image of that uniformity and routine that had repulsed him back in America. How, he asks, could he get on when 'they're all the same' when 'the only difference you can find between people is their *volume*' (46). Her world is not his. She is ironic and witty. England, she explains to him, is not a good place to be looking for God. She mocks his desire for freedom – 'Pining for freedom when you have more of it than anyone in the history of the earth' (56) – while she has to struggle to survive, to find something more fulfilling than bar work.

He does finally find an answer of sorts when he is introduced to Tamyra's flat mate, an accomplished sculptor called Harry who inducts him into drugs, dancing and alcohol, but also into his craft, becoming his instructor when he pays their rent. He is Eliot's stranger who will point Ken in a new direction, the stranger who, in *The Family Reunion*, releases a new force. In explaining why his statue of Tamyra is not an exact likeness of her, he offers what could be Letts's justification for his own approach: 'Sometimes it helps to exaggerate just a bit . . . There's no point in producing Tamyra *again*: she already exists . . . yes, you want to have the *ability* to do that: that's *craft*. But your belief, your expression of your belief: that's *art* . . . objectivity is craft, subjectivity is art' (74–5). Beyond a description of art it is a clue to Ken's problem of belief which is less the routine repetition of external gestures, which he had previously settled for, than a sense of the real transformed. So, formerly ignorant of poetry, he comes to recite verses from Pablo Neruda which underscore daily facts re-energised:

> The sky folds its wings over you,
> Lifting you, carrying you to my arms
> With its punctual, mysterious courtesy.
> That's why I sing to the day and to the moon,
> To the sea, to time, and all the planets,
> To your daily voice, to your nocturnal skin. (76)

When his mother dies, Ken, a continent away, sees her figure in a darkened room; he feels guilty, suddenly, that he had relegated her to a home and guilty, too, that he had wished her dead. He flees to Harry's flat, where he destroys the sculpture he had been working on and creates a new one, leaving immediately to return to his American home and to Nancy, having rediscovered God, albeit not the same one in which he had lost faith. They sit in the same car with which the play had begun, holding hands as the stars appear above them where earlier Ken had confessed 'I don't understand the stars. The stars in the sky. Don't make sense' (15). In the words of Reilly in *The Cocktail Party*, 'I can reconcile you to the human condition / . . . Become tolerant of themselves and others.'[43]

Has Letts then settled for a sentimentality? Is this like the ending of Eliot's *The Elder Statesman*, which concludes with reconciliation? Is the wound healed? Perhaps not. Perhaps the crisis was not Ken's alone. In *The Cocktail Party*, Celia remarks, 'I must tell you / That I should really *like* to think there's something wrong with me – / Because, if there isn't, then there's something wrong with the world itself – and that's much more frightening! That would be terrible. So I'd rather believe there is something wrong with me, that could be put right.' There is this feeling in Letts's work that the dislocations he stages in family life, the lack of some inner coherence, reflect not only those in the wider society but more fundamentally in human experience as his characters look for some ruling principle, an order that can make sense of their existence. Plots, conspiracies, religion are their way of creating narratives offering what is manifestly not otherwise evident to them: purpose.

With *August: Osage County*, Letts would both broaden his canvas – it has thirteen characters, runs for three-and-a-half hours and has a three-storey set– and narrow it in the sense that at its heart is a family gathered in what had once been their family home, simultaneously attracted and repelled by memories less shared than wielded as weapons. This is *Who's Afraid of Virginia Woolf?* and *Long Day's Journey into Night* as full orchestra rather than mordant quartets. It is also his most personal play, rooted in his family's history with at its heart a figure, Beverly Weston, based on his grandfather; Letts's own father would play the role of Beverly until his death in 2008. Somewhere in the play you can sense Letts is an invisible figure, observing the emotional mayhem he himself had witnessed growing up in a family fiercely addicted in one way or another, involved in an undeclared war that would flare up and subside. This is a family, in Tom Lehrer's words, 'sliding down the razor blade of life'.

Beverly is married to Violet, a woman modelled on Letts's grandmother, shaped by poverty, a survivor of the Dust Bowl, and survival is one theme of a play in which its price is sometimes high and its virtue debated. The tension in the family echoes that in Letts's own which may account both for his clinical dissection of a family at war with itself and for his sympathy for those who are products of their circumstances if also of their own perverse self-destructiveness. Perhaps that is why he has described its writing as the hardest thing he has done. Violet and Beverly have had to struggle with poverty and make sacrifices, but, as Violet observes of her daughters, 'You never had real problems so you got to make them all for yourselves' (95). Letts has said that his own mother thought he had been kind to his grandmother, and he agreed explaining that if he had made Violet as 'accurately horrible' as she was in life, the play would have been difficult to take. 'There's a moment in the play', he has explained, 'when Violet snaps at Jean, the granddaughter, at the kitchen table – if you say another word I'll knock your damn head off your shoulders – and the actors playing the parents always wanted to comfort the child, reach over and stroke her hair. And I wouldn't let them do it'.[44]

Something has been passed down the family line in *August: Osage County*, and it is not an instinct for natural empathy. Most of the characters have escaped this dark house on the Great Plains, but they have not escaped the forces that shaped them. Addiction is fact and metaphor in a play in which characters deny the truth of present circumstances by retreats of one kind or another, by denials, evasions, even as secrets are gradually revealed. Albee's George, in *Whose Afraid of Virginia Woolf?*, speaks of a process whereby it is necessary to get through the skin and muscle, down to the bone and the marrow. That is the process at work in *August: Osage County*, a county named for the Osage Indians, the Osage Reservation in Oklahoma registering a population of 156 in the 2010 census, survival being an issue for them too. An Indian woman, indeed, is a presence in the play, an observer of the cruelties on display yet ready to step forward at a moment of need.

In the 2008 presidential election, Barack Obama once referred to small-town America as a place where they 'cling to guns or religion, or antipathy to people who aren't like them'.[45] It was a political mistake not least because it collided with a basic myth having to do with integrity, eternal values, stable families – a timeless quality. It all depends which fiction you prefer. Sarah Palin, after all, winner of the Miss Wasilla pageant, came from such a place – Sandpoint, Idaho, and then Skagway, Alaska – where 'gee, shucks' hospitality co-existed with cold calculation.

August: Osage County, which Letts has described as 'a true story of my family and the place I come from and the people I come from' but which is also 'an embodiment of pretty much everything I believe about the theatre and ensemble work',[46] features a family in small-town America, Pawhuska, Oklahoma (population in 2010 3,589, a sharp decline from fifty years earlier), described as a 'flat hot nothing'.[47] Letts has spoken of the paradoxical sense of claustrophobia that comes from living in a place where you can see fifty miles to the horizon. Not for nothing is it set in August. The heat is all but unbearable, and there is no air-conditioning in the house where the play takes place, only blacked-out windows. Nor is this the only thing blacked out. The heat itself is an imprisoning force, and nothing is permitted to relieve the temperature – literal and symbolic. Those who live there are inured to pain – literal and symbolic. When their family is assembled for a funeral, less out of a residual loyalty than a custom void of real meaning, it is clear that Violet and Beverly have engendered offspring marked by the same human failings, the same undignified skirmishes in battles they are bound to lose.

When Beverly disappears, later to be fished up from the nearby lake, the rest of the family gather, led by the three sisters who are the couple's daughters, and over time we learn of the emptiness of their lives (serendipitously, Letts would later adapt Chekhov's *Three Sisters*). Not for nothing is the play framed by a quotation from T. S. Eliot's 'The Hollow Men', and Eliot is very much in the air in this play. Something has been evacuated from these lives and, it seems, from a national family that has equally lost its way. The fear, as one of the characters remarks, is that 'We're all just people, some of us accidentally connected by genetics, a random selection of cells. Nothing more' (102). They are characters trapped in an idea of communality that is no longer functional, performing roles in which they no longer believe. Their only true north lies in their own necessities. Abandonment, or fear of such, is paradoxically what links them.

The family consists of daughters, Barbara, whose marriage to Bill is falling apart because he is having sex with a student and whose daughter, fourteen-year-old Jean (named for Jean Seberg, the actress who killed herself), is an enthusiastic marijuana smoker; Karen, who had never found a partner until now, only for him to turn out to be three times married, involved with mercenaries and off-shore accounts and with a liking for under-age sex; Ivy, who falls in love with Charles Aiken, son to Violet's sister, Mattie Fae, and Charlie, who despite his being thirty-seven years old they refer to as Little Charles, not least because they know he is not in fact their son, being a consequence of Mattie Fae's relationship with her brother-in-law. The only two figures who represent some kind of order and hope are both outsiders. One is the housekeeper, Johnna Monevata, a Native American, the other the Sheriff, Deon Gilbeau, who seems a possible partner for the bitter Barbara who had earlier announced, 'Thank God we can't tell the future. We'd never get out of bed' (54). The first act ends with Violet dancing and repeating the same words – 'and then you're here, and then you're here' – in a frenzied and fragmented aria as she tries to avoid confronting the fact of her husband's death, a death in which, we will later learn, she is implicated, failing to make a crucial call because she had another priority, securing their money.

There is a great deal of contempt here. Any obligation for kindness and empathy has seemingly been laid aside, lost somewhere down the years because that would involve opening themselves up to others where survival depends on slamming doors, a closing off. No wonder marriage proves fragile. They have witnessed what that can mean. In *Who's Afraid of Virginia Woolf?* what seems open warfare between husband and wife conceals a curious respect and even love, tenuous, openly denied, but privately, and finally, conceded. There is little of that here beyond the presence of the Indian woman who brings something to this place on the plains, something the other characters have evacuated from their lives. She does more than feed them physically, offering, as she does, what they have abandoned.

There is a compacted history here. They know one another's vulnerabilities, are as they are because they have been shaped by an unforgiving place and an unrelenting family. Things have happened, and there is no need to invoke them. They are what they share. This is their common ground, having little else that pulls them together beyond some residual ritual as they mark the death of a man none understand and none, bar one, Charlie, husband to Violet's sister Mattie Fae, seem to have liked. They have all fled a house closed in on itself and parents who have done much the same. There is little sign of grief, no evident sense of loss. No tears are shed, except, perhaps, for Charlie, each locked up in their own psycho-dramas. Not even Violet laments the disappearance of a man with whom she has shared nothing beyond a sense of quiet desperation. At the same time, they are more than they seem, more than they themselves allow to be seen. The instinct to protect still survives even as they seem to be spiralling down.

This acid tragi-comedy slowly dissects not just a family but a country. The different generations have sought love, direction, purpose, apparently losing all three. Beverly, the man who ushers us into the play, suggests that much the same could be said of America, himself having embraced alcohol and his wife pills which have 'made burdensome the maintenance of traditional American routine: paying of bills, purchase of goods, cleaning of clothes or carpets or crappers' (11). Letts himself has said, that his characters 'were representative of the country on some level',[48] the very name of the Westons echoing the promise once offered in the move west, an irony to be found in *The Grapes of Wrath*, which he would later be asked to adapt for the cinema.

Once a poet as well as a professor, Beverly has never recaptured the talent of his youth, content only with his books but finding in them an echo of his own sense of lost purpose, direction, meaning, equally true of the country. As Robert Frost's poem 'Provide, Provide' observes, 'No memory having starred / Atones for later disregard / or keeps the end from being hard', a warning Beverly embraces; 'Die early and avoid the fate' the poem continues, but 'go down dignified', advice Beverly seems to take. It was Philip Roth's Everyman who remarks of the force that was once his and of the fact that once upon a time he was a full human being. Beverly is no longer that.

The house itself is tired. All structural care, we are told, ceased in 1972. There are cheap plastic shades, sealed by duct tape. A chandelier is 'tatty' casting 'a gloomy yellow light' (9). Outside, the grass is dead and scattered with discarded newspapers. The patriarch of the family contemplates the fate of Hart Crane and John Berryman, both suicides, a fate he is about to embrace. Sitting alone, he quotes Berryman's lines: 'By night within that ancient house / Immense, black, damned, anonymous'(13). This house may not be anonymous, but it is black, closed off against the light, and those who inhabit it are perhaps damned for all that most of them have moved away, if only to lives masquerading as purposeful. Beverly recalls further lines from Berryman: 'The world is gradually becoming a place where I do not care to be anymore' (11). 'Here we go round the prickly pear', he intones as the Prologue ends, the first act opening with his disappearance.

Eliot's 'The Hollow Men' speaks of the dead land, the cactus land, of a hollow valley of dying stars and a meeting place where people grope together. It talks of the shadow that falls between emotion and its response and that sets the tone for what follows in *August: Osage County* as those drawn together by the idea of family reveal the gap between the conception and reality. This is a family reunion but an epigraph from Robert Penn Warren's *All the King's Men* suggests that this will be less than a warm renewal of relationships: 'The child comes home and the parent puts the hook in him . . . the good old family reunion, with picnic dinner under the maples, is very much like diving into the octopus tank at the aquarium' (7).

August: Osage County echoes that retreat into literature and handy opiates familiar from *Long Day's Journey into Night*, here recast in part to humorous effect. There is something wonderfully absurd about the bran tub of distractions its characters seize on, from drugs and alcohol to sexual waywardness of one kind or another. They are distracted from distraction by distraction, as Eliot suggested in 'Burnt Norton', the poem in which he observed that humankind cannot bear very much reality, a truth equally rehearsed by Letts. In the course of the play, whatever has been repressed breaks surface, this being a family much given to repression, if equally to the exposure of secrets. What in Edward Albee's *Who's*

Afraid of Virginia Woolf? formed a last act called Walpurgisnacht here becomes the whole play.

Death is a present and future fact only partly concealed in the vaudeville performances that pass for engagement. Violet quotes lines from an Emily Dickinson poem, although not the lines that precede them: 'Because I could not stop for Death / He kindly stopped for me'. At times characters rise to a sudden articulateness, momentarily pinning truths in place. A second later and language slides uncontrollably as if mocking such seriousness. Violet is suffering from mouth cancer (she is not the only one with cancer we later learn) and finds it difficult at times to articulate, although when she does, her words are razor sharp. This is a play whose surging energy can make us forget the current moving the other way, for there is an undertow and it is that which gives it its particular force. This is not a play that is liable to move to tears, like that other small-town American play whose spun candy surface conceals a concern with mortality: *Our Town*. What it is liable to do, in its humour and sudden dislocations, is to freeze the smile for a moment as something else leaks into this hermetic house.

There is a counter force at play in the figure of Johnna. She brings light into the house, literally, as the shades disappear and daylight penetrates. She intervenes when Karen's fiancée is about to seduce the young Jean. She puts food on the table and offers support to those in moral collapse. When everyone else abandons Violet, she stays behind. However, it is she, as Violet repeatedly intones the lament 'and then you're gone' (138), who utters Eliot's words: 'This is the way the world ends.'

This is a play that requires a deal of choreography as the focus shifts from one conversation in one part of the house to another. Indeed, there is a three-and-a-half page passage in which those conversations overlap one another in a three-part disharmony. At times it is as much how language is delivered or not as its lexical meanings or truth value that is significant. Violet alternates between inarticulacy, a rapier-like delivery and a scream, as she evades, accuses, despairs. Truths are concealed, denied, flourished. Characters are, as Bill says of his wife Barbara, 'in attack mode' (47), or they are conciliatory, shouting, whispering. Although they are all deeply flawed, there are no villains, except, perhaps, the egregious Steve Heidebrecht, conman seducer. As Karen declares, 'it's not cut and dried, black and white, good and bad. It lives where everything lives: somewhere in the middle. Where everything lives, where all the rest of us live' (121), although she excepts Barbara, who herself delivers a jeremiad about more than this house of disappointed dreams. Her father, she declares, had despaired, of himself, perhaps, of his house and his family but also of a wider lost promise that reached out to the country itself, 'As if it had already happened. As if whatever was disappearing had already disappeared. As if it was too late. As if it was already over. And no one saw it go. This country, this experiment, America, this hubris: what a lament, if no one saw it go . . . Dissipation is actually much worse than cataclysm' (123–4). 'I'm still here' (124), she declares, as if she might hold the line, only to leave. Johnna's final recitation from Eliot seems another version of Barbara's remarks, although it stops short of the words that follow – 'this is the way the world ends' – not with a bang but a whimper.

John Malkovich said, 'I took my wife and kids to see *August: Osage County*. I didn't want my kids to not know what Steppenwolf was. I wanted them to see *August: Osage County*, to see what Steppenwolf actually did – to see the ensemble in full attack mode. [It] captured who we were and what we did.'[49] Much the same could be said of the play itself. Its New York transfer ran for 648 performances.

If his earlier plays had been located in the world of his upbringing, in 2008 Steppenwolf opened his next play, an affecting comedy – *Superior Donuts* – in the city that had become his home town. He had written the first act of the play when *August: Osage County* intervened and he nearly failed to continue with it.[50] Nonetheless, he has said that '"Superior Donuts" is very important to me. I wrote it after the year I had huge success with "August" but also after my father had died. I felt like I didn't have it in me to put something dark into the world.'[51]

It is set in the historic Uptown neighbourhood of Chicago, more particularly Jefferson Park, once a popular entertainment centre with elegant houses before people moved onto the suburbs and immigrants from the South and elsewhere moved in. It has a large Polish community. At the time of the play, it is being gentrified, although the characters – Polish-American, Irish-American, African-American, Irish/Italian-American and Russian – represent that earlier community. Originally doubting that he knew enough about the immigrant experience, he realised that his own journey from Oklahoma to Chicago was itself a kind of immigration, so different were the two worlds.

At the centre of the action is a donut shop, apparently the last independently owned donut shop in Uptown (in actuality, there are now none), recently vandalised and beginning to lose customers to a nearby Starbucks. Its owner, Arthur Przybyszewski, who was born the year the donut shop opened, seems what the local drug dealers regard him as being: an aging hippy who had dodged the Vietnam War. Certainly he is laid back enough to open the store on a haphazard basis and dress in unwashed and wrinkled clothes, although a black policewoman evidently finds him attractive, something of which he is oblivious. Both are in a sense misfits.

Arthur has retreated, as he had earlier to Canada to evade the draft, and seems to be drifting, suffering from wounds having to do with the collapse of relationships and a sense of loss. He has clearly withdrawn so that the shop is a refuge, a place frequented by a limited clientele who themselves evidence damage of different kinds. We learn his background in a series of direct addresses. His life is transformed when he hires a young black man, Franco, who, it turns out, besides being smart and having ideas to update the store, has been writing the Great American Novel. Whatever has gone wrong in the past, he leans into the future as Arthur seems frozen in the past. They are potentially separated by race but both evidence sufficient irony not to make that a central concern. This, after all, is a mixed neighbourhood. The real distinction is generational. Arthur's divorced wife is dead and his daughter distant. Franco becomes a surrogate son.

When Franco is badly beaten, having failed to pay a bookie his debts, and the typescript of his novel is destroyed, Arthur sells his shop to settle those debts. There is a spasm of violence, as Arthur does battle with the drug dealer – a fight described as long, painful, sweaty and bloody – but this is the moment he abandons his air of detachment, having been stirred back into life. He may have evaded serving in the Vietnam War and engaging with life beyond the walls of his shop, but now he steps forward. The shop is lost, but something more important has been found, a family implicitly assembled. Arthur has stepped back into life, and in handing a blank notebook to Franco and inviting him to re-create his novel, he brings him back into life too. Again it is tempting to quote Eliot who, in *The Family Reunion*, has Harry remark, 'You do not know what hope is until you have lost it.'[52]

Letts has said that he was having to deal with the death of his father when he was finishing the play and that may have fed into it, offering, as it does, an act of generational reconciliation that implies a more positive view of human nature and social possibility. In the past lie personal and social problems whose echoes are still faintly to be heard, but something has changed and is changing. There is an urban tension in the play, although this is largely played as comedy. The characters all have their needs but are treated with understanding. The police are unthreatening, one attending Star Trek conventions in full costume. A Russian who exudes the potential for violence is polite if not intelligible. In this play, as opposed to *August: Osage County*, America, too, is offered the grace of reconciliation Arthur writing, and speaking, the title of Franco's novel, once destroyed but now to be re-created: 'America . . . Will be' (93).

In 2014, Letts announced that he was working on a new play *The Scavenger's Daughter*, the title coming from a sixteenth-century instrument of torture, designed to compress those who were its victims. It was, he explained, to be about the end of a great man's life and, after what he described as his other 'story-heavy' plays, more free form. His next produced play, too, was free form. *Mary Page Marlowe* opened at the Steppenwolf Theatre in 2016. This enters the life of its principal character at different stages, with six actors playing her as she moves from the age of sixteen to sixty-nine. It was born from Letts's own sense that he had been a different person at different moments of his life, hence the epigraph from Joan Didion:

I think we are well advised to keep on nodding terms with the people we used to be, whether we find them attractive company or not. Otherwise they turn up unannounced and surprise us, come hammering on the mind's door at four A.M. of a bad night and demand to know who deserted them, who betrayed them, who is going to make amends.

There are, perhaps, faint echoes of Edward Albee's *Three Tall Women*, which featured three actresses marking different stages in a woman's life; the various versions of the woman in *Mary Page Marlowe* do not, as in Albee's play, comment on one another, however, although the different selves are on occasion mute observers. What we witness is the extent to which she changes with time, to which youthful expectations are modified, frustrated, subject to irony. Frank Kermode observed that what we call a plot is an organisation that humanises time by giving it form and that is what is in play here. The meaning of a life is elusive. It is more, obviously, than an accumulation of details not least because it is never stable. It is tempting to say that the story of a life only becomes clear with its ending except that it is a story told from a particular perspective, as much imposed as an imminent truth finally emerging.

Mary Page confesses to her psychiatrist, 'The truth is you and I pretend I make decisions about the direction of my life. I don't. I haven't. I didn't decide any of it. All of it happened *to* me, and I went along with it.'[53] How far does she – how far do we – have agency? How does she exist independent of the roles she plays? As she explains, 'I just think that as a woman, a lot of our roles just get stipulated for us, and there's only one way to be a wife, be a daughter, be a mom, Be a lover . . . I'm not the person I am. I'm just *acting* like a person who is a wife and a mother' (36).

In a memoir, *Ammonites and Leaping Fish*, the British novelist Penelope Lively looked back through her own life at age eighty and, in doing so quoted, approvingly, Sir Thomas Browne writing in *Urn-Buriall*, a book she had discovered earlier in her life when she was the same person only different: 'such a compass of years will shew new examples of old things, parallelisms of occurrences through the whole course of Time, and nothing monstrous unto him, who may in that time understand not only the varieties of Man, but the varieties of himself, and how many Men he hath been in that extent of time'.[54] The phrase that particularly struck her was 'varieties of himself', even as she believed in what she called a 'coherence over time'. *Mary Page Marlowe* engages with a similar awareness, raises a similar question to do with how a life unspools, identity morphs or retains its inner coherence.

The play's title seems so definite, the announcement of its subject as a seemingly fixed identity, yet we watch as she is formed, deformed, reformed, as her name changes, from Mary to Mary Page, her last name changing with her husbands. She is an actor in a drama whose plot can only seem clear in retrospect, as if happenstance could be seen as ordained, or simply absorbed. Who, in the end, is Mary Page Marlowe, ever becoming rather than being until, at last, time, having speeded up, begins to slow, yearning ceding territory to acceptance, desire dulled as if it were a phase, a drifting tide leaving her at last what she is when a line is finally drawn across the ledger. History is a tidying up of events to give them a shape few experience at the time. A life lived forwards is understood backwards or seen through a glass darkly. What we become reorders what we were as if that had an inevitability which can only be factitious. Charles Dickens's Scrooge is shown his former life and shocked by what he sees. To travel back in time is to encounter a self that can seem alien, with always a shadow world of what might have been but was not. We are judge and jury when it comes to our lives, ever inventing pleas in mitigation or simply invoking a failed memory. The essence of Letts's play, however, is that the past is summoned as it was rather than as it is remembered, even as the times visited contain their own indicative meanings. In that sense, it is pitiless; in that sense, it is forgiving.

Lively has said that autobiographical memory 'is random, non-sequential, capricious, and without it we are undone . . . never mind that [it] is full of holes – it is meant to be like that. There is what we remember, and there is the great dark cavern of what we have forgotten'.[55] Who, in *Mary Page Marlowe*, either remembers of forgets? It is Letts who performs that function for her, but he is equally conscious of the non-sequential and the capricious as he is of the necessity to acknowledge past moments whose immediate significance is lost but that lodge somewhere in the mind, so many hidden clues to a puzzle that can only be seen as such with time and by then irremediable.

Age demands summary, a sense not just of an ending but of what that ending means in terms of a life, more especially when the evidence gathered consists only of fragments brought together as if they should make a whole, contradictory though they may be, dismaying even. Is a life completed a triumph or the moment when failure must be acknowledged, regrets no longer functional, successes modified by subsequent failures? We never remember a clean narrative. We return to moments, sometimes inexplicable in their seeming inconsequence, sometimes burnished with a happiness suddenly recalled and sometimes the source of a guilt with a gravitational pull. Lively recalls that Joseph Brodsky insisted that the process of recollection is never linear and that for Vladimir Nabokov it was a series of spaced flashes. The story of a life, she suggests, is entirely unsatisfactory: 'The novelist in me – the reader, too – wants shape and structure, development, a theme, insights. Instead there is this assortment of slides, some of them welcome, others not at all, defying chronology, refusing structure.'[56] That is essentially how *Mary Page Marlowe* works. There is a tension between a life recalled in the arbitrariness of events retrieved, snatched from the continuum, and the playwright's shaping imagination.

Mary Page Marlowe's is a life that, like everyone's, ebbs and flows. Wrong paths are taken, wrong decisions made, and their consequences echo through her life. She bears the marks of her own family past even as she convinces herself that she will forge her own future. A marriage is made and broken – more than one, we learn. Children change, their own futures hard to predict as they are also marked by their own pasts, products in part of choices made by others. Regret and reconciliation contend. There is a continuity to her existence but equally a disturbing flux. Who, in the end, is Mary Page Marlow? 'I don't know', she confesses. Like everyone, she is a different person to different people, but she is also a stranger to herself as we glimpse her over time.

The play is not sequential. It is about a person but it is also about time, time which itself is not constant from the perspective of an individual, recalled not as an unfolding story but a series of moments. It begins with her at forty, her life at a moment of crisis as a marriage collapses and she has to explain to her children that their lives, too, will change and, in the case of the son, we discover, not for the better. Then she is back in college charting a future we already know will not be hers. Everything seems possible except that every subsequent decision will narrow possibilities. As a child she was raised by a cold, bitter, alcoholic mother who had been abandoned by her husband, who was himself suffering from the trauma of war, and abandonment is to be part of Mary Page Marlowe's life. There will be three marriages and a litany of lovers as she searches for fulfilment or perhaps simply contentment, happiness being too strong a word, although there have been moments of such.

There comes a time when she turns to drink, a sign, perhaps, that her family past has left its mark, and suffers the consequence of driving while intoxicated, justly punished, she thinks, acknowledged guilt perhaps offering its own consolation. Her life, like a quilt in need of attention, is a patchwork, so many disparate moments that she, and the audience, have to sew together since the playwright consciously forbears to do so beyond presenting seemingly random fragments of a life. She, as an accountant, took pleasure in assembling her clients receipts as if they were part of a puzzle, and this stands as a metaphor for a play in which fragments slowly coalesce, except that, as with a kaleidoscope, a shake might have produced a different pattern.

Here Mary Page Marlowe's life is condensed into a bare ninety minutes. It is not a remarkable life, and therein lies its power. 'I *am* not exceptional', she declares (34). We are not invited to watch that life because she commands a social significance. The small change of life co-exists with times of emotional drama, as it does for all. There are moments of anger and moments of silence, each charged with meaning if that meaning were ever fully apparent. There is, she feels, an emptiness to her existence, and she turns to a psychiatrist to make sense of things, as if events could be reshaped into a coherent story, and the play ends without a real resolution, as lives, perhaps, are prone to do, not least because the final scene catches her not at sixty-nine, as in an earlier scene, but suspended at the age of fifty-nine. At sixty-nine she has achieved a kind of equanimity, though that had never been her ambition when her eyes were bright with life's possibilities. It has been said that all politicians' lives end in failure. Could that be generalised in that death is hardly a triumph? In the double entry accounts of a life, the columns rarely match. Was there a perfect life that might have been led, falling short, therefore leaving a residue of disappointment? And if perfection was never possible, how to judge a life in which chance plays a role, in which decisions were never wholly in her hands, some moments leaving a mark and others not? Mary Page Marlowe is not wholly her own invention. She had accomplices. She betrayed and was betrayed. There was darkness and light, a full spectrum of colours and dismaying monochromes. Is mere survival, therefore, a virtue, or are we to understand that all lives are defined by confusion, dismay, exultation, resignation? *Mary Page Marlowe* does more than humanise time by giving it form; it humanises a life by like means.

Israeli novelist David Grossman noted that 'inside of each of us there is the potential for so many other selves, but because of conventions we congeal into one story line. Writing', he explained, 'gives me the pleasure of melting into the others that are within me'. That could be seen not only as applying to Mary Page Marlowe but equally to Tracy Letts, as both actor and playwright.[57]

Notes

1 Tracy Letts, 'How to Live a Creative Life', *Chicago Ideas*, 2016. www.chicagoideas.com/videos/how-to-live-a-creative-life
2 Suzy Evans, 'Tracy Letts in Conversation about "August: Osage Country"', *Backstage.com*, 10 December 2013. www.backstage.com/interview/tracy-letts-conversation-about-august-osage-county/
3 Bruce Weber, 'From an Okie Playwright and Actor, A Life with a Drama of Its Own', *New York Times*, 14 April 2004. www.nytimes.com/2004/04/14/theater/for-an-okie-playwright-and-actor-a-life-with-drama-of-its-own.html?_r=0
4 Hermione Hoby, 'Tracy Letts: 'If You're Not Entertaining, What the Hell's the Point', *Telegraph*, 31 January 2014. www.telegraph.co.uk/culture/theatre/10607247/Tracy-Letts-If-youre-not-entertaining-what-the-hells-the-point.html

5 Sarh Ruhl, *100 Essays I Don't Have Time to Write* (New York, 2014), p. 213.
6 Missy Kruse, 'Billie and Tracy Letts Talk about Their Award-Winning Careers', *Tulsa People*, December 2009. www.tulsapeople.com/Tulsa-People/December-2009/Online-exclusive-Billie-and-Tracy-Letts-talk-about-their-award-winning-literary-careers
7 Ibid.
8 Quoted in David Lodge, *Lives in Writing* (London, 2014), pp. 90–1.
9 Alex Witchel, 'Tracy Letts Is Still Haunted by His Past', *New York Times*, 21 March 2014. www.nytimes.com/2014/03/23/magazine/tracy-letts-is-still-haunted-by-his-past.html?_r=0
10 Ibid.
11 Tony Adler, 'Mr. Danger', *Chicago: Arts and Culture*, 27 July 2007. www.chicagomag.com/Chicago-Magazine/July-2007/Mr-Danger/
12 John Moore, 'Tracy Letts on the Origin of the Poison in "August: Osage County"', Denver Center for the Performing Arts, *DCPA Newsletter*, 15 August 2015. www.denvercenter.org/blog-posts/news-center/2015/08/05/tracy-letts-on-the-origin-of-the-poison-in-august-osage-county
13 T. S. Eliot, *Collected Plays* (London, 1962), p. 110.
14 John Mayer, *Steppenwolf Theatre Company of Chicago* (London, 2016), p. 48.
15 Ibid, p. 68.
16 Ibid, pp. 104–5.
17 Ibid, p. 151.
18 Rashid Razaq, 'Homeland's Tracy Letts: "Performing in London Helped Me Feel I'd Made It"', *Evening Standard*, 10 August 2016. www.standard.co.uk/showbiz/celebrity-news/homeland-s-tracy-letts-performing-in-london-helped-me-feel-like-i-d-made-it-a3316676.html
19 Richard Christianson, 'Killer Joe Unfolds As a Bizarre, Gut-Twisting Thriller', *Chicago Tribune*, 4 August 1993. http://articles.chicagotribune.com/1993–08–04/news/9308040062_1_killer-joe-tracy-letts-ansel
20 Locke Peterseim, 'Interview: Killer Joe Screenwriter and Playwright Tracy Letts', *Open Letters Monthly*, 3 August 2012. www.openlettersmonthly.com/hammerandthump/interview-killer-joe-screenwriter-and-playwright-tracy-letts
21 Ibid.
22 Stephen King, 'Big Jim Thompson: An Appreciation', p. ix in Jim Thompson's *Now and on Earth* (New York, 1994).
23 Locke Peterseim, 'Interview: Killer Joe Screenwriter and Playwright Tracy Letts'.
24 Ibid.
25 Tracy Letts, *Killer Joe* (New York, 1999), pp. 16–17.
26 Ibid, p. 26.
27 Ibid, p. 37.
28 Locke Peterseim, 'Interview: Killer Joe Screenwriter and Playwright Tracy Letts'.
29 Steve Prokopy, 'Capone Talks to Renowned Playwright Tracy Letts about His Works', *Ain't It Cool News*, 30 July 2012. www.aintitcool.com/node/57323
30 Stephen King, 'Big Jim Thompson'.
31 Locke Peterseim, 'Interview: Killer Joe Screenwriter and Playwright Tracy Letts'.
32 Ibid.
33 Hermione Hoby, 'Tracy Letts: "If You're Not Entertaining, What the Hell's the Point"'.
34 Olivier Père, 'Interview with William Friedkin on *Killer Joe* and His Previous Films', *Arte Cinema*, September 2012.
35 Jason Zinoman, 'Theater: Excerpt; Bug', *New York Times*, 29 February 2004. www.nytimes.com/2004/02/29/theater/theater-excerpt-bug.html?_r=0
36 Tracy Letts, *Bug* (New York, 2005), p. 40.
37 Philip Roth, 'Writing American Fiction', *Commentary*, 1 March 1961. www.commentarymagazine.com/articles/writing-american-fiction
38 Tracy Letts, *Man from Nebraska* (Evanston, 2006), p. 21.
39 T. S. Eliot, *Collected Plays* (London, 1962), p. 134.
40 Ibid, p. 135.
41 Ibid, p. 189.

42 Ibid, p. 65.
43 Ibid.
44 Alex Witchel, 'Tracy Letts Is Still Haunted by His Past'.
45 Ed Pilkington, 'Obama Angers Midwest Voters with Guns and Religion Remark', *Guardian*, 14 April 2008. www.theguardian.com/world/2008/apr/14/barackobama.uselections2008
46 Alex Witchel, 'Tracy Letts Is Still Haunted by His Past'.
47 Tracy Letts, *August: Osage County* (London, 2008), p. 29.
48 Katey Rich, 'Tracy Letts: "August: Osage County" Has Always Only Ended One Way', *Guardian*, 16 January 2014. www.theguardian.com/film/2014/jan/16/august-osage-county-always-ended-one-way
49 John Mayer, *Steppenwolf Theatre Company of Chicago*, p. 159.
50 Ibid, p. 185
51 Daisy Bowie-Sell, 'Tracy Letts Interview: "Saying 'I'm an Important Writer" Is Deadly', *Time Out*, 17 February 2014. www.timeout.com/london/theatre/tracy-letts-interview-saying-im-an-important-writer-is-deadly
52 T. S. Eliot, *Collected Plays*, p. 79.
53 Tracy Letts, *Mary Page Marlowe* (New York, 2016), p. 34.
54 Penelope Lively, *Ammonites and Leaping Fish* (London, 2013), p. 41.
55 Ibid, pp. 122–3.
56 Ibid, p. 125.
57 Daniel Asa Rose, 'I Always Prefer Books That Are Inevitable: David Grossman on "Falling Out of Time"', *Barnes and Noble.com.*, *April 9, 2014*. com/review/i-always-prefer-books-that-are-inevitable-david-grossman-on-falling-out-of-time

6

David Lindsay-Abaire

I will always be the working class kid. I have a deep respect for hard work and people trying to make their lives better. I hope it informs my work ethic. My sense of humor is *very* Southie – dark and inappropriate.[1]
– David Lindsay-Abaire

David Lindsay-Abaire is a dramatist whose first plays were like three-ring circuses, wildly inventive farces with a gothic touch, anarchic, funny, fast-paced, reveling in offending against good taste, indeed not acknowledging the existence of such a thing. Plot, character and language are all put under pressure to the point that they become ironic gestures, mocking their own conventions. His is a world of bizarre conspiracies, wild coincidences and unlikely relationships. Audiences are likely to be left trailing behind, desperately trying to piece together a narrative line that is no less absurd once the fragments seemingly cohere. He takes special pleasure in dispatching his characters by inventive means or disassembling them. They often disguise themselves and their motives – in so far as they are aware of them. Then things changed.

Having resisted the naturalistic, rebelled against characters who compel empathy and shown little interest in private pain and public concerns, he began to write a different kind of play. Where his early work had appeared Off-Broadway, he now found himself, with *Rabbit Hole*, on the Great White Way and the recipient of a Pulitzer Prize. He was back on Broadway with *Good People*, which won a New York Drama Critics' Circle Award as well as an Outer Critics Circle Award, a Drama Desk Award, a Tony Award and a New York Drama Critics' Circle Award for Frances McDormand, its leading actress. He also wrote the book for a musical, *High Fidelity*, and subsequently the book and lyrics for *Shrek the Musical* as well as writing a series of screenplays. So where did it all go wrong?

It may be that your idea of Boston is shaped by Dennis Lehane, born and raised in Dorchester on the edge of South Boston. He came from a working-class Catholic background and watched as priests sexually molested children. He wrote crime novels that he insisted is where the social novel went, urban novels that explored another side to a city that presented itself to the world as the cradle of the Revolution. David Lindsay-Abaire (born David Lindsay, in 1969, adding Abaire on his marriage), also came from the working class. His mother was a factory worker while his father worked in a fruit market. He was raised in South Boston, seeing himself as defined by that fact. The world he wrote about, though, he has explained, had little to do with Whitey Bulger, the notorious murderer of nineteen people and head of the Boston Irish Mob, or with Lehane's sagas of the underside of the American dream, which led him to be a writer on the television series *The Wire*. On the other hand, in Lindsay-Abaire's first play, we do learn of a man murdered with an axe whose feet are cut off by a serial killer, but this was in the context of an absurdist play in which a son is urged by his mother to avenge his footless father.

Lindsay-Abaire lived in the same house where his mother had been raised but, at the age of eleven, won a scholarship that lifted him out of that world. It was awarded by the Boys and Girls Club of South Boston, and it took him to Milton Academy, which today lists him as one of its distinguished alumni, alongside T. S. Eliot, Buckminster Fuller and both Robert and Ted Kennedy. He mixed, in other words, with people from a class remote from his own and as a consequence never felt entirely at home there, nor in the house to which he returned. It was a scholarship, however, that set him on a path substantially different from the one he might have followed even as he is convinced that he would have made his way irrespective of what he was inclined to feel was a stroke of luck.

While at school he took Modern Drama, reading two plays a week, beginning with Aeschylus and proceeding to David Mamet and August Wilson. Asked to choose a play-wright as a model for exercises, he selected Eugène Ionesco. He also wrote plays, his first being *Mario's House of Italian Cuisine*. He ended up the valedictorian and was thought of as the class comedian. Asked if that meant that he was the class clown, he explained that, 'The class clown is the guy who runs across the football field naked, and the class comedian is the guy who talked him into doing it. I was that guy. Still am.'[2] At Sarah Lawrence College in New York, he studied acting and took playwriting classes. His play, *A Show of Hands*, was well enough received to encourage him to continue with writing rather than acting.

After graduating in 1998, he entered playwriting contests and submitted his work to a range of theatres, accustoming himself to rejections. Later, he would advise writers to take every opportunity offered in the knowledge that they would be rejected 99.9 percent of the time, casting their lines in the hope that one day they would land a fish. He then applied to the Juilliard School, one of its chief attractions being that there was no tuition fee (although there is tuition for other programs at Julliard, tuition is free for playwrights; of note, Lindsay-Abaire was named co-director of the program in 2016). It was not a degree programme, and while there he was working full time at the Dance Theater Workshop in Chelsea. One of a handful accepted into the Lila Acheson Wallace American Playwrights Program at Julliard every year, he studied with Marsha Norman and Christopher Durang, one of whose plays he had acted in at the Milton Academy. Students were required to deliver ten pages a week. One by-product of that process was *Fuddy Mears*, written in ten-page increments. On leaving Julliard, he was approached by 20th Century Fox to become a contract writer on a weekly salary and produced a screenplay with Hugh Grant being lined up to star. It had a producer, the man who had produced *Forrest Gump*, but it went the way of many such projects. His contract came to an end.

His early plays were what he called absurdist comedies, deliberately turning his back on naturalistic drama. *A Devil Inside*, which he wrote before going to Julliard, opened at the Soho Rep in 1997. It was, he said, an 'over-the-top take on 19th-century Russian novels that I set in present-day New York, Lower East Side', a 'crazy play'.[3] Compared with the work of Ionesco, whom he confesses to be his idol, it is a farce on accelerant, a work that winds the spring of its comedy tighter as it goes.

A tumble-dryer of satire, parody, pastiche and absurd comedy, *A Devil Inside* is an intricately contrived comic tour de force whose absurdities deliberately implode. Its plot mocks the idea of plot intricacies, its characters the very notion of three-dimensional figures. Here is Russian literature as Jackson Pollock, Raskolnikov as tortured Woody Allen, a collision between Wes Craven's *Scream* (which opened a year before *A Devil Inside)* and TV crime series in which victims are killed in ever more unlikely ways, their limbs often liberally scattered around cities here, though, in the Lower East Side rather than a neon-glossed Las Vegas or the sunlit Miami of *CSI*.

It is not difficult to feel the influence of Christopher Durang who was given to parodies (*The Idiots Karamazov, For Whom the Belle Tolls*, a parody of *The Glass Menagerie*, *A Stye of the Eye*, a take-off of a Sam Shepard play), who described some of his early plays as having exploded out of his head and as having a nihilistic energy even as their exaggerations were a reflection of the fact that people's behaviour beyond the theatre was not without its absurdities. David Lindsay-Abaire seems at times to breathe the same air as Joe Orton and with a similar pleasure in disrupting expectations. This is a jigsaw that becomes more menacing with every added piece, a paranoid vision in which everything does indeed connect except that in doing so it proposes an alarming conspiracy, the underlying principle of which is entropy.

Durang, in speaking of his own play *The Nature and Purpose of the Universe*, has referred both to its cruelty and the need for actors to say outlandish things in a normal tone of voice even as their timing allowed the comedy to be evident. Sometimes, he suggested, the rhythm of the play was itself the source of humour. Much the same could be said of *A Devil Inside*, in which there is a comic relentlessness in the way in which horror is built on horror, as if there were no limit, no outrageous event that could not be capped even as the characters seemed capable of taking outrageous things in their stride, unaware of the absurdities they express and experience. Here, the non sequitur becomes sequitur, and vice versa.

At the same time, as I pointed out in a study of Joe Orton, farce 'has always been concerned with the elimination of character, with the creation of an almost hysterical intensity in which character is flung off by the sheer centrifugal force of language and action'.[4] There is a frenzy to it, its pace alternately concealing or boasting of its implausibilities. It is essentially parodistic, mocking the very form, methods and assumptions of the drama it subverts. Nor is it without a certain cruelty, humiliation being laced through its humour. Figures of authority and respectability are exposed, order is inverted, logic required to perform arabesques. This is the world of Lindsay-Abaire's early plays, owing less to Beckett than the Marx Brothers or *Hellzapoppin'*.

It is also worth remembering that one writer he admired was Tina Howe who, while claiming that she earthed herself in the European tradition – invoking Pirandello, Ionesco and Beckett, and seeing the absurdists as groundbreakers – also referred to the Marx Brothers films in which 'going berserk was *allowed*', works that featured performers who 'didn't just celebrate lunacy, they turned it into a high art form . . . The whole point was to keep piling excess on top of excess – more props, more pratfalls, more dizzy language'. Why, she asked, 'shouldn't it be the same in the theatre?'[5] Interestingly, it was her humour that in her early plays seemed to rattle critics and blind them to aspects of her work which that humour engaged and Lindsay-Abaire would probably share her observation that 'it's very tricky to be true to your darker self and still get laughs'.[6]

A Devil Inside received a positive review from the *New York Times* while it divided others. Lindsay-Abaire would later complain that critics were disinclined to pay the kind of attention that they would to naturalistic plays while nonetheless acknowledging that his early plays were 'pretty ridiculous'.

In an ironic introduction to *Fuddy Meers* he imagines a conversation in which he explains that he writes comedies and stages them Off-Broadway, something that mystifies the woman he is talking to and for whom Broadway musicals are the template of good drama. In fact that play began at Juilliard while he continued to work on it, in 1998, at the National Playwrights Conference at the Eugene O'Neill Theatre Center, where it was workshopped before opening the following year at Off-Broadway's Manhattan Theatre Club.

The idea for the play occurred to him when he saw a television programme about a man who suffered from amnesia. The action takes place in the course of a single day in which Claire, the woman at its centre, slowly discovers the truth, or competing truths, of her life. Because Lindsay-Abaire wrote it in fits and starts, following the rhythm of his Julliard assignments, he was at first unsure how it would develop: 'I thought of the first scene and then the very last one. Otherwise, the play unfolded itself to me as it unfolds to Claire – as a series of surprises. I tried not to know where I was going with it.'[7] At one point, a masked man appears from beneath a bed, although Lindsay-Abaire confessed that he had no idea who he was or why he was there, so he later had to return to the script and retrospectively establish his identity and how he fitted into an evolving, if byzantine, plot.

Lindsay-Abaire has referred to *Fuddy Mears* as akin to his own experience of fairgrounds, which always seemed to him to combine enjoyment with threat: 'They had this giddy, joyous quality and at the same time were horribly frightening. Those kiddy roller coasters were great, but they could burst apart at any moment, and the guys working at the game booths were obvious ex-cons. Those places were just filled with the scariest people.'[8] 'Claire's world', he explained, 'is like a funhouse, where anything can happen. A floor can drop . . . Something terrifying can pop out of the darkness. Giddiness can turn into horror at the turn of a corner.'[9] He invited designers to reflect this fact, creating 'a world of incomplete pictures and distorted realities'. As he has explained, at that time in his career 'the more absurd the better'.[10] It was, he confessed, written for the amusement of his fellow Julliard students while 'trying to write outrageous farce with an underlying sadness, a real weight that peeks through the silliness'.[11]

Fuddy Meers has something to say about memory and language, albeit in the context of an increasingly wild plot. It opens as Claire awakes to be told by her seemingly caring husband, Richard, who she is and what her life has been, because a past event resulted in all of her memories disappearing each night when she goes to sleep. Her surly son, Kenny, is, it appears, a self-concerned observer, though we later learn that he is not Richard's son. The action then shifts into another dimension as a man in a ski mask appears from under her bed, a man who walks with a limp and talks with a lisp. He has appeared, he explains, to rescue her, claiming to be her brother, Zack (in fact long dead), and indeed they drive off together heading for her mother's house where a grizzled old man called Millet appears, along with a puppet that he engages in conversation while trying to strangle it. Both Millet and the Limping Man are wearing manacles and, it slowly emerges, have escaped from prison.

Richard and his 'son' set off in pursuit, only to be intercepted by Heidi, a police officer who stops them for speeding. When she draws her gun, they seize it and force her to go with them. By degrees it emerges that the Limping Man, masquerading as her brother, was Claire's first husband, sent to jail for his violence towards her, having burned down their house. He has escaped from jail with the assistance of Heidi, who is not in fact a police officer but a lunch lady at the prison whom he has promised to run away with even as he tries to re-establish his relationship with Claire. The reason he is blind in one eye and has a damaged ear is because Claire poured hot bacon fat over him in response to one of his attacks in which he threw a model of the Empire State building at her, leading to his lifelong aversion to bacon.

In a confused tussle, Gertie (Claire's mother) stabs the Limping Man and the puppet, and Kenny is shot in the arm. Richard, it turns out, is no less a criminal than the other men, having been an addict and robber. The play ends as Claire, Richard and Kenny drive home, only for her to go to sleep with no guarantee that when she wakes she might not have to begin her life all over again.

There is a stage direction that underlines the farcical nature of the action: 'MILLET chases RICHARD into the darkness of the basement. From a different part of the basement, GERTIE comes running out of the darkness with a raised shovel. She runs into an oblivious MILLET. Offstage we hear the metallic thwack of a shovel hitting his head. Lights out' (112). Claire, unsurprisingly, remarks, 'it's so hard to keep it all straight' (102). Meaning is apparently constructed as it is deconstructed. A seemingly coherent story emerges that is at heart incoherent, a fact underlined by the general mayhem. Secrets are exposed quite as if this were an Ibsen-esque drama in which the past boils to the surface only for those secrets to expose random violence and a house of mirrors.

Lindsay-Abaire's characters are all in denial – suppressing truths, telling lies. As he observed, they are figures with 'debilitating, awful pasts' in escape from themselves as much as others. Meanwhile, with one suffering from a lisp, another unable to articulate following a stroke and a third incapable of remembering anything, much of the humour derives from a series of linguistic misunderstanding that underscore other failures to connect.

Six months into the production, which would run successfully for nine, he recalled that his grandmother had suffered from cancer and had her voice box removed, making communication impossible, but the essence of farce is that pain can be turned into humour. Death is a joke, an absurd product of passions that are literary constructs. Characters lack depth because this would subvert a form in which we are invited to enjoy surface even as the intricacies of plot mock the actual complexities of life, its misdirections those encountered in a world in which emotions are real.

At the hands of Orton, farce became a conscious assault on society, deliberately subversive of a culture that reduced him, as a gay man at a time when his sexuality was illegal, to caricature – a smutty joke. He responded in kind. This is where Lindsay-Abaire parts company with him, for all his sense that farce retains the ability to comment on a life whose absurdities can be exposed if pushed to the extreme. In his farces, absurdist comedies, there is no moral stance. Causality is mocked. Coherences are factitious; violence, often a product of misfortune, is no more than an irony. The pleasure offered is that of watching figures, unaware of their absurdities, walking into situations that baffle them, insensitive to the hidden pattern of their relationships. Acts have disproportionate effects, while inanimate objects have the power to threaten, mocking the belief of the characters that they inhabit a rational world. In Beckett and Pinter, for all their elements of vaudeville, the threats are real enough and engage with metaphysical, social and even political anxieties. Lindsay-Abaire may be commenting on the suspect nature of human communication and the fragility of relationships, but his primary pleasure seems to lie in creating works whose internal intricacies are themselves the source of humour.

At the same time, and in the context of his next play, he has said, 'Most of my writing ends up being about people desperately trying to navigate the strange environment they find themselves in. People who are trying to make sense of a confusing and terrifying new world. On the surface, *Wonder of the World* is a ridiculous comedy where absurd things happen and people's lives are turned upside down, but that's also exactly what happens in real life – everything makes sense, then something awful occurs, and in an instant our world is blown apart, and we're left to figure out how to put the pieces together again.'[12]

Wonder of the World (2001) features couples whose marriages break along unlikely fault lines, who try to transform themselves, conceal their true identities and motives and inhabit a world stranger by the moment. Its cast of characters includes a suicidal woman intent in going over Niagara Falls in a barrel, a man who gets sexual pleasure from swallowing and evacuating the decapitated heads of Barbie dolls, a couple masquerading as private detectives but happy to work as shoeshine operatives, a therapist dressed as a clown in a play set on a train, in a motel room, on a boat on the Falls and in a helicopter over the Falls.

Lindsay-Abaire began *Wonder of the World* with nothing more than the image of a woman packing a suitcase knowing nothing of who she was or how things would develop, as before discovering the play in the course of writing it. Once more it was an anarchic farce in which unlikely deaths accumulate and characters are connected in ever more complicated ways. His initial stage direction – 'Most importantly, nothing should stop the flow of the play' – underlines the accelerating pace of the action.

Cass, a woman in her thirties, decides to leave her husband, Kip, unimpressed, we subsequently learn, by his habit of ingesting Barbie Doll heads. She has developed a wish list, which she divulges to Lois, an alcoholic who is carrying a barrel, heading to Niagara Falls to end her life. The list consists of 266 items including 'Learn Swedish . . . Wear a large wig . . . Drive cross-country . . . Have a baby, Wear overalls. Go parachuting'.[13] In the motel room they share Lois practices for her forthcoming plunge by sitting in the barrel with a shower cap on. The two women visit the falls, the sound of which makes communication difficult, but it is here that she encounters Barbara, a woman, judging by her accent, from Texas wearing a large wig, which Cass buys, thus ticking off one item on her list.

On board the *Maid of the Mist*, the boat that sails below the falls, Cass meets Captain Mike, with whom she forms a relationship, insisting that she is not married, 'Torrid fling' being on her to-do list. He explains that he had lost his wife when she was struck by an outsized peanut butter jar she was putting away. Back at the motel, Karla and Glen appear, having begun a career as private detectives and hired by Kip to find his wife. They are in couples therapy and formerly had run an ice cream store and groomed dogs. They wear stolen bellhop uniforms. Their sudden appearance forces Lois to try to conceal her barrel, before hiding in a closet.

The scene then switches to a sightseeing helicopter in which the pilot grows increasingly concerned at Lois's behaviour ('somebody give this lady her lithium'). They are shadowed by another helicopter with Carla and Glen on board before returning to the motel where Kip appears. Cass and the Captain, Lois and Karla, Kip and Glen then retire to separate restaurants in what is a comic tour de force. The first is a medieval restaurant requiring the wearing of medieval clothes, complete with a serving wench speaking with a cockney accent. The second is Native American, where the server is called 'Walks-with-a Tray'. Asked whether people might find it offensive and boycott it, the server replies, 'You wanna order or picket?' (43). The third is gothic themed. The waitress is dressed as a vampire, and they order Grave-Robber Nachos and the Chicken Wrap of Doom.

The play rushes towards its conclusion as they all gather together to be joined by Janie, dressed as a clown thus terrifying Kip, who has clown phobia (in case Lindsay-Abaire's world seems remote from American reality, 'fear of clowns' in fact comes eighty-fourth in Chapman University's survey of American fears, fear of zombies coming in at eighty-second).[14] She responds by stabbing him with a fake knife. Her own qualifications as a therapist, meanwhile, are dubious given that she is on parole, her sister is an alcoholic, her husband has been having sex with a meter maid while she had sniffed glue until experiencing an epiphany on the *Maid of the Mist* when she had caught a watch, dropped by Lois, inscribed 'Love Always'. When Lois produces a gun, Captain Mike disarms her, but as he is putting it in his pocket, Karla opens the door, causing him to shoot himself. He dies.

We learn that one of Janie's sisters was the very person from whom Cass had bought the wig, and that Karla, who confesses to being bisexual, had provoked the death by peanut butter. Kip picks up the gun, but the play ends with Lois and Cass lodged against a rock in the barrel on the very edge of the falls. Lois's suicidal urge has disappeared, and she celebrates their survival, pointing to the sun. 'Do you see that?' she asks. 'It came up. And you're breathing.' As the stage direction comments, 'Cass has no response. Lois has made a good point. Something changes' (69). They discuss having breakfast in Canada, even as the roar of the falls sounds and the light fades.

Henri Bergson suggested that 'farce . . . is in striking contrast to reality' but that 'the higher it rises, the more it approximates to life; in fact, there are scenes in real life so closely bordering on high-class comedy that the stage might adopt them without changing a single word' (148–9).[15] Describing his own early work, Lindsay-Abaire has said that

I view the world in a very off, skewed way. People have called it absurdist. I don't think it's so ridiculous. In my plays there are real people, real dilemmas. Yeah, they're over the top sometimes, because the characters' needs are so desperate, or their situation is so odd. That's real life to me. Life just seems ridiculous to me sometimes. I don't want to write a realistic play set on a back porch . . . not my thing. I think theatre has an obligation to be theatrical. It's not real. Don't pretend it's real. I'm not a realist. For some, the game is how real can you make it. That's silly to me. It's a play.[16]

Speaking of his own work, John Guare remarked,

Durrenmatt's *The Visit* . . . had a profound effect on me. To have a play draw you in with humor and then make you crazy and send you out mixed up! When I got to Feydeau, Strindberg, Pinter, Joe Orton and the "dis-ease" they created, I was home. Pinter's plays had the rhythms of high comedy trapped in the wrong surroundings; I identified with that. I loved the strictures of farce, besides liking the sound of audiences laughing . . . I have always liked plays to be funny and early on stumbled upon the truth that farce is tragedy speeded up . . . The intensity puts it on the edge.[17]

It is a statement with which Lindsay-Abaire would surely agree, even the observation that farce can be tragedy speeded up. Certainly the markers of tragedy are there in characters who are simultaneously the victims of fate and of their own misdirections, but the very pace leaves profundity trailing in the wake.

Ben Brantley, in the *New York Times*, described the play as 'exceedingly whimsical', granting Lindsay-Abaire the talent for finding 'the acid in sugar and spice', and crediting him for 'deftly bizarre jokes . . . outlandish symbols' and a 'double-edged tone of voice' while lamenting that the characters 'rarely cohere into a three-dimensional landscape',[18] on the face of it a curious response to a play in which Barbie dolls have an unlikely fate and a large jar of peanut butter becomes the agent for a journey into the afterlife. At the same time Lindsay-Abaire's own description of his characters as 'over the top sometimes' hardly does justice to a play whose pleasure lies precisely in the degree to which he presses plot, character and language to their limits, satirical set pieces embedded in a celebration of contingency.

Lindsay-Abaire has explained that the idea for his next play, *Kimberly Akimbo*, first produced by the South Coast Repertory in Costa Mesa in 2001, came to him when he asked a friend how his niece was and he replied, '"Oh, she's incredible. She's eight months going on 80. She's just this wise, tiny little woman trapped in a baby's body." Being the very literal-minded person I am, I immediately pictured this tiny old woman trapped in a baby's body. And that, in turn, reminded me of a documentary I had seen as a child about this disease, progeria, which is a very sad disease that afflicts kids. They look like old people.' It was not the condition itself which interested him: 'I knew I wasn't going to fictionalize it because it's a dark sort of subject and I didn't want to write a disease-of-the-week story.' What did occur to him was 'What a great role – for an older actress to play a kid or a teenager.' As was his habit, he began the play not knowing a great deal more about what would happen than that. What he did know was that 'I wanted to have a bunch of sort of upside-down roles in the play, where adults acted like kids and the kids acted like adults . . . There are all sorts of things that are askew in the play.'[19]

In F. Scott Fitzgerald's 'The Curious Case of Benjamin Button', a story supposedly inspired by Mark Twain's observation that it is a pity the best part of life comes at the beginning and the worst at the end, a man grows steadily younger. In *Kimberly Akimbo*, it is the sixteenth birthday of the central character, Kimberly, the average age of death for someone suffering from her condition, which involves ageing at four-and-a-half times normal speed. It is a birthday forgotten by both of her parents, whose own feuds and self-absorption leave little room for sentiment.

Nor is she the only one afflicted. Her pregnant mother's hands are bandaged because of trouble with her carpal tunnel, which means that her alcoholic father has to wipe her bottom for her when not staggering in drunk in the early hours. She had formerly worked for sixteen years pumping cream into 'Ding-Dong knockoffs' and believes, on the basis of no evidence, that she has cancer and diabetes. Oblivious to her daughter's fate, she believes she is going to die even as she accuses Kimberly of being 'self-involved'.

Her husband, Buddy, works in a service station. Her sister, Debra, is a bag lady fresh out of jail but already planning a criminal enterprise that will involve her niece. She is implicated in the death of a former neighbour, who it turns out was Kimberly's real father, hence the family's swift exchange of one nowhere-in-particular, a town called Secaucus, for another nowhere in particular called Bogota – as it happens both real places and doubtless blameless. Since the first in reality has a population of 14,000 and the second of 8,000, this has not, as Buddy observes, turned out to be 'the someplace I had in mind' (43). The family lives on take-out food, the mother incapable of cooking and the father too drunk to do so. A jar into which they have to pitch a nickel every time they swear gradually fills in the course of the play, eventually requiring a second. When Kimberly suffers a heart attack and her hair turns white, her mother steps outside the hospital for a smoke and falls off the loading bay, breaking her leg.

This is not a world in which anyone evidences empathy for others. Thus Jeff, a sixteen-year-old boy on Ritalin, accomplished at anagrams if little else, questions Kimberly on her condition for his high school project: 'So your disease is like progeria without the dwarfism, the beaked nose and the receded chin' (15). Meanwhile, his father, we learn, works the tollbooth on the turnpike while his brother, having been in a juvenile detention centre, is now in rehab on methadone. Kimberly, it seems, is not the only damaged character in a play in which there is no moral code to break and language barely connects. Sex does not worry the ostensible sixteen-year-old because she has already passed menopause as her life picks up speed towards an inevitable and fast-approaching end. The play concludes as Kimberly and Jeff, clutching the proceeds of a bank scam directed by Debra, drive through a wildlife park, he still sixteen, she now old, the radio playing 'swing music as the lights slowly fade on the giddy teens' (69), except that Kimberly is no longer a giddy teen and the slowly fading light is expressive of a life ticking down towards its end.

In these early plays, pain exists, but there is no sense that suffering is real. People die but usually in bizarre circumstances, disasters accumulating rather as they do in the *Scary Movie* franchise. Illness becomes material for laughs, inadequacy inviting collusive enjoyment. For Bergson, comedy is born out of a growing callousness towards social life. Characters resist empathy because they exist to serve the humour even as, for Freud, the joke hints at what is repressed or suppressed, offering licensed anarchy. With Lindsay-Abaire's next play, however, that revelling in the unlicensed was about to end. He had long distanced himself from anything resembling naturalism, except mocking its determinisms, but with *Rabbit Hole* (2006), that would change, and that change had something to do with his personal circumstances as the father of a young boy of four.

Having long before been advised by Marsha Norman to write about what frightened him most, he found himself being told stories of young children dying suddenly and unexpectedly. Where once that might have provided material for farce, now it struck home, and that coincided with his desire to show that he was fully capable of writing plays in a different mode – in doing so explaining that he thereby discovered different muscles. *Rabbit Hole* may have been born partly out of a desire to show that he could write the kind of play against which he had previously set his face, but clearly his personal investment in the subject made this a minor concern. The dark farceur now stepped aside, and what followed was a play of great subtlety in which the simplest of gestures and sudden silences are freighted with meaning. The pace slowed.

The play opens with a scene that could have been an echo of one of the best known of naturalistic dramas as a woman is seen ironing clothes, John Osborne's *Look Back in Anger*. In both cases, it is that very domesticity that conceals latent passions. Indeed for the woman at the heart of *Rabbit Hole*, even cooking is not just a skill but an evasion. If those early plays bypassed feeling now it is tempting to think that he would have agreed with Osborne's observation, 'I want to make people feel'.[20]

The play is set in what seems a comfortable Westchester middle-class milieu. Although it begins in a kitchen, this is not the world of kitchen-sink drama. Everything here is upmarket. On offer are paillard, crème caramel, a torte or home-prepared cake, which ought to carry overtones of comfort but do not. A couple spend an evening drinking wine, except that there is an edge that quickly becomes apparent. The most significant event has already taken place many months earlier, the death of a child. The play opens with Becca, who previously worked for Sotheby's, ironing and folding clothes preparatory to their being given away. What we only subsequently discover is that they are her dead son's clothes and that this gesture is itself compacted with grief, not quite a letting go but perhaps an acknowledgement, although even that will be shaped into an accusation as she is charged by her husband with removing all evidence of their child to dull the pain they mutually feel.

When her sister Izzy announces that she is pregnant, it is a twist of the knife. A stage direction indicates, 'Silence. Becca looks at the stacks of folded kids clothes'.[21] Dialogue is redundant. There is another silence as friends fail to call, not knowing how to address the fact of their loss. They are isolated from others but increasingly from one another. When her husband, Howie, later says of Izzy's pregnancy that the baby might get her back on track, that it 'can wake a person up. It did us' (28), this hints both at something in their past that had already divided them even as it says something about their present, their own child no longer being there to awaken whatever it was that was asleep. Howie has been off work, and she has not returned to hers in eight months. In that time, they have not had sex and have been in group therapy. Becca now suggests that they should move because 'He's everywhere . . . Everywhere I look, I still see Danny' (46). He is in the toys left behind, the smudged fingerprints on the door jams. Howie's suggestion that they should try for another child merely intensifies her sense of the one who is not there, the absence always present. Meanwhile, the pet featured on a family video has been handed over to her mother – one more reminder of what cannot be faced.

If Howie seems less vulnerable, when his wife goes to bed, carrying one of Danny's toys, he puts a video of their child on and watches, an action, we are told in a stage direction, he has repeated many times already. Unseen by him, Becca appears at the top of the stairs as they separately mourn. Such is their state that anything can take them back to the place they would evade. A family discussion of the fate of the Kennedys leads to her mother, Nat, hardly the most sensitive person, expressing her sympathy for Rose Kennedy who had lost her own sons. The stage direction indicates a pause before Becca offers cake in an attempt to deflect her, although this does not prevent Nat from recalling Onassis, whose son had died in a plane crash. Becca offers cake once again.

There is a reason, though, for Nat's remarks, as she goes on to observe that Onassis, failing to find any reason for his loss, had died a few years later because 'he never came to terms with it' (68), an implicit rebuke aimed at her daughter. When she objects that she was 'just talking', Becca insists, 'You never *just talk*. It sounds like you're just talking but it's always so much more.' The same could be said of Lindsay-Abaire's play, in which everything, no matter how apparently oblique, bears on the central absence at its heart. Urging her daughter to undertake therapy Nat insists, 'I always thought talk was healthy' (71), having just proved the opposite. For her part, Becca resists attending a group of people who have also lost children because looking for meaning, they find it in God's will. The fact is that, for her, there is no reason, no plan, no coherence, no comforting anodyne. She has lost a child and is being asked to find a way to move on when, for her, there is no convenient passage through or out. Danny, it transpires, was killed chasing his dog – the dog in the video – into the street while her brother, whose death Nat asks her to compare him with, 'was a thirty-year-old *heroin* addict who *hung* himself', although, as Nat says, 'he was still my son' (75).

When the tape of Danny gets accidentally erased, Howie accuses Becca of trying to remove all evidence of their son, getting rid of his clothes, sending his dog away, packing up his paintings, 'erasing' him – and erasure becomes a central image and focus in the play – while his bedroom remains as it always was. Howie is reduced to tears. They are pulled together by their mutual feelings of guilt but pushed apart by their different responses to loss. Their son has gone, a fact that might have united them in grief but seems to separate them. Why did their son die? Because Izzy telephoned to complain about her mother, leading Becca to run to answer the phone, leading Danny free to run through a gate, which his father had failed to secure, in pursuit of a dog they need not have bought. There is guilt enough to go around in a seemingly unbroken logical chain. There are no accidents without an 'if only'. But there is someone else who feels guilt, or at least some sense of responsibility: seventeen-year-old Jason, who drove the car that killed Danny, driving, he confesses, perhaps a little too fast. Howie, who works in risk management, learns that in some way risks can never finally be managed. Contingency can always trump rational planning, as it can emotional bonds.

Two months on and the house is on sale, although still with Danny's room kept as a shrine or perhaps as a way of putting off the buyers Howie does not want. Becca, who claims to have 'had a bunch of good days in a row' (108), still finds that supermarket shelves remind her in some way of Danny, a supermarket where she has slapped a woman for ignoring her own son. She is clearly still struggling to keep things together. Later, Becca and Nat sort through Danny's room, deciding what to keep and what to abandon even as the memories attached to them are not so easily abandoned.

Izzy and Nat could almost have come out of his earlier work, given as they are to alcohol-fuelled insensitivity. Izzy punches a woman in a bar. Nat blunders through conversations, seemingly oblivious of their effect, although as the play progresses so their own vulnerabilities are exposed. Nat's constant references to her own son are so much a part of her that they can seem no more than a conversational gambit, except that she, too, has tears to shed emerging suddenly from the figure of a vaguely overbearing, interfering person, as someone harrowed by her own sense of loss. When Becca asks her whether the pain ever goes away, there is a beat before, in a deeply affecting response, she says,

No. I don't think it does. Not for me it hasn't. And that's goin' on eleven years . . . It changes though . . . The weight of it . . . At some point it becomes bearable. It turns into something you can crawl out from under. And carry around – like a brick in your pocket. And you forget it every once in a while, but then you reach in for whatever reason and there it is: "Oh right. *That*." Which can be awful. But not all the time . . . it's what you have instead of your son, so you don't wanna let go of it either. So you carry it around. And it doesn't go away, which is . . . Fine . . . actually.

(129–30)

Her speech is followed by a silence in which mother and daughter come together before continuing to clear the room.

There is a subtlety to this transition that makes it the more moving. Contempt, suspicion, anger, the whole panoply of feelings that have come between them, vanish in a sudden mutuality. Becca is transitioning along the same line as her mother in a way that Howie is perhaps not. There is the guilt that springs from a feeling of responsibility failed, and there is the guilt that comes from letting go. Becca's mother has travelled that path before her and is offering not only her own experience but a kind of absolution. Surviving is not a legitimate source of guilt; neither is living itself.

Izzy, who first appears as wild, with dubious relationships, emerges as more sensitive and supportive than she had at first seemed, while Jason, who comes from a single-parent family and is the immediate agent of Danny's death, visits Becca, wishing to clear his conscience even as he is oblivious to the effect of his account of his high school prom, an occasion Becca's own son has been denied. He has dedicated a science fiction story to Danny, a story about a boy who goes in search of his father through rabbit holes into alternative universes. To Becca it seems to be a reflection of Jason's search for his own dead father, an echo of Orpheus's failed search for Eurydice, wishing to retrieve him from death. Jason, though, offers a more optimistic version, believing that in alterative universes things can turn out differently. So this, Becca says, 'is just the sad version of us', and 'somewhere out there I'm having a good time' (144–5).

The play ends back in the kitchen and on a note of reconciliation. Izzy has been inducted into baking, Howie has abandoned group therapy and he and Becca have been invited by a family that has kept them at arm's length, although largely because Howie has called them to open the way. Their daughter has just turned four, as Danny's birthday approaches, and they discuss a possible present, understanding and accepting the implications of that. The house will now probably not be sold. Something has changed. They have not come out the other side, but they have begun to understand that a new stage has started. At the very end they come together, rather as George and Martha did at the end of *Who's Afraid of Virginia Woolf?*, scared but 'holding one another's hands, tight', as the lights fade.

If restraint had hardly been a mark of Lindsay-Abaire's early plays, it is certainly a virtue in *Rabbit Hole*. These are characters struggling to maintain control, to avoid their grief making its way into language. It is not that they are in denial but that they know that a wrong word, a gesture, an object, could send them spinning into a reflexive despair. In the film version, Lindsay-Abaire would open up the action, following characters beyond the family home, something Edward Albee allowed to happen in the film version of *Virginia Woolf*. The virtue of the stage version, in both cases, is that there is no escape – no air can enter. As in *Long Day's Journey into Night*, they have to recycle their sense of lost purpose within the constraints of what should have been a place of safety. There is, indeed, that same rhythm of comfort and accusation, love and distrust, that same desire to transcend past experience while seemingly tied to it. This is a family thrust apart and held together by the same forces. It is a play in essence about a physical absence that translates into an emotional one. What is invisible to others is manifest to them. Everything circles around their son who is what is not there, except that he remains a constant presence.

There are echoes of their plight in the Israeli novelist David Grossman's *Falling Out of Time*, except that in his case the dead son was real, killed in Lebanon. Here is that same sense of an absence that divides and brings together. The son's death, we are told, 'bore a hole in me'; he and his wife 'couldn't bear it any longer . . . giving his dog to a boy on the street'.[22] For him, too, everything in his son's room is a reminder, life a tearing off of bandages until at last the moment comes when he can finally say:

'The boy is dead.'
I understand, almost,
The meaning of the sounds:
The boy is dead. I know.
Yes, I admit it: he is dead.
But his death – it swells,
Abates,
Fulminates.
Unquiet,
Unquiet
Is his death.
So unquiet.

(106–7)

Lindsay-Abaire's achievement is that he imagines himself into the situation that Grossman inhabited from within. It is not that there is no spiritual analgesic on offer. Various strategies are tried out beyond the merely anodyne. Becca eventually packs away her son's toys as she has tried to pack away different aspects of her own life, but there is no box for the loss that threatens to disable her. There is even a hint that Howie may have turned his affections elsewhere, but once again it is the subtlety, the restraint around what is no more than a hint, that adds to its effectiveness.

This is a play of pauses into which a disturbing meaning threatens to pour, only to be ended by a momentary change of direction, an attempt to restore a seemingly untroubled normality. Lindsay-Abaire annotates his text with the word 'beat' as an indicator of a moment in which his characters refuse to follow the logic of a conversation, register the implications of what is spoken. There is a current of desperation flowing that breaks surface from time to time, the more dangerous because it contrasts with the placidity of daily life.

If irony is the conscious use of understatement, here emotional understatement serves to underscore the fact that nothing is commensurate with a loss that blots out all sense of coherence. The irony is potentially cosmic as they debate the extent to which any sense of purpose can be derived from the merely contingent, whether chance has a hidden agency, whether there is a master story into which their own story of disaster could be said to fit. There are tears in the play but Lindsay-Abaire warns against shedding them except as he directs. It is true that the very situation has an emotional charge, but he was anxious to avoid sentimentality, anxious, too, to draw attention to the humour that co-exists with pain. As he has said, 'Yes, *Rabbit Hole* is a play about a bereaved family, but that does not mean they go through the day glazed-over, on the verge of tears, morose and inconsolable. That would be a torturous and very uninteresting play to sit through. The characters are, instead, highly functional, unsentimental, spirited and, often, funny people who are trying to maneuver their way through their grief and around each other as best they can . . . It's a sad play. Don't make it any sadder than it needs to be.'[23]

Sentimentality is equally what the characters struggle to avoid for fear that they will lose themselves as well as their child. At the same time, not to give way can seem a betrayal.

It is a delicate balancing act. Peter Nichols had reached for the same strategy in his 1967 play *A Day in the Death of Joe Egg*, concerned not with the death of a child but with the raising of a girl with cerebral palsy and the strains that caused on a marriage. This, too, has its comic moments. A revival opened on Broadway in 2003. At the same time, it is difficult for audiences of *Rabbit Hole* to mobilise a defence against a sense of desolation, the more acute for being registered through silences, aborted conversations, the flickering images on a television screen, the holding of hands by two people who had previously denied themselves such a consolation.

It is tempting to recall another play in which loss is registered with that same sense of numb bewilderment. It is King Lear who laments, 'Why should a dog, a horse, a rat, have life, / And thou no breath at all? Thou'lt come no more, / Never, never, never, never!' while Albany acknowledges what Becca and Howie, in their different ways, accept 'The weight of this sad time we must obey; / Speak what we feel, not what we ought to say.'

The *New York Times* review by Ben Brantley reported copious weeping among the audience even as, for the most part, it praised both production and play for its honesty, accuracy and humour, while oddly adding, 'it never rises to greatness' because it deployed 'clichés, involving sibling jealousy, conjugal estrangement, the rivalry of grief and the urge to blame'.[24] It is hard to see how the commonalities of human experience can be said to be clichéd, or even their representation on the stage. This is, and always has been, the stuff of drama, but that is because it is equally the stuff of life, hence the connection audiences felt to a play that embodies them. It went on to win the Pulitzer Prize for drama in 2007, one of whose judges, ironically, was Ben Brantley.

There is another absent child in Lindsay-Abaire's next play, *Good People* (2011), or if not quite absent, then unseen. In fact there are two, one the child of poverty, the other of wealth. It was a play that took him back to his South Boston origins. He had himself escaped from Southie, which he describes as a working-class, salt-of-the-earth place, and this is a play about those who did and those who did not. As he has said, 'I was this poor kid from Southie and a lot of the feelings I had growing up – and things that I've wrestled with since – were funnelled into the play . . . Southie is a neighbourhood rich in characters and stories and humor . . . Humor was a coping mechanism, and that – and storytelling – was in my blood and sinew.'[25] It was an area rich in humour but not in much else, and he was conscious of those who had not had his advantages.

He was drawn to set his play there, he explained, in part because the economy had taken a downturn, and it was those at the blunt end of society who tended to suffer; and because he was increasingly struck by his own luck in escaping what others still had to wrestle with. The scholarship he had won had been a piece of luck, coming up only once every six years so that a shift of birth date might have led to a different path. He had worked hard and felt justified yet was aware that what he now took for granted had once seemed out of his reach. As he explained,

I kept hearing about English playwrights who were writing about class, and people kept asking why American playwrights don't. But then I went back to Southie and thought, "If I write about the old neighborhood, the subject of class will inevitably bubble to the surface because it's so present to the community." Also, the economy is in a really crappy place right now, and I thought if I was ever going to write about class, this was the time to do it. What's most interesting to me is that, before I wrote the play I thought, "Why would you do this? It's going to be irrelevant in three years." But the play has actually become *more* relevant and hums in a way that it didn't when it was on Broadway two years ago.[26]

The questions he had asked himself, and did again in this play, are: 'Have we stepped on people along the way to get where we are? And what do we owe a neighborhood? Yes, people can succeed on their own because of hard work but a lot has to do with luck, too . . . The difference between me and one of the characters in the play is I recognised that luck played a major part in my success, and I recognize that every day . . . One little hiccup and things could have ended up much differently. One character in the play doesn't feel that way, and feels he earned every single bit of success, but I don't feel that way.'[27]

In that sense, there is an echo of *The Price* in which Arthur Miller had explored the price of success and failure and the justifications advanced for both.

Good People is a play he felt required a realistic treatment, not least because he had learned his capacity for writing such with *Rabbit Hole*. Beyond that, he was writing about people he had known, acknowledging that the central figure of Margaret, along with her friends Jean and Dottie, shared characteristics with his mother, a fact confirmed when she saw it.

Good People opens in an alley behind a Dollar Store in South Boston, a store that, according to one of the characters, has 'nothing but shit in it'.[28] There is a dumpster and a rusty chair. Margaret, a woman of 'about fifty,' is fired from her dead-end job by her manager, Stevie, a man in his late twenties who himself comes from a poor background, his father having served time in prison, his mother stealing from food stores when he was young. In a desperate attempt to hold on to her job she tells him a story of his mother's attempt to steal a frozen turkey, hoping to invoke a bond between them, staving off what she knows is coming. She is fired nonetheless because of constantly arriving late, although this is a consequence of having a disabled daughter whose minder, Dottie (also Margaret's landlord) fails to arrive in time to look after her. Behind on her rent, she is a danger of losing more than her job – jobs in Southie anyway being hard to find unless, like an ex-soldier noted, you have had half your face blown away in Iraq.

Dottie, like Lindsay-Abaire's own mother, earns money on the side by making cheap toy rabbits, while the highlight for her, and a friend, Jean, again as for the playwright's mother, is a night of bingo. This is a world in which people hang on to the hope that they will win even as a former friend is a wino who sleeps in the street and dies. Chance, however, seems to present a solution. Margaret had a boyfriend for a brief period in high school, and he returns as a doctor; Jean suggests that he might be the source of a job – or if not that Margaret should claim her disabled daughter was actually his. 'You have to be a selfish prick to get anywhere' (19), she explains.

The idea of any doctor in Southie seems unlikely enough to Margaret. When one is invoked, indeed, she turns out to have been a vet's assistant, whose job is to hold dogs down when they are put to sleep. Desperate as she is, though, Margaret goes to see him. To her, he is a desperate gamble. To him, she is an intrusion. They encounter one another across a gulf both social and linguistic. When she asks what kind of a doctor he is, he replies, 'a reproductive endocrinologist', to which she replies, 'I don't know what you just said . . . Was that even English?' (29). She accuses him of being 'lace-curtain Irish' like the Kennedys. To her, he is still Mikey Dee from the projects even though he has exchanged that world for Chestnut Hill and an expensive house. Old bonds have been broken, though he gives to a local charity – the very charity, incidentally, that won the playwright's free pass out of Southie. He has moved on in a different sense having married a woman nearly twenty years younger than himself and black, a teacher from Boston University.

Margaret goads him into inviting her to his birthday party, thinking that one of his friends might have a job to offer. When he calls to cancel on the grounds that his daughter is sick, she takes it for a brush-off and turns up anyway, only to discover that their child is indeed sick, although evidently not sufficiently to justify the cancellation. Her feeling on entering the house is one Lindsay-Abaire recognised from his own past when he travelled to his private school: 'past the winos and the projects, and took a train out to the suburbs, and sat in classes in these beautiful ivy-covered buildings . . . listening to these other kids discussing their vacations in the Bahamas. And then I'd take the train back every night, and walk past the projects and the winos, and do it all again the next day. So that thing that Margaret feels when she walks into Mike's house in the second act of *Good People*? I know that feeling REALLY well.'[29]

What follows is scarcely a relaxed evening. Mike is anxious for her to leave, his wife, Kate, equally concerned to be hospitable. The house is plainly expensive. They are seemingly wealthy and happy but are in therapy and as the evening develops, so the cracks begin to open up. When Margaret offers a counter-narrative to his sentimental recollections of his time in Southie, explaining that he had once beaten a black boy severely and had asked her not to mention the fact that they had once had a relationship, this plainly strikes a chord with Kate: 'Are we actually having this conversation again? . . . And you wonder why I don't wanna stop seeing the counsellor' (93). Finally, and increasingly desperate, Margaret tells Mike that he is her daughter's father, a story, though, which quickly falls apart. Not only does her attempt at blackmail collapse, but so, too, does the story she has told herself, that she had once been loved and that their relationship had ever offered a chance to escape.

The play ends as Margaret and her friends are once again playing bingo, hoping that something will come up. When it does, it takes the form of a stack of bills with a note attached saying, 'Margaret's rent' (106). The money, however, comes not from Chestnut Hill but the man who had fired her, charity coming from Southie. The play concludes as a priest intones not the liturgy but bingo numbers.

While this is a work in which people are divided by class, it is not a play about class in the sense of examining why it exists and persists, what its mechanisms are, even as on the one side are those struggling to pay the rent, aware of the trap in which they are caught, while on the other are those seemingly insulated by education and money. The gulf is real enough, but there are other spaces in the lives of these characters. In Lindsay-Abaire's Southie, men tend to drift away from their women, while in Chestnut Hill, they stay in hope that therapy will address failed relationships. Something is wrong between men and women, and in both cases a child is what shapes decisions.

It is in part a play about the strategies people use to survive, the stories they tell themselves and others, the lies with which they protect themselves. It is about guilt and responsibility, a past that is never quite abandoned, sentimentalities dissolved by experience, hope clung to in the face of evidence. Margaret and Kate are both strong women living with compromise, subsisting on the possibility of change, even as the latter has very little understanding of the person who has just stepped into her world, apologising for only being able to pay $15 an hour for babysitting when this is nearly double what this Southie woman was earning as a cashier. Lactose intolerance, clearly a fashionable concern in Chestnut Hill, has yet to reach South Boston, where they have more serious intolerances to deal with.

Mike, seemingly so sure of his own accomplishments, is aware on some level that he could have moved in a different direction. He made it. Margaret did not, chance playing a central role, though he wishes to reject his own lack of agency. At one moment, she explains the series of incidents that accounts in part for her difficulty in getting work. She was hungry but lacking time or money ate peanut brittle. As a result she broke her tooth but could not afford a dentist, thereafter developing an abscess. Now she had to choose between seeking medical help or keeping up the payments on her car. As a result she lost her car, which in turn meant that she had difficulty in travelling to work while paying someone to look after her mentally damaged daughter. As a result she lost her job. When, then, did she have a real choice?

At one stage Kate invokes Upton Sinclair, and there is a sense in which Margaret and her friends are regarded as disposable units in an economy they do not understand and which has no place for them except at the margin, but this is not where the play lives and breathes. There is a resilience that resists irony, a humour never simply seen as a working-class resource. They are aware of the forces that constrain them but refuse to accept them as definitional. There is certainly no faith in an American dream that suggests that everyone has an equal chance. Getting by is a central preoccupation, and getting by requires a certain mutuality. All the time, though, a young woman lies unseen doing little more than survive while her mother does whatever is necessary to sustain her. Miles away, another girl lies in bed while her parents work out how and on what terms they can stay together. There is a level on which they share a common fate no matter the radical differences of their circumstances.

What constitutes good people when there are those who lie, betray, abandon? Margaret, after all, is vindictive, devious, aggressive. Dottie is self-concerned, Jean immoral when she suggests blackmail. Mike is inclined to give himself too much credit for his rise while apparently being ready to betray his wife. Kate's tolerance of him is hardly a virtue, her understanding of Margaret less than complete. Stevie alone offers help. Good people, however, are not those who show familiar virtues. They are those whose loyalties are clear, who work with what they have, endeavour to survive without a cost to others.

With a certain inevitability, it did not appeal to Terry Teachout in the *Wall Street Journal*, who rejected what he took to be its sociological narrative, its promotion of the idea that success is a product of pure luck rather than hard work. It fared better with Ben Brantley in the *New York Times* who regarded it as a fine new play, one of the treats of the season, while *Slant Magazine* found Lindsay-Abaire as sensitive a modern playwright as could be heard and *Variety* predicted a potential hit.

If there is a thread that runs through all his work, it is an awareness of the human comedy. In fact, in 1999 he had written another play, *How We Talk in South Boston*, an outrageous comedy presented almost entirely in the Boston accent with speeches written out phonetically along with a glossary. The play features a man who enters with his arm stuck in a car door whose window he had been trying to fix. Norman is an Archie Bunker figure, profoundly prejudiced and shocked to learn that his son is gay and has been living in the basement with his Asian lover, Ping, for three months, and that his daughter is marrying an African-American man who incidentally speaks in standard English and finds his new putative father-in-law's language all but impenetrable. Norman spits in his face and explains that there is 'No tollarinse in dis house. Dis is Southie! We doan tolerate nobidy heah! Not da niggas, not da japs, not da chinks oah da spics, oah da fags, nobidy! Day all wanna take us over Dah fohced bussin was da first step.'[30] When he has a heart attack he refuses to allow Ping to treat him, demanding 'an American doctor' and not to be taken to what he characterises as 'dat nigga hospital in Roxbury!' (64). On his death, his wife declares that he had not in fact been father to his children, introducing Frankie Grey Hawk, in full Native American regalia, who turns out to be a professor of linguistics at Northeastern.

As is apparent, at times Lindsay-Abaire has a fondness for the gross. In *Baby Food*, inappropriate as it would seem in a 2004 production in aid of Working Playground Inc, a not-for-profit organisation bringing the arts into public schools, a man has died because of inserting an air pump up his rectum. 'I wouldn't let a baby within ten feet of that pervert', observes a somewhat drunk woman, 'He'd probably try to shove it up his ass'.[31] Guests invited to become god parents to a baby turn out to be on the verge of divorce while they are served lasagne made in part from its placenta, a fact that provokes immediate vomiting as evidence of attempts to serve curry, similarly laced with afterbirth, to other prospective godparents is to be seen on the floor. The play ends as the couple contemplate other possible godparents to look after the spiritual welfare of their child, the man in question now being out of rehab. Happily, they still have the umbilical cord to make kebabs.

In *Crazy Eights*, in aid of the same non-profit as *Baby Food*, a woman is stalked by a man who has been her probation officer and who climbs up the fire escape to cook her a meal. He demands that she provide a urine specimen only for her to throw it in his face. In *That Other Person* (2005), he identifies the characters as 'sweet, beautiful, thin, and can't swim; a man with regrets in search of hope; an occasionally mean woman who never stands up; a guy in every sense of the word; a generally good-natured lad who has been pushed too far tonight' (37). We are seemingly in the world of farce except that in some ways, it anticipates *Good People:* after many years, a woman accuses a man of having fathered her now-troublesome child as a result of a one-night stand, refusing to confront him at the time because she did not want to spoil his chances as he went off to university. That he could move from this play to *Good People* says something for his capacity to shift gears from farce to a sensitive engagement with those for whom abandonment is not a plot device and an absent child is a genuine constraint as well as an obligation. The humour does not disappear; it changes its tone and function.

In 2015, his next play, *Ripcord*, a comedy, opened at the Manhattan Theater Club. Set in what is described as a 'Senior Living Facility' in suburban New Jersey, it features two women, Abby Binder and Marilyn Dunne, both in their seventies or eighties. They are an odd couple, by no means winding down intellectually, their chief pain and pleasure lying in their rivalry. What is at stake is the room over which Abby, cynical, apparently self-centred, wishes to claim proprietary rights. She insists that Marilyn, who is described as 'warm and pleasant', should move into a room vacated by a 'fat woman on the first floor' who has died or that if she must share, it should be with a woman who has lost her voice box. What follows is a bet. If Abby can make Marilyn angry, the latter will leave the room; if Marilyn can frighten Abby, she will lay claim to the better side of the room with its bed by the window. What follows is an ever more inventive contest.

Abby puts Marilyn's telephone number on line, with an announcement that she is happy to give away a list of desirable goods. The result is a series of calls that make Marilyn unplug her phone. Abby then leads Marilyn to believe that her family will be making a visit, so that she looks forward to seeing them, only to be disappointed – except that Marilyn is one step ahead of her. For her part, Marilyn drugs Abby and forces her to sky dive, later persuading her son to stage a mugging before faking her own suicide; Marilyn finally wins when Abby is genuinely frightened as she is told that she has died of a heart condition.

As their lives are winding down they are invigorated by their competition, grudgingly admiring each another's ploys. There comes a moment when they confess that they had each long since lost the contest but concealed the fact, and this is not the only truth that emerges. Abby, it turns out, is in the facility because her money has gone to her drug-addicted son, who, unbeknownst to her, at Marilyn's initiative, now visits her with a picture of his new baby. Although Abby turns him away, reconciliation seems possible not least because Marilyn insists 'You can't give up on people. Once you do it's all over.'[32] Abby has lost her sense of taste but under Marilyn's direction seems to recover it, as she has also recovered something more significant. Having, as Marilyn says, 'chased off everyone else who dared walk in here' (50), including the staff, she has stepped out of the isolation she thought necessary to who she was. Her cynicism is how she kept herself together in the face of her disappointments. They now declare the contest a draw, although not without a final stage direction by Lindsay-Abaire, which sees Marilyn looking at the bed by the window, perhaps not entirely having given up on the contest after all.

There are elements of his early plays in *Ripcord*. The scene in an aircraft has echoes of the helicopter in *Wonder of the World*. There are farcical set pieces including one in *Beelzebub's Den*, in which an actor dressed as a zombie seemingly electrocutes a prisoner for the entertainment of guests. But, beneath the playfulness, it is a work in which the characters are doing more than what George, in *Who's Afraid of Virginia Woolf?*, calls walking what's left of their wits. Abby is in need of the company she shuns. Her son needs the mother he has betrayed. Marilyn may be the redemptive figure, but there is a sense in which her mobilising of her family as part of her plots underlines the fact that, here she is, no longer with them but in a senior living facility for those who will eventually share the fate of the fat woman who has died, freeing up a bed.

Lindsay-Abaire can draw with a broad brush and with fine brushstrokes. His humour can be touched by vaudeville. He can revel in the absurd but equally register what may lie beneath that humour, which is frequently a sense of disappointment, regret, an awareness of something lost along the way.

What the Scottish novelist Ali Smith said of the novel could equally be said of Lindsay-Abaire and his plays: 'You never know what you're going to end up with when you sit down to write something. At the end, if it holds, it can do this multifarious thing – which is to open things rather than close them, to make them bigger rather than smaller, to cross those divides which we live every day of our lives. Kafka was right: we have to break whatever is frozen inside us. That's what books are for.'[33]

Notes

1 Charles Haugland, 'An Interview with David Lindsay-Abaire', Huntington Theatre Company'. www.huntingtontheatre.org/mobile/Articles/?depth=1&srcid=2564
2 Evan Hughes, 'Truthful, Honest – but Funny', *Milton Magazine* (Winter 2003), p. 17.
3 Robin Pogrebin, 'Theatre; A Playwright Who Casts His Muse', *New York Times*, 2 February 2003. www.nytimes.com/2003/02/02/theater/theater-a-playwright-who-casts-his-muse.html?pagewanted=all
4 C. W. E. Bigsby, *Joe Orton* (London, 1982), p. 17.
5 Tina Howe, *Coastal Disturbances: Four Plays by Tina Howe* (New York, 1989), n.p.
6 Philip C. Kolin and Colby H. Kullman, *Speaking on Stage: Interviews with Contemporary American Playwrights* (Tuscaloosa, 1996), p. 273.
7 Celia Wren, 'Lost in the Funhouse: An Interview with the Playwright', *American Theatre*, July/August 2000. www.tcg.org/publications/at/playindex/?fuddy
8 Ibid.
9 David Lindsay-Abaire, *Fuddy Meers* (New York, 2001), p. 17.
10 Sandra Hosking, 'Interview: Playwright David Lindsay-Abaire', *Stageways*, 25 January 2014. https://stageways.wordpress.com/2014/01/25/interview-playwright-david-lindsay-abaire/
11 Celia Wren, '1st Stage's "Fuddy Meers": Long on Laughs, Short on Meaning', *Washington Post*, 19 February 2011. www.washingtonpost.com/wp-dyn/content/article/2011/02/18/AR2011021806807.html
12 E mail to the author from David Lindsay-Abaire, 17 July 2017.
13 David Lindsay-Abaire, *Wonder of the World* (New York, 2003), p. 10.
14 America's Top Fears 2015. https://blogs.chapman.edu/wilkinson/2015/10/13/americas-top-fears-2015
15 Henri Bergson, *Laughter* (Baltimore, 1956), pp. 148–9.
16 Evan Hughes, 'Truthful, Honest – but Funny'.
17 Anne Cattaneo, 'John Guare: The Art of the Theatre IX', Paris Review, 125 (Winter 1992), p. 85.
18 Ben Brantley, 'Setting Forth, the Wind in Her Sails', *New York Times*, 2 November 2001. www.nytimes.com/2001/11/02/arts/theater/02WOND.html
19 Robin Pogrebin, 'Theatre; A Playwright Who Casts His Muse'.
20 T. Masschler, ed., 'They Call It Cricket', in *Declaration* (London, 1957), p. 65.
21 David Lindsay-Abaire, *Rabbit Hole* (New York, 2006), p. 23.
22 David Grossman, *Falling Out of Time* (London, 2014), pp.103, 136.

23 Ibid, p. 159.
24 Ben Brantley, 'Mourning a Child in a Silence That's Unbearably Loud', *New York Times*, 3 February 2006. www.nytimes.com/2006/02/03/theater/reviews/mourning-a-child-in-a-silence-thats-unbearably-loud.html
25 Frank Rizzo, 'Theater Works Explores the Morals of "Good People"', *Hartford Courant*, 7 August 2016. www.courant.com/entertainment/arts-theater/hc-good-people-0531–20150531-story.html
26 Charles Haugland, 'An Interview with David Lindsay-Abaire'.
27 Frank Rizzo, 'Theater Works Explores the Morals of "Good People"'.
28 David Lindsay-Abaire, *Good People* (London, 2014), p. 15.
29 'An Exclusive Interview with "Good People's" Pulitzer Prize Winning Playwright, David Lindsay-Abaire', *Walnut Street Theatre*, 7 March 2013. www.facebook.com/notes/walnut-street-theatre/an-exclusive-interview-with-good-peoples-pulitzer-prize-winning-playwright-david/10151292911990741
30 David Lindsay-Abair, *How We Talk in South Boston* in *Great Short Comedies, Volume 1* (New York, 2007), p. 63.
31 David Lindsay-Abaire, *Three One-Acts: Crazy Eights, Baby Food and That Other Person* (New York, 2006), p. 28.
32 David Lindsay-Abaire, *Ripcord* (New York, 2016), p. 50.
33 Erica Wagner, 'We Are a Selfish Idiot Generation', *New Statesman*, 26 February 2015. www.newstatesman.com/culture/2015/02/we-are-selfish-idiot-generation-ali-smith-talks-scotland-politics-and-why-audiences

7

Lynn Nottage

I think of myself as a playwright who is socially engaged. It's important. I get very frustrated when I go to the theatre and it feels like we're in some sort of bubble that has no relation to what's going on in the world . . . I don't understand how young playwrights choose not to be actively in conversation with the culture.[1]

– Lynn Nottage

History is entirely created by the person who tells the story.[2]

– Lin-Manuel Miranda

In 2015, to mark the centenary of his birth, Penguin books published a collection of Arthur Miller's plays. It had an introduction by Lynn Nottage presented in the form of a letter to a young playwright. On the face of it, this might have seemed a strange choice. Nottage is a black woman playwright, and black characters do not abound in Miller's work. But this is to misunderstand something about Nottage who, whatever the subject of her plays, does not choose to be defined only by her race and gender, important though both are. 'He was someone', she explained in interview, 'who understood that you really had to be engaged in order to be a writer'.[3] She was drawn to a man who saw the theatre as offering an opportunity to have a dialogue with America.

In her introduction to *The Penguin Arthur Miller*, Nottage recalls that when looking for inspiration and guidance as a young writer, she had frequently turned to a well-worn copy of Miller's plays, albeit alongside the work of Lillian Hellman, Tennessee Williams, Clifford Odets and August Wilson. What she learned from Miller was how he used language to shape characters, how 'effortlessly he conjured the worlds of ordinary men, transforming the minutiae of their day-to-day lives into epic tragedies . . . He used the small rebellions and conflicts of the common man in order to stage a larger conversation with history'. He wrote, she said, with an 'overarching concern about the shifting moral fault lines that threatened to fracture the foundations of American culture'. Beyond that, he had 'great empathy for the disaffected souls that hovered on the edge of darkness, light-seekers trying to negotiate a world that was rapidly redefining itself in the aftermath of the Depression and World War II'.

It was, in other words, the social dramatist who attracted her, writing about those who pursued the American dream without ever quite grasping what it might mean in lives often lived on the margin. He was intent to unsettle 'and ultimately pry people out of their complacency'.[4] What finally impressed her was his idea that art should be a place of transformations, probing social and emotional truths. At the same time, she noted that Miller was committed to more than a realistic presentation of life and not only in the memory scenes of *Death of a Salesman*. Ahead, after all, lay plays in which he was happy to deconstruct that reality, asking (in *Two-Way Mirror*, *Danger: Memory!*, *The Archbishop's Ceiling* and *Mr. Peters' Connections*) how it might be constituted.

Although not quite a manifesto for her own writing, there are points of contact. Drama is, by its nature and context, a social art. At the same time, the route into the social lies through the personal. The nature of the American dream, or the state of an oppressive society enforcing its arbitrary rules, only matter because we are persuaded to care about the fate of Willy Loman or John Proctor. Betrayal is a public fact but equally a private reality, denial by the state echoing denial by the individual. Miller's characters sometimes fail to understand themselves or the true nature of the world they inhabit, but that is a familiar psychological and even metaphysical truth that extends beyond the realm of the theatre and certainly applies to Nottage's plays, which also have something of Miller's shaping of ordinary speech into lyricism. Perhaps she also learned from him his theatrical tactic of entering plays through reassuring comedy, only subsequently to edge in another direction. Characters in Miller's plays, but equally in Nottage's, stand on thin ice, the quotidian concealing suppressed truths.

Her work is equally concerned with characters sometimes trapped in their own rhetoric or the ideas and myths presented to them as social truths. White or black, they are liable to be exposed for the narrowness of their view of the world, even if she is sympathetic to the extent that those views have been forged by social and cultural presumptions. They are products of history, although a number of them seek to transcend that history. Their dreams may be shaped by the images offered to them, by a rhetoric that limits rather than expands possibilities, but there is a counterbalancing desire to move beyond the given, their sense that there must be more to life than is proposed by those bruised by experience or cowed by constrictions and distinctions they are told are ineluctable. She is concerned with the pressures of the past, like Miller but unlike the society she inhabits dedicated, as it is, to deferred meaning, history less inspected than declared irrelevant to the national project. She grants significance to that past as a shaping force as she denies it final authority.

Her characters struggle to navigate their way through a society inclined to press them to the edge, to escape what others would make them. That she often does this with humour and irony is a sign of her ability to step back from the world she chooses to dramatise, she herself not being contained by the categories in which critics sometimes choose to locate her and which her characters often embrace to their detriment. Although she admires August Wilson, the ground on which she stands is not the same as his. He was focused not merely on staging black life through the twentieth century but on looking for a black theatre with, where possible, black directors, although his audience extended far beyond a racially defined one precisely because behind the particular truths, the distinctive experiences and cultural specifics, lay certain human truths.

Lynn Nottage's theatrical heritage embraces both Miller and Wilson who, as it happens, died in the same year. Like both of them, she is happy to infiltrate non-realist elements into her work while she explores the texture and substance of a society seemingly so confident in itself and what it takes to be the self-evident nature of its social constructions. Her plays examine the American past, but she has also stepped outside that seemingly familiar world, or a world she makes familiar, tracking her interest in the fate of women or the politics of identity into other countries and continents. She is, however, conscious of the absence of black playwrights in the American theatre and never forgets that her own work may help open spaces formerly closed.

Running through her work is a concern with identity, and in that context, she could scarcely be more American, inhabiting, as she does, a country in which national identity is loudly proclaimed and yet always in flux. As she has said, 'Our notion of selves is dynamic. It shifts from year to year. How I identify myself changes every decade.'[5] In all contexts she is an African-American woman, but both parts of that description are relevant and entering the sensibility of others the essence of a writer's remit. She has said that she feels liberated from the need to write what she calls 'race plays' in which race is central and, coming from a happy middle-class home, is able to create characters who reflect that background while 'looking for a middle-class African-American audience'.[6]

In the 1990s, Thelma Golden, director of the Studio Museum of Harlem, coined the term 'post-blackness'. It was intended to respond to her sense that a certain obligation had been lifted from the black artist, the obligation to speak for the race. In 2011, the journalist Touré, in his book *Who's Afraid of Post Blackness? What It Means to Be Black Now*, extended this to describe what he saw as a new condition – culturally and politically – basing his work on interviews conducted with a wide range of people in the arts, politics, business and academia. This was a generation that had grown up after segregation, beneficiaries of the Civil Rights movement of which the most significant was the first black president of the United States, although the descriptor 'black' is curious as applied to the son of a black man and a white woman, suggesting that history had yet to relinquish its grasp on the American mind. Likewise, the description, in the cinema, of Halle Berry as black conveniently filters out aspects of her background, but, then, America has always had a tendency to round up fractions to whole numbers.

It was not that colour had suddenly become insignificant or that history had lost its relevance, but that identity was now seen as more complex, a series of negotiations no longer defined by past battles. A significant middle class had emerged, although it has been pointed out that Touré's choice of interviewees was largely restricted to that class so that his thesis was not without its flaws. In society at large, racism has scarcely disappeared, as is attested to by police actions and the country's prisons, but the rhetoric has changed, and black writers are no longer patrolled for evidence of allegiance to approved models as James Baldwin had been attacked for *Giovanni's Room* in which there were no black characters and sexual preference trumped racial identity. The past is still to be explored, its absences peopled, for what else does the present rest upon, and Lynn Nottage has journeyed there while doing so with a sense of irony and humour (she is an admirer of Richard Pryor as well as Toni Morrison), which time and her own experiences have gifted her; but to her, black identity is heterogeneous and that heterogeneousness is in part what interests her, exploring as she does the various strategies of those struggling to make sense of their own situation. Her plays are set in different times and places. She has what she has described as a nomadic imagination. Baldwin had warned himself of the danger that his own articulacy would be seen as aligning him with those who oppressed him, even as that articulacy would be his claim on attention. Such fears have long since faded.

At the same time, history is not to be denied. In 2007, and drawing on slave narratives assembled under Roosevelt's Works Progress Administration (WPA) in the 1930s, along with period advertisements, newspaper articles, speeches, sermons and music, Nottage crafted a drama she called *One More River to Cross: A Verbatim Fugue*. The narratives, she explained, put a human face on an inhumane system. It was a process she found painful to confront, confessing that 'I hadn't quite realized the extent to which the experience still reverberates inside me'. She offered the play because slavery was still a fact around the world, because that particular past had been evaded as the source of pain, and because she believed the theatre could be 'a place of catharsis and healing'.[7]

Lynne Nottage's father, a psychologist interested in prison reform, was born in Harlem and her mother in Brooklyn. She was a schoolteacher and became a principal in the same elementary school she and her mother had both attended. They were art lovers, collecting the work of African-American artists, and art was part of the young Lynne's life growing up in the Boerum Hill area of Brooklyn. Boerum Hill consists largely of three-story brownstones and is close to Atlantic Avenue. Today it has been gentrified, but then it consisted of boarding houses and one-family homes. Nottage remembers it as 'a multicultural neighborhood, which was unusual at the time. It was primarily black and Latino, but it was a neighbourhood where everyone fleeing their other neighbourhoods went. So you ended up with this unusual group of hippies, queers, Latinos, Irish, blacks, Mohawks, artists, merchant marines, and junkies. We were a neighbourhood of others. That was what defined us.'[8] It was, she claimed, what would make her more adventurous as a writer, both stylistically and in terms of her subject matter. It was a neighbourhood as economically as it was racially diverse, though not without its problems. Her family home, she recalled, was robbed eight times, and it was wise to have some mugging money available.

She has said that her journey to becoming a playwright began 'downstairs at the kitchen table of my house. Down there was a gathering place for so many women.' When she came home from school, 'my grandmother would be sitting at the table, and my mother would be sitting at the table. The woman from across the street would be sitting at the table. And they all had stories to tell.'[9] Nottage herself began writing short stories as a child and her first play at age seven or eight, casting herself as a princess and her brother as a prince. They performed it for her parents.

At New York's High School of Music and Art, a long subway ride away, she was a music student, playing the piano, but she also became interested in drama, going to see Broadway and Off-Broadway productions. In her senior year, she explained to Alexis Greene,[10] with others at the Dramatists Guild, she wrote a musical about a group of Midwestern high school students who come to New York. She also wrote a play titled *The Darker Side of Verona* about an African-American Shakespeare company. On graduating in 1982, she went to Brown University, although she had been told she would be wasting her time applying to an Ivy League school. There, along with journalism, she studied playwriting, inspired by George Bass, a graduate of Fiske University and Columbia and secretary to Langston Hughes. At Brown, he had established Rites and Reason, the research theatre of the African-American Studies Programme responsible for more than fifty plays, some of which he had written. He insisted that his plays were concerned with exploring black people's contributions to understanding how people perceive the world and how they have maintained their humanity in the face of what they have suffered.

In her senior year, Nottage worked with Paula Vogel, who had just arrived at Brown; in 1986, she went on to the Yale School of Drama, largely, she has confessed, because she did not know what else to do. Indeed she has said that she might have been better off working for a while and finding herself; instead she did so among students who were better informed about theatre than she was. Her previous exposure to theatre had either been productions at the Negro Ensemble or Broadway musicals.

What she did learn was something about playwriting by watching a play move through to production. College, she has said, was her laboratory. At the same time she was disillusioned with theatre, feeling it to be decadent and irrelevant to the culture and so wished to do something different. At Yale, she was only the second African-American woman to graduate from the playwriting programme, and, on leaving in 1989, took a job with Amnesty International working in the public relations department. It was, she has said, one of the most important formative experiences she could have had. She ended up doing advocacy work, and there is an element of advocacy in her plays, although she maintains an objectivity that is sometimes exposed through her humour.

After four years, she changed her mind about theatre, although her experience at Amnesty clearly had an impact on her, even if she had been frustrated at the difficulty of finding an audience for the organisation that, with the end of the Cold War, seemed to have gone off the media's agenda. Amnesty was also not at the time mandated to engage with women's issues, so when she was presented with photographs of women at a shelter for battered women, there was nothing she could do. As a result, she wrote a monologue, *Poof!*, while still at Amnesty, which went on to win a Heideman Award, worth $1,000, given each year for a ten-minute play written by someone between age eighteen and twenty-eight and hosted by the Actors Theatre of Louisville. It opened in Louisville in 1993. Brief though it was, it was critical in bringing about her change of direction. It seemed to her that in theatre, she could find an audience, no matter how small. She had attended a theatre workshop, but the job had got in the way of her revived ambitions. Having sold her own computer, she typed *Poof!* on a work machine.

Hers is a career that has largely fallen after the turn of the millennium, and later she was inclined to look on this, and another play, *Por' Knockers*, as 'not ready', but they do stake out what would become her territory. So in her case, a twenty-first-century career began seven years before the Millennium Bug, when it was feared computers would reset themselves back a century – as it happens not without a certain symbolic truth as fundamentalist religion returned as a force and racism proved resistant to millennial optimism.

Slight though it is, *Poof!* is a play that already identifies what Lynn Nottage is and is not. Hers is a satirical take that nonetheless grants the significance of what she satirises. What she is not is ideological. Her characters are themselves prone, like Gatsby, to see the world through a single window, whether of race, politics or gender, and not without justification, but also reach for a broader perspective, engage in a conversation with themselves as much as with others. Theatrically, she is liable to step outside the conventions she appears to establish, break the fourth wall, allow characters to move from one reality to another or from reality to enacted thoughts.

A workshop production of *Por' Knockers* at the Dance Theater Workshop in New York City took place in 1994, followed by a production the following year at the Vineyard Theatre at East 15th Street in Manhattan. Like *Poof!* it mixed a familiar environment with seeming fantasy. The idea for the play was prompted by Nottage seeing a television documentary. The play has an epigraph from Wilson Harris explaining that por' knockers, or pork knockers, were gold prospectors in Guyana, descendants alike of slaves and great navigators, who, when times were bad, used to hammer on the barrels that contained pork in the hope that this would dislodge any remaining scraps of food. Such figures, who were seen as asserting kinship with the poor of all races and were generally of mixed heritage, in time became father figures of a 'new wilderness in great cities' as the twentieth century drew to a close.

The image from the television documentary that stayed with Nottage was of a man with only a scrap of clothing panning desperately for gold. What, she asked herself, was the modern equivalent? So 'I threw these people together in a room . . . who represent aspects of the African-American activist community . . . an intellectual professor, Tamara, who's married to academia. There's Kwami, who is a black nationalist from the 1960s and can't let go of that rhetoric' . . . Ahmed . . . flirting with the Nation of Islam' and 'James . . . a conspiracy theorist'.[11] The very variety of responses was Nottage's resistance to the notion of a single black voice, suggesting that 'it's in the interest of the establishment to keep us as The Blacks'.[12]

The play, Nottage explained, initially written as a comedy, was produced the following year by the Vineyard Theatre, but in the meantime, the Federal Building in Oklahoma City had been bombed so that the humour in a play that involves the incompetent destruction of a building by the ironically named Diasporic Folks Revolutionary Collaborative for Justice and Equality, was potential blunted by the new social context and the play closed early, nobody staying for the promised post-show discussion. Bomb threats were called into the theatre. At the same time, she came to feel that the play was prescient in that, social satire though it was, its portrait of the anger felt by the disaffected would return in a different guise.

The production led to a commission by Second Stage to write *Crumbs from the Table of Joy* (1995). It ran for two-and-a-half months, and she noticed the audience changing from a subscription to a more mixed and ultimately a black audience. Looking back, she was inclined to count this as her first real play, more especially when she rewrote it, in a version shortened by twenty minutes, for South Coast Repertory, based in Costa Mesa, California. The play looks back to the 1950s, a period she confessed to know little about, capturing the tone and voice through her reading of James Baldwin and Langston Hughes. It is a play in which the racial situation in New York provides a backdrop but, as in *Por' Knockers*, is treated with irony. This, she has noted, was a time before the Civil Rights movement was underway, before the feminist revolution. The play was offered as 'an allegory in some ways of the African-American experience in the 1950s, of the issues that people were grappling with' in 'a very, very volatile period'.[13]

The various characters feel the pressure of white oppression, but Nottage's concern is more with the way they struggle to define themselves. For the young James Baldwin, religion had represented an escape; so it does for Godfrey, the father in *Crumbs from the Table of Joy*. For his sister, it is radical politics, while for his daughters, caught at a moment of change, it is in part the small rituals of daily life, high school graduation, visits to the movies, as they slowly learn something about the world they have entered and the fallibility of their father as a guide. Nottage locates the play in her own neighbourhood, the street names real enough and the characters no less so, even as her realism is infiltrated by fantasy.

The Crump family, headed by the patriarch Godfrey, have moved to Brooklyn from the South, where his wife and their mother had died. He travels inspired by, and in search of, Father Divine, who he believes will answer all his questions. The real Divine (who called himself the Reverend Major Jealous Divine) claimed to be God and was widely regarded as a fraud. In *Crumbs from the Table of Joy*, he is the Godot who never arrives, although his picture dominates the sparsely filled Brooklyn basement apartment where they live. Godfrey works nights in a downtown bakery, forced to tolerate the racism he encounters, while his daughters walk fourteen blocks to school. Ernestine Crump, a seventeen-year-old African-American, sister to fifteen-year-old Ermina, like Tom in *The Glass Menagerie*, acts as a guide, sharing her memories and fantasies with the audience, commenting on the family's lives and that of the community.

Coming from the South, she and the other members of the family are strangers in a strange land, learning as they go. In the background, heard through the apartment wall where their white Jewish neighbours live, a radio mentions Senator McCarthy before the station is changed so that 'Some Enchanted Evening' plays. It being Sunday, they are not allowed to listen to their own radio, denied the simple pleasures because Father Divine would disapprove, a man who, Ernestine points out, has married a white woman while requiring adherents, including Ernestine and Ermina, if Godfrey gets his way, to wear the letter V for 'Virtue, Victory and Virginity'. For the girls, the cinema is their recourse, watching Joan Crawford, white but alluring (Nottage confessed that when she was growing up, she had seen *Mildred Pierce* a hundred times, finding there a strong woman, albeit one to whom she could not relate). Their father, meanwhile, is conscious of external threats, recalling the fate of the Scottsboro Boys, sentenced for rapes they did not commit.

Into the apartment comes their Aunt Lily, worldly wise, dressed, as Ernestine remarks, like a white woman (wearing a smartly tailored suit and white gloves) and bringing all the allure of someone who has been to Harlem. She explains that she had bought her clothes from Fifth Avenue to spite the white women who 'hate to see a Negro woman look better than they do', her 'subversive mission' being to 'outdress them' (24). She had plainly once had a relationship with Godfrey and now announces that she will move in to chaperone the girls, bringing with her subversion as opposed to Godfrey's withdrawal. There should, she says, be a Black Scare rather than a Red Scare. Her motives, though, are unclear. She has lost her job and arrives hungry. Little by little the fancy clothes disappear as she spends her time drinking and apparently has a reputation, which sits uneasily in a home dominated by a fraudulent god. While demanding racial justice, she works to straighten Ermina's hair. Ernestine, though, is intrigued by her ideas. She writes a school essay on 'The Colored Worker in the United States', only for her teacher to tell her that her father should stop mixing with the Jews at work, though the workers are in fact all black and 'the Jews on our block won't speak to us' (34). Godfrey insists that she should apologise to the white teacher, anxious, as ever, to avoid giving offence as well as aware of danger.

Lily is the antithesis of Godfrey, locked up as he is in his fears and religious enthusiasms. She plays at being a revolutionary, failing to answer Ernestine's question of whether the revolution would set black against white or rich against poor. Reminiscing about the South, she recalls gentlemen callers quite as if she were Tennessee Williams's Blanche Dubois or Zelda Fitzgerald. But she is not the only intrusion into this basement apartment. Godfrey disappears only to return with a white German wife called Gerte, whom he had met, as Nottage says, 'riding a subway literally to nowhere'.[14] She brings love into his life.

For Nottage, the characters 'represent different ideas . . . Godfrey . . . is an assimilationist . . . Lily . . . is somewhat of a separatist', while the girls 'are trapped in the middle. There's a tug of war for them. And what Ernestine discovers is that her path is right down the middle'.[15] Lily was marginal in both the South and the North, but in 1950s America, what other role was there? Meanwhile, Ernestine has the capacity to substitute her imagination for regular disappointments, as reality falls short of her hopes. When they all attend a Peace Mission banquet at which Father Divine is supposed to make an appearance (as ever, those waiting to see him are disappointed), the staid Gerte sheds her normal clothes to reveal a cocktail dress, climbs on a table and sings 'Falling in Love Again' except that this is no more than the enacting of Ernestine's fantasy.

Gerte, though, introduces a different perspective to the play. She is also a woman who grew up in a small town and moved to a city, discovering a new world. She is a lover of jazz: 'it was freeing to know that someone so far away could give a musical shape to my feelings.' She had grown up under the Nazis and, like the black girls who are now part of her new family, found that 'things happen just as you're finding yourself' (64). She had nearly starved to death. When she asks Lily, 'can't we forget our differences?' and Lily replies, 'I see a white woman, and when I look in the mirror, I see a Negro woman', she invokes her own experiences: 'I have seen what happens when we permit our differences' (66). Indeed when she and Godfrey go out, he is beaten by those who will not tolerate an interracial couple. Part of the strength of the play lies in its recognition of contending forces, briefly reconciled in Ernestine's imagination as Lily and Gerte dance the mambo together, although only in the world as she fantasises it. One thing Gerte does succeed in doing, however, is to tear up the scraps of paper on which Godfrey had listed the questions he wished Father Devine to answer, lists that fill the closet and represent the accumulation of his false hopes.

In an epilogue, Ernestine glimpses her future. She cares, she says, 'very much about the status of the Negro in this country' (87) and, standing by City College, which will be her route to that future, is carried forward to the time when she will ride the Freedom Bus, argue about the Vietnam War and the Black Panthers before sending one son to a New England college while losing another to drugs. Meanwhile, though, she will be 'walking as far as these feet will take me' (88).

Crumbs from the Table of Joy is alternately disturbing and moving, painful and funny, realistic and non-realistic. It is a play that withholds judgement. The responses of the characters are humanly understandable as they look for solutions to personal and public issues, struggling to find a basis on which to live. If there are false gods, religious and political, there are also missteps born out of differing needs and hopes. The introduction of Gerte locates racial tension in a wider context. They are all immigrants trying to find their feet in a society that seems not to offer them what they desire. It is a play whose dramatic strategy turns on the figure of Ernestine. In finding her way, she leads the audience into a world now more than half a century away but disturbing in its continued relevance. She is, though, coming of age, and her glimpse into the future is what would lead to a writer like Lynn Nottage.

Towards the end of the play, Ernestine recalls what she imagined to be the communal world that existed in Africa and which she believes offers a potential model. In 1996, though, Nottage staged another play, *Mud, River, Stone*, set in southeast Africa, in which that communal world has seemingly long since disappeared. It was inspired by an article she read that described the situation in Mozambique where a war had been raging for nearly two decades. In particular, it described the kidnapping of people at gunpoint by those who had been fighting and had now been demobilised. Their demands were for food and blankets.

Mud, River, Stone is a play in which she draws on her experiences at Amnesty International, where she had been involved in interviewing Africans, although at the time she wrote it she had yet to visit the continent. That lay ahead in preparation for *Ruined*, her second play set in Africa, a continent, she has noted, that rarely impinges on American consciousness, decades-long conflicts barely registering. For African-Americans, however, it has a particular significance even as it is re-invented by those who lay claim to it. For some it is the starting point of a journey. For others, it is Conrad's heart of darkness, a place of colonial exploitation, a tourist destination. When Nottage herself later went to West Africa she sensed a certain familiarity but in central East Africa felt a foreigner and was treated accordingly.

For the most part, the play is set in a decaying hotel in the middle of the African countryside (modelled on Mozambique), in which a single bellboy, Joaquim, a former guerrilla, seems to be the only surviving member of staff, along with a lone guest, a white South African businessman. They are joined by an African-American couple, David and Simone, on holiday looking for their roots; a Belgian tourist adventurer, who convinces himself that he has become native embracing what he takes to be local dress and myths; a West African aid worker and, eventually, a naïve United Nations negotiator. They are stranded there by heavy rains, with no access to a telephone or radio, and are eventually taken captive by the bellboy. Every character is deeply compromised. Under stress, civility and order itself collapse. Whatever this place was, whatever they were, is no longer true in this anteroom to nowhere. No sentimentalities, no values survive here, even as survival itself becomes the only necessity. These characters may be the product of history, but history seems to have ended, given the anarchy without and within. Here, roads turn into rivers, and the land is mined. Death by disease, starvation or bullet awaits.

Outside the hotel there is hunger and the distant sound of gunfire. The centre cannot hold because there is no centre, only the consequence of empire and the broken promises of African leaders. If the African Americans are quickly stripped of their fashionable clothes, they are equally stripped of their assumptions. Those who struggled in the 1950s may now have risen to wealth, having escaped what had oppressed the Crump family, but they are now threatened by the very Africans Ernestine had rhapsodised over, the community she celebrated having collapsed. When the former child soldier takes over, it seems as though power has been reversed, but he has no clear objective beyond relishing the power he has momentarily seized.

The setting may be Africa, but in this place truths about elsewhere are disclosed. David, the African-American music journalist, is described by his wife as non-voting 'non-tax-paying, this country can kiss my black ass' while himself insisting that 'I've put up with people putting me down for my entire life, for not being black enough'. At the same time he wishes to be seen as 'an African person . . . we fought too hard for that hyphen' (215). Pointing to his heart, the white Belgian asserts that 'I may not be a black man outside, but I am a black man. Here' (216), only to be told that he cannot become the African he wishes to be. Identity here is fragile.

The play ends melodramatically when Joaquim is shot dead, except the final irony has already been signalled in the opening scene as David and Simone relay their experiences at a dinner party back in America, she with Armani sunglasses on her head and he holding the stone with which he had struck the doomed child soldier. Nottage herself has suggested that they have been changed by their experiences, that they recognise their complicity in events and that their telling of the story of their trip is 'giving voice to the struggle',[16] David acknowledging that he is part of the problem, but it is hard to see this as their adventure is reduced to a dinner party anecdote. They had gone to Africa to see it 'without the filter' while in effect taking it with them. Looking for Africa, as James Baldwin discovered in travelling to Europe, underlined how American they are. David may have been tempted by the thought of seeing the mud and stone ruins of his ancestors, but in fact they were looking for a romantic tourist experience with slightly more edge than their previous holidays in the Caribbean and Martha's Vineyard. If it turned out to be otherwise, they nonetheless end where they began, the stone a symbol of complicity but equally a curio, a reminder of a world from which they are once more insulated. Their idea of Africa may have changed, but there is no suggestion that their understanding of it has. Off stage a war is being fought, but we never learn, and they never enquire, what its cause is. It exists as a threat – in their case another reason to want to get back to the safety and comfort of America. Nor, as the play suggests, is there one Africa, homogenised in the eyes of others but in fact as various as Europe, with different languages, myths, loyalties, identities, and identity is as much at the heart of this play as of her earlier works and, indeed, as it is of her next, *Las Meninas* (2002).

This was a play prompted by an essay she came across that mentioned in passing a relationship between Queen Marie-Thérèse, Spanish wife to Louis XIV of France, and a black dwarf, a gift delivered to court in a box. She set herself to research what seemed an unlikely story but turned out to be true, a fact that had largely been erased from history and accounts for the play's epigraph, supposedly a Yoruba proverb: 'The white man who made the pencil also made the eraser.' Erasure is indeed a theme of much of her work, wherever it is set, in that the stories she sets herself to tell are often of those lost in larger narratives. She looks for the spaces, here in history, elsewhere in accounts of social change. In 2016, the story would be resurrected in *Versailles*, a British-Franco-Canadian television series.

The play's title comes from a painting of the same name by Velázquez which features a court scene in which the young queen-to-be is seen surrounded by maids of honour or ladies in waiting. It features two dwarfs and a painter (Velázquez himself being court painter), although painters were not highly regarded in social terms. The picture itself, like the story Nottage retrieves and invents, has faded over the years.

In Nottage's play, the young girl is now wife to Louis. She has grown fat and, as a Spanish woman in a French court, is treated with disdain. Her husband meanwhile is busily engaged in serial affairs, and not those to do with the state. Their two children having died young, he no longer evidences any sexual interest in her. A box arrives as a gift, and from it is extracted a black dwarf who is to be her jester; in time, however, she requires him to carry out another function, becoming pregnant as a result. Despite his lack of contact, Louis is persuaded that the child, a girl, is his but when it is born, to general consternation, it is black and swiftly sent to a convent to be raised in seclusion and secrecy. The jester, whose joke, it turns out, had been on himself, is equally dispatched, although to death rather than a religious institution. Once grown, and shortly before becoming a bride of Christ, the one-time child is inducted into the truth of her origin. Just as the ladies in waiting in Velásquez's painting had been on the margin of events, so those in the play are likewise, the queen largely ignored, a painter seemingly invisible to those around him, the dwarf literally below the eye level of those in the court. The story is even told from the remoteness of a convent cell by one abstracted from the world.

While it ends with a death and a step back into obscurity, it is not a play without humour from the credulous king, here little more than a wandering irrelevance, to a queen, lost in the labyrinthine rooms of an alien palace whose command of the language is inadequate and whose techniques of seduction are laughable if menacing. The dwarf, whose name, Nabo, she will no more accept than slaveholders would those of their African slaves, is brighter and funnier than anyone else, clever enough, indeed, to recognise inevitability when he sees it, although none of the characters know, of course, that they are contained within a story told by an abandoned child as the king and queen are captured in a painting that will outlast them, a lie of propinquity and shared majesty to be bequeathed to a future that will take it for truth.

As characters, of course, they are not free, though the queen remarks, with uncharacteristic acuity, 'if every man had a free will, then imagine the chaos that would be imparted' (263). Iris Murdoch once claimed that in her novels she wished to create a house fit for free characters to live in, meaning by that that they would develop their own logic, generate their own stories, except that she also claimed to plan every novel down to each comma and full stop. The rhetoric of freedom often contains its own contradictions. In *Las Meninas* everyone has his or her roles prescribed – king, queen, jester, nun – yet somehow an enlivening leaven of anarchy manages to infiltrate the grand confection, which is the court and play alike.

In 2003, Nottage once more turned to the past, this time prompted by her own family's history. In a note significantly entitled 'Lives Rescued from Silence', she recalled clearing her grandmother's brownstone in Brooklyn preparatory to a sale. She had learned little of her family history from her when she was alive as though a door had been deliberately closed on a past she chose not to revisit. 'I imagine', Nottage says, that 'the act of forgetting was how she survived, for to remember was to embrace the painful legacy of oppression. The pain was inherent in her reticence... In order to transcend the past, we'd let it go. Hence, the names of my ancestors were rarely spoken, and subsequently forgotten.'[17]

As it happened she had been researching the lives of African Americans in the early twentieth century, although those of ordinary people remained, in her words, 'memoir-less', omitted from public accounts beyond the required records of life and death. What was missing was what lay between those two markers of mere existence. This only served to underline her lack of awareness when it came to her own family except that she recalled being told that her great-grandmother had been a seamstress from Barbados who had created underclothes for women and that she had corresponded with a fellow Barbadian who was working on the Panama Canal, resulting in a brief marriage. Further research identified the ship on which she had arrived at Ellis Island. She finally allowed 'their memory to breathe' (6). The play that emerged was not specifically about them, although she names them in a note, thereby granting them their place in history.

Intimate Apparel was commissioned and first staged by South Coast Repertory in 2003. She wrote it just after the death of her mother and has said that it reflects her feelings of love, loneliness, sadness and a loss of self. It is set 1905 in Lower Manhattan. A woman sits at a sewing machine in a simple bedroom as the sound of a ragtime melody filters through from the next room along with those of a party marking a marriage. She refuses to join them feeling that no one will dance with her. The woman is Esther – a version of Nottage's great grandmother, Ethel – thirty-five, unmarried and 'rather plain'. She has been working since she was nine 'with barely a day's rest',[18] her mother dying when she was seventeen and her father, a one-time slave, two years later, having lost his tongue in a fight and therefore unable to express love.

Her skill, like Nottage's great-grandmother's, is as a sewer of intimate garments, and intimacy lies at the heart of the play, each scene taking place in a bedroom with a bed centrally located, unavoidably keeping the focus on relationships, sexual and otherwise. She makes lingerie both for a woman in a brothel and for one on Fifth Avenue, while herself being lonely, convinced that love has passed her by, not recognising it when she encounters it coming, as it does, from where she least expects it. She has lived in the rooming house for eighteen years making clothes for those whose lives she presumes are more vital and vivid than her own, until a letter arrives that changes her life, a letter from George Armstrong, a handsome Barbadian who is working on the Panama Canal. He is revealed reading the letter (Esther being illiterate). In the following scene, Esther is seen fitting a corset to a white woman, the childless Mrs Van Buren, who is evidently intent on attracting the attention of her wandering husband, divorce being socially unacceptable. She undertakes to write letters on Esther's behalf, letters that open the door to what she comes to believe is love, having no experience of it.

Love of another kind, though, is available, except that Esther cannot see it as such. Every Tuesday she visits Mr Marks, an Orthodox Jew in his thirties from whom she buys material for the clothes she sews. They meet in their love of material, which itself is lovingly made but when their hands accidentally touch, he withdraws, rabbinical law, he explains, forbidding such touching except between man and wife, his own fiancée, whom has never met, living in Romania. A spark that might have flamed thus seems extinguished, and when she visits Mayme, a prostitute whose clothes she also makes, she explains, albeit unconvincingly, that she couldn't be drawn to him because 'he a Jew' (26). Yet the attraction remains – subtle, so subtle it can be denied and not acted upon except that she confides to Mrs Van Buren that 'I touched someone . . . who I knew I wasn't supposed to touch. I touched them because I wanted to. It was wrong but I couldn't help myself' (38), even as Mrs Van Buren reaches out to Esther, touching her hand with tenderness, no less in need of love than the woman who serves her.

Mayme and Esther share their dreams, the former of being a concert pianist, the latter of owning a beauty parlour while Mayme fosters Esther's other dream, like Mrs Van Buren writing a letter on her behalf to the man who only exists in words until, one day he writes back proposing marriage. So Esther leaves the boarding house as her landlady, Mrs Dickson, recalls her own mother's warning against love – 'Look what love done to me' (44). Mayme, Mrs Van Buren, and Mrs Dickson have all traded themselves for comfort, security, possessions, survival – all realising too late the consequences of such a deal. Even as she prepares for her marriage, Esther is still drawn to Mr Marks, neither able to articulate their feelings except in the cloth they mutually caress.

The first act ends as we glimpse Mrs Van Buren, Mrs Dickson, Mayme and Marks in their separate bedrooms as George appears and Esther wears her wedding dress. The lights fade again, leaving the couple looking at one another as there is the flash of a camera and a projected title appears: 'Unidentified Negro Couple, ca. 1905', a sepia photograph such as Nottage had discovered when searching through her grandmother's possessions.

The second act begins with the couple in a studio flat with an iron bed dividing them, a division that swiftly grows. His parents, George explains, 'were chattel . . . born to children of chattel' (52), but his mind is only on sex. As he pulls Esther onto the bed, Mayme and Mrs Van Buren stand over it dressed in their corsets, present as a warning if not in fact. For Esther, her new husband offers comfort except that he quickly begins to reveal another side. He had no more written his letters than had she. He takes all her money for an unlikely investment, as Walter had done in *A Raisin in the Sun*, and spends it on gambling and sex with Mayme, even giving her the smoking jacket Esther had presented to him on their wedding night. The money spent, he leaves and she confronts Mayme before returning briefly to Marks, giving him the jacket, a marriage of minds that leaves them both more solitary than before. She ends in the same room in which she had started, beginning work on a new quilt as she had sewed the original in which she had stored the money she had spent her working life earning and was to have given her a new life. A gentle ragtime tune plays as the lights shift 'creating the quality of an old sepia-toned photograph'; a title appears: 'Unidentified Negro Seamstress, ca. 1905.'

The achievement of *Intimate Apparel* lies in its gentle touch in a play where touch has a special significance. These are all characters reaching for something they cannot grasp, divided from one another by race, class, religion. The most powerful relationship is one that cannot be articulated, its intensity suggested in what is not said. The question asked in Langston Hughes's poem 'Montage of a Dream Deferred' – 'What happens to a dream deferred' – used as an epigraph to *A Raisin in the Sun*, could apply equally to this play in which no one realises his or her hopes and the end mirrors the beginning, except that we are told that 'ESTHER lightly touches her belly', a gesture that carries more meaning than speech. Words, anyway, as she has learned, are suspect, the letters between husband and wife being written by others. The characters lie to one another. Intimacy is precisely what is lacking. As to the intimate apparel, for the prostitute it is part of a financial transaction drained of meaning. For Mrs Van Buren it is a desperate attempt to lure her husband back as it is for Esther, except that for her, it has its own beauty. She caresses the various materials as she has not been able to caress the one man whom she genuinely loves but who is constrained by custom and edict.

Does Esther's return to the room where she started, and what appears to be her pregnancy, mark simply another turn of the wheel or a new possibility? Is persistence a virtue in itself or the source of irony? It is unclear, except that Nottage has said that, to her, 'Esther's journey is about becoming empowered'[19] and Nottage's own present owes a debt to a similar past, as, generations on, one of the seamstress's offspring, now fully in command of language, embraces her.

Nottage has remarked that, her father aside, she comes from a family in which men have deserted their women, and Esther is deserted and by more than a man. Meanwhile, her story had been abandoned, surviving only in a sepia photograph that had been the playwright's portal into the past. What Nottage has done in this play is to reach back and animate that photograph.

In *Fabulation, or, the Re-Education of Undine* (2004), written at the same time as *Intimate Apparel*, she would carry the story forward in what amounted to a comic fable. As she explained, 'For *Fabulation*, I tried to imagine Esther 100 years later, after she's enjoyed the benefits of the women's rights and civil rights movements and become a fully empowered African-American woman, like Condoleeza Rice – and that was Undine.'[20] Undine, however, was not her real name, changing it, on graduation, when she became embarrassed by her family.

At the beginning of the play, she is a seemingly rich owner of a public relations company currently seeking anyone resembling a celebrity for a charity event in aid of Fallopian Blockage: 'Gangsterish enough to cause a stir but not enough to cause a problem.'[21] As she explains to the audience:

I left home at thirteen. I was a bright child. I won a competitive scholarship through a better chance program to an elite boarding school in New England. I subsequently acquired a taste for things my provincial Brooklyn upbringing could no longer provide. I went to Dartmouth College, met and mingled with people in a constructive way, built a list of friends that would prove valuable down the line. And my family . . . they tragically perished in a fire . . . Fourteen years ago, I opened my own . . . boutique PR firm catering to the vanity and confusion of the African American nouveau riche.[22]

Her family, though, did not die, this being a lie she told the press, editing them out of the story of her own success, a success that comes to an abrupt end as her husband, having made her pregnant, absconds with all her money, Esther's story repeated. What follows is a tumble down the social ladder as she returns home only to find herself arrested for buying heroin on behalf of her grandmother, who has convinced everyone that she injects herself because of diabetes. She is briefly imprisoned and finds love with a man she encounters in a meeting for recovering addicts before, as the play ends, giving birth.

Fabulation is not so much a companion piece to *Intimate Apparel* as an antidote offering, as it does, a comic version of history and the aspirations of those who celebrate their escape from their origins, in her case from Brooklyn's Walt Whitman projects. The African heritage becomes little more than a backstory to a vacuous success as Undine now, according to her accountant (with whom she had had a sexual encounter in a men's room), faces bankruptcy: 'My ancestors came shackled in wooden ships, crossed the Atlantic with nothing but memories! But I'll spare you my deprivation narrative. Let's just say their journey brought me here, their pain, their struggle established me behind this fine expensive teak desk . . . a rare, strong and endangered wood. And now you want me to declare bankruptcy because that Argentine prick has run off with my money' (11). Desperate to turn things around, she pays a thousand dollars to a Yoruba priest with a divination board.

Like Esther, in *Intimate Apparel*, she ends up back where she started. If she, too, is empowered, it is only by virtue of having lost everything not worth retaining in a play of comic set pieces in which actors play multiple roles and Nottage takes pleasure in satirising bourgeois pretensions, academe (an addict used to attend panels on the symbol of the tomahawk in *The Dearslayer*), African myths, drug counselling and social services. For her next play, however, Africa would be more than the source of humour.

In 2004, the night after *Fabulation* opened, she and the director Kate Whorinsky took a plane for Uganda. Some time earlier they had discussed the possibility of Nottage writing a version of Brecht's *Mother Courage* set in the Congo where a war had been raging. She abandoned the idea in favour of something more direct. Her time in Amnesty International had sensitised her to overseas conflicts but also to the difficulty of interesting the American public in distant events. What had initially attracted her to the idea of *Mother Courage* was the ambivalent character at its heart. There was, though, little ambivalence about the women she now set herself to interview over the process of two weeks, who had suffered in a war in which every conceivable standard of human behaviour had been breached and those who had survived had somehow resisted giving way to despair. On their trip, they indeed witnessed the positive as well as negative aspects of a traumatised community, and Nottage determined that the work she created would reflect that fact. She returned the following year, interviewing those who had fled from the Sudan and Somalia as well as Uganda and the Congo. The women had been sexually abused. What emerged was a play, *Ruined* (2008), that would prove politically influential and artistically accomplished, winning the Pulitzer Prize.

This was not, though, to be a docudrama, a verbatim play, such as those written by Anna Deavere Smith, Emily Mann or Moisés Kaufman and members of the Tectonic Theater Project. At the same time it does hurry news from the front line and was written with an urgency informed by what Nottage had learned from interviews that distressed both interviewer and interviewees. If she had written about the plight of women before, it was not in the context of such brutal and unapologetic violence as she now encountered. The same requirements, however, remained in that what she learned had to be transformed into a drama convincing in structure, language and character. The stories she had heard required a narrative form, and although the soldiers who appear in it are irremediably evil, it was still necessary to resist simple melodrama. The moral centre is to be found in the young women at its heart, but the other characters are not entirely bereft of a surviving humanity even if the evidence for it is tenuous.

The play is set in a bar in a small mining town in the Democratic Republic of Congo, a place of former colonial theft and present corruption. The bar, which provides 'beer and distractions', is run down, the audio system powered by an old car battery, yet with a deceptively cheerful air. Presiding over it is Mama Nadi, an attractive woman in her early forties and in many respects a Mother Courage figure, running her bar/brothel, trading with all sides. The young women who service all comers are survivors of multiple rapes, rejected by their families and neighbours as 'ruined'. They are delivered and sold by a travelling salesman, ironically called Christian, an uncle to one of the girls, who seems to have a limited immunity, like a diamond dealer, Mr Harari, who bribes his way past innumerable road blocks in a country permanently at war, the causes of which are never clear, even, it seems, to those who fight it. It is, as Mama, declares, a war that 'keeps fracturing and redefining itself' (88). There is, though, no guaranteed immunity when both of the contending sides have been brutalised, miners being shot dead and buried in their own pits for failing to surrender what little they have, children forced to kill their parents, men murdered at will, women regarded as trophies to be carried off damaged in body and soul.

Of the two girls Christian delivers, one is eighteen-year-old Sophie, described as a luminous beauty with an air of defiance who had been about to sit for her university exam when she was seized and raped with a bayonet. She is in pain. The other is Salima, nineteen, illiterate, 'a sturdy peasant woman whose face betrays a world-weariness'. Beauty, though, as Sophie has discovered, carries its own dangers, while Salima's world weariness is bone deep, having spent nearly five months in the bush as the plaything of the rebels who have done 'ungodly' things to her while her child was killed when a soldier stamped on her head with his boot, an echo of O'Brien's prediction in George Orwell's *1984* that if you want a picture of the future, you should imagine a boot stamping on a human face forever.

Time moves on and they are now part of a place whose festive air conceals a constant tension. Drunken rebels and their leader listen as Sophie sings a song whose lyricism is at odds with the brutality of their situation even as it comments on it.

> The liquid night slowly pours in
> Languor peels away like a curtain
> Spirits rise and tongues loosen
> And the weary ask to be forgiven.
> You come here to forget,
> You say drive away all regret
> And dance like it's the ending
> The ending of the war.
>
> *(20)*

Asked if she finds relief in singing, she replies, 'While I'm singing, I'm praying the pain will be gone' (32), and indeed, music and song carry some of the play's meaning. Thus a stage direction indicates that Josephine, another of 'Mama's girls', should dance to a furious drumbeat, seductively at first and then in a frenzy: 'She releases her anger, her pain ... everything. She desperately grabs at the air as if trying to hold on to something. She abruptly stops, overwhelmed' (64). If words and action can play against each other, so inner tensions break surface in movement. In this bar, located nowhere in particular, in which two sides compete in atrocities, meeting injustices with injustices, exchanging cruelties as though they were a common currency, human beings struggle to negotiate a space in which they can survive, even as the need for survival is what leads to the compromises that can slam the door on hope. If this is a play about the extremes to which people may be pressed, it is also a play in which some spark of possibility flickers darkly.

Part of the power of the play, indeed, lies in its staging of inconvenient truths, alongside attempts to deny them, as it does in a lyricism that momentarily glows at the heart of horror.

Here, love is for sale, carrying a taint as one girl disappears with AIDS, even as love is sought when Salima's husband appears begging for the wife he had rejected. Even Mama has her hopes, Christian being attached to her as Mr Harari is to Sophie, who is obliged to dance and sing for the pleasure of those who constitute a continuing threat to her. Hope, though, is too easily corrupted, contaminated, the source of irony. Thus although Salima becomes pregnant, it is with 'the child of a monster' (70).

At the end of the text, we are offered a list of Swahili translations but if instead of reading horizontally from Swahili to English one reads vertically, what emerges is a brutal poem that summarises the action and tone of the play:

> Stop the noise
> Fear death
> Shut her mouth
> Welcome
> Dummy
> Come here
> Shit
> Stupid
> Cheers
> Quick
> Okay okay

Africa was probably called the dark continent for the first time in the nineteenth century by American journalist Henry Stanley, dark because unexplored but also because of its assumed savagery, compared with the supposed sophistication and civilisation of the Western powers that plundered it. When Conrad titled his book *The Heart of Darkness*, however, that darkness was seen as located in a Europe that suspended its Enlightenment values when it came to profit. Today Africa is still seen as rich for exploitation, a fact invoked in *Ruined*, and this is surely not a play only about a distant place despite the specificity of the crimes committed there. It is not just that women have always been seen as the spoils of war, the victims of calculated revenge or passed around as evidence of an unchallenged power. It is not just that neighbour turns against neighbour, as they did in Rwanda but as they did equally under the great dictatorships of twentieth-century Europe, as they did in the former Yugoslavia. It is that there is a more general point being made. As Christian declares, 'Our leaders tell us: "Follow my rules, your life will be better", their doctors say, "Take this pill, your life will be better", "Plant these seeds, your life will be better", "Read this book, your life will be better", "Kill your neighbour, you life will be better" . . . someone has to say it, otherwise, what? We let it go on . . . One day it will be at your door' (76).

There comes a moment when Mama lays aside her cynicism, pressing a diamond into the hand of Mr Harari, the proceeds to go to Sophie whom he is taking to safety, to a place where she can have an operation to heal her wounds, but she is too late, as the soldiers return, bringing with them a chaos underlined by gunfire and explosions. Their threat comes to nothing, though, because Salima has already anticipated their violence by inflicting it on herself, entering with blood running down her legs and dying in the arms of the husband who had abandoned her but then sought her out.

In *Ruined* hospitals are destroyed and patients killed. So they are in Syria. We hear accounts of torture and see their victims, but this play was written when George W. Bush was making torture American policy. Living with terror has become the experience of many. Here, race, gender and ideology are invoked to justify inhumanity, common ground across the planet.

For all this, Nottage allows herself to end the play on a note of grace as the poet salesman, Christian, returns and, in effect, proposes to Mama who despite insisting that love 'is a poisonous word' that will cost more than it returns, succumbs. Suddenly vulnerable, she declares that she is ruined, but she has encountered a man who, like Salima's husband, will not desert her: 'I don't know what those men did to you, but I'm sorry for it' he insists, 'I think we, and I speak as a man, can do better' (101). They begin to dance as the light fades, and Josephine watches 'joyfully'.

The evidence for men doing better in this play, and perhaps beyond its boundaries, is not strong. One woman is dead, another in thrall to what she is told is necessity, reading romantic stories so remote from her as to seem merely ironic. Yet the play also celebrates a resilience that is not that of Mother Courage, who will sacrifice anything as she profits from war including, crucially, her humanity. African-American women had first to survive before they could reclaim themselves and those they engendered. Slavery was built not only on labour but on sexual exploitation. There is, in other words, another history beyond that in contemporary Africa that Nottage invokes.

If there is any doubt about Lynn Nottage's ability to spin on a dime in dramatic terms, already evidenced in *Fabulation, or the Re-Education of Undine*, it should be dispelled by a visit to a website called www.meetverastark.com, not to be confused with another site, bythewaymeetverastark.com. This tells the story of an actress called Vera Stark whose career is celebrated by, among others, Peter Bogdanovich, credited as author of *Who the Devil Made It*. Billed as a documentary titled 'A Leading Lady in a Maid's Uniform: A Closer Look at *The Belle of New Orleans*', it explores the life of an African-American woman, Vera Stark, who appeared in the film *The Belle of New Orleans*, set in a brothel. The film was directed by the Jewish Maximillian Von Oster and banned by the Hays Office, which indeed precipitated the Hays Code. The film starred Gloria Mitchell, who plays the part of a white woman alarmed to discover that she has black blood, gasping, 'I'm an octoroon'.

In the 1950s Von Oster was blacklisted and faded into obscurity, writing jingles for toothpaste. In that same decade and into the 1960s, Stark is credited with being active in the Civil Rights movement. Indeed there is a photograph on the website, unfortunately taken from the rear so that only the back of her head is visible. Staying at a hotel in California, she used the swimming pool, which led to it being emptied and refilled when white guests complained. In 1973, after a short-lived run in Las Vegas, we are told, Vera Stark disappeared, although she does have a star on Hollywood Boulevard. Those in the documentary all identify a single line as the most memorable and meaningful she uttered: 'Stay awake and together we will face a new day.' The site offers information about the date and place of a Vera Stark symposium, although the link unfortunately leads to a message that 'The requested page cannot be found', itself something of a profound comment on the ephemeral nature of fame.

At bythewaymeetverastark.com, we learn that Vera's grandmother had been a contortionist and that she might have been cousin to Gloria Mitchell. *The Belle of New Orleans*, we discover, was based on a southern novel conceived as an indictment of slavery and publicly burned in front of the state capitol in Louisiana. Vera Stark was rewarded for her performance by being the first African-American to win an Academy Award for Best Supporting Actress, although her subsequent career offered only bit parts in film (*God's Fitfull Chilluns*) and television (*Lumus and Larry*). Her two marriages proved unsuccessful; one was to a trumpet player who beat a man to death with his trumpet, the other to a middleweight boxer; Vera took to drugs and alcohol. In Las Vegas she stripped naked while singing 'Heat Wave' and was arrested for public indecency before disappearing. Once again there is a documentary, this time introducing her gay agents, whose company is captioned as Scottie Hudson Affiliated Talent (S.H.A.T). Her last film, they explain, was *Blacula*, in which she played the mother, except that her part was cut. Her final acting job was on a radio advertisement for tobacco, recorded when she was drunk.

Unsurprisingly, none of this is true. Vera is Nottage's invention, the websites extending that fiction out into the world, ironically making her more real by virtue of a virtual history. The play, she has explained, was written out of a need to 'go somewhere light' while writing *Ruined*, although that lightness has an edge to it, the humour changing its tone and target.

By the Way, Meet Vera Stark, whose premiere was at Second Stage Theatre in New York City in May 2011, is, Nottage suggests, in the 'tradition of the screwball comedies of the 1930s' with the first act 'very fast-paced, whimsical and always buoyant. Breathless', while the second is 'no less fast-paced' but reflects 'the comic sensibilities of 1973 and 2003'.[23] The first scene takes place in a stylish room in Hollywood in 1933. Gloria Mitchell is a 'white' starlet, a little more bulky than perhaps she might be and nursing a glass of gin, while Vera is a twenty-eight-year-old African-American, dressed as a maid and speaking with an exaggerated black language of a kind familiar from films of the time. It is not immediately clear but Vera is rehearsing the actress for an audition for which she is clearly unprepared, oblivious to the fact that she is to play the part of a dying virgin in a brothel. The word 'white' in quotation marks is a clue to what seems to be her ambiguous racial heritage.

The second scene takes place in a dishevelled apartment that Vera shares with two other women, Lottie and Anna Mae, the latter described as 'very very fair-skinned,' angling to get into films by attaching herself to directors while passing as white by pretending to be Brazilian. In fact, all three are desperate to get their foot in the door to Hollywood, Lottie having 'shimmied' in New York in a show called *Blackbirds* and played Juliet to a group of Pullman porters. Alongside the witty dialogue, however, another world exists beyond the movies or the radio drama and music they listen to as Vera refers to police 'swarming all over the place . . . plucking Negroes off the street like cotton' (17). Vera herself hopes to persuade Gloria to help her get into the film, which offers the prospect of 'Slaves with lines' (22), with black actresses getting to say 'something other than "yes 'um" and "no 'um"', her own eye being on the part of the maid we have already seen her play.

On a studio back lot, she meets Leroy, apparently an assistant to the director who she asks to arrange for her to audition for the part of Tilly, a slave girl who cares for her ailing mistress. He 'does a spot-on impression of Stepin Fetchit' and asks, 'why we still playing slaves . . . it was hard enough getting free the first damn time' (32). Unsurprisingly, he is not the director's assistant but his chauffeur, and in the fourth scene, when the head of studio and director meet for drinks in Gloria's apartment, comedy gives way to farce as friends, and now rivals, Vera, Lottie and Anna Mae (desperately struggling to maintain the fiction that she is Brazilian), present themselves as potential actresses adapting to whatever roles they think they might be asked to play, Vera presenting herself as a poor girl from the South whose mother had died in childbirth and whose father was a blues singer. Asked to sing the blues herself, she desperately improvises.

The studio owner is nervous about a picture to be filmed in an actual brothel, asking if the whores could be 'less, prostitutey', afraid that 'if our lead is a whore and we have a bunch of Negroes running around selling misery, we won't be able to open the picture in New York City'. If he had 'wanted a critique of antebellum New Orleans', he objects, he would 'have checked a book out of the library' (49). At a time when 'the economy is dying and good folks are being forced out of their homes and into the fucking gutter', he explains, 'People want to laugh . . . All I'm asking is that if you're gonna give 'em slaves, give 'em happy ones' (50). When *By the Way, Meet Vera Stark* was staged in 2011, the US economy was still struggling to recover from the 2008 crash while 6.8 million homes had already been lost to foreclosures with a further 2 million expected that year. Whenever it is set, and despite the comedy, it was not wholly removed from the present.

The second act starts with a clip from the movie *The Belle of New Orleans*, with Gloria playing the octoroon mistress of a wealthy merchant and Anna Mae playing her friend, a French singer, obviously having won her battle to make her way into movies. Vera herself has only won the part of the slave girl, delivering her lines in the way she had at the beginning of the play. Nonetheless, the film, a direction explains, is not to be a parody but in the style of the 1930s, although in truth parody it surely is with Vera pleading, 'Oh Lawdy, Mis', please don't die on me' as Gloria declares, 'I'm free, Tilly, I'm free.' She does indeed die despite Vera imploring her to 'Stay awake, and together we'll face a new day.' She is joined not only by Anna Mae but also Lottie who has obviously managed to stake her own claim to a part as a slave woman and has the last words: 'She in he'ben now.'

When the film ends, however, we have moved forward to 2003 and a colloquium titled, 'Rediscovering Vera Stark, the Legacy of *The Belle of New Orleans*' conducted by Herb Forester played by the same actor who had earlier play Leroy and, indeed, a number of the parts are doubled. It is a colloquium in which a professor of media and gender studies, who is also a semiotician and classically trained actress, together with a 'slightly masculine' poet and performer whose book is titled, *Interrogating Mammy, the Parenthetical Negro Dilemma*, try to squeeze Vera into their particular jargon. For the former, she represents, '"Das unausgesprochene", to cite Arnhelm Machenhauer, "The Unspoken!"', while for the latter she had been 'battling patriarchal hegemony' (73–4), both all too familiar from academic conferences around the world.

As part of the colloquium, a 1973 recording of a chat show is played, featuring Vera and Gloria, Vera now in her sixties, hardened by drink, Gloria coming off the back of three marriages. They still upstage one another and come close to revealing Gloria's racial heritage. The play ends as they step down for a moment from the movie as their young counterparts debate whether Gloria's line about being free might have meant being free from prejudice before stepping back onto the set for the movie to resume.

In 2010, there was an actual symposium at Arena Stage in which African-American playwrights and theatre practitioners came together to discuss the state of black theatre. It revealed familiar tensions between those who looked to define themselves by colour and who called for theatrical institutions in which they could flourish, and those who resented being defined purely by colour rather than a national identity that contained a plurality of voices. There was concern expressed about the need for black women to write plays that reflected backgrounds and experiences capturing more than deprivation, to tell their own stories rather than conforming to models preferred by artistic directors, black or white, or even by what had once been an assumed consensus about the role of black playwrights and the legitimacy of their subjects.

At the same time, there was the feeling that there remained an anxiety about staging dysfunctional families, not because of any pressure from a presumed black community (whose homogeneity had always been suspect and perhaps was more so now) but because of fears that that this might not be seen as acceptable. A black *August: Osage County*, one contributor observed, would be unlikely to get a reading. Concern was expressed about the role of comedy, on the one hand because of a history in which humour had been seen as embedded in stereotypes designed to appeal to white audiences, and on the other because of the nervousness of politically correct white audiences unsure of the legitimacy of laughing until validated by black members of the audience.

Those in the symposium met two years after the election of President Obama, and there was a sense that something radical had changed. Some obligations had been lifted. History had not been transcended, but, for the playwright Pearl Cleage, the direction of travel had changed. The pressure to write as a representative of anything but her own experience had been lifted. She was, she declared, an American playwright concerned with what it means to be that.

The problems of the American theatre remained, the tendency of artistic directors to include a single work by a black American writer as a gesture, a token of multiculturalism, and the absence of roles for black actors, hence the continuing need for black theatrical institutions. At the same time, the conversation had changed. For Lynn Nottage, black playwrights remained a community in that, sometimes in radically different ways, they did, and do, share common problems if not subjects, so much so that she proposed a mentoring system. Yet she is an embodiment of an approach to writing that is not bound by any one subject, model, convention, genre. She self-evidently engages with painful and urgent issues but equally has a powerful sense of irony and a playful manner, her humour being as essential to her view of experience as her commitment to telling the stories of those who have found themselves excluded through their race or gender.

Marsha Norman, in an essay regretting the barriers to women playwrights, observed that 'A theatre that is missing the work of women is missing half the story, half the canon, half the life of our time . . . Telling the stories of women is the first crucial step in insuring their safety and their work . . . Lynn Nottage's beautiful play *Ruined* is a perfect testimonial to the power of a storyteller to make a difference'.[24] At the same time, it was Sarah Ruhl who observed the need to 'write outside our gender . . . write outside of our culture sometimes . . . write about mythologies that are much larger than us . . . expand what you know'.[25]

That is what Nottage did with *Sweat*, a play that resulted from a commission by the Oregon Festival and Arena Stage; it opened in Oregon in 2015 and at Arena Stage, Washington, DC, in 2016. It was a play that had a particular resonance as the presidential election of 2016 astonished and depressed by equal measure except that, in many ways, *Sweat* had identified what would turn out to be a key issue in that election: the sense of alienation felt by many of the middle and lower-middle classes in those states that had seen their industries collapse long before the 2008 financial crisis. The immediate inspiration came from the realisation that a nearby friend was struggling with poverty, from the Occupy Wall Street movement and from a *New York Times* article about Reading, Pennsylvania, a town of 88,000 people in which, according to the 2010 census, 41.3% were living in poverty.

For two-and-a-half years, she and her assistants travelled to Reading and conducted interviews with a number of those struggling to get by. As she explained to the *Los Angeles Times*, 'It's what I call the de-industrial revolution' the 'shifting from a manufacturing base . . . When you rip that out from under the country, how do we redefine ourselves? . . . What I heard repeatedly, regardless of race or class, was that people felt a sense of being trapped and isolated. The city had lost its tax base, and they could feel the city decaying and crumbling around them.'[26] The play that emerged would reflect what she had found, which was a population of people who were marginalised, disenfranchised, ignored. Where once that would have defined the plight of many African Americans, now it was a shared experience.

Sweat opens in 2008 with two young men, Jason and Chris, one white (with white supremacist tattoos), one black, meeting their black parole officer. They share a crime but differ in their expectations, the former angry and bitter, the latter sustained by religion and optimistic about his future. The action then moves back to 2000 and a bar where three women factory workers, two of them the men's mothers, meet. Cynthia and Tracy have managed to find jobs at the plant for their sons. They have known one another since high school and feel a loyalty not only to one another but to their place of work, no matter how hard that work may be. This is a site of camaraderie, truth telling and, ultimately, accusations and betrayals, presided over by a barman who carries the physical wounds of a factory accident while in the background are those whose desperation has led them to torch their home or commit suicide.

The women have worked in a metal tubing plant for many years. They feel secure, although their fate is being determined by others. Management develops plans to downsize while a television set, tuned to cable news, brings political realities into this supposedly protective environment. Trade deals are being done that will reach out to Pennsylvania. The drama that plays out reflects the entropy of the community as the plant where they work winds down and tensions develop as one of the women, the African-America Cynthia, looks for promotion even as others face layoffs. Marriages have proved no more secure than employment. Drink and drugs have their attraction as gaps open up between those who had once seemed so close. As the tension builds, fractures appear along the lines of race. As Nottage explained,

I wanted two generations to be in conversation. And I wanted to understand how the impact of the parents' choices played out in the lives of their children. And that's how I came upon the two time periods. So it's set in 2000 and 2008 and it begins with a very cohesive group of people who are slowly fractured over a period of time, and then in 2008, you see all the repercussions of the choices that they made in 2000. So that's how the structure took shape.[27]

For Nottage, the play began with 'the last image of the play, in which you have four men who come from very different backgrounds standing on the stage in a moment of crisis and trying to find the vocabulary to communicate across the divide. That's what I began with, and I thought, how did I get there?'[28]

Sweat is bridged by two elections and reached New York on the edge of another. What had begun as a history play suddenly lived on the pulse. The plight of those in such places as Reading was invoked at one end of the political spectrum by Bernie Saunders and at the other by Donald Trump, who went on to win the area of which Reading was the county seat and had previously voted for Barack Obama. The play is open-ended not least because the issues at its heart have not been resolved and do not offer themselves for resolution except in the rhetoric of politicians or those who present themselves as anti-politicians nonetheless seeking public office. That is in part the strength of a play that takes a cold look at the real, reflected through the lives of individuals, while resisting an ideological stance. Nottage was determined to embrace the conviction she had learned from Arthur Miller – to engage in a conversation with America, something whose relative absence in the American theatre she regretted. As she has remarked,

What I see in New York is that shows are shrinking down. I don't see a lot of politics on stage . . . it's not about ideas and ideologies being challenged . . . I think that provocation is when you enter in the space and everything you believe in is challenged . . . I think that what surprises people with this show is the alliances they forge with characters that are then undermined . . . the whole show exists in the gray area. Everyone in the play makes a compromised decision that ends up having implications that hurt someone else. There's no character in the play that doesn't do that, and I think that's challenging.[29]

Sweat won the 2016 Susan Smith Blackburn Prize for women playwrights, awarded in previous years to Annie Baker, Katori Hall, Sarah Ruhl and Naomi Wallace. It also won the Pulitzer Prize, in 2017 opening on Broadway where it ran for 105 performances.

Notes

1 Victoria Myers, 'An Interview with Lynn Nottage', *The Interval*, 14 October 2015. http://theintervalny.com/interviews/2015/10/an-interview-with-lynn-nottage/

2 Lin-Manuel Miranda and Jeremy McCarter, *Hamilton: The Revolution* (New York, 2016), p. 33.

3 Victoria Myers, 'An Interview with Lynn Nottage'.

4 Lynn Nottage, 'Introduction', *The Penguin Arthur Miller* (New York, 2015), pp. xiii–xv.

5 Alexis Greene, *Women Who Write Plays: Interviews with American Dramatists* (New York, 2001), p. 359.

6 Ibid, p. 360.

7 Lynn Nottage, *One More River to Cross: A Verbatim Fugue* (New York, 2015).

8 Dwyer Murphy, 'History of Omission', *Guernica*, 1 May 2013. www.guernicamag.com/interviews/history-of-omission

9 www.encyclopedia.com/education/news-wires-white-papers...nottage-lynn-1964

10 Alexis Greene, *Women Who Write Plays* (New York, 2001).

11 Alexis Greene, *Women Who Write Plays*, p. 350.

12 Ibid, p. 351.

13 Ibid, p. 347.

14 Ibid, p. 349.

15 Ibid, p. 345.

16 Ibid, p. 356.

17 Lynn Nottage, *Intimate Apparel* (Bristol, 2014), p. 4.

18 Ibid, p. 17.

19 www.encyclopedia.com/education/news-wires-white-papers...nottage-lynn-1964

20 Ibid.

21 Lynn Nottage, *Fabulation or, The Re-Education of Undine* (New York, 2005), p. 9.

22 Ibid, p. 13.

23 Lynn Nottage, *By the Way, Meet Vera Stark* (New York, 2013), p. 5.

24 Marsha Norman, 'Not There Yet', *American Theatre*, 9 November 2009, p. 79.

25 Bianca Garcia, 'Playwright Sarah Ruhl on "The Oldest Boy"', *Stage Buddy*, n.d. http://stagebuddy.com/theater/theater-articles/interview-playwright-sarah-ruhl-oldest-boy

26 Daryl H. Miller, 'What Happens When Factory Jobs Disappear? Playwright Lynn Nottage investigates in "Sweat"', *Los Angeles Times*, 28 October 2016.

27 Victoria Myers, 'An Interview with Lynn Nottage'.

28 Jeffrey Brown, 'Steelworkers' stories of disappearing jobs comes to life onstage in "Sweat"', *PBS Newshour*, 10 February 2016. http://pbs.org/newshour/bb/steelworkers-stories-of-disappearing-jobs-come-to-life-onstage-in-sweat

29 Holly L. Derr, 'Lynn Nottage Talks Research, Collaboration, and the Fracturing of America', *Howlround*, 28 January 2016.

8

Sarah Ruhl

I'm interested in poking holes in naturalism.[1]

– Sarah Ruhl

... we shall not aim at imprisoning the comic spirit within a definition. We regard it, above all, as a living thing... we shall treat it with the respect due to life.[2]

– Henri Bergson

For Sarah Ruhl, playwriting is in part about play, theatre as artifice. In her work the real has less to do with simulation than metaphor. Her instincts are meta-theatrical. Humour works to crack open an art of surfaces. She is drawn to the Dionysian. She resists the gravitational pull of naturalism and is interested in the performed self, in *Passion Play*, the membrane between actor and role proving disturbingly permeable. In *Dead Man's Cell Phone*, a character is slowly created in front of us. *The Last Kiss* features a play within a play. Physical objects are liable to become animate or transmute. Indeed, she revels in the capacity of theatre to effect transformations, to disturb our sense of the fixity of experience. In her adaptation of Virginia Woolf's *Orlando* (2010), a man changes into a woman. In her plays, stones can talk, a woman transforms into an almond. Humour can become method and subject, comedy edging towards farce, although neither without an undercurrent of seriousness. She deals, indeed, with fundamental issues. Her 2016 play *Peter Pan on her 70th Birthday* (staged first as part of the Humana Festival of New American Plays), for all its vibrancy and imaginative freedom, starts with the death of a father and mortality is one of its themes.

For Ruhl, language becomes an object to be explored, an inheritance, perhaps, from her mother who has a doctorate in language, literacy and rhetoric, if also from her father who had a fascination with words. The poet in her is a felt presence, sometimes, as in *Orlando*, in a literal form, presented in verse, but equally in the rhythms of ordinary speech. In her adaptation of Chekhov's *The Three Sisters* (2011), she set out to capture the rhythms of his prose.

Sometimes, as with *In the Next Room (or the Vibrator Play)*, it could take years for plays to come into focus. They could equally change in the process of development as she listened to actors inhabiting the roles and to audiences who in her work are often asked to become confederate, their presence acknowledged, their role integral as rather than be wholly external to the action they are invited to revel in the mechanics of theatre, its claim simultaneously to offer simulation and truth. She has said that she is a lover of poor theatre, happy with a play with no more than a couple of chairs and language.

Sarah Ruhl was born in Wilmette, Illinois, a village in Cook County, four miles north of Chicago's northern border on the western shore of Lake Michigan, also the birthplace of Charlton Heston and Bill Murray. Speaking of her early years, she has said that 'Bookish-ness and difference are not terribly rewarded in the Midwest ... You really had to hide any interest in the intellect – guard it with your life, especially at elementary school.'[3]

Her mother was an actress in Chicago in the 1960s, appearing in plays by María Irene Fornés and Megan Terry before becoming a teacher. She continued to act in and direct plays, taking her daughter to rehearsals. Ruhl was enrolled in classes at the Piven Theatre Workshop in nearby Evanston, whose alumni, as John Lahr points out in a *New Yorker* interview, included John Cusack, Joan Cusack, Aidan Quinn and Polly Noonan, the last subsequently appearing in Ruhl's plays. The group was heavily influenced by Viola Spolin famous for the acting exercises she called theatre games. As Ruhl explained, 'We acted stories, myths, fairy tales, folktales, then literary tales – Chekhov, Eudora Welty, Flannery O'Connor, Salinger.' It was not a theatre that used props or sets. 'Language did everything. So, from an early age: no fourth wall, and things can transform in the moment.'[4] It was the theatre that in 2002 would stage her *Melancholy Play*.

Her father sold toys but had a love of language and music. He used to take Sarah and her sister (who later went on to be a psychiatrist) to a pancake house for breakfast and teach them words and their etymology.[5] They 'were encouraged to play at home, so that art-making didn't seem like an escape from family or a retreat but very much a part of life'. They saw Shakespeare at Stratford, Ontario, while her mother explained to Lahr that 'One of the most intense theatrical experiences for her was when I directed "Enter Laughing" [a 1963 two-act farce by Joseph Stein] ... She got to know all the actors. By that point, people would ask her for her notes. She was six or seven.'

Rulh has recalled the plays she saw growing up, including *A Midsummer Night's Dream*, set by her mother in the 1920s; from that production, she learned 'an early love of theatrical magic and transformation',[6] as she did an interest in minor characters when her mother played the Nurse in *Romeo and Juliet*. Meanwhile, these productions in a community theatre taught her something of theatre's significance to a community, later reflected in her own *Passion Play*. Memories from these years, indeed, would stay with her when she wrote *Peter Pan on her 70th Birthday*: 'When I was growing up, whenever I visited [my mother's] family house in Iowa, there were these pictures of her as Peter Pan, in green tights, flying ... So it was part of my association with my mother, and also part of my association with what theatre was.'[7]

As a child she would tell stories, which her mother duly typed. Apart from an attempt at playwriting in the fourth grade, there was little evidence she would become a dramatist. Indeed, her first published work was a volume of poetry, which appeared when she was twenty. She renewed her interest in theatre when, as a student at Brown University, she saw a student production of Paula Vogel's *The Baltimore Waltz*, a play that reduced her to tears and from which she derived elements that would become important to her own work:

How she uses gesture and language in that play, and how there was no fourth wall. How she used fragment. How she changed modes and styles quickly, seamlessly. How language itself can be a source of solace but also a mode of alienation. How the personal can coexist up against the iconic and become even more personal for the contrast . . . how arbitrary are our distinctions between the real and the unreal. How she sees theatre as a place for memory, and for ghosts.[8]

During her first two years at Brown, she spent part of her time travelling to Chicago, her father having been diagnosed with advanced metastatic cancer in her freshman year. When he died, she took a semester off. On her return to Brown, she was in a state of some confusion until she took a course with Vogel. It was her father's death that prompted her first play. Vogel has explained that in her own case, 'If someone asked me to write a play about my brother Carl, who died of AIDS, I'd never have gotten out of bed. Instead I wrote about a kindergarten teacher taking a trip through Europe, which became *The Baltimore Waltz*. And I was able to write about my brother.'[9] She now suggested that Ruhl should write a play with a dog as protagonist. Ruhl used the play – *Dog Play* – to address the fact of her father's death, picturing a dog waiting for the return of a family that, in fact, is at its master's funeral. It moved Vogel to tears, and she offered to work with her on her drama.

At first, she resisted, spending a year at Oxford University. When she returned it was initially to write a senior thesis on representations of the actress in the Victorian novel. Instead, Vogel suggested she should write a play. It turned out to be the first part of *Passion Play*, which would not be completed for another twelve years. During that time she had thoughts of being a poet but came to feel that she had exhausted her possibilities in that direction. As she explained to Lahr, 'I didn't know what a poem should be anymore . . . Plays provided a way to open up content and have many voices. I felt that onstage one could speak lyrically and with emotion, and that the actor was longing for that kind of speech, whereas in poetic discourse emotion was in some circles becoming embarrassing.'[10]

Speaking of the works of Arthur Miller and Tennessee Williams, Ruhl has suggested that the former built scaffolds to reach a moral ('They were all my sons'), while the latter stressed that every moment is emotionally or aesthetically important for its own sake. This distinction between what she calls the architect and the poet she sees as reminiscent of the old contrast between morality and mystery plays, with the morality plays having a clear moral and the mystery plays having an emotional impact that is hard to capture cognitively. In modern drama, she sees one as represented by Shaw and the other by Beckett.[11]

While not disparaging the architect, her own work would seem to privilege the poet. In particular, she was suspicious of an American dramaturgy that favoured the morality play presented as realistic drama in which characters go on a journey, come to an understanding: 'don't,' she urges, 'make your play into a reform school' (18). Her characters do change, but often in the moment and in ways that do not serve an objective. Their interior worlds are not disguised to serve some ultimate revelation. The boundary between interior and exterior can indeed be factitious. When her own child was growing up, she was struck by her ability, in play, to change roles and moods in a moment, to contain different identities, fundamental to theatre but equally to that sense of empathy that is a pre-condition for any community, large or small. To her, psychological realism made emotions so rational that they no longer seemed like emotions.

In offering advice to actors in her plays, she said, 'please, don't think one thing and then say another. Think the things you are saying . . . Perhaps it is because I am from the Midwest, but I think it is ontologically impossible to truly think one thing while saying another thing. It creates an acting muddle in the theatre and a sociopath in life.' It is not that there is no subtext but that what is not said is best looked on as 'to the left of the language and not underneath it'. She recalls Maria Irene Fornes objecting to method actors saying, 'What does my character want in this scene?' remarking, 'Who always wants something from someone else? Only criminals. And Americans.'[12] It is not that her characters lack objectives. Indeed they sometimes oblige by announcing them. It is not that they lack interior lives but that she sees language in its immediacy, emotion as not requiring an act of recall, emotional speleology.

For her, naturalism imposes limits not least because it underestimates the capacity of audiences. 'One declares the imaginary world into being. Method acting has the opposite philosophical stance. Saying one thing, the actor assumes that the real truth is buried or hidden under the language. Rather than having language bring to life the invisible world, in naturalism the visual lie is attempted scenically, and language is a cover for the invisible world of feelings.' What is understood by a five-year-old, she asserts, 'that language invents worlds – is assumed by producers to be intellectually ungraspable by an audience of well-educated grown-ups, who, it is thought, need to see spigots and so forth to represent kitchens, because holding a mirror to nature – or the sink – is thought to be transcendent' (78–9). For her, drama involves dialectic rather than conflict, contrasts and surprise rather than linguistic duelling. She favours the Dionysian over the Apollonian, because it leaves space for the irrational. She quotes approvingly Virginia Woolf's observation to Vita Sackville-West that style is all rhythm, and there is a rhythm, or rather there are rhythms, to Ruhl's plays.

She did not find placing her plays easy and, indeed, has recalled crying as she received rejection letters, one accusing her of being too conservative, another of being too radical, yet another suggesting that her work hardly constituted a play. Finally, though, in June 2002, the Piven Theatre, where she had watched her mother act, staged *Melancholy Play*.

W. G. Sebald once observed that melancholy 'is a very respectable mood to be in, whether you are a philosopher or a writer . . . Even comedians . . . tend to be of that dark bent'.[13] Of *Melancholy Play*, Ruhl has said, 'I was fascinated by the rise of the pharmaceutical approach to depression, and wondered if we had caught up culturally . . . I wondered if a whole aesthetic category of melancholy was being altogether lost in our efforts to eradicate depression more broadly. I was also interested in sudden emotion; that in the pharmaceutical era, you could be happy very suddenly and neurochemically, without a rising action . . . and I wondered if our plays had caught up to this more biological model of emotion.'[14]

Melancholy Play, which Ruhl describes as 'a contemporary farce' and which would later become a musical, is, in part, to do with transitions, emotional and literal. There has to be sadness, she explains in a note on the tone of the play, inside the farce even as melancholy is to be bold and outward. The set calls for specific props even as they are used to mark transitions. The world of the play, she explains, 'is less about scenic illusion and more about seamless entrances and exits, so that one scene floats into another'.[15]

The play, we are told by Frank, a tailor, is to be a defence of melancholy, although Ruhl has said, 'I was thinking about depression rather than melancholy . . . The character (Tilly, a bank teller) is so depressed she seals herself off from the world with a very hard shell and disappears into a small object.'[16] In one sense the hard shell is the almond-shaped amygdala, that part of the brain, we are told in an epigraph, that attaches emotional meaning to sensations and can be the source of feelings of sadness or fear. For all Ruhl's preference for the word 'depression', Tilly explains to the psychiatrist who is treating her, Lorenzo, that she is feeling melancholy. For his part, Lorenzo confesses to having feelings for her, nor is he the only one to feel this way, melancholy, it seems, having a certain allure. We are not, though, in a realistic world as one character turns into a literal almond, another is accused of being like an almond because he is 'dry – like bark', while at one stage a letter warns people to stay at home for fear that they, too, might turn into almonds. Ruhl has written about her interest in the transformations of Ovid. Here it is as easy to feel the influence of Kafka.

It is a play that almost defies summary and certainly not a work in which plot can be said to be central. The characters at times address the audience directly, sometimes simultaneously, repeat words and phrases, tread on scattered almonds. Characters have been abandoned, separated, reunited, drink from a vial of tears. As the other characters fall in love with Tilly so her melancholy transfers to them while she becomes increasingly happy and the play ends with a dance of joy, melancholy giving way to happiness. Ironically, when the play was turned into a musical, the composer's name was Almond. Somehow, given the logic of the play, that seemed inevitable, music in her plays, meanwhile, being seen by Ruhl as an antidote to naturalism.

Just a month after the initial production of *Melancholy Play* came *Passion Play*, the first two parts of which were written with the encouragement of Vogel. The first draft of the third part came years later, before the 2004 election and, she has said, was written with a great sense of urgency. As she explained, 'Paula . . . and I would sit at a little café in Providence . . . and she would buy me a cookie and read ten pages of *Passion Play*. Had Paula not said: "I think you should write that play", with the characteristic gleam in her eye, I would now be dissecting the imagery of wax in the Victorian novel. I would never have had the strange audacity to write the first sentence of a full-length play. At that time I wrote primarily poetry and fiction, and Paula snuck *Passion Play* into the New Plays festival at Trinity Repertory Company.'[17] That was 1997.

Ruhl recalls that she had been obsessed with the passion play since she was a child: 'Maybe it was being raised a Catholic, but I was also definitely interested in how whole towns would get involved, or religiosity could be used as a cloak for other things. In that sense my play is much more about theatre than it is about religion.'[18] Religion, though, is theatre, as is politics, a point made by Arthur Miller in a contentious speech he made in Washington in which, in front of the city's elite, he analysed American presidents as actors – and not only the actor-president, Ronald Reagan. Ruhl confessed to being fascinated by 'how leaders use, misuse and legislate religion for their own political aims, and how leaders turn themselves into theatrical icons' (8). Thus Queen Elizabeth I, Hitler and Ronald Reagan enter the play, consummate performers, while the line between performance and being is sometimes blurred for those who play parts that are sometimes at odds with their lives, and sometimes in alignment.

In 2000, James Shapiro published *Oberammergau: The Troubling Story of the World's Most Famous Passion Play*. As he explained,

Oberammergau is justly celebrated as one of the few places in the world where theatre still matters. Communal and personal identity have become inextricably bound to the Passion play . . . Oberammergau is also notorious for staging a play – praised by Hitler himself and sharply attacked by Jewish organizations – that has long portrayed Jews as bloodthirsty and treacherous villains who conspire to kill Jesus. That it is performed in the country responsible for the Holocaust has only intensified criticism.[19]

Ruhl may have said that *Passion Play* is not a political treatise, but when she wrote the second and third parts, there was no doubting the deepening political intensity, although even the first part was rooted in a political context, religion, over the centuries, being what brought a society together by excluding those whose faith differed. England's history, which provides the backdrop to the first part, was one in which religion and the state were one, a stark melodrama in which rites, customs and practices were patrolled to exclude the potential for subversion. Theatre itself had to tread carefully or could become an agency of power, favoured or not by monarchs for whom religion was the very basis of their legitimacy.

The original passion plays were never simply community dramas that did no more than celebrate. In re-enacting Christ's passion they were deeply embedded in the forces that defined the private and public world. One dimension in particular united passion plays wherever they were staged: anti-Semitism. Sometimes unconsciously, more often consciously, they could reflect history or become its motor. They were performed by townspeople who thereby gained prominence, and often some recompense besides. They were amateurs who performed the same plays for years, actors whose roles often permeated their everyday lives as though the borderline between acting and being were flexible. No wonder that those who sought or assumed political power have always been drawn to the theatre, recognising in the figure of the actor someone seeking to convince the public that appearance and essence are the same.

The characters recur in the three parts that also share imagery, from puppet figures to a threatening red sky. Over the years the passion play at Oberammergau, and indeed human nature, remains the same even as its social and political context changes. It acts as a barometer of the times. For all its political resonances, however, Ruhl's triptych is laced through with humour, although it is scarcely the 'religious-themed romp,' described by the *Los Angeles Times*, as though it were a cross between *Noises Off* and *Murder in the Cathedral*.

The first section is set in England in 1575, shortly before the passion plays enacted in various cities were shut down by Queen Elizabeth, anxious to purge the last remnants of Catholicism from the land. And, indeed, a priest disguised as a friar appears, covertly taking confession from those performing in the drama. Ruhl was initially inspired by re-reading James Shapiro's book about Oberammergau's own passion play, first performed in 1634. What struck her, she explains in an author's note, was the fact that the man who played Christ was in fact holy, while the woman who played Mary was 'in real life, just as pure as the Virgin', which made her wonder 'how would it shape or misshape a life to play a biblical role year after year' and, beyond that, 'How are we scripted? Where is the line between authentic identity and performance? And is there, in fact, such a line?'[20]

That blurring is evident in Ruhl's play as the first part moves between scenes in which the actors perform their roles, often addressing the audience directly, and scenes in which they enact their own dramas, the young woman playing the Virgin Mary becoming pregnant by a fish gutter playing both Pontius Pilate and the Devil. To avoid scandal, she announces that she has actually been impregnated by God. She, in turn, lusts after a fisherman whose roles in the passion play are Jesus and Adam. Ironically, while offering to marry her, he believes her claim and hence promises not to touch her as she herself begins to believe in her own lie, thus thwarting her desires. Mary Magdalen, meanwhile, is, it seems, a lesbian dreaming of a life with the erstwhile, and now misnamed, virgin.

In one sense this is a passion play as Pirandello farce, a drama designed to celebrate purity and sacrifice devolving into a work of confused identities, religious passion into casual sex, the parts of Mary and Eve finally being taken by the Village Idiot as the director insists that 'the play must go on!' It ends with the arrival of Queen Elizabeth, hunting Catholics and banning passion plays, and with the deaths of Mary, who has drowned herself, and the Fish Gutter, fish puppets lifting him up and carrying him off as a red sky turns blue. The mechanics of the theatre are on display, as they were, of course, in the genuine passion plays, and that inevitably foregrounds the question of performance, the nature of passions staged as well as felt.

Part Two of the play takes place in Oberammergau in 1934, at the time of the rise of Hitler, who himself endorsed the 1934 production and who makes an appearance in *Passion Play*. The passion play's anti-Semitic dimension was such that in the 1970s, changes were made to a production as a result of representations made by Jewish organisations and the Catholic church. Arthur Miller was one of a number of Jewish intellectuals, including Leonard Bernstein and Lionel Trilling, who condemned its portraits of Jews. For Elie Wiesel, 'the artist cannot be silent when the arts are used to exalt hatred'.[21] Abraham Foxman, director of the Anti-Defamation League, remarked, 'if it's about a Crucifixion in which the Jews kill Christ, you can never clean it up enough'.[22] In the 1970 production, indeed, an ex-Nazi had become artistic director, while no Jew had ever appeared in it, for most of its history parts being restricted to Catholics.

Now, in 1934, a play in which a Jew is condemned by Jews has a sudden relevance, the daughter of the man playing Christ saying, 'I wanted with all my heart to run onstage and fight the Jews' (70). As they enact a scene in which Christ overturns the tables of the money changers in the temple, the Jewish chorus intones, 'My money, ah, my money!' (71). Violet, a young girl who is an outsider referred to as the Village Idiot, has a story of her own, re-imagining that of Hansel and Gretel, although when she speaks of the witch wishing to cook Hansel in an oven, the contemporary relevance is clear: 'Wouldn't you be scared? If someone wanted to push you in an oven' (72). In fact, and outside the play, the man who designed and built the crematoriums at Auschwitz lived in Oberammergau.

Eric, the man who plays Christ, wishes to become a soldier and, indeed, this is something of a militarised Oberammergau, with a German officer seducing the Virgin Mary and Pontius Pilate played by a foot soldier, a man who no longer believes in plays because the 'soldier's boot – that's real' (77). They are, he says, 'building a new Germany – there's hope for the future'. Mary 2, who plays Mary Magdalen, remarks that he should spend less time 'dreaming of wars that are never going to happen' (78). Even the play's director, in talking of his function, suggests the wider theme when he remarks that 'There are times in every man's life . . . when he needs a director . . . He needs someone with vision . . . someone stronger – me – to tell him what to do' (79). It is Eric, as Christ, who offers the warning: 'false Christs and false prophets shall rise. The sun shall be darkened, and the moon shall not give her light . . . Take heed. Watch and pray . . . And this is what I say unto you all: watch' (90). When Pilate hands over Christ, responding to the violence of the crowd, and they shout, 'We take it upon ourselves. His blood is upon us and our children!' guilt of another kind is implied. The irony is perhaps a little too calculated, but the passion play itself deals in betrayal, the arrival of a redeemer, a community focussed on a single purpose.

When Eric forgets his lines as Christ, Violet, hidden under the Last Supper table, prompts him, adjusting the speech as she does so. He dutifully repeats the words she whispers: 'In time you will crawl around like pigs snorting in the mud looking for the answer to this fundamental question: is there a God? And if you decide that there is no God, will you need someone with vision, someone stronger, to tell you what to do? Resist, I say unto you! And finally, I want everyone at this table, eating my blood and my body, to remember that I am a Jew' (82).

The second part opens with the figure of a visiting Englishman who is writing a book about theatre and who suggests that those involved in what has become a commercial passion play 'do not have a very complex understanding of the relation between art and life' (60), a relationship that is precisely what interests Ruhl and in fact dominates Oberammergau itself despite the fact that the play is only performed every ten years. Those playing the Virgin Mary were expected to be virgins while any scandal attaching itself to would-be actors could secure their disqualification, happily not a requirement of theatre around the world and not, in truth, in Ruhl's play despite the Virgin Mary's observation that 'here in Oberammergau, everything is as it appears to be' (89). Here, Christ and Pilate are sexually attracted to one another, and the Virgin Mary is prepared to submit to a German officer, while earthy humour co-exists with Christian melodrama, identity and role sometimes coinciding and sometimes diverging. As James Shapiro observed in his book about the town and its passion play,

> In Oberammergau people don't say someone acted or played the part of Caiaphas; they say he was Caiaphas; in the minds of many of the performers – and of their fellow villagers – acting goes well beyond ordinary impersonation. When a cyclist whizzes by, a local is likely to tell a visitor, 'There goes Pilate.' Everyone seems to know who had which of the hundred or so speaking parts in the play, and how well they performed, going back decades. And they are frank in their judgments. It's like living in a village populated entirely by theater critics ... As a former director of the play once put it: 'No Oberammergauer can talk about the village without talking about the play. No native in the village can think about his life without thinking about the play. The play is a part of us. It controls the rhythms of our life, like it or not.'[23]

Part two concludes, or nearly so, with the arrival of Hitler, duly saluted by all but Violet and the Englishman. His speech, Ruhl notes, is a direct quotation: 'One of our most important tasks will be to save future generations and to remain watchful in the knowledge of the menace of the Jews. For this reason alone it is vital that the Passion Play be continued at Oberammergau; for never has the menace of the Jews been so convincingly portrayed' (920). The sound of a whistle, and a train speeding across the tracks, justified by the fact that the Englishman is writing a letter from a train, is calculatedly ominous. In the final scene Eric, as Christ, enters wearing a Nazi uniform, talking to Violet who is being taken away because she has 'different blood'.

The third part of the play is set in the small town of Spearfish, South Dakota (population 11,000), which, until 2008, had its own passion play in a six-thousand-seat amphitheatre. It was founded by a German émigré whose family had played in a local passion play and left Germany when Hitler came to power. The time now is 1969 and the context not only the Vietnam War but also, at the time *Passion Play* was staged, the Iraq War. Asked by Arena Stage in Washington to write a play about America, Ruhl felt that a work that combined religion, politics and theatre was especially appropriate 'when it seemed as if we were in the midst of an unacknowledged holy war, conducted by a man who felt himself to be appointed by God (he must have been appointed by someone, he wasn't appointed by the popular vote in 2000) ... what is the difference' she asked herself, 'between acting as performance and acting as moral action. It is no accident that we refer to theatres of war' (8).

Closer in time than the first two parts, this has a sharper political edge. Humour has, for the most part, drained away, along with lyricism. Its middle American setting underscores the obvious gap between heartland values and the brutal realities of a war sanctioned in the name of those values. The leaders who precipitated war in the first two parts – Elizabeth and Hitler – appear alongside an American president, not because there is a proposed equivalence in the scale of the deaths for which they bare responsibility but because they all justify their actions in terms of national necessities. As to the passion play itself, for one of the amateur actors, it is about love. It is also, though, plainly concerned with betrayal and violence justified in the name of religion.

Ruhl has indicated that the three parts can be played separately but that they gain from being performed together (with a running time of more than three hours) in that it underlines the degree to which, whatever the changing context, there is a depressing continuity in human affairs even as, beneath the level of state violence, individuals continue to live the kind of messy existence that gives those lives their energy. The fact of communities coming together to serve art is also a counterbalance to the purposeful dislocations and divisions fostered by religion, which offers transcendence but too often breeds the opposite.

P, the man playing Pontius Pilate, who proposes to Mary 1, the woman playing the Virgin Mary, is off to Vietnam. As they wish him on his way, Queen Elizabeth enters, declaring that a famous victory is at hand and urging him to 'Go forth into battle, my son! And go with God!' (108). While he is away, though, J, his brother, the actor playing Christ, introduces Mary 1 to marijuana and begins an affair with her even as P is shot in Vietnam, appearing in uniform dragging a fish across a blood-smeared stage. The sky is red and the music associated with the puppet fish that had appeared in part one plays. Queen Elizabeth enters, expressing surprise that in this age men are ready to die for leaders who themselves know nothing of war.

J, who has been taking acting classes at university and has an ambition to be a professional actor, has plainly absorbed the language of theatre departments, looking, as he does, for the arc of the play, wishing to play the moment and feel it. Trying to motivate himself to play the part of a betrayer, he is asked by Mary 1, with whom he has betrayed his brother, whether he knows anyone who has been betrayed.

P returns from the war traumatised. He can no longer connect with his family. He has a vision, visible to the audience and to his daughter Violet, of Elizabethan ships and a chorus entering with wind machines. Violet claims to have lived before and insists that there have always been wars.

In time, a new professional director appears, a man who has avoided the draft by moving to Canada. The show is now complete with special effects. P is back in the play but sees blood everywhere, having memories of holding a child, a victim of friendly fire, whose brains had covered him. Hitler appears, but P alone can see him. P now objects to the play's anti-Semitism, even though the new text has been approved by the Anti-Defamation League. He explains that he no longer believes in God and that when he plays his part, he wants to be real, hammering a nail through his hand wishing, he explains, to nail the bad man for once.

The action then moves to 1984. Reagan is in power, and, now divorced, P has spent time in ten veterans hospitals in ten cities. He returns to Spearfish wishing to play Pontius Pilate again, feeling he now knows what it is to be responsible for killing someone. When he declares that he had killed people on the orders of the president, and his ex-wife reminds him that there is now a new president, he replies, 'A likeable man becomes a tyrant just like any other man . . . In a democracy, it is a *likeable* man who gets elected. It is a *likeable* man who sends you to your death . . . there's no difference between a nice guy and an evil guy who sent you out to kill. One of them is *photogenic* – the other one isn't – they both take you and they go ZIP' (144).

His brother, now a famous actor, returns to play in a special performance of the passion play for Ronald Reagan campaigning in the area, who now addresses the crowd in a speech that contains familiar Reagan phrases along with prophecies of the last times. Like George W. Bush, he believes God has a plan for him and for the country. The passion play, he announces, is about American values – family, God, baseball. He warns against homosexuality and AIDS (which, for years, Reagan famously failed to acknowledge) and then watches what has turned into a musical in which the Virgin Mary and Jesus seem embarrassingly like the lovers they are. When P shouts out from the audience, Reagan salutes him, another president who himself had not experienced war: 'I never did serve in the military' he declares, 'but I feel as though I did' (152). P then pulls a gun out, and as the Secret Service close in on him, he points it at his own head.

Passion Play, in its early form, was first produced in workshop in July 2002 at the sixty-seat Tristan Bates Theatre in London, named for the son of actor Alan Bates who died at age nineteen. Its world premiere followed in 2005 at Arena Stage in Washington, DC. Subsequent productions were at Chicago's Goodman Theatre in 2007, Yale Rep in 2008 and the Epic Theatre Ensemble at Brooklyn's newly established (2008) Irondale Center in 2010, an appropriate setting given that the space had previously been used for Sunday school lessons for the Lafayette Church.

In 2003, Ruhl opened *Late: A Cowboy Song* at the Ohio Theatre on Wooster Street in New York, a converted factory with high ceilings and a large space interrupted by columns and occasionally rats. As playwright Adam Boch observed, 'It didn't look like a normal theatre, so why would you expect normal theatre to come out of it?'[24] It was produced by Clubbed Thumb, a company whose name was derived from a book on palmistry.

Late: A Cowboy Song, Ruhl explains in a note reminiscent of Tennessee Williams, is a 'play for all the lady cowboys of heart and mind who ride outside the city limits of convention' (219). It features three characters, Crick and Mary, childhood sweethearts, who in the course of the play produce a child, get married and finally part, and Red, a woman described as a cowboy. Crick loses the only job he has, working as a museum guard, fired for touching a painting. Art, indeed, fascinates him, though partly as an investment.

When Crick and Mary's child is born, it has an indeterminate sexuality, a boy who surgeons intervene to make a girl. Mary wants to call her Blue, inspired by her growing relationship with Red, a butch woman who teaches her to ride a horse. Ruhl has said that the play was her love letter to transgender people and butch actors who seldom have parts to play.

Blue, the horse and the painting should, she says, be suggested or abstracted, while insisting that she would not say no to a real horse. There comes a moment when time speeds up until the play ends as Mary takes Blue's hand and leaves her husband for Red, together singing a cowboy song whose final verse is: 'Oh, find me a child / Who grows into a girl / Who rides like a man – / With a mask' (219).

Crick and Mary often deploy a language that implies affection and commitment (the sentimental *It's a Wonderful Life* playing on television in the background) while a current is moving in the other direction. Crick exudes an air of menace, baffled by her growing disaffection as by his own unfocussed existence, which he justifies to himself as much as her. Their exchanges lack precisely what exists between Mary and Red, a commonality. Mary is less seduced by her new cowboy friend than by the alternative world she offers. Learning to ride, she ventures into the dangerous and the free. She longs to be defined by something other than habit and convention. In a play in which gender is unstable, she searches for an identity and this in a form – theatre – which itself raises questions of identity. As elsewhere in her work, Ruhl's images work as hard as words – the painting (whose detail we never see), the horse (which may be no more than a saddle) being meta-theatrical gestures. The play, she has explained, was in part prompted by her reading of Brown University professor Anne Fausto-Sterling's *Sexing the Body: Gender Politics and the Construction of Sexuality*, which explored the social construction of gender and the treatment of intersex people.

The first act of *The Clean House* (2004), the play that would mark Ruhl's breakthrough, was commissioned in 2000 by the McCarter Theatre Center in Princeton, the full-length version following four years later at Yale Repertory Theatre before, another two years afterwards, opening at the Goodman Theatre. A subsequent production was staged by Lincoln Center. It was prompted by an overheard conversation at a cocktail party. As Ruhl explained, 'A doctor walked in and said, "I've had such a hard month . . . My cleaning lady from Brazil wouldn't clean, and I took her to the hospital and got her medicated, and she still wouldn't clean. So I had to clean my own house. I didn't go to medical school to clean house."'[25] What emerged from this, as might be imagined, was a comedy in which she required that everyone in the play should be able to tell a really good joke. In a 'Note on Jokes', she thanks those who contributed them while allowing for new ones to be added in subsequent productions. She later recalled the importance of humour in her own house when her father was dying. Now she was interested in what happened if you pushed humour, or funniness as she preferred to call it, to a reductio ad absurdum. Meanwhile, she asked herself of that cocktail party conversation: 'What does this mean about gender and class? . . . What about the poor woman? Is she clinically depressed or does she just hate cleaning? . . . The question is, how much responsibility do you have, not just literally, for the mess of your own life, and how much do you try and avoid chaos?'[26]

In his study of comedy, Mathew Bevis recalls that it was Ludwig Wittgenstein who claimed that a serious philosophical work could be written that would consist entirely of jokes and that the beginning of Aristophanes' *Frogs* sees Xanthias turn to Dionysus to ask, 'Shall I tell them one of the usual jokes, master, the ones that always get the audience laughing?'[27] *The Clean House* does not consist entirely of jokes, but it does feature a character in search of the perfect one and does, indeed, start with one, albeit told in Portuguese, itself something of a joke. Ruhl wanted, she explained, to see whether it would be funny in another language, an idea that María Irene Fornés found absurd. In the end, she indicated it could be subtitled.

The initial joke is addressed directly to the audience, as is the first speech of Lane, a doctor in her early fifties, who uses virtually the same words Ruhl had heard at the cocktail party while the answer to her own question is that the maid does, indeed, hate cleaning, having ambitions to become a stand-up comic coming from a family in which humour was a lingua franca and her mother literally died of laughter at one of her father's jokes, leading him to shoot himself. As a result, she wears black where her employer, Lane, wears white.

Lane, her sister Virginia, and Matilde, the Brazilian maid, all speak directly to the audience, explaining their respective positions. Virginia, it turns out, loves cleaning as much as the maid hates it, seeing it as a way to avoid morbid thoughts of a kind she immediately demonstrates as she speaks of the possibility of slashing her wrists and describes hospitals as 'places for dead human waste. Places to put dead bodies' (10). For her, cleaning is a way of bringing order to a disordered world.

Ruhl has said that the 'monologue dramatizes privacy, and yet, not really, because one is saying one's thoughts aloud to the audience, in an open admission that there is an audience . . . I like plays that make visible the interior'.[28]

This is indeed a play in which the mechanisms of theatre are made evident, not least in that the actors playing two of the characters also play two others and in which a stage direction requires that 'space should transform and surprise', a white living room morphing into an operating theatre, the balcony of a house by the sea into that same living room, objects thrown from the one landing in the other. Characters are given to bursting into song. As Ruhl has said, 'I enjoy the sensation of being read to in a theatre as opposed to watching people behave behind glass . . . So to break the fourth wall, or the implied wall of glass, for the actors to read to, speak to, sing to the audience, is an ancient form of communication, which now seems almost revolutionary. Don't make a wall of glass between your play and the people watching.'[29]

In that sense she has something in common with Edward Albee, who explained the reason he had actors speak directly to the audience:

In my mind, this is a way of involving the audience; of embarrassing, if need be, the audience into participation. It may have the reverse effect: some audiences don't like this; they get upset by it quite often; it may alienate them. But I'm trying hard to *involve* them. I don't like the audience as voyeur, the audience as passive spectator. I want the audience as participant . . . I am very fond of this because voyeurism in the theatre lets people off the hook.[30]

Lane's husband, Charles, is described as a compassionate breast surgeon, although plainly not carrying that over into his private life since he decides to leave his wife for a patient, Ana, a sixty-seven-year-old Argentinean woman who we are told is impossibly charismatic if also suffering from breast cancer. He loves her, he explains to the audience, 'to the point of invention' (53). His justification for leaving Lane is that under Jewish law, he has discovered, those finding their true soul mates are legally, 'metaphysically', and objectively justified in ending their existing marriage, information he has apparently derived from a programme on PBS. 'They fall in love', a stage direction indicates, only for another a moment later to indicate that 'They fall in love some more' before seconds later 'They fall in love completely', time compressed and, indeed, moving around, Scene 5 in Act II picking up where Scene 14 in Act I concluded.

When Charles brings Ana to meet his wife and her sister, Angela, Ana and Matilde immediately strike up a rapport, one speaking Portuguese and the other Spanish, the former proving an ideal audience to the latter's jokes, indeed inviting her to join her and Charles. In a scene together on a balcony they talk in a combination of Portuguese and Spanish, with English subtitles, as they throw apples into the sea except that the sea is also Lane's living room, space evidently being as plastic as time.

Ana is dying of cancer but refuses to go into hospital, leading Charles to travel to Alaska in search of a tree with medicinal properties, while Lane is persuaded to treat Ana, becoming reconciled to her and welcoming her into her home. Ana, recalling that Matilde's mother had died on being told a perfect joke, asks her to do the same for her. To the background of 'sublime' music, the maid – and would-be stand-up comic – whispers the joke into her ear. A subtitle is projected reading, 'The Funniest Joke in the World'. Ana laughs and collapses, dead. Lane washes her dead body as Charles returns from Alaska, carrying an enormous tree before collapsing over her.

At this point, Ana and Charles transform into Matilde's mother and father, wearing their clothes under their own, Matilde recalling the circumstances of her birth, which had been consequent on her mother laughing at her father's joke. The play ends on a note of reconciliation or, as Ruhl indicates, 'completion', Matilde finding herself in tune with her parents declaring, 'I think maybe heaven is a sea of untranslatable jokes. Only everyone is laughing' (109).

For Ruhl, self-evidently, play is a verb as well as a noun and in *The Clean House* she plays with theatrical conventions, modes of presentation. Thus characters transform, subtitles are projected. Not only are jokes told, sometimes at length and in a foreign language, they are functional both in terms of character and the spirit of a piece in which death is subsumed in life. She has said that she once wanted to be a portrait painter, reproducing the exact details of faces. In the end, though, she became suspicious because 'I was unable to paint *not* from life'.[31] What seems to fascinate her is not character as psychologically coherent, observably familiar in a recognisable social environment in which the solidities of the set offer to ground events in an unproblematic sense of the real. She wants instead to defamiliarise, to create rather than reflect a world that remains recognisable in its engagement with emotional needs but displaces these into a space in which anything can happen, perhaps rather as the novelist David Mitchell does in *Cloud Atlas* where character and time are fluid.

This can represent a challenge to those trying to place her work. In a play in which apples play a role, passing from one dimension into another, it is tempting to see reflections of Magritte, or hear echoes of Eric Satie who composed humorous miniatures for piano and kept a file of imaginary buildings in a filing cabinet. In other words she is an inventor of worlds rather than a chronicler. She has a dislike for the words 'whimsy' and 'quirky', both of which have been applied to her work, the former because it is 'a way of making feminine and therefore trivial a whole school of aesthetic fabulation. We do not' she adds, 'call Shakespeare whimsical, although his fairies flew and his witches chanted.' As to 'quirky' that seemed to her a word applied to anything with a perceptible aesthetic, as though 'in a homogenized culture, difference has to be immediately defined, sequestered, and formally quarantined while being gently patted on the head.'[32]

One scene in *The Clean House* has a stage direction that reads, 'it will be fun' (115), surely a promise rather than an injunction. Comedy, she has noted, may teach us 'to laugh at ourselves even as we weep for others'. Her worry, she explains, 'is that if plays (in order to be high art) ought not to be funny, or not funny in a certain way, because it cheapens their aesthetic status, then theatre is relegated to the mode of ballet or opera – neither of which is funny . . . If plays have their roots in vaudeville as much as they have their roots in Passion plays, then their roots are cut off when laughter is viewed as cheap.'[33]

Her next play, *Eurydice*, opened in 2003 at Madison Repertory Theatre and was subsequently produced by Berkeley Rep in the following year and at Off-Broadway's Second Stage Theatre in 2007. By her count it had fourteen staged readings on its way to full production, stabilising only with the thirteenth, after which nothing changed. Its first professional production was at Madison Rep. What interested her in particular was the emotional life of the characters. To a degree, in *Euridice* she was still dealing with the death of her father, and one of the play's characters is simply called Father. 'I think', she has said, 'I was trying to have more conversations with my own father by writing this story.' Beyond that, though, 'We live in a culture that's totally afraid of death . . . But it does seem to be a preoccupation of mine, this tenuous link between living people and dead people . . . I started writing seriously when my father got sick, and he died fairly young. That was a crucible through which a lot of my impressions were formed. When you have a loss like that, I think you keep re-experiencing it until you finally just don't.'[34]

Eurydice herself, scarcely given a voice in the original work, now has one and becomes the focus. When she dies and enters the underworld, she meets her father, who teaches her words as Ruhl's own father had taught her. When Orpheus is granted permission to enter the underworld to bring her back to life, she has to decide where her loyalty – her love – lies.

Perhaps understandably with Ruhl, she suggests that the underworld should have more of *Alice in Wonderland* about it than Hades, although frequently her images, casually described as surreal simply because of their unlikely juxtapositions of qualities, are rooted in the familiar. Thus when Eurydice descends into the underworld via an elevator in which rain is falling, it was because 'the experience of going into the underworld involves an alienation or unfamiliarity. Not in a devilish or horrible way, but in a contemporary way. Like when you go to a mall and you're in an elevator. It smells funny and it's tinny. Then you walk out and you're in a corporate hell.'[35]

Once in the underworld, she is met by her father who, mysteriously, had been able to write to her before she joined him. Because she has been through the River Lethe, at first she remembers nothing. People engage in normal activities, but there is no love save for that felt by Eurydice's father. A chorus of stones, indifferent, reminds those who come of where they are and the rules that apply, although even they are moved to tears when Orpheus descends playing a pure music to the accompaniment of raspberries, plums and peaches that fall from the ceiling into the river. Love, the father insists, is the joy of life, the love of father for daughter, a man for his wife. He creates a room for his daughter out of string, yet ultimately there is no avoiding death, Orpheus disobeying the injunction of the Lord of the Underworld (who rides a red tricycle and is accompanied by a heavy metal band) by looking back when he has been given permission to guide Euridice back to life. The play ends as she urges Orpheus to marry again and writes a letter to his next wife before she steps into the Lethe, which will purge her of her memories. Orpheus appears in the elevator, the rain streaming down, as he picks up the letter he cannot read because it is written in the language of the dead.

Ruhl re-forges the familiar myth, shifting its emphasis. As she remarked, 'There's an archetypal recognition of the story, which has been told through so many bodies and voices . . . I think there's something about the notion of a lifetime of remorse and regret being contained within the smallest thing – that one iconic gesture of looking back . . . At the same time, while we know a lot about Orpheus, we have so little information about Eurydice that in a way it's like writing the thing completely from scratch.'[36] Relieved of the responsibility of forging a plot that, she has confessed, is not her forte, she focuses instead on inventing a world out of music, images, a blend of the prosaic and poetic which makes the myth her own. She is not interested in reflecting the solemnities of Greek drama with its broad passions and conscious poetry. She operates on a smaller scale, as she brings the drama down to everyday and familiar emotions played out, although against a background of sometimes startling images. At the same time, she is more than happy that companies, sometimes strapped for cash, should find simpler ways of presenting the raining elevator and talking and weeping stones, theatre audiences happy to bring their imaginations to meet those of actors, designers and directors.

Her next play, *Dead Man's Cell Phone*, was first staged by the 265-seat Woolly Mammoth Theatre Company in Washington, DC, in 2007, before moving to Playwrights Horizon and Steppenwolf Theatre the following year, Ruhl acknowledging that 'a play needs a third production to finish the thing'.[37] It has the advantage of a title that is an entirely accurate description of a play in which a cell phone repeatedly rings turning out to be a portal into the life of a dead man if also an agent of revelation, consolation, irony and humour. Its published version carries three epigraphs. The first is from Charles Dickens's *A Tale of Two Cities* and underscores the degree to which people are mysteries to one another and pain a consequence of broken connections. The second is from John Donne, which praises someone for performing a brave act, the braver for being concealed. The third is from a study of Edward Hopper whose paintings feature characters 'whose parts have deserted them and now, trapped in the space of their waiting, must keep themselves company'.[38] Hopper's characters are pictured in their silence, communicating nothing but their isolation, discovered in bleak rooms or a night-time diner.

The play, indeed, begins in what could have been a Hopper setting, an almost empty café. A woman, Jean, with what a stage direction tells us is 'an insular quality', sits drinking coffee, while at another table a man, Gordon, is still – except that his stillness turns out to be that of death. His cell phone rings. When he fails to answer, Jean is at first irritated, then believes he may be deaf and answers the phone taking a message only, finally, to realise he is dead. That broken connection, though, leads her to make new ones as this isolated woman becomes involved in the life of the dead man, meeting members of his family, inventing spurious messages of love that she believes will offer them comfort, in the process discovering the truth of Dickens's observations while, like Donne's figure, concealing her efforts to console those she encounters. At a mass to commemorate the dead man, she prays, 'Help me to comfort his loved ones. Help me to help the memory of Gordon live on in the minds and hearts of his loved ones.' However, if she does so by inventing spurious conversations with him, she has an equal capacity to lie to herself, explaining that 'I only knew him for a short time, God. But I think that I loved him, in a way' (14). Nor does the phrase 'loved ones' quite ally with what we discover is a man who trades in human organs, a fact of which he assumes his wife is ignorant as she tells enquirers that he is in waste management.

Ruhl has remarked that cell phones have changed not simply behaviour but the way we relate to the world and other people. 'We're less connected to the present', she has said. 'No one is where they are. There's absolutely no reason to talk to a stranger anymore – you connect to people you already know. But how well do you know them? Because you never see them – you just talk to them. I find that terrifying.'[39] In fact Jean does talk to strangers, underscoring another aspect of electronic communications, that instant familiarity which breaches old conventions of address, a familiarity to which she lays claim as she assumes a specious intimacy. In a world in which people are 'friended', connections become a way of bolstering a sense of personal significance, even as the word 'friend' is drained of meaning.

In the first act she encounters Gordon's irascible mother, Mrs. Gottlieb, at a funeral that ends with the playing of 'You'll Never Walk Alone', which turns out both to be an accurate comment in a play in which a cell phone constantly rings and people walk around with other people's transplanted organs, and ironic in that Gordon has long since ceased to return his mother's calls, and this in a family characterised by alienation. Jean's efforts to assure the family that Gordon had thought of them all at the last become ever more desperate. At one stage she presents the family with gifts, insisting that they had been Gordon's last minute bequest, although these turn out to be no more than objects she had picked up in the café, including a salt shaker ('he said you were the salt of the earth'), a cup ('Because you can hold things . . . And they don't pour out') and a spoon ('Because of your cooking'), the last being unfortunate in that it is offered to Mrs Gottlieb whose cooking is apparently a subject best forgotten (39–40). Later she asserts that Gordon had written a letter to his wife before he died, drafting it on a series of napkins the waiter had thrown away but that she now recalls in its elaborate entirety.

Jean works in the Holocaust Museum (where, incidentally, Ruhl lost her own phone) because, she explains, 'it's good . . . to remember. I want to remember everything. Even other people's memories' (47). Indeed, she herself seems to exist through others. When she is alone, she is described as being small and tired, 'An Edward Hopper painting' (43). She has no cell phone of her own because she likes to disappear even as those who do have them seem to have the ability to tune out those around them. So long as Gordon's phone rings, though, it is as though he were still alive, something not unfamiliar to those who lost people on 9/11. Five years after Arthur Miller died, his voice was still on the answer phone for anyone who called, kept there by the young woman with whom he had a final relationship.

Behind the humour of *Dead Man's Cell Phone* are questions about presence and absence, the need to feel connected, the substitution of the virtual for the actual, fragments of conversations overheard becoming part of a tessellated reality, silence being invaded and even feared, meaning being constructed, innocence compromised by the mere process of living ('the goodness rubs off you if you so much as leave the house. Life is essentially a very large brillo pad') (83). Memory is what is left when a person dies, yet memory is itself manipulable, invested in a necessary act of reconstruction. Gordon's mother has long waited for a call from her son, which has not come, yet she loves him. A stage direction refers to a sound like an animal in pain as she cries out at the loss of him, as Ruhl had heard her grandmother respond to the death of her son, Ruhl's father: 'The sound of age grieving for dead youth, the sound of age not having gone first.'[40] Comedy is no defence against genuine feeling, indeed it may be a means of accessing it.

The play's action is constantly invaded by the ringing of the phone, although we never hear what is said at the other end. She and Gordon's brother, Dwight, discuss whether messages in the air have any substance, he running a stationary store selling paper on which people once declared themselves with a sense of permanence. What does 'I love you' mean, Dwight asks, if it is no more than so many informational bits in the air that disappear with the utterance?

The first part of *Dead Man's Cell Phone* ends with a shift in style and tone as 'stationary moves through the air slowly, like a snow parade. Lanterns made of embossed paper, houses made of embossed paper, light falling on Jean and Dwight, who are also falling' (56). The dead Gordon appears, opening his mouth as though to address the audience. He describes his final day and offers a justification for his profession as human organ salesman in a manner reminiscent of Blake's speech in the film of David Mamet's *Glengarry Glen Ross*:

Truth for its own sake – I've never understood the concept. Morality can be measured by results: how good do you make people feel? You make them feel good? Then you're a good man. You make people live longer? Great. Is it my job to stop executions in China? I don't have that power. What I *can* do, however, is make sure that these miserable fucks who die for no good reason *have* a reason – I make sure their organs go to someone who needs them.

(59)

Struck down with a heart attack, he considers calling his wife, mistress, brother, mother but can find no reason to do so, being alienated from them all in one way or another, as they are from him. He dies, again.

Later, to the background of film noir music, the phone rings with the offer of an organ trade to be conducted at Johannesburg airport where Jean goes to be met by a contact who is Gordon's mistress in disguise. She hits Jean with a gun, who then finds herself in a café with Gordon as though they were doomed to repeat their first encounter 'for eternity' (80). This,

Gordon explains, is a hell reserved for those selling organs on the black market and those who lied to help others. Although dead, they can still hear cell phones, and Ruhl indicates that there should be a 'cell phone ballet' with people moving through the rain speaking on their phones. Gordon disappears, leaving Jean 'alone in the afterlife' (89), only to re-materialise on earth, having been missing for months, and be taken to his mother's home by Dwight. On learning that her son is alone, Mrs. Gottlieb immolates herself on a barbeque to return to him, her alienation having given way to love, a word now drained of any irony it may have acquired. The play thus ends as Jean and Dwight pledge their love, the latter invoking the John Donne poem of the epigraph, a poem about a love that is the greater for not relying on appearance but on essential virtues.

Dead Man's Cell Phone is a comedy that encompasses the banal and the mystical, trade in human organs and in human emotions. Its characters enact a morality play about the uses to which we put one another, our failed and imperfect connections, but also the possibil-ity of redemption. Lies (although Ruhl prefers to call them 'confabulations') are used to conceal and console. If its conclusion seems to have overtones of an Ovidian faith that love conquers all, this is a sentimentality tempered by evidence of its failure in the most intimate of relationships.

Its characters both maintain and betray their privacies in a society that itself does much the same and a daily life in which cell phone chatter seeps into the air as if silence were to be feared. It is a play that features the exploited and the exploiters. In explaining the Edward Hopper moments, Ruhl explains, 'These are about the solitary figure inside the landscape or architecture. They are about being alone inside of or in relation to the modern' (103). Transitions, she indicated, 'are fluid. Space is fluid. There is not a lot of stuff on the stage.' Her final remark, in her note to any director, is 'enjoy yourself'. Her plays are serious not despite being comedies but because they are comedies. As she has asked, 'Tragedy has a long history of ethical enquiry, but does comedy have its own ethics?' Her answer is that 'ethical comedy might teach us to embrace ordinary efforts to overcome folly over and above the tragic impulse' (137).

Ruhl has said that there are ways in which *Stage Kiss*, her later play, and what was originally to have been called the *Vibrator Play*, are companion pieces while conceding that the former is more chaste. To be sure, there are kisses in what she eventually called *In the Next Room (or the Vibrator Play)* (the changed name deriving from the fact that it was not to be seen as a sex farce about vibrators), but as the subtitle suggests this is a work in which osculation plays less of a role than masturbation or at least the aid to such, featuring, as it does something called the Chattanooga vibrator, which may sound like something Glenn Miller might have used to tune an instrument but is a prototype of something people find handy in more ways than one. It was, Ruhl has explained, prompted by her reading of a book called *The Technology of Orgasm*, a history of the vibrator, a device that, to her surprise, was used by doctors to treat women with what was perceived to be hysteria; however, as she has said, 'I set out to write about vibrators . . . and it ended up by being about marriage and all kinds of other things.'[41] The other things include race, social class, and the extent to which art embraces or exploits sexuality.

It is certainly a comedy in which a space opens up between the physical and the emotional – and not only in the 1880s when it is set. As Ruhl has said, 'I think it's actually ontologically impossible to write about the past and not write about the present.'[42] It is, she has remarked, a play about intimacy in more than one sense. It is about the body. It is also a play that because of its subject matter she thought few people would go to, that would make a brief appearance at a small theatre and then disappear from view. It ended up with a Broadway production and as a finalist for the Pulitzer Prize.

The play (first staged at Berkeley Rep in 2009 before its Broadway opening the same year) is set in a prosperous spa town outside New York City, Ruhl suggesting Saratoga Springs both because a similar treatment did, indeed, take place there and because of its African-American community in a play that introduces a black woman who is to act as a wet nurse and, in some sense, a moral compass. The action takes place, sometimes simultaneously, in two adjoining rooms, a living room and a doctor's surgery. Unusually for Ruhl, it is a set with all the solidity of a nineteenth-century play. Dr. Givings specialises in gynaecological and hysterical disorders. It is the dawn of the age of electricity, a time when people wondered at the seeming miracle of electric light. Givings, when not delighting in news of animals being electrocuted, has developed an electric vibrator. This is to replace the manual manipulation with which he had previously treated patients, relieving them of their symptoms by precipitating orgasms, equally miraculous to those for whom they are a mystery and certainly not part of their normal experiences with husbands to whom the very idea would have seemed perverse if not incomprehensible. There is electricity in the air, to be sure, but it is in the sense of a repressed sexuality that until now has not been earthed in actual experience.

He himself maintains a scientific detachment that unfortunately extends to his relationship with his wife, oblivious as he is of her sexual needs, seeing no connection between the treatment he offers and the supposed intimacies of married life. To him, the treatment has no sexual implications, even as he reaches under a woman's skirt or inserts the vibrator into a man's anus. When the machine fails him, he asks his female assistant, Annie, to use her fingers, on occasion himself stepping in to assist.

The comedy of the play is in part generated by embarrassment, audiences scarcely believing what they are watching (observing multiple orgasms, the nurse revealing her breast and two of the characters stripping naked, leading to a conversation between Ruhl and her director as an actress complained that the actor's penis was upstaging her). It also comes from the innocence of characters who have no language to describe what is happening to them but who respond with growing enthusiasm, his patients Sabrina and Leo desperately returning for further treatments, constantly claiming to have left various items of clothing behind as an excuse. Dr. Givings engages in small talk as those he treats quickly lose interest having other things to concentrate on. His wife, meanwhile, forbidden access to the surgery while listening to the cries of pleasure emanating from it (never acknowledged as such), finally picks the lock and enters with Sabrina, who has, apparently inadvertently, left her gloves behind, and who now inducts her into the pleasures of the vibrator, only to have the courtesy returned as they both 'look heavenward', the hum of the device being accompanied by transcendent music as the first act climaxes.

Sabrina has been unable to play the piano, and one is to be seen in the living room as untouched as Mrs. Givings, whose husband, when he is not in the other room performing actions to which she is not privy, spends his time in his gentlemen's club. It is, she laments, just dead wood until played, clearly herself wishing to be played without yet understanding how, sex being only for procreation. Now, following her treatment, Sabrina plays and is joined in song by Mrs. Givings. When at last she persuades her husband to apply the same treatment to her as to his patients, she begs him to kiss her when he applies the vibrator, leaving him baffled as to why she should wish any such thing. When later she asks him how he loves her and tempts him to kiss her he does so, except that he enumerates each part he kisses by its correct anatomical designation, even though that does open him to a tenderness that surprises him. Until that moment, a hand on the cheek was no more than a matter of muscles and skin. He inhabited a world of facts, an observer of life rather than a participant in it.

From Dr. Givings's perspective the treatment is working. His patients are cured, but what they suffer from is less hysteria, or the need for relief, than a life without passion. They have been living partial lives. Now that life has been breathed back into them, they seek to bring their emotional and physical lives into alignment, Mrs. Givings being attracted to Leo, who, much to her alarm, is drawn to Elizabeth, as Mr Daldry is to her, while Annie kisses Mrs. Daldry, a series of pairings reminiscent of Schnitzer's *La Ronde*. Farce is not far away, with doors opening and closing, Mrs. Givings listening at a keyhole ('You are acting the part of a madwoman in a play', her husband objects) (123) and people getting dressed and sometimes precipitately undressed.

The play ends, however, as the set, with its actual and symbolic separate rooms, dissolves, and, amidst winter snow, Dr. Givings and his wife strip one another, in doing so stripping off their misunderstandings, removing the barriers that have separated them, she having never previously seen her husband naked. They lie down with her on top of him. In a play in which the reality of sexual lives has been denied, characters and audience alike are confronted if not with unaccommodated man then with a sudden level of reality, for as Ruhl has observed, 'nakedness is always real on stage'.[43]

John Lahr, in the *New Yorker*, greeted the play as her best to date revealing 'an impish intelligence' and observing that in 'a low-key but daring way, Ruhl has extended the geography of the comedy of manners' responding, in particular, to 'its thrilling, poetic final image'.[44] For Charles Isherwood in the *New York Times*, it was an 'inspired new comedy . . . Insightful, fresh and funny . . . as rich in thought as it is in feeling'. Sarah Ruhl, he observed, was 'one of the most gifted and adventurous American playwrights to emerge in recent years'.[45] When it opened in England, first at the Ustinov Studio in Bath in 2012 and then the following year at London's St James Theatre, Michael Billington, in the *Guardian*, while doubtful about 'a slightly improbably, feelgood ending', hailed it as a 'brilliant play . . . a serious comedy' with a 'modern relevance'.[46] Charles Spencer, in the *Daily*

Telegraph, declared that 'the American dramatist Sarah Ruhl has come up with something rather wonderful: a period drama that is funny, original and genuinely touching'.[47]

Ruhl called *Melancholy Play* a contemporary farce. The surprise is that she does not describe *Stage Kiss* (2011) in the same way, given that it can seem a blend of S. N. Behrman, Noel Coward and Michael Frayn, with a dash of Neil Simon. Indeed, she acknowledges a line taken from Behrman's *No Time for Comedy* ('I don't mind hiding in a bedroom but hiding in a library seems kind of dry') while, beyond a possible reference to *Private Lives*, it is tempting to hear an echo from Coward's *Hay Fever* as a character declares, 'I love you. I love you. I love you . . . I want to kiss you all over' where Coward's character says, 'I should like to kiss you and kiss you and kiss you.' Indeed in an essay, she recalls a game the characters play in *Hay Fever* called 'the adverb game' in which they have to perform in the manner dictated by a particular adverb. The context for the essay is her dislike of what she calls adverbial acting, for which she offers the example, 'SHE (jubilantly) Hand me the broom',[48] despite the fact that in *Stage Kiss* an actress designated as SHE is required by a stage direction to 'laugh mordantly', to 'look around wildly' and 'cough loudly'. The Director of the play within a play, also called *Stage Kiss*, has crossed out all stage directions, something, as it happens, to which Ruhl herself objects. But then this is a play in which she makes fun of many aspects of theatre, even as she explores the relationship between artistic and social performance. The play opened at the Goodman Theatre in 2011, its New York premiere following in 2014 at Playwrights Horizon.

It is, she has confessed, 'one of my sillier plays . . . a bit of a soufflé in the way that 1930s plays are, but I think I really wanted to think about illusion and love'. It is 'such a beast written for actors to do all the things they can do – like kiss each other in various ways that could never have been imagined'.[49]

A couple, former lovers now in their forties, and designated simply as HE and SHE, come together to appear in a revival of a 1930s play, *The Last Kiss*, a flop on Broadway at the time and now unaccountably being revived for a production in New Haven. They had been lovers but had plainly not parted on good terms. She has not, she explains, worked for some while because she had a child, but since that child is now sixteen, it is clear that the theatre has not been overanxious to employ her. Indeed she laments, 'If you are an actress in this country you are either Juliet or Lady Macbeth and there's nothing in between.'[50] In ten years she has only had two auditions, one for a maid and the other for an anti-depressant commercial, securing the latter part. 'You were very good', HE says, 'you seemed depressed – and then you seemed happy' (22).

The Last Kiss features a woman given a month to live who cables a former lover, now living in Sweden, inviting him to join her for what she assumes will be her last days. Her husband tolerates the arrangement. The rekindled affair miraculously restores her health, but unfortunately her lover now falls in love with her daughter and disappears back to Sweden. It is a play in which the characters are required, often at curious moments, to burst into songs whose lyrics have a stultifying banality ('No one says farewell these days / They all just say good-bye / No one says farewell these days / They hire a car, or fly') (76). The

Director is a one-time teacher of the Meisner technique. 'Trust your instincts', he tells HE, sometimes advice too willingly embraced by his actors.

HE and SHE spar with one another as they rehearse, memories of their joint past infiltrating not least because of parallels between their own situation and that in the play. Indeed there come moments when they speak both as the characters and as themselves as they rekindle their relationships, stage kisses turning into real ones. Since they parted, she, like her character, has married a businessman, her mother having told her not to marry an actor: 'never marry a man who looks in the mirror more than you do' (61). Since this is a farce, there comes a moment when HE trips and breaks his leg, having to perform on crutches, which in performance leads to a slip of the tongue as he substitutes crutches for clutches. The play is a success with the audience but not with the critics.

The second act moves from the elaborate set to a cramped studio apartment in the East Village, the morning after the first night, a packet of bad reviews on the floor. HE and SHE remain in costume even as the sounds of the city can be heard. Her husband and daughter arrive, as does his girlfriend. They then effectively reprise the play declaring that they have fallen in love again quite, her husband remarks, as though they were in a 1930s drama as, of course, they are since this is precisely a play in which life and art perform an odd dance. They now break into song, singing 'Some enchanted evening' in perfect harmony.

Finally, the Director arrives to ask them to audition for a play he has written to be performed in a small theatre in Detroit. It is titled *I Loved You before I Killed You, or Blurry*, a work of breath-taking absurdity. She is to play an aging whore who wants to become an ophthalmologist and will have to do nude scenes, while he is to be an IRA man running guns to Belfast. They are, the Director explains, to fall in love and plan to open an eye clinic for poor children, but her pimp kills her and IRA gang members kill him, a small child entering, as the men sing a hymn, to remove the dead man's glasses so that he can finally see.

When they rehearse the play in Detroit, the set is an exact copy of his New York apartment. Their opening night performance ends in confusion as they conduct a personal conversation between delivering their lines. It turns out that the play had been commissioned by her husband, who wanted to see her play the role of a whore and him that of an 'asshole'. The play ends as husband and wife are reconciled, with a kiss that Ruhl's stage direction indicates should be 'as simple as it is real', and this in a play in which reality is hard to pin down. In a play of echoing ironies, artifice piled on artifice, the word 'real' is hard to take entirely seriously. It was Bergson who said that laughter has no greater foe than emotion. It should, he said, demand 'something like a momentary anaesthesia of the heart'.[51]

Ruhl has said, though, that 'Lightness isn't stupidity . . . It's actually a philosophical and aesthetic viewpoint, deeply serious, and has a kind of wisdom – stepping back to be able to laugh at the horrible things even as you're experiencing them.'[52] *Stage Kiss* is hardly about horrible things but is concerned with the fact that a kiss is not just a kiss, that the real is a performance as a performance may be real. If this is, as she says in her acknowledgements, a love note to actors, it is perhaps because they will recognise the problem of bringing authenticity to the deeply inauthentic but also because they will understand that there are moments when artifice becomes something more on the stage as behaviour beyond the stage may be heavily invested with artifice.

In 2014, Ruhl followed *Stage Kiss* with *The Oldest Boy: A Play in Three Ceremonies*, based on a story told to her by her Tibetan babysitter, this being the first play she had written following the birth of her twins. Yangzom had escaped from Tibet and eventually ended up in Queens. The story she told, Ruhl explains in an afterward to the published version, was of a Tibetan couple in Boston who had run a successful restaurant. One day two monks arrived and told them that their son was a reincarnated lama, or high teacher. They had consequently closed the restaurant and moved to India so that the child could be educated in a monastery.

The idea of surrendering a child was, Ruhl confessed, difficult to understand, beyond the fact that every day she would send her own children to preschool, nervous for their safety even as she knew the need for them to learn independence. To hold on, to let go, these are the opposing feelings every parent knows. What was lacking, in terms of writing a play, was a sense of dramatic conflict. The original couple had simply submitted. It occurred to her, though, that if one of them had not been raised as a Buddhist, this would potentially create a tension that could work in dramatic terms and incidentally involve questioning notions of parenthood currently fashionable in America. What she did not know, as she began to write, was whether that mother would agree to surrender a three-year-old child even if the two lamas who arrive at their house explained that he was reincarnated and hence older than they are.

The play calls for, if possible, a chorus of traditional Tibetan dancers, preferably women. It includes brief speeches in Tibetan, something of a challenge to directors and actors alike. Ruhl solved the problem of presenting a three-year-old child who is also the incarnation of an older and now dead person by the use of a puppet. In the original production a *bunraku* puppet was used, operated by an old man who acted as the person the boy had once been, a teacher who had died three years earlier.

The Oldest Boy can read like a poem. Nearly all the speeches are brief. One of the longest sounds suspiciously like Ruhl as the mother describes being raised as a Catholic, losing faith and then feeling the need for it with the death of her father. Rehearsals for the Lincoln Center production began with five minutes of meditation, and the play itself starts with the mother meditating, even as beside her is a book about 'attachment parenting', attachment being the very thing she will have to learn if not to sacrifice then to redefine.

The play, as its subtitle indicates, is in three ceremonies. The first begins with what seems a traditional marriage, except that this is no more than an acting out of what might have been. In fact, in America, the ceremony of the central couple designated as Father and Mother takes place with the boy's mother already pregnant and in City Hall. The witness is a stranger, the wedding photograph an iPhone picture. The second ceremony follows the death of Father's mother, while the third marks the enthronement, in India, of their son, the puppet now dressed in monastic robes, with the puppeteer dressed as a monk. The parents are blessed by their son until the puppet disappears to be replaced by the adult puppeteer, now a lama, the teacher reborn. Mother is again pregnant, although this time with a girl, grateful that she will not have to surrender her.

In an epilogue we learn that Mother and Father returned home and reopened their restaurant. At night Mother feels her son return, and the boy puppet does so. In the morning they part, and the puppet walks away, as he does so cutting his own strings and collapsing even as the puppeteer stands, arms apart, to embrace her, becoming the boy she feared she had lost. The final direction is 'The end. The beginning. The end. The beginning. The end' (135).

The play expresses a felt lack of transcendence. We live, Ruhl implies, in prose when we once lived in poetry. The theatre, meanwhile, is itself a ceremony, a play in some sense taking place outside of time, or in which time is redefined. This is a space in which a puppet can be real and experience shared. The characters acknowledge the importance of teachers as Ruhl has acknowledge the importance of her own who may disappear in the rear-view mirror but leave a residue.

Ruhl's is a theatre of transformations, transitions, fabulations. Sets can overlap or dissolve if also establish a seemingly naturalistic context. Puppets can appear, cell phones dance, music play, yet even as she disavows psychological realism – and her characters tend to display a comedic and even farcical artifice – she is nonetheless interested in making the internal manifest. Emotions are at times real enough even as she explores them for their capacity for humour. When one woman laments the lack of a child and another the death of her own in *In the Next Room (or the Vibrator Play)*, the tears are real enough. No matter how tart the mother in *Dead Man's Cell Phone* may be, there are times when her sense of loss breaks through the comedy. A woman in a café holds the hand of a dead man, an impossible connection and yet the impulse for connection remains.

Ruhl is fascinated by the performed life as by theatre's capacity to stage such. The calculated acts of drama and those of the quotidian blend. She is conscious of the politics of the moment, as is manifest in *Passion Play*, even as she sees a connection to the past. In her work language can be pulled towards the lyrical but can equally be exposed for its capacity to seduce, to deceive. Love can be real even if it is felt by characters who are players in a human charade. Ruhl, in short, is conscious of the multiple meanings of the word 'play' and revels in them.

Notes

1 John Lahr, 'Mouth to Mouth: Sarah Ruhl on Attraction and Artifice', *New Yorker*, 30 May 2011. www.newyorker.com/magazine/2011/05/30/mouth-to-mouth

2 Henri Bergson, *Laughter, in Comedy* (Baltimore, 1956), p. 61.

3 Emma Brockes, 'The Vibrator Play: The Woman behind the Buzz', *Guardian*, 3 April 2012. www.theguardian.com/stage/2012/apr/03/vibrator-play-sarah-ruhl-interview

4 John Lahr, 'Surreal Life: The Plays of Sarah Ruhl', *New Yorker*, 17 March 2008. www .newyorker.com/magazine/2008/03/17/surreal-life

5 Ibid.

6 Ben Hodges, *The Play That Changed My Life* (New York, 2009), p. 125.

7 Tara Anderson, 'Taking Flight: How Sarah Ruhl's "For Peter Pan" Got Off the Ground', *American Theatre*, 20 June 2016.

8 Ibid.

 9 Sarah Ruhl, *100 Essays I Don't Have Time to Write* (New York, 2015), p. 167.
10 John Lahr, 'Surreal Life'.
11 Sarah Ruhl, *100 Essays*, pp. 34–5.
12 Ibid, pp. 66–7.
13 Christopher Bigsby, *Writers in Conversation* (Norwich, 2001), pp. 160–1.
14 Olivia Jane Smith, 'Six Questions for Sarah Ruhl', *New York Theatre Review*, 16 July 2012.
     http://newyorktheatrereview.blogspot.co.uk/2012/07/six-questions-for-sarah-ruhl-posed-by
     .html
15 Sarah Ruhl, *The Clean House and Other Plays* (New York, 2006), p. 27.
16 Terry Byrne, 'Sarah Ruhl's "Melancholy" Is Anything But', *Boston Globe*, 21 May 2015. www
     .bostonglobe.com/arts/theater-art/2015/05/21/sarah-ruhl-melancholy-play-anything-but/
     W313zQ7fvHtsGATylfBcPJ/story
17 Sarah Ruhl, 'Acknowledgements', *Passion Play* (New York, 2010), p. 155.
18 Celia McGee, 'Sarah Ruhl's Sunday School Lessons', *New York Times*, 13 April 2010. www
     .nytimes.com/2010/04/18/theater/18passion.html?_r=0
19 James Shapiro, *Oberammergau: The Troubling Story of the World's Most Famous Passion Play*
     (New York, 2000), pp. ix–x.
20 Sarah Ruhl, 'Preface', *Passion Play*, p. 7.
21 James Shapiro, *Oberammergau*, p. 13.
22 A. J. Goldmann, 'New King of Passion in an "Alpine Jerusalem"', *Forward*, 26 May 2010.
     http://forward.com/news/128345/new-kind-of-passion-in-an-alpine-jerusalem
23 James Shapiro, *Oberammergau*, pp. 4–5.
24 Eric Grode, 'Remembering the Ohio Theatre', *Village Voice*, 18 May 2010. www.villagevoice
     .com/arts/remembering-the-ohio-theatre-7134381
25 Dinitia Smith, 'Playwright's Subjects: Green Myth to Vibrators', *New York Times*, 14 October
     2006. www.nytimes.com/2006/10/14/theater/14ruhl.html?_r=0
26 Ibid.
27 Matthew Bevis, *Comedy* (Oxford, 2013), p. 10.
28 Sarah Ruhl, *100 Hundred Essays*, p. 42.
29 Ibid, p. 110.
30 Matthew Roudané, 'Albee on Albee', *RE: Artes Liberales* 10 (Spring 1984), p. 1.
31 Sarah Ruhl, *100 Essays*, p. 133.
32 Ibid, p. 125
33 Ibid, p. 138.
34 Dan Bacalzo, 'Death Becomes Her', *Theater Mania*, 30 May 2007. www.theatermania.com/
     new-york-city-theater/news/05–2007/death-becomes-her_10860.html
35 Wendy Weckwerth, 'Sarah Ruhl', *Theatre*, 34, no. 2 (2004), p. 28. https://muse.jhu.edu/login?
     auth=0&type=summary&url=/journals/theater/v034/34.2weckwerth.html
36 Dan Bacalzo, 'Death Becomes Her'.
37 Sarah Ruhl, *Dead Man's Cell Phone* (New York, 2008), p. vii.
38 Ibid, pp. 5–6.
39 John Lahr, 'Surreal Life'.
40 Sarah Ruhl, *100 Hundred Essays*, p. 148.
41 Dinitia Smith, 'Playwright's Subjects'.
42 Ibid.
43 Sarah Ruhl, *100 Hundred Essays*, p. 51.
44 John Lahr, 'Good Vibrations', *New Yorker*, 30 November 2009. www.newyorker.com/magazine/
     2009/11/30/good-vibrations-2
45 Charles Isherwood, 'Beyond Electricity, Toward Female Emancipation', *New York Times*, 19
     November 2009. www.nytimes.com/2009/11/20/theater/reviews/20innextroom.html?_r=0
46 Michael Billington, 'In the Next Room (Or the Vibrator Play)', *Guardian*, 26 November 2013.
     www.theguardian.com/stage/2013/nov/26/in-the-next-room-review

47 Charles Spencer, 'In the Next Room or the Vibrator Play', *Daily Telegraph*, 22 November 2013. www.telegraph.co.uk/culture/theatre/theatre-reviews/10467679/ In-the-Next-Room-or-the-Vibrator-Play-review.html
48 Sarah Ruhl, *100 Hundred Essays*, p. 73.
49 Bess Rowan, 'Ruhls of Play: An Interview with Sarah Ruhl', *Huffington Post Arts and Culture*, 19 April 2014. www.huffingtonpost.com/bess-rowen/ruhls-of-play-an-intervie_b_4805944 .html
50 Sarh Ruhl, *Stage Kiss* (New York, 2014), p. 22.
51 Robert Corrigan, ed., *Comedy: Meaning and Form* (Scranton, 1965), p. 473.
52 John Lahr, 'Mouth to Mouth'.

9

Naomi Wallace

. . . the work of imagination is itself a political act . . . The very act of writing or of artistic creation is one of making peace. War causes people to become an undistinguished mass. Literature recognizes each human being and shows how there are actually a huge number of options available to every single person. In a very real way, literature is an anti-war act. To write about a human being helps you to feel empathy for people who are quite different from you, even those who are your enemies.[1]

– David Grossman

Politics is history and history is what sparks my imagination. That's where my fire comes from. For me, politics and art can never be divided. Once you see that politics affects our daily lives – our loves, our desires, our needs – that's terribly exciting.[2]

– Naomi Wallace

If people want a label, they can call me a socialist.[3]

– Naomi Wallace

In March 2016, President Barack Obama announced that American citizens would be free to travel to Cuba, no longer requiring advance permission from the government and able to devise their own 'educational' programmes. Until then, it had been illegal. A decade earlier, an American playwright openly defied the ban. Returning to the United States, she was detained for four hours by Homeland Security interested in her supposed communist sympathies. Because her daughter had drawn a picture of a knife in a notebook she was also seen as a potential threat, an official claiming to be aware of her views by virtue of consulting Wikipedia. Her name was Naomi Wallace, and in one sense they were not wrong: she did, indeed, embrace radical opinions and as a writer was that relative rarity in twenty-first-century American drama, a political playwright interested in exploring class, racism, human rights and America's adventures abroad.

It is certainly not every American playwright who attracts the attention of *The Socialist Worker* and *Revolutionary Worker*, the latter quoting her remarks that 'Today it is, once again, war and empire. And it is with these monstrosities that we [playwrights] should engage in one form or another. What would Euripides, Marlowe or Brecht have done? They would have made these times strange, to use a Brechtian formula, so that an audience could see their society anew and possibly act on those new visions. Why settle for a lesser goal?'[4]

She was, though, also a poet and, besides publishing a collection, poetry would stain the prose of her drama sinking deep into a language reshaped to serve something more profound than the immediacies of her subjects. Her writing was engaged not simply ideologically but in so far as it acknowledged forces at work in the past and present alike, at first finding a receptive audience outside her own country in England, where radical politics were not regarded with the suspicion they tended to be in her own country.

Certainly, not many American writers would open their first volume of poems with one titled, 'Looking for Karl Marx's Apartment, 28 Dean Street', celebrating a man who had lived in such poverty that he had to pawn his coat and shoes while three of his children died 'on the floor of filth'.[5] She followed it with a poem as told by a strike breaker who is spat at by the man whose job he took – 'The Company rolls the coin into the centre / of the strike and we have no choice but to kill for it' (11) – and one as told by a woman in a sweatshop. 'Execution in the Country', carrying the place and dateline 'Nicaragua, 1986', is the last testament of a man about to be killed by the Contras, secretly funded by an American government happy to deny its culpability, although this last is not referred to in a poem in which a flood of memories transform the moment of death into a sudden beauty.

Her poems appeared in a variety of magazines in the United States and Britain and, in 1993, she won the U.S. National Poetry Competition, coming second in the United Kingdom's equivalent. Her poetry collection was published in 1995 by the significantly named Peterloo Poets, based in Cornwall in the west of England (the Peterloo Massacre of 1819 being the occasion of the death of those urging the extension of suffrage to working men). It carried as an epigraph a poem from Thomas McGrath, which in some ways captures the essence of her belief in the function and purpose of her own work:

> Bring all the darkness level with our eyes.
> It is the poem provides the proper charm,
> Spelling resistance and the living will,
> To bring to dance a stony field of fact

The poems are dramatic monologues covering, among other subjects, Anne Frank; the Westerbork Transit Camp, where the Nazis gathered Dutch Jews preparatory to transporting them to concentration camps; the American-owned tungsten mines of Quiruvilca, Peru, about which César Vallejo had written in *El tungsten*, focusing on the exploitation of the indigenous people; a witch burned to death in 1503; war against the Indians ('Framing the Thoughts of a Forefather before the Pequot Battle'); a miners' demonstration in London's Hyde Park; the First World War ('Battle for Gallipoli'), and war in the Middle East ('Kentucky Soldier in the Saudi Desert on the Eve of War'), the last as seen by a racist at home and abroad. Although they range in time and space, there is a common thread to do with violence perpetrated on the vulnerable and in the service of suspect values.

In amongst them, though, are more personal poems about what it is to bear and care for children – lyrical, celebratory; yet even children can prompt darker thoughts as she writes of a school bus hit by a truck and bursting into flames. In other words, as exemplified by this collection, hers is an imagination that, even as moments of beauty distract her, is drawn towards a more pervasive darkness. What is also apparent is that this is a poet committed to entering the minds, imaginations and language of those who are actors in a series of dramas, sometimes victims, sometimes collaborators in a tainted history, submitting because not fully unconvinced they have the power or will to resist, even as resistance is a necessity. The dramatist was already present in the poet as the poet would persist in the dramatist.

Naomi Wallace is aware that the phrase 'political playwright' carries negative connotations for some as if plays were blunt weapons, hectoring diatribes that fail to pass beyond their immediate causes. The suspicion deepens if the playwright shows an interest in political theory, reaches back into history to re-interpret it, discovers parallels to a present too easily assumed to have severed itself from that history. It does so if she writes polemical essays about art and the current state of a society whose divisions may go unchallenged and in which individuals are assumed to be complicit in national policies that work to the disadvantage and worse of others. She writes, in other words, about power in its various guises while rejecting the notion that the political excludes an interest in the individual, in the private passions and needs of those who function within a world they do not command. The political, for her, excludes neither the poetic nor the humorous, both of which have the power to subvert or elevate.

She is not merely a writer of political drama, in the broadest sense, but also an advocate. At times, perhaps, she protests too much. The vast majority of writing, she has said, delves into the human soul and has produced a great deal of what she describes as bad, bad stuff. It is not clear which plays she is thinking of or what the 'human-soul' school of writing is. Yet her own position is clear: She looks for a theatre that is oppositional, defamiliarising; a theatre that breaches boundaries, is continuously curious; a theatre of praxis. She listens for voices that are absent, that whisper from the past or a disregarded present. This, in turn, makes her impatient with mainstream American theatre, which remains largely white and middle class, although she is herself both while convinced that the theatre offers the possibility of feeling and breathing through characters who are not.

The objective is to infiltrate the sensibility of others as, of course, it is the function of all writers. The difference is that for her there is a moral imperative behind this opening of doors, this refusal to acknowledge boundaries of gender or race, in the past or present. There is a reason she is often inspired by the reading of history or political theorists. Both offer a way of structuring understanding, although there comes a moment when research becomes flesh and characters speak for themselves. The body is the site of sensual encounters, but it also bears the marks of labour, violence and social condition. Can anyone, she asks, be said to be private if they are contributors to a society whose values distort the self or a world required to be subject to its fiat? Just how do we live as individuals and co-operative selves in a world that can be so hostile to both?

She does not believe that we live in comfortable times. For many, she suggests, and witnessed in growing up, her own country's national dream of endeavour rewarded is no more than a fantasy. Inequity persists, indeed grows, prejudices retain their hold, civic freedoms and spaces are threatened, the stranger regarded as a threat, whether at home or abroad. At such a time, she believes, the imagination is a resource with the power to penetrate beneath pieties, bland assurances and modern myths too easily embraced because they offer sanction for inaction. Suggesting that the principle purpose of mainstream theatre is to keep the peace, she sees her own responsibility as to disrupt it. She is, as those immigration officials suspected, a disturber of the peace. She disturbs it in part by looking again at a past assumed to be discontinuous with present tensions and exploring a present in which the individual struggles to find an uncompromised place on which to stand.

To her, the individual is not a simple by-product of history, a cog in the machine, even as the scars of that history and machine may be evident, but a site of resistance, reinstating sensuality, reasserting agency. Her central assumption is that change is not only possible but necessary and that a theatre which itself deals in transformations can become both metaphor and instigator. Social roles are just that. They are performances that assume the guise of ineluctability. Class, race and gender roles are social constructions. There is a theatre to social life in which individuals are assigned parts to play, theatre by its nature making that manifest.

Her interest in the past is in part because it gives her a sense of perspective and in part because it establishes causality – a link between act and consequence that is the basis of morality and political awareness. Like Arthur Miller, she is inclined to believe in the return of the repressed, that the past is not a foreign country in which they do things differently but a reality to which we are umbilically attached. In her work the past literally haunts the present, ghosts recalling what was thought safely buried, disinterring offences, a manifestation of guilt denied

Behind that, of course, lies a question about the ability of theatre to challenge power. In the mid-1970s David Hare briefly stopped to re-evaluate his career. Writing from the left, he saw society moving in the opposite direction, as if to mock the pretentions and presumptuousness of those who thought drama an agent of revelation that could precipitate change. He had sought to create a new audience, travelling the country and performing in unlikely venues, but theatre remained stubbornly a minority concern. Society, anyway, has also always had the ability to absorb the rebel, consumerise the resistant spirit. He subsequently re-emerged offering an insight into the past while staging plays that explored the systems of power in British society. This would equally prove Wallace's concern, conscious that the playwright stands on a particular ground and writes from that position. Her work would not always prove popular with some critics who saw ideas looking for embodiment, convictions seeking validation in figures required to perform exemplary roles. The vitality of those figures, however, would prove resistant to the didacticism some affected to detect.

Naomi Wallace was born in 1960 in Prospect, Kentucky, population some four and a half thousand and largely conservative. Her father, once a *Time-Life* reporter, was now what he described as a gentleman farmer. Like his wife, he was involved in the civil rights movement and was a protestor against the Vietnam War, Naomi, as a child, taking along a pet sheep on an anti-Vietnam rally. She has recalled that at the time she knew more about Vietnam than she did about any children's show on television. Her mother was Dutch, from the working class and had once been a member of the Netherlands Communist Party, the family being involved in the resistance movement during the Second World War, hiding Jews and communists alike.

Wallace's family were comfortably off. The same could not be said of the nearby communities, one poor white, the other black. She recalled playing with children from both not recognising, at that age, the difference between her own family's circumstances and theirs. Unsurprisingly, her family were thought of as radicals even as it was class that divided them from many of those around them, more particularly in a time of depression. It was clear to her even then that her fate would differ from theirs. At age fourteen, her mother gave her a copy of James Baldwin's *Another Country*, and although she has said that she was perhaps too young to fully appreciate it, she nonetheless had the feeling that the country she had grown up in was not the country she thought it was.

Eventually, her mother returned to Holland, and the couple divorced. Wallace began writing poems in second grade and saw her first play at the Actors Theatre of Louisville at age nineteen. People, she discovered, dressed up to go to theatre as if it were part of a social world to which she did not aspire. As a result, it would be many years before she went again, having in the meantime realised that 'good theatre' could 'terrify you, or break you, or spin you topsy-turvy'.[6]

She graduated from Hampshire College in Amherst, known for its alternative curriculum and its liberal politics, relying on narrative evaluations rather than grades. Her master's degrees are from the University of Iowa, where she was part of the Iowa Playwrights Workshop. It was here that she began to write both poems and plays, coming late to the latter. As she explained, 'I surprised myself in really liking to work with other people, working in a community with people to create something. I was this loner. I wrote poetry but I found out my work was better in working with others, and I had an audience to dialogue with.'[7]

The kind of plays that interested her, though, were not those that engaged other members of the workshop. The turning point seems to have been a week that Tony Kushner spent with them in which he said, 'I want each of you to write a political manifesto of what you believe about the world.'[8] Half the class, she remembered, either left or went to complain. Kushner himself recalled that,

The students were all OK, smart, talented, some of them better than OK. And then there was Naomi. I'd given them all this theory, Marx and modern drama . . . that stuff doesn't go over well in playwriting courses. She not only loved it, went right for it, she already knew a lot of it. I remember thinking, 'Who is this?' She gave me 'War Boys' to read, and I was blown away. The power of language in it! And the way she thought, the things she was thinking about . . . she walked into class the next day and I gushed: 'This is the most astonishing play by a student I've ever read.'[9]

It is hardly surprising that Kushner responded to Wallace and she to him. He also came from a small town in the South. For him, the political was embedded in experience and hence not remote from the business of family life. Indeed for those who lamented the lack of political theatre, he pointed to the classic works of the 1940s and '50s. To him, *Long*

Day's Journey into Night was about the Irish immigrant experience in which money was the currency of conversation. *A Streetcar Named Desire* had at its heart a woman who lacks economic power and is raped not only by Stanley Kowalski but by a system that has driven her to despair. *Death of a Salesman*, meanwhile, was 'probably the greatest play about money ever written'.[10] Kushner is a socialist because he believes in economic justice, is conscious of the body as the site of conflict, but acknowledges a moral obligation to transcend despair, while as a playwright he warned against writing 'what you are absolutely certain of' (47). More than anything else he believed in the necessity for a play to entertain. Wallace would have dissented from none of these principles.

The War Boys received its first production not in the United States but England, and for a number of years her career was essentially a British one. The British theatre had always been comfortable with politically engaged work, a fair percentage of writers being on the left, from David Hare and Howard Brenton through to Edward Bond, Trevor Griffith, David Edgar and Caryl Churchill. Indeed, in 2006 Nicholas Hytner, artistic director of the National Theatre, would confess to the difficulty of finding right-wing plays. *The Observer*'s drama critic, Susannah Clapp, confessed that she could not recall reviewing a single play coming from the right while there were plays about the miners' strike, events in Northern Ireland, the Iraq War, Guantánamo. Theatre was, in a sense, oppositional, challenging right-wing governments for their injustices and left-wing governments for falling short of an ideal. Sir Peter Hall has said, 'I don't believe drama is necessarily about conflict, but it is always about confrontation leading to change . . . If you write a play saying let nothing change, you could be celebrating the Right, but it would make for poor drama.'[11]

In 2008, Neil LaBute recalled that while at university, his dramatic heroes had been British because they 'shook the very ground I walked on, the ideals I believed in'. Now, it seemed to him, that American writers were workshopped and '"staged-readinged" to death'. He acknowledged Christopher Shinn, who explored the impact of 9/11 and the Iraq War, and pledged a certain faith in David Mamet but saw few others. If playwrights wrote political plays, he assumed they had them hidden in a drawer but suspected that they had simply stopped writing them. In England, he suggested, they were taken out of the drawer and addressed major issues, not least because the British theatre was not one that relied on subscriptions.[12]

In truth, America, as suggested earlier, is not short of oppositional voices despite LaBute's accusation that Americans were writing 'tiny plays' with 'tiny ideas.' Indeed it could be argued that this is its central tradition. Add to Kushner's list of classic plays the work of Lorraine Hansberry, Amiri Baraka, David Rabe, August Wilson, Sam Shepard, Emily Mann and many more, and the distinction between the two dramas tends to blur. Wallace herself, in an article in 2008, invoked Rebecca Gilman, Suzan-Lori Parks, Tarell Alvin McCraney, Kia Corthron, Erik Ehn, Maria Kizito, Richard Montoya and Howard Zinn as evidence to the contrary. Only judged by Broadway fare, she suggested, could it be said that American political theatre was moribund.[13]

Even so, while Wallace found a ready audience in Britain, it took her some time to establish a reputation in America. *The War Boys* was staged at the Finborough Theatre in

February 1993, not that this was a major institution, boasting, as it did, only fifty seats and located above a pub – pub theatres, however, often proving significant venues. The play is set on the Mexico/Texas border, although it is implied that what is acted out here is a drama that could be staged anywhere people pay a price for trying to flee poverty or violence. It features three men, Greg, a working-class Mexican-American; David, college-educated, having spent four years at Stanford, 'privileged' and white; along with George, described as a 'homeboy', also white. They are a vigilante group out to catch those trying to cross the border for the reward of $10 for every one they catch and turn over to the police, although they have evidently run into trouble with the authorities.

In the course of the play, they catch no one, even as they offer a running commentary on those they see. What they do is play the War Boys game, acting out scenarios of their own devising. There is a Pinteresque air of threat throughout in a play, which is less psychological study than an account of the coercive pressure of the group and the common currency of a denatured language. People are objects to be converted into cash. The body is liable to assault, the place where public tensions are enacted. Speaking of *The War Boys*, Wallace has said,

That play I wrote when I first entered theatre. I was taking a critical look at the kind of psychology we use on the stage, 'character-building': 'I'm so and so and this is what happened to me when I was little, and everything that I am now is because of this incident or that incident.' It's the idea that we are so tied to these experiences that we can't become anything else, and how we manipulate those experiences to excuse ourselves. You see this in more mainstream theatre, that moment where, 'When I was a child', and you go, here it comes. Or 'my father when I was this or that age did this to me.' It's predictable, a certain way of psychologically looking at people and how their past creates them.[14]

It is not that she denies the impact of the past on the present but that she is more interested in how we choose to shape that past to justify ourselves. She has spoken of the ease with which people can be caught up in a system in such a way as to deform their humanity. Those deformations are displayed in *The War Boys*, the implications of its title extending beyond a bunch of disaffected men patrolling America's southern border. In this, her first play, she was staking out her territory with a work that addressed a political issue of the moment but also explored the mechanisms of power, a sense of personal and national privilege.

While still a student in 1994, she followed *The War Boys* with *In the Heart of America*, which appeared on the front cover of *American Theatre* magazine, thus it is not quite true to say that she was ignored in the United States. Nonetheless, although Wallace was told that the attention from the cover would mean the play would be widely produced in regional theatres, she found no takers. This was an experience later replicated when she won an Obie Award. In 2014, she could still say, 'Only a handful of theatres produce my work in this country. No complaint. It's just how things are for me … As playwrights we don't need mainstream American theatre to acknowledge our work.'[15]

This was a feeling that Britain's left-wing playwrights embraced for many years, as if major companies must be embedded in the very system against which the writers were in rebellion; they would, in time, change their minds, however, not least because those companies often offered a platform and were run by those not unsympathetic to their views. Radical writers can often be suspicious of too easy a success, as if they were at risk of its seductiveness. When Arthur Miller began to receive money from his first success, *All My Sons*, he took a minimum wage job, suddenly feeling guilty that he had betrayed his values, even though some on the left saw the play as an assault on capitalism.

Like Wallace's first play, *In the Heart of America* was first produced in London, at the Bush Theatre, but three months later it reached America where it was staged at the Long Wharf Theatre in a production directed, significantly, by Kushner. The published text carries a dedication to her mother, 'who gave me a conscience'. Wallace has confessed that she began writing the play knowing only the first and last scenes, discovering the middle by writing, although she had spent two years researching. It is a play that brings together two American wars, Vietnam and Iraq, and is set in a Kentucky motel room, a military camp in Saudi Arabia and the Iraqi desert. It features a ghost, 'but more solid', and the soul of Lieutenant Calley, responsible for the massacre of between 347 and 504 unarmed citizens in a South Vietnamese hamlet. Sentenced to life imprisonment, he ended up under house arrest before being pardoned by President Nixon. It took him forty years to apologise. He haunts this play, as he does the American conscience, although plainly he had not had such an effect on President Nixon. The ghost is the spirit of a Vietnamese in whose village sixteen people had been killed.

The United States is a country that invests in the future. For Arthur Miller and Gore Vidal alike, its disregard for the past, except at the level of myth, amounted to amnesia, a word Wallace herself uses. For Miller in particular, the present would remain a mystery if the past was not acknowledged, which is one reason he was drawn to Ibsen. For Wallace, too, 'so much of what we're questioning now can be better understood by looking at the past . . . For me, writing about the past is a way of learning about this moment . . . There's so much that has been buried . . . The past is what is with us this very moment, that's where I get my fuel'.[16] That past contains not only war but also class and race divisions in a country that declares 'e pluribus unum'.

The story of America's wars is not one narrative. In a country of multiple identities, which nonetheless insists on a singular one, the fault lines easily break surface. For Wallace, political power has always challenged and subverted the autonomy of the self, asserted presumptive rights over the body which is, perhaps, why protest movements so often involve deliberately confronting power with that body – in marches, on picket lines, blocking the transportation of weapons. That same body, however, is implicated in the deeply personal, in private passions and encounters that somehow survive in a world where human kindness has no place as weapons are designed to invade and shred the body but are given names that make them seem no more threatening than products in a supermarket.

In the Heart of America intercuts between these different experiences and functions in a collage of violence and love, tracing back and forth through time in an attempt to lay bare the origins of a disturbing sense of loss, damage done by assaults on the body being simultaneously assaults on a notion of right action. Characters are drawn together by the fact of war even as their relationships are a denial of its legitimacy. Their loyalties are divided. To what are they committed, beyond one another, and what is the true nature of their feelings? They are in part shaped by their origins, by the roles they are required to play, by personal awareness of violation or their failure to intervene at crucial moments. It is a play about the need to understand what it is that has shaped them and by implications the country in whose heart they supposedly live even as that country reaches out across the world in defence of a liberty that is itself compromised.

In the Heart of America is clearly a political play. For Wallace, though, it was 'just a love story – or rather, a triangle of love stories interacting in war ... What happens', she asks, 'to two people who fall deeply in love in a situation of war ... One comes into conflicting loyalties. The same body that loves also kills. How does one deal with that? ... When does love become violent? ... When is violence assumed to be an act of love? This happens on a personal level, but also politically. The Gulf War was presented by the media almost as an act of love – to restore peace and democracy in a troubled nation.'[17] In an essay, Wallace quoted Randall Jarrell's poem, 'Losses':

> In bombers named for girls, we burned –
> The cities we had learned about in school
> Till our lives wore out; our bodies lay among
> The people we had killed and never seen.[18]

As Terry Eagleton observed, 'Military technology creates death but destroys the experience of it.'[19]

Throughout her work, Wallace has been concerned with the body as the marker of oppression, scarred by a political and social system, even as it is the expression of love, the site of a redeeming sensuality. Its vulnerability is both the avenue to intimacy and evidence of an oppressive power that underscores its mortality. As Eagleton has observed,

The body, that inconvenient reminder of mortality, is plucked, pierced, etched, pummelled, pumped up, shrunk and remoulded. Flesh is converted into sign, staving off the moment when it will subside into the sheer pornographic meaninglessness of a corpse. Dead bodies are indecent: they proclaim with embarrassing candour the secret of all matter, that it has no obvious relation to meaning. The moment of death is the moment when meaning haemorrhages from us ... Capitalism too, for all its crass materialism, is secretly allergic to matter ... It is a culture shot through with fantasy, idealist to its core, powered by a disembodied will which dreams of pounding Nature to pieces.[20]

For Wallace, the logic of mortality may be irresistible, but not those forces that are complicit with it. Meaning may be negated by the very terms of existence, but that merely creates an obligation to construct that meaning and to resist those forces that are in alliance with absurdity. Capitalism constructs its own paradigm whereby possession of the world is to be equated with possession of one's soul, a bargain Eugene O'Neill observed with his usual clear-eyed cynicism, enrolling citizen/consumers in ventures that serve the purpose of consumption – industrial servitude, foreign wars to secure the products that keep the machine of state in motion. For Wallace, the siren call of a progress that requires its opposite to be achieved, a simple pragmatism, a doffing of the hat to inevitability, is to be resisted, resistance itself being generative of meaning.

The American novelist and artist William Wharton (real name Albert du Aime) published a memoir about his experience of the Second World War during which he was wounded at the Battle of the Bulge. It appeared in Poland and failed to make its way into publication in English until 2012, four years after his death, which was surprising given the success in 1978 of his novel *Birdy*, about a traumatised soldier of working-class origins who finds solace in birds, a work subsequently made into a film by Alan Parker in 1984. The memoir told of his participation in the execution of a number of German soldiers. When they were dug up from the shallow graves in which they were buried, he vomited. In 1997, Wallace's adaptation of *Birdy* was performed first at the 175-seat Drum Theatre in Plymouth before transferring to the Lyric, Hammersmith, and thence to the Comedy Theatre in London's West End – incidentally the mainstream theatre she had felt no need for in her own country. It opened the following year at the Philadelphia Theatre Co., but it was 2001 before it reached New York, where it was produced by the Women's Project Theatre then at 55th Street and now at 76th.

It is something of a tone poem, a celebration of a friendship between two men, Birdy, named for his love of pigeons, and Al. When young they had welcomed danger, always treading on the edge. Al is regularly beaten by his father, waiting for the moment he can hit him back. The army seems to offer a solution, but the war leaves both of them damaged. Birdy, seemingly catatonic, is now detained in a Kentucky cell for psychiatric investigation. It is up to Al to lure him back to life, although when at last he does so, Birdy has lost his youthful confidence having learned that 'we can't accept the idea that things happen for no reason at all', that life is 'just a row of hurdles we have to get over somehow'.[21] The play ends as Birdy is perhaps about to launch himself into the air, a bird liberated at least in his own mind, except that it is not entirely clear that liberation is a possibility.

Wallace was attracted to the original book, she explained, by 'its seeming simplicity, coupled with a complex examination not only of the repercussions of war on the human psyche, but of the dehumanizing process boys are forced to undergo in order to become acceptable "men" in our society. Sensuality and eroticism, compassion and intimate community between men are repressed, while rugged or slick male individualism, with its macho veneer and casual violence, are cultivated.'[22] What was at stake was conformity, which, in war and peace, she saw as a 'process of brutalization'.

Three hundred pages had to be reduced to a play that would run for less than two hours. Birdy and Al are seen both as teenagers and young men, and her first decision was to have both their parts played by two actors, thereby permitting them to be simultaneously present, the gaps between their younger, confident selves and their damaged later versions closed. The result is a strained nostalgia, a painful irony. One of the two, Al, represents the physical; the other, Birdy, a dreamer who wishes to follow the trajectory of his imagination. They are both outsiders pulled into the restrictive world of the military, both, when young, thrilled by life's possibilities only later to discover that the battle they are required to fight is not only a literal one against the country's enemies but one against the very terms of their existence, life inflicting wounds that have to be accepted unless the imagination still has the power to transcend circumstance. The search for meaning is a journey which leads down unfamiliar paths.

Trauma exists in the domestic world of these characters as much as it is a product of the more immediate wounds of war. It is a play, then, for which war is a context but which also identifies the scars picked up along the way as they test the limits of possibility while being pulled down by those who limit their freedoms. There are repressed truths, and a price is to be paid. Past and present are woven together, two parts of their lives forging a metaphor.

Wallace's interest in war is not detached from her social concerns at home. As she has explained, 'I'm interested in war and violence because, in Kentucky, a state of violence and war is inflicted daily on the majority of people through poverty and the class system . . . I'm not an issues writer . . . The subjects I choose determine what I write about. I am interested in long-term ideas about history and war and class struggle.'[23] Ironically, Bernie Sanders, the unlikely contender for the Democratic presidential candidacy in 2016, being a self-declared socialist, virtually dead-heated in the Kentucky primary while, in December 2015, the *Merriam-Webster Dictionary* announced that the most looked-up word online was *socialism*, although whether that was in a spirit of enthusiasm or alarm was difficult to say. Perhaps Wallace, then, is not quite that voice crying in the wilderness she might seem, although her next play, which also engaged with history, once again had its premiere in Britain, opening at the Bush Theatre in October 1995, reaching the Public Theatre in New York in February 1997.

Perhaps appropriately, this was a play that reached back into British history, the time of the plague, 1665, although Wallace has said that its inspiration came from closer to home, the Los Angeles riots of 1992:

I'd been reading Daniel Defoe's 'Journal of the Plague Years' when the riots broke out and I began to see them both – L.A. and the London plague – as the same event. A time of crisis. A time when rich and poor get thrown together – and, suddenly, one sees alternatives. I began to think what happens when the containment of a presumed danger through the regimentation of space breaks down, such as when South-Central L.A. began to 'invade' Beverly Hills. I wanted [to] foreground a society in crisis. By writing about a time other than our own, it's possible for issues that have become locked in rhetoric, or dismissed as too over-determined for the stage, to become visible anew.[24]

In *One Flea Spare*, it is the time of the plague. The court has left the city, along, in actuality, with two-thirds of Londoners, although a couple – William and Darcy Snelgrave – have failed to follow, effectively trapped in their own 'comfortable' house, which is invaded by a sailor, Bunce, back from impressments, having fought in a series of wars on different sides, and by Morse, a twelve-year-old girl, a maid masquerading as her mistress. Outside is Kabe, both their protector and guard, the latter because without a pass it is impossible to leave for the supposed safety of the countryside. They bribe him for food and free passage, never achieving the latter. They come from different classes, now bound together, as their blood might be in a flea, by circumstance even as money still has a certain power. The plague is supposedly kept at bay by stripping the furniture and regularly washing everything in vinegar, although they will try any remedy rumoured to work.

The couple has long since ceased to be held together by something as mundane as love and certainly not by physical intimacy. William regards Darcy as redundant, a woman who has passed her utility. The working-class Bunce brings sex into her life, something which, although only momentarily, vitiates class differences, as does disease, a leveller despite the money with which they hope to buy immunity. At a time of plague, power shifts. In *Licking Hitler*, David Hare wrote about the effect of war on social roles, with the classes being forced together; power would quickly revert to the former state of affairs with the end of hostilities, however, and other kinds of hostilities would re-establish themselves.

Both Bunce and Darcy carry wounds, visible evidence of physical and mental assaults, and Wallace seems fascinated with the way social roles can effect damage. She has referred to *One Flea Spare* as a 'dark little play' while stressing an ending that sees the young girl damaged but surviving and even feeling sympathy, and perhaps love, for those who have made themselves monstrous or at least deprived themselves of feeling. It is a tenuous resolution, however, as Morse, looking back, recalls seeing the dead body of a child drift by on the Thames. Kobe, she recalls, had told her, 'Our lives are just a splash of water on a stone. Nothing more', as if he were a figure out of Beckett. 'Then I am the stone on which they fell', she declares, 'And they have marked me . . . Because I loved them, and they have marked me'.[25] Wallace has conceded that this is a 'terribly fragile' hope even as she is equally inclined to claim that her work is 'irresponsibly optimistic', a phrase used by Edward Bond in a preface to *Saved*.

The play picked up three awards, including the 1997 Obie for Best Play, although this did not prevent John Simon from eviscerating it in *New York Magazine* – Simon who once greeted a play with the words 'more trash from Louisville'; those back at the Humana Festival of New American Plays in Louisville made those words into badges they wore with pride (I was there at the time to witness this response), Simon not being a critic who commanded their respect. True to form, he greeted *One Flea Spare* as pretentious, boring, pointless and preposterous, the product of a Marxist, presumably because it dealt with people from different classes and the rich died while the poor did not, a somewhat reductive version of Marxism.

Wallace's determination to root a number of her plays in a carefully researched past is evident in the bibliography she adds to the published versions, as if to underline the degree to which her imagination rests on a factual foundation. Plays have their own truth, but to her there is another to be served. One of the listed texts is indeed the *Communist Manifesto*. Beyond this, she has something of the naturalist's determination to identify the pressures exerted on the self by an actual environment. That was especially so in a play originally staged by the Royal Shakespeare Company, *Slaughter City* (1996), which, given its location in a slaughterhouse, has echoes of Upton Sinclair's *The Jungle*, although set at some indeterminate time in the past, not least because time proves spectrally fluid as figures from the past carry forward old conflicts. At times two key figures, manifestations of history, are invisible to those they move among, raised to consider themselves its victims, even their rebellions seemingly in the command of forces to which they accede as they glimpse the need to speak their own lives. In developing the play, she interviewed strikers in Indiana and Kentucky, from whom, among other things, she learned of the injuries they carry from their work.

At its heart is the figure of the sausage man who flits in and out of time, the embodiment of a self-made man who unmakes those who work for him. Here, in the slaughterhouse, men lose limbs, cut themselves, become literally and figuratively diminished as they work to feed the line, speeded up from time to time, careless of the consequence. His agent is Cod, cut from the dead body of her mother, who died in the Triangle Shirtwaist Factory fire of 1911 and who, as a result of a bargain made by that mother and despite moments of resistance, bends to his command, appearing at the site of different industries, a strikebreaker or whatever he wills. Years pass but are always the same. 'Whatever happened to that animal called hope?' asks Cod, only to have Maggot, a worker in his mid-thirties, reply, 'First it got stunned, then it got slaughtered. Seems like for years I just wake and work and shit and sleep. It's a good life. Nothing to disappoint me' (237). The slaughterhouse is not merely a place of work, it stands as a metaphor, a place where promises prove void and dreams die.

Is it too crude, too direct in segueing past conflicts into present despair at capitalism's eternal motor of consumption? Certainly it requires that we accept that little has changed from the early twentieth-century strikes that float in the background and gave impetus to her time-travelling characters. The dream, to be sure, is still sold as people labour with the promise of an incremental climb towards liberation that for many never comes, America currently ranked twenty-eighth in the world for inequality. Something has changed to be sure, but not in any essential way. As Cod remarks, 'What you see here is deregulation so that workers have no way of protecting their rights. When we make a stink 'cause we're offered part-time jobs with twelve-hour shifts, big business ups and moves across the border or across the sea', but 'we're one of the only industrialized nations where illegal firings and the hiring of Scabs are common practice . . . We're back to the Depression . . . Back to the Victorian age . . . Robber Barons are again free to trade – eat! – over our dying bodies. Everything and nothing has changed' (215).

For Wallace, the individual lives in the context of others. Her last play before the millennium, *The Trestle at Pope Lick Creek*, carries an epigraph from Percy Bysshe Shelley that might stand as an epigraph for all her work: 'Nothing in the world is single.' She had already written a poem with the same title, something she would do with *In the Heart of America* and *Slaughter City*. Staged at the New York Theatre Workshop in June 1999 and then at the Traverse Theatre in Edinburgh in February 2001, it is set during the Depression when hope, along with jobs, is running out. Once again, characters carry the marks of their oppression on their bodies – cuts from a glass factory, burns from steel making, hands stained with chemicals. In the North, police have killed strikers, while here violence is turned on themselves out of a frustration at how things are. Drained and despairing, they no longer touch one another with intimacy or ease, alienated from each other as from a community in a state of collapse.

At the centre of a play in which the real and fantasy intertwine is the relationship between two teenagers, male and female, Dalton and Pace, testing themselves and their emotions, playing dangerous games. The trestle is a bridge across which a locomotive and train pass and which they dare one another to face, racing for safety before it arrives, as another had before them. That other had died. They stand on the edge of more than a train track, simultaneously wanting and afraid of contact and with no sense of anything waiting for them beyond the moment. The train has an implacability as, it appears, does their future, rushing toward them and they in a race to survive.

The story has something of a myth about it, even as it was based on an actual event she had been told and is suffused with a poetry both linguistic and visual. Despite the setting and the time, it is not a simple Depression play, although the harsh realities of deprivation exert their power, distort lives and occlude the future. It is a play that explores the poetry and the prose of lives, the desire to reach out to others whose mysteries can seem impenetrable even to themselves. Almost inevitably, it seems, one of the teenagers, Pace, dies, daring too much, but she remains a presence, someone who defied the limits and paid the price but who also opened herself to another. There is a moment of grace and stillness even as the seemingly irresistible train roars by. There are also moments of reconciliation – Dalton with his father, a husband with his wife – and moments of resistance. Workers are taking over their factory. Something continues; something survives.

For, Anita Gates in the *New York Times*, reviewing the 1999 production at New York Theater Workshop, the dialogue was 'self-consciously portentous' at times and the play 'just short of being fully enthralling', but by the end she thought it had 'built up a head of steam and we feel its power'.[26] On the other side of the Atlantic, Elizabeth Mahoney in the *Guardian*, reviewing the Traverse Theatre production, saw Wallace as 'the finest of writers . . . weaving poetic symbolism into her tale [of] . . . two teenagers growing up in the Depression'. Wallace was 'a thrilling writer, handling the vilest emotional darkness with grace. As a portrayal of teenage angst and lust, this would be hard to better',[27] although she had doubts about the symbolism. It was an ambivalence that would be familiar in reviews of Wallace's work as critics debated with themselves the particular virtues of a writer who took them beyond their comfort zone.

With *The Inland Sea* (2002), once again set in England, she turned to the past and to a specific time, the 1760s, a moment of social change when many who had worked the land for themselves found it increasingly enclosed and the countryside reshaped. She does so not simply because of a fascination with the period but, inevitably, because it holds a key to the present, hence the epigraph she chooses from James Baldwin: 'The great force of history comes from the fact that we carry it within us, are unconsciously controlled by it in many ways, and history is literally present in all that we do.'

The play also has something to say about culture in that Capability Brown, hired here by the fictional Lord Heywood to redesign his estate, was not only replacing one aesthetic with another in sweeping away Italianate and French influence on the British landscape, he was also offering the opportunity for people to admire an art designed to appear artless, while oblivious to what was not on show, for culture deals in exclusions as well as inclusions. His plans involve the destruction of a village and its relocation (something still familiar around the world as master plans require similar sacrifices) and hence the elimination of memories and experiences rooted in place. His brother, Asquith Brown, invokes the painter Claude Lorraine, famous for the Claude Glass, a small tinted mirror that would act as a frame when held up to nature, abstracting the subject from its surroundings. The artist would turn away from the actual scene and address instead the image in the mirror, the colour itself being simplified. So, nature was turned to art by exclusion. It is those exclusions that interest Wallace. A landscape artist, Simone, paints the scene before Brown reconstructs it but places a peasant, who 'represents the fruits of honest labour, a body at one with the natural world',[28] in the distance because 'he didn't pay for this painting' and is 'lucky he makes an appearance at all'. He is, therefore, doubly misrepresented.

Painting, she explains, is 'not about how things are' but 'how we would like them to be' (42). For Wallace, who herself places invented figures in her landscapes, the question is the degree to which such transformations retrieve what is omitted, bring into the foreground those relegated to the margin. As the workers dig the land, to bring about the changes Brown wishes to effect, so they disinter the dead but are instructed to re-bury them because the past is precisely what he wishes to conceal, the more especially because the dead were a villager and his daughter, the latter haunting the play. He wishes to create untroubled pleasure, an apparently natural scene in which no memories will intrude, although his fictional brother, Asquith, observes that the 'simple question is how to make the world stay with us a little while so that we are not alone' (74). While he is bewildered in the present, especially when it comes to sex, his remark surely reflects Wallace's own conviction and one of the reasons for her interest in history. Without the past, we believe ourselves unique. Without the past there is no moral logic to be respected, no acknowledgement of a common bond.

The workers' bodies, once again, carry the marks of the past. Hesp, a village woman, has lost a thumb to pigs while her palm is scarred from cutting meat: 'My mother says our hands, our bodies even, are the history of insults that have been inflicted against them' (45). The landscape of their bodies cannot, like the actual landscape, be reconfigured to eliminate pain.

Wallace's commitment to writing about class is clear. She looks for moments of conflict and resistance. She is not interested in staging victims. What concerns her is those who refuse such a role, albeit at a cost not only in the public world, which they challenge, but the private sphere where relationships are as liable to bear the marks of the labour required to survive. If her work can have a lyrical quality, she insists that the poetry of her work is 'tough' and not 'decorative'. If her language is constructed so, she insists, is all stage language. She looks to art to change people, to be, as she has said of herself, more dangerous citizens.

With *Things of Dry Hours* she turned from the rebellious workers of eighteenth-century England to early 1930s America. It is a play in which two books dominate: the Bible and the *Communist Manifesto*. For Wallace, books have always been central, 'you open them up and there's this entire floating world in there and it can radically change the way you think in seconds . . . pieces of you are no longer the same'.[29] There are, however, those who are too completely committed to the world as it is rather than as it might be, and so it proves here. The play was inspired by her reading of D. G. Kelley's book *Hammer and Hoe* about Alabama Communists during the Depression of the 1930s. The movement largely consisted of poor blacks, most semi-literate and religious, but it also attracted a few whites, including industrial workers who had lost their jobs. This was a time, during the Depression, when the Party seemed to represent possible hope. As Wallace has noted, this is a familiar story when it comes to New York intellectuals. Communism thrived in universities. But there was another struggle, less sophisticated, less acknowledged.

In 1924, the Soviet Comintern instructed the American party to organise African Americans, attacking the NAACP as accommodationist, a class enemy. Organisers were sent into the South, focusing on Birmingham, Alabama, as an industrialised city. They met violent resistance. 1931 saw the scandal of the Scottsboro Boys in Alabama when nine black men were falsely accused of rape and sentenced to death. The Share Croppers Union was doing battle. There was hunger for food and hope alike.

The play takes place in 1932 in a small cabin in Birmingham. Tice Hogan is a preacher and communist, a unit leader of the state party paying his monthly dues of two cents even while unemployed. Those who are working are paid in scrip rather than money, scrip they can only spend in company stores. He is father to a twenty-nine-year-old daughter, Cali, who earns money by taking in washing and refuses to join the Party or engage with his religion. Into their world intrudes the white Corbin Teel, who is looking for temporary sanctuary having, he claims, killed a foreman at Tennessee Coal and Iron. Suspicious of him at first, Tice sets himself to teach the apparently illiterate man the rudiments of communism even as his daughter feels herself drawn to him. At Tice's instruction, Corbin reads out sections from the *Communist Manifesto* (in fact, illiterate, merely remembering them), and Wallace introduces direct quotations as she would in *The Fever Chart*. So, we learn that 'Differences of . . . age and sex have no longer any distinctive social . . . validity for the working class'.[30]

Tice argues that race is a social construction – 'You became a white man' he says to Corbin, 'only 'cause I was said to be coloured . . . the slave trade gave me that definition' (63). If this seems an unlikely analysis from a Party member, beyond the play the Party itself underwent a series of changes, at one moment arguing for a separate black state in the South and at another that race was irrelevant, so that Richard Wright, once embraced, would find himself ousted.

For Tice, words themselves, a secular catechism, are important but 'what's driving those words comes from the motor right here under our feet, what we learned fighting a slave-owning culture with something you could never imagine: spectacular resistance and spirit' (59). Beyond quotations from the *Manifesto*, though, Wallace interleaves factual details (those of the 1930 election campaign among much else) and historical texts (Cali even quoting verbatim from a speech by Communist leader John Owen to be found in *Hammer and Hoe*) as if this earthed the play more completely, gave it a sense of authenticity even as its real authenticity lies in the characters and their interactions, a human immediacy that the enunciation of political theory can serve to blunt unless her point is precisely that texts remain inert until embodied. Indeed, at the end of the play Tice distances himself from both the Bible and the *Manifesto*: 'Take a look at yourselves. You're just damn books' (86). There is certainly an irony given that what happens is that the pupil, who himself has very little interest in the Bible or *Manifesto*, attempts to gain power over the tutor.

For anyone familiar with Richard Wright's short stories, particularly 'Bright and Morning Star', in which a white man betrays Party members, there is an inevitability to the plot as it emerges that Corbin has been sent to discover the names of Party members. In Wright's stories, a man's legs are snapped. In *Things of Dry Hours*, we learn that a man's fingers have been broken one by one, once again the body becoming the site of a social drama.

The betrayal fails because father and daughter prove more resilient and intelligent than Corbin anticipated, although Tice had believed he might change a man he suspected of being a traitor because if he could it would prove the fallacy of those who said that 'human nature doesn't change' and 'you can't remake the world' (82). Corbin, given false names rather than those of actual party members, is beaten when he presents them to those who hired him and returns to Tice and Cali looking for help, only to die. Cali, meanwhile, has joined the Party. In an epilogue, Tice, seemingly now dead, looking back asks, 'what lasted?' (91). It is the question Wallace herself poses. She is, though, 'an optimist, an angry optimist . . . The small things we can all do; that's enough for me. I don't look for goals or wins; my history is longer than that'.[31] She has said, 'we can see more about today if we look into the past. That's why I felt it was important to go back to previous struggles about race and class – and the two are always intertwined. It's about a time when people dreamt about a radically different kind of America . . . a commitment to justice that is all too easily dismissed as naïve and utopian today . . . it is not just about the particular struggles out there – we need to be involved in some kind of resistance to oppression in order to maintain our humanity within a brutal system'.[32]

The play was originally produced by the Pittsburgh Public Theatre in 2004, opening three years later in England at Manchester's Royal Exchange Theatre. It was dismissed by Charles Isherwood in the *New York Times* as 'static, lifeless and achingly literary',[33] while the *Socialist Worker* found it a 'stunning piece of radical theatre'.[34] The divergent responses can hardly have come as a surprise to her.

From eighteenth-century England and 1930s Alabama to twenty-first century Palestine can seem more than something of a jump, but the question remains power – who wields it, who suffers from it, what forms it takes. In some ways her trilogy, *The Fever Chart: Three Visions of the Middle East* (2008), takes us back to the world of *In the Heart of America* in that it is about war, as is her ten-minute play *One Short Sleepe*. The plays that make up the triptych were produced separately over a period of five years, the first commissioned by the Scottish radical group, 7:84 (7 percent of the population of the United Kingdom own 84 percent of the wealth), originally founded by John McGath, the second written for the Hot Bed Theatre Festival in Cambridge and the third for the McCarter Theatre in Princeton.

There could hardly be a more contentious, divisive, intimidating subject than the relations between the Palestinians and the Israelis, more especially in the United States where politicians are required to declare unequivocal support for Israel even as they are aware of the tinder box that is the Middle East. Wallace, though, is interested in entering the story obliquely. These are, after all, visions and by now audiences were likely to be attuned to characters who have a spectral existence, although the plays are based on true events, albeit seen through a prism. In *Vision One: A State of Innocence*, written as a response to 9/11, we are seemingly in a zoo. The apparent keeper is Yuval, a twenty-seven-year-old Israeli soldier who nonetheless is aware that 'Something is wrong with this zoo.'[35] The animals appear to shed parts of themselves only to be reconstructed. In reality, and in response to the killing of seven Israeli soldiers in Rafah, Israeli tanks destroyed Rafah's zoo in the Gaza Strip in 2004, killing animals, crushing tortoises under tank treads. It had been a place that had been a resource for children. Forty people were killed in the assault, including two children shot in the head by an Israeli sniper, and forty-five buildings destroyed. But the setting for Wallace's play is only 'something like a zoo . . . a space that once dreamed it was a zoo'.

Into this space comes Um Hisham Qishta, a Palestinian woman from Rafah, and although she and Yuval engage in conversation, they frequently fail to look directly at one another, occupying their own psychological no less than political realities. He accuses her of wanting to throw him into the sea, to which she replies, 'I just might. But I can't get to the sea. Seventeen and a half check points keep me from it' (9). A third character, an Israeli architect, Shlomo, is literally charged with constructing the nation as his buildings in the settlements are destroying another nation, that of Palestine. Once again, Wallace drops information into their conversations as if this were a blend of myth and Living Newspaper. So we are informed of the origin of Tel Aviv (the Hebrew title of Theodore Herzl's novel *Altneuland*) while Shlomo quotes verbatim from Ariel Sharon before he was prime minister: 'Move, run and grab as many hilltops as you can to enlarge the Jewish settlements because everything we take now will stay ours . . . everything we don't grab will go to them' (14). Quotations from Plato are invoked.

Um Hisham's account of the attack on the zoo is an accurate description of the actual event: 'you and your buddies crushed the rest of the zoo. The ostrich was flattened, as were the squirrels, goats and kangaroos. The single deer lay on her side all night, paddling with her broken legs as though she were swimming . . . The only place for children to go to touch animals and hear their sounds.' This is a virtual transcription of contemporary reports. As in *In the Heart of America*, the characters discuss the precise nature of the weaponry deployed as if facts have an immutable power (17).

Yet none of the characters are what they seem, or they are more than they seem. Shlomo, supposedly in his fifties, claims to be in his nineties with a past reaching back into Europe. He can smell destruction. Slowly, it emerges that Um Hisham's daughter had been shot by an Israeli sniper and that Yuval himself is dead, shot in like manner at her home, a home subsequently destroyed in revenge. He and Um Hisham come together because they share something, no matter how divided from one another they are. She had cradled him on his death, singing to him. The first section of the play ends as they re-enact his death.

Vision Two takes place in the waiting room of a West Jerusalem medical clinic, although this is not, a direction indicates, 'realistic'. Mouri Kamal, a Palestinian, confronts Tanya Langer, an Israeli. A third character, Sami, an Israeli of Moroccan descent, is a cleaner.

This time the connection between two people from different sides of a divide is physical as we learn that Tanya, as a result of a transplant (she has cystic fibrosis), carries the lungs of Kamal's son, shot twice by Israeli soldiers, the bullets carving out half of his brain.

This is a play (based on a true story) that literally embodies Wallace's sense that we inhabit one another – that, whatever the divisions, there is a level on which human instincts survive, that we breathe the same air, no matter how contaminated that air may be by calculated aggression, and breath becomes an image in this and other of her plays. She herself has said that she is a citizen of empire and 'was born and raised in the belly of this beast, in all its myriad forms . . . Because somehow the beast still gets inside us. Somehow it takes up residence, leaves its residue, in our most intimate thoughts, our most personal actions. How to write with that? Against that? Sometimes, how to write against our own minds.'[36] She speaks out of that belly, as the dead boy 'speaks' out of Tanya, controlling her breathing. Tanya's body does not reject the transplanted lungs because there is a level at which they are compatible, and not merely in medical terms. Mouri, meanwhile, is not only a father seeking out the remnants of his dead son. He hears future and present, knows more of Tanya than he could by normal means. The second section of the play ends with Tanya following Mourid's breathing lessons, breathing in unison. *Vision Two* has a subtitle: 'Between This Breath and You.'

Vision Three, subtitled *The Retreating World*, written at the request of the McCarter that she should write a ghost play, was a response to the ten-year embargo against Iraq. It is a monologue by an Iraqi pigeon fancier. In 1991, he had served in Saddam's army as bombs 'incinerated every living thing' (61). Attempting to surrender to the Americans, his fellow soldiers are shot with an anti-tank missiles as he is struck by a bullet. With the end of the war, he had been forced to sell his pigeons and books, including Arabic and English-language copies of Shakespeare, to buy prescription drugs prohibited by the embargo, children dying around him. His world spirals down. He no longer has books to read or pencils with which to write. He itemises the weight of bombs that have fallen, along with their types, this by now being a familiar trope as if these names haunted Wallace. He and his fellow Iraqis have been reduced to ghosts, haunting their own lives. Other troops are buried alive by bulldozers. The play ends with the rattle of bones.

In 2008, at the Humana Festival, she added a brief ten-minute play, *One Short Sleepe*, featuring a monologue by a Lebanese man who is first seen digging a grave and who describes the messages dropped by aircraft taking off from Tel Aviv and Haifa, warning everyone to leave the area, but not in time to prevent his father and sister being killed by cluster bombs built in Nevada, Wisconsin or Indiana, indeed not in time to prevent his own death, this being yet another of Wallace's characters who speaks to us from beyond death as do characters in a thirty-minute play, *No Such Cold Thing*,[37] one of thirteen by different authors on the subject of Afghanistan presented by London's Tricycle Theatre in 2009. It is set in what is described as 'a possible desert' near Kabul and features two teenage girls, Meena and Alya, the former of whom has apparently returned to Afghanistan from England. They discuss the cruelties of the Taliban and the possibility represented by escape even as they encounter an American soldier, Sergio, a Chicano, who wakes convinced he is in Indiana, except that nothing about this is real. Meena has not been in England nor Sergio in America. None of them are alive. Sergio has shot Meena while Alya dies, apparently at the bottom of a well, Sergio being killed by a landmine. Whatever hopes they might have had, no matter their cultural differences, their individual needs, their stories end here in a possible desert, casualties of a war but also of the narratives, the myths, in which they are trapped.

These are plays written out of anger. Are they more than polemics, identifying those guilty of crimes, giving voice to those whose deaths would have rendered them mute unless given eloquence by Wallace? They are, to be sure, about loss and even love and are not devoid of a certain humour, but there is clearly a desire to bear witness, to record more permanently what had otherwise appeared briefly in newspaper accounts. This is a theatre of action and reflection aimed at transformation. At times the plays seems to bring the real on stage, actual events retrieved from a news cycle that has revolved too many times to be recalled. Yet her strategy is to lift these moments from their particularity in search of some underlying pattern, to explore what it is that links those otherwise separated by actions seemingly too absolute to be demystified, interrogated for their component elements.

Death, in these plays, is not personal. It is delivered by distant aircraft, by invisible snipers, those in tanks and bulldozers. There is no space for tragedy, rather as Hemingway remarked of those killed in the First World War by shells while eating macaroni. There is, to be sure, a politics but the risk is that there can seem an inevitability as if the gods were punishing those who can do no more than articulate their suffering, doing so, moreover, as spectral presences. Those who issue the orders are remote, to be acknowledged only in quotation, seen only through the consequences of decisions whose nuances, if such there are, remain closed to us.

It is not that there are those who act and those who suffer. There is more than one kind of guilt, more than one kind of trauma. Death may be one-sided but it has a common denominator. Clearly, Wallace aligns herself with those lacking immunity. She turns, after all, to a conflict that is asymmetrical when it comes to power. It could hardly be otherwise. She does, however, ask whether it is always clear that anyone, finally, is immune in that the damage done spreads out from the moment a child is killed as she plays with a spider, when animals or people are crushed by tanks. There is no containing force.

It was anger that fuelled Arthur Miller's *The Crucible*, a desire to rush the news out. He gained control of his material by a spatial displacement. The witch-hunts of 1950s America were best seen through the lens of 1692. Wallace attempts something similar by lifting her characters out of time altogether, allowing them to see with a clarity denied by the moment, their anger not diminished or allayed but seen from a different perspective.

There was anger, too, behind her next play, *The Hard Weather Boating Party* (2009), written for and set in Louisville. It differed from her earlier work, however, in seeming a cross between David Mamet's *American Buffalo* and Tracy Letts's *Bug*, that is to say it features a failed robbery and an apocalyptic vision. It is set in Rubbertown, a neighbourhood of Louisville that is home to eleven chemical plants, including American Synthetic Rubber, along with Borden Chemical and DuPont Dow, notorious for spilling pollution into the environment leading to health problems for those in the vicinity. This, in turn, led to the 2005 Strategic Toxic Air Reduction Program, but Louisville still comes fourth in the country for the emission of toxic chemicals and there continue to be the odd explosion and what are called shelter-in-place advisories. That apocalyptic tone is captured in Wallace's play in which three men gather in a seedy motel room to plan a robbery murder.

They are led by Standon Vance, a member of management, and include the Latino Lex Nadal and African-American Coyle Forester. It slowly emerges that all are suffering from their time in the plant, Lex coughing up phlegm that smokes or glows while Coyle has difficulty with his limbs, his feet at one time smouldering: 'It took years on that work floor to happen. First I lost the memory of my feet . . . Then I lost the memory in my hands. The feel of water. Gone.'[38] Standon is similarly afflicted. They itemise their complaints and how they acquired them, but the damage extends beyond them. The whole city seems to be suffering, slowly falling apart. What appears to be snow falling on the roofs and sidewalks is actually pollution from the smoke stacks. Spring no longer comes to Rubbertown as the trees are blighted. There is a crack in the motel floor that in the course of the play gradually widens.

It was not, she insisted, an environmental play but one about the poisoning of bodies in the very place people live and love, although that sounds very like an environmental play. The proposed murder is an act of revenge on the man who came in 'as top manager, fresh out of Princeton' and who makes 'the shareholders money . . . Wages capped . . . Unions out'.[39] The murder is to be sweetened by stealing his money. They fail in both respects, their challenge futile. They end up turning against one another, killing Standon at his request as he recites lines from Sir Philip Sydney's 'Ye Goat-herd Gods'. A verse from the same poem, not quoted, reads:

> Meseems I see a filthy cloudy evening
> As soon as sun begins to climb the mountains;
> Meseems I feel a noisome scent, the morning
> When I do smell the flowers of these valleys;
> Meseems I hear, when I do hear sweet music,
> The dreadful cries of murdered men in forests.

The Hard Weather Boating Party is a dark comedy featuring three men whose lives and relationships have been blighted and have nothing in common with one another beyond their situation. Coyle is prone to quote Gerard Manley Hopkins and, with Staddon, George Herbert, while the irresponsible Lex can improvise a song. There are moments when their bravado is stripped away and they are revealed in their vulnerability, their absurdity momentarily laid aside. Meanwhile, strange things are happening. Water is beginning to well up, filling a drawer, until finally the floor of the motel room opens and the hull of a boat appears, a 1960s speedboat, the embodiment of their dream of the freedom they seek but have despaired of finding.

The play got short shrift from Charles Isherwood in the *New York Times* in a review of the Humana Festival of New American Plays. It was, he thought, portentous game-playing, although with some sharply funny dialogue. It certainly had the familiar markers of a Wallace play, combining caustic social observation with vivid imagery. Perhaps it was this that left Isherwood unimpressed. It is not hard to imagine a naturalistic play which would have staged lives shaped by the environment, and elements of this are plainly present, but her approach has always been to find some theatrical correlative that disturbs expectations, to expand the imagination rather than laying stark facts before an audience expected to believe they are in touch with the real because offered a simulation of it.

If *The Hard Weather Boating Party* was written for a particular theatre, *And I and Silence* was commissioned by a company that had a specific remit. Clean Break is a feminist theatre company begun by two women when they were prisoners in Her Majesty's Prison (HMP) Askham Grange in Britain. It was written to tell the stories of women in prison. As part of the process of writing the play, Naomi Wallace, together with Lucy Morrison, head of Artistic Programme, ran a series of playwriting workshops in HMP Morton Hall in 2008. The play opened at the Finborough Theatre in London in May 2011, the same theatre that had produced *The War Boys*.

The play, she has said, was in part inspired by a friendship from her youth and in part by a desire to capture the relationship between two woman in the 1950s, indeed a requirement of the commission was that the characters had to be female because the play was designed to tour women's prisons. It is worth registering the fact that this was not a play immediately designed to reach a general audience, although it would later be staged by Signature Theatre in the season dedicated to her work in 2014–15.

And I and Silence features two women, as in so many of her plays of different racial backgrounds, who find solidarity as they meet in prison and plan a future that both relieves their present and projects possibility and hope. We see them first in 1950, at the age of seventeen, and then in 1959 when they are released and rent a room together. They take menial jobs, still confident that they can rebuild their lives around one another. Sexual assault, however, closes that option while romance proves deceptive. For the most part speeches are brief, exchanges in prison being snatched moments as later they are attenuated in part because their communication is not only verbal. There comes a moment when the younger selves appear alongside their older selves, the gap between hope and disillusionment closed.

There are times when they join in song, echoing similar moments in her earlier plays, times, too, when they act out scenarios, like actors coming together in a necessary mutuality, again a familiar trope in her work. These are the moments of harmony their situation works to disrupt. Their mutual deaths are finally the only way they can stay together, command their own fate, the only freedom available – an echo, perhaps, of Martha Norman's *'night, Mother*. It would be interesting to know what the actual prisoners who formed the initial audiences for the play made of a work that staged the solidarity of two women but projected a future as airless as their own cells.

It was greeted by Charles Isherwood for the *New York Times* as striking a dirge-like note, grim and elliptical, which rather misrepresents a play in which a friendship forged in adversity is touched with a lyrical intensity even as it is conducted in a world that leaves its characters trapped first in a cell and then a small room as they struggle to discover a way to find meaning in necessity. It is true that shades of the prison house do close upon them when once they seem to have escaped their literal imprisonment. Perhaps that is why the reviewer of the *Huffpost Arts and Culture* found it 'doggedly nihilistic'. There is, though, a delicate balance in her work between a desire to resist portraying her characters as no more than victims and her acknowledgement of a system that allows so little room for manoeuvre. *The Hard Weather Boating Party* had ended in a death. So, too, does this play, as if death retrospectively adds significance to everything that precedes it, transforming the social in the direction of the tragic.

Wallace has said that she has never begun a play only to abandon it but confessed that she discarded the whole third act of *The Liquid Plain* and indeed continued to work on it in rehearsal. It was part of a cycle of plays commissioned for their American Revolutions cycle by the Oregon Shakespeare Festival in Ashland, where it was staged in 2013. This was to be a series of plays designed to mark moments of change in American history. It was directed there by the black British actor and playwright Kwame Kwei-Armah as it was two years later where it opened at the Signature Theatre in February 2015.

Explaining its origins, Wallace has said that it was about 'the foundations of this country, the building of wealth, of capitalism, and how it was largely created on the backs of black labor' and that it was prompted by her reading of Marcus Rediker's *The Slave Ship*, an earlier book having inspired the creation of the character of Bune in *One Flea Spare*. It introduced her to the world of former captives, runaways and sailors who inhabited the docks of Rhode Island, a place, she explains, 'of violence and the threat of violence . . . a predatory, ferocious environment with ragged edges that cut at every turn'.[40]

Here different nationalities came together in a trade in human beings, which she likens to the exploitation of labour in today's world marketplace. She wanted, she explained, to reflect that hybridity, the fluidity of a violent world, as she did the resistance to a seemingly implacable system, the play being set in 1791 and 1837. That resistance exists in the play on the level of language, in unlikely alliances, surprising moral stands, a sensuality that may be exploited but is also a key to solidarity. Desire is to be denied, relationships fractured, yet there is a counter-current.

Once again, the human body is the site of conflict, bearing the marks of oppression, even as it is a recourse for those who forge a personal alliance against what is presented as brute fact. It is a play in which low cunning and illegality are weapons, as are subtle skills and shared hopes. As in many of her plays, these are characters whose existence is presumed to serve the interests of others, live lives at a tangent to those who believe themselves the shapers of history but who stake out their own territory, work for principles abnegated in the society from which they are excluded and who slowly shape that society by their refusal to accept what they are told is the given.

When *The Liquid Plain* was staged by the Signature Theatre, several historians whom Wallace herself has invoked responded. For Marcus Rediker, it reflected the fact that the slave trade continues to haunt America, its residue being evident in today's poverty, racialised incarceration and public violence as it captured the multi-ethnic nature of those who built the Atlantic economy based on enslaved workers. For Robin D. G. Kelley, whose

Freedom Dreams: The Black Radical Imagination was another inspiration for Wallace, it was a 'magnificent play' that offered an 'understanding of, and sensitivity to, how the system of slavery pulled everyone into its bloody fold . . . She grasped immediately what most historian have yet to understand – that slaves only existed in the white imagination, and that Africans refused to become slaves'[41] even as everyone was bonded together by the system.

The Liquid Plain opens at Bristol, Rhode Island, on a dock where Dembi, born into slavery, and Adjua, ostensibly a man born in West Africa, drag what they take to be a drowned white man called Cranston from the water to rob him of his clothes. As it turns out, he is not dead and, a sailor, had spoken out against the killing of a slave on board the ship on which he served, a woman who turns out to have been Adjua's sister, whose spirit haunts the play, another of Wallace's accusing ghosts. Dembi and Adjua have been saving what little they could to return to Africa and when they are joined by Balthazar, an Irishman who had been paid to kill Cranston, and Liverpool Joe, a black sailor, they set sail. When Adjua announces that she is pregnant, however, Dembi stabs her, aware that the child must be Cranston's because, although dressed as a man, she is a woman.

The action then moves on forty-six years. Bristol, Adjua's daughter, returns looking for the person she assumes to be her father, although she has heard he is dead. We learn that she has been raised by Liverpool Joe and Balthazar who had told her that Dembi had saved rather than killed her mother. What follows is a vision of her aunt's death at sea.

The final act begins in the home of Senator De Wolf, the man who had paid to have Cranston drowned and who had financed eighty-eight voyages that transported ten thousand Africans (a figure, incidentally, based on the real James De Wolfe). He still owns plantations and is, he admits to Bristol, the man who 'made all that's formed you' (88). In particular, he was the captain who had ordered the death of Adjua's sister, strapped tight to a chair whose loss mattered more to him than the woman it carried to the depths. Bristol comes to kill him but forebears, his death being shifted from the literal into the symbolic. Cranston, who now runs a nearby inn, had always been infected by a worm. It finally escapes him as he uses the knife she had readied for assassination. That same worm, then emerges from a painting of utopia the senator has on his wall and invades him.

As for Dembi, required to wear a dress until escaping, he has learned that 'being is not what you're born, not about what you seem or speak. Who you are is what you carry . . . no one make Dembi. Dembi, he make himself' (96), the pronoun itself being a claim of autonomy. Bristol finally accepts him as her father. The play ends as the spirits of Adjua, Balthazar, Joe and Cranston appear as their younger selves, and we hear the sound of sails as they catch the wind. Bristol is freed of her nightmares, knowing, now, who she is. She was not 'made' by De Wolf but is her own invention.

Like her other plays, *The Liquid Plain* is scarcely realistic. As the lights come up at the beginning of the play THE SHADOW sprinkles powder around the stage. It is haunted by more than one ghost, including that of William Blake. Scenes are introduced with projected texts, sound is liable to be distorted, characters turn to verse or song, sets not simply the context for action. The worm that infects Cranston infects society and can only be slowly extracted. A play of metaphors is itself a metaphor, the slave trade standing for international trade and its human costs, for the loss of self, the scars left by dereliction, the assault on feeling, emotion. The play's second part is set when slave trading was illegal but slavery not. Now slavery, at least in America, has passed into history, but its contaminating residue has not. Once again, Wallace turns to the past because it is unfinished business even as a journey is under way.

It was not embraced by New York's critics. For Charles Isherwood in the *New York Times*, it was soggy and convoluted. The *New York Theatre Guide* thought it lacking in action and too clever by half, sacrificing story and plot to history lessons. She fared no better in the *New York Post* or *Time Out*, the latter finding it mannered, disjointed and unintentionally mawkish. In truth, Wallace has often found a cold response to her work in the United States but, as she has said, the news she brings is itself not always welcome, more especially her commitment to retrieving a disregarded past or challenging the values and myths of the present. She laces together realism and fantasy, has an urge to educate through having characters quote directly from theorists and poets, not, as in *Long Day's Journey into Night*, as a means of side-stepping the moment but as a way of earthing her fictions. Her characters bend language in the direction of the poetic, deploy a vocabulary not immediately accessible even as it forges a connection between her characters. As American artist Doug Aitken said, 'I don't separate social and political work as different from any other art. The value of any art is to be curious and to forge new languages and questions.'[42] That, in essence, would seem to be Naomi Wallace's position.

Her next play, though, would turn to the present and the darkness that can lie at the heart of personal relations. *Night Is a Room* (2015), which Wallace claimed was based on a true story and concluded the Signature Theatre season devoted to her work, is set in England. The title comes from a William Carlos Williams poem: 'Night is a room / darkened for lovers', a poem in which a woman is 'perhaps vomiting, perhaps laboring' to give birth to her tenth child and doing so in 'misery', though the narrator watches 'with compassion'. *Night Is a Room* features a seemingly happy couple, Liana and Marcus, content in every way, the latter on the verge of his fortieth birthday. As a surprise, she decides to reunite him with his birth mother, Doré, a cleaning lady who, at age fifteen, had given him up for adoption. It turns out not to be such a good idea.

Liana is a successful and elegant advertising executive, while Doré lacks any trace of elegance but is intelligent and possesses an inner strength. Two worlds, two classes come together, the former stylish, at times condescending, the latter blunt, direct, although their exchanges are not without humour even as there are subtle warnings of what lies ahead. No sooner is this family re-assembled than it is disassembled, love proving dangerous as a taboo is broken. More than one critic noted the Greek theatre's fascination with incest as a marker for social collapse and tragedy alike, and here moments of overt sexuality and violence leave emotional detritus as eventually the two women reverse roles.

When Doré appears in their apartment, she calls Marcus by the name she had originally given him and announces that he will be leaving with her and not returning. He explains that the arrival of his mother has infused him with a new sense of life. They leave together. Time passes. Liana has now aged. Her home and job have gone. By contrast, Doré is the one who commands her life, as elegant as Liana had once been. It is she who offers the compassion noted in the William Carlos Williams poem, although the two women come into confrontation even as they acknowledge the fact that lives are flawed.

Marcus, as becomes evident, is not what he appeared, although there are hints that make his behaviour not entirely out of character, even as this hardly reduces the shock that drives a play that ends with a dying fall and a sense of resignation as they accept that whoever they have turned out to be, whatever they have turned out to be is what they must now live with.

There is perhaps, as her critics, have often suggested, a certain superfluity, a desire to pull into her work facts and observations which link private lives to wider issues. You can sometimes feel the pressure of her discoveries as if she were eager to share them. Although she is happy to respond to directors and actors when it comes to her texts, there is equally a fierce commitment to their integrity. Her themes and subjects might invite melodrama because they often address situations in which social conflicts assume a melodramatic form, but she largely resists this precisely by her elliptical, metaphoric approach. She is a political writer, but for her the political is as precise as a needlepoint and as wide as God's eye.

Notes

1 Marilyn Cooper, 'David Grossman: The Dissenting Patriot', *Moment*, May-June 2016. www .momentmag.com/david-grossman-dissenting-patriot
2 Vivian Gornick, 'An Exile in America', *New York Times*, 2 March 1997. www.nytimes.com/ 1997/03/02/magazine/an-american-exile-in-america.html?pagewanted=all
3 Alexis Greene, ed., *Women Who Write Plays* (Hanover, 2001), p. 451.
4 Connie Julian, 'Naomi Wallace: Looking for Fire', *Revolutionary Worker*, 14 March 2004. http://revcom.us/a/1232/naomirwinterview.htm
5 Naomi Wallace, *To Dance a Stony Field* (Calstock, 1995), p. 10.
6 Jen Clark, 'The Hauntings of History: An Interview with Naomi Wallace', *Signature Stories*, vol. 9, Summer 2014. https://issuee.com/jdennaclarkembrey/docs/signaturestoriesvol9final
7 Connie Julian, 'Naomi Wallace: Looking for Fire'.
8 Ibid.
9 Vivian Gornick, 'An Exile in America'.
10 Jill Taft-Kaufman, 'A TPQ Interview: Tony Kushner on Theatre, Politics, and Culture', Text and Performance Quarterly, vol. 24, no. 1, January 2004, p. 44.
11 Jay Rayner, 'Why Is Nobody Doing the Right Things?', *Observer*, 11 November 2007. www .theguardian.com/stage/2007/nov/11/theatre1
12 Neil LaBute, 'How American Theatre Lost It', *Guardian*, 15 January 2008. www.theguardian .com/world/2008/jan/15/usa.theatre
13 Naomi Wallace, 'Beyond Broadway, American Theatre Is Alive and Kicking Ass', *Guardian*, 18 January 2008. www.theguardian.com/commentisfree/2008/jan/18/usa.theatrenews
14 Connie Julian, 'Naomi Wallace: Looking for Fire'.
15 Christie Evangelisto, 'An Interview with Naomi Wallace'.
16 Ibid.
17 Clare Bailey, 'Make Love, Not War: A Play About Vietnam . . . Written by a Woman', *Independent*, 2 August 1994. www.independent.co.uk/arts-entertainment/theatre-make-love-not-war-a-play-about-vietnam-written-by-a-woman-clare-bayley-meets-the-playwright-1381124 .html
18 Naomi Wallace, 'Let the Right One In', *American Theatre*, January 2013. www.tcgcircle.org/ 2013/03/let-the-right-one-in

19 Quoted in David Lodge, *Lives in Writing* (London, 2014), p. 139.

20 Ibid, p. 139.

21 Naomi Wallace, *Birdy* (London, 1997), pp. 67–8.

22 Ibid, p. v.

23 Ibid.

24 Vivian Gornick, 'An Exile in America'.

25 Naomi Wallace, *In the Heart of America and Other Plays*, p. 74.

26 Anita Gates, 'In Dullsville, Playing Chicken with Life', *New York Times*, 3 July 1999. www
.nytimes.com/1999/07/03/theater/theater-review-in-dullsville-playing-chicken-with-life.html

27 Elizabeth Mahoney, 'Tragedy beneath the Trestle', *Guardian*, 22 February 2001. www
.theguardian.com/stage/2001/feb/22/theatre.artsfeatures2

28 Naomi Wallace, *The Inland Sea* (London, 2002), p. 42.

29 Connie Julian, 'Naomi Wallace: Looking for Fire'.

30 Naomi Wallace, *Things of Dry Hours* (London, 2007), p. 42.

31 Lyn Gardner, 'Enemy Within', *Guardian*, 6 February 2007. www.theguardian.com/culture/
2007/feb/06/lyngardner.features11

32 Lorna Brown, 'Writer Naomi Wallace and Director Raz Shaw on "Things of Dry Hours"',
Socialist Worker, 17 February 2007. https://socialistworker.co.uk/art/10476/Writer+Naomi+
Wallace+and+director+Raz+Shaw+on+Things+Of+Dry+Hours

33 Charles Isherwood, 'Supplying Shelter and the Gospel of Marx', *New York Times*, 8 June 2009.
www.theguardian.com/culture/2007/feb/06/lyngardner.features11

34 Lorna Brown, 'Writer Naomi Wallace and Director Raz Shaw on "Things of Dry Hours"'.

35 Naomi Wallace, *The Fever Chart: Three Visions of the Middle East* (New York, 2009), p. 8.

36 Betty Shamieh, 'The Art of Countering Despair', *Brooklyn Rail*, 6 May 2008. www.brooklynrail
.org/2008/05/theater/the-art-of-countering-despair-naomi-wallace

37 Naomi Wallace, *No Such Cold Thing* (New York, 2016).

38 Naomi Wallace, *The Hard Weather Boating Party* (New York, 2014), p. 58.

39 Ibid, pp. 35–6.

40 Naomi Wallace, *The Liquid Plain* (New York, 2015), p. 2.

41 Nathaniel French, 'A Nautical Interweaving: An Interview with Naomi Wallace', *Signature
Stories*, Spring 2015, p. 17.

42 Doug Aitken, *The Observer: The New Review*, 11 September 2016, p. 10.

Index

7:84, Scottish radical group, 210
9/11 attacks, 73, 184, 199, 211
410 [Gone] (Cowhig), 31–5
4000 Miles (Herzog), 76, 82–5

Abbott, Paul, 12
absurdist theatre, 122
Abu Ghraib prison, 36
Actors Studio, 15
Actors Theatre of Louisville (Kentucky), 3, 146, 198
Afghanistan, 212
After the Revolution (Herzog), 76–7, 78–82
Agamemnon, 55
Ai Weiwei, 41
Aitken, Doug, 218
Albee, Edward, 1, 16, 24, 36, 77, 95, 132, 178–9
Aliens, The (Baker), 17–20, 27
All My Sons (Miller), 74, 94, 201
All the King's Men (Warren), 111
Allen, Joan, 95
Allen, Woody, 92
Als, Hilton, 26, 90
Altneuland (Herzl), 211
American Buffalo (Mamet), 213
American Repertory Theatre (Cambridge, Massachusetts), 49
American Theatre, 48, 200
Amherst, Jeffrey, 7
Ammonites and Leaping Fish (Lively), 115
And I and Silence (Wallace), 215–16
Angels in America (Kushner), 35
Another Country (Baldwin), 198
anti-Semitism, 75, 172, 173, 176
Apple, 42
Arcadia (Stoppard), 75
Archbishop's Ceiling, The (Miller), 143
Arena Stage, 69
Arney, Randy, 95
As You Like It, 49
Atlantic Theatre Company's Stage 2 theatre, 9
August: Osage County (Tracy Letts), 92, 93, 94, 96, 108–13

Baby Food (Lindsay-Abaire), 138
Baker, Annie, 2, 165
   Aliens, The, 17–20
   Body Awareness, 6, 8, 9–12
   Circle Mirror Transformation, 12–16
   creative approach, 6–7
   early life and influences, 7–9
   Flick, The, 6, 7, 20–4
   John, 7, 24–7
   Nocturama, 16–17
   reasons for choosing the theatre world, 27
Baldwin, James, 144, 145, 151, 198, 207
Baltimore Waltz, The (Vogel), 34, 168, 169
Baraka, Amiri, 199
Barrett Browning, Elizabeth, 87–8
Barrow Street Theatre (Greenwich Village), 20
Bass, George, 146
Bassett, Angela, 59
Bates, Alan, 177
Battlestar Galactica, 73
Beckett, Samuel, 20, 51, 123, 169
Behrman, S. N., 188
Belleville (Herzog), 85–7
Bennett, Alan, 93
Bergson, Henri, 127, 129, 167
Berlin Wall, fall of, 75
Bernard B. Jacobs Theatre (New York), 59
Bernstein, Leonard, 173
Berry, Halle, 144
Bevis, Matthew, 178
Bible, 26, 208
Bikindi, Simon, 65
Billington, Michael, 60, 187
Birdy (adaptation by Naomi Wallace), 203–4
Birdy (Wharton), 203
Birthday Party, The (Pinter), 101
Blood Quilt, The (Hall), 50, 54, 69–70
blues music, 49
Boch, Adam, 177
Body Awareness (Baker), 6, 8, 9–12
Bond, Edward, 199, 205
Boston Globe, 54

Braff, Zach, 92
Brantley, Ben, 59, 60, 62, 105, 127, 134, 138
Brecht, Bertolt, 157, 194
Brenton, Howard, 41, 199
Bright Room Called Day, A (Kushner), 49
Brittain, Victoria, 36
Brodsky, Joseph, 116
Broken Glass (Miller), 59
Brooklyn College, 9
Bug (Tracy Letts), 94, 97, 101–5
Bukowski, Charles, 18–19
Buried Child (Shepard), 94
Burnt Out Case, A, 6
Bury the Dead (Irwin Shaw), 74
Bush Theatre (London), 96
Bush, George W., 36, 177
Butterworth, Jezz, 58, 60
By the Way, Meet Vera Stark (Nottage), 161–4

Cage, John, 19
Capability Brown, 207
Cartier-Bresson, Henri, 50
Castillo Theatre (New York), 63
Chang, Leslie, 42
Chekhov, Anton, 9, 20, 87, 168
Cheney, Dick, 36
Cherry Lane Theatre (New York), 49, 50
Chicago Tribune, the, 59, 96
Chicken Soup with Barley (Wesker), 78
Children of Killers (Hall), 62–5
Children's Hour, The (Hellman), 90
Chimerica (Kirkwood), 41
Christiansen, Richard, 96
Churchill, Caryl, 9, 199
Circle Mirror Transformation (Baker), 12–16
Civil Rights movement, 75, 144, 197
Clapp, Susannah, 199
Classical Theatre of Harlem, 52
Cleage, Pearl, 163
Clean Break theatre company (London), 215
Clean House, The (Ruhl), 178–81
Clockwork Orange, A, 94
Cloud Atlas (Mitchell), 180
Clubbed Thumb company, 177
Cocktail Party, The (Eliot), 106, 108
Color Purple, The, 59
Comedy Theatre (London's West End), 203
Commentary, 104
Communist Manifesto, 208
Communist Party, 74
Confidential Clerk, The (Eliot), 106
Conrad, Joseph, 150, 159
Corner, The, 73
Corpse Walker (Liao Yiwu), 45
Corthron, Kia, 199
Coward, Noel, 188

Cowhig, Frances Ya-Chu, 2
410[Gone], 31–5
Chinese and Irish heritage, 29–30
continuing journey, 45–6
early life and influences, 29–30
journey to become a playwright, 30–2
Lidless, 35–41
The World of Extreme Happiness, 41–5
Crazy Eights (Lindsay-Abaire), 138
Crèvecoeur, J. Hector St. John de, 30
Crowded Fire Theater (San Francisco), 35
Crucible, The (Miller), 3, 50, 66, 74, 78, 213
Curious Case of Benjamin Button, The (Fitzgerald), 128
Cusack, Joan, 168
Cusack, John, 168

Dacre, James, 58
Daily News, 60
Daily Telegraph, 41, 45, 59, 188
Dance Theater Workshop (New York), 147
Danger: Memory! (Miller), 143
Darker Side of Verona, The (Nottage), 146
David Callichio Award, 45
Day in the Death of Joe Egg, A (Nichols), 134
Dead Man's Cell Phone (Ruhl), 167, 182–5
Dearslayer, The, 157
Death of a Salesman (Miller), 143, 199
Defoe, Daniel, 204
Delicate Balance, A (Albee), 95
Dell'Arte International School of Physical Theatre (Blue Lake, California), 31
Devil Inside, A (Lindsay-Abaire), 122–3
Dickens, Charles, 115
Dickinson, Emily, 7, 16, 112
Didion, Joan, 114
Dog Play (Ruhl), 169
Donne, John, 15, 182, 185
Dracula Has Risen from the Grave, 93
Drama Desk Awards, 120
Dreiser, Theodore, 62
Drum Theatre, Plymouth, 203
Drusky, Roy, 26
Durang, Christopher, 121, 122
Durrenmatt, Friedrich, 127

Eagleton, Terry, 202
Ecclesiastes, 106
Edgar, David, 199
Edinburgh Festival, 96
Edinburgh Fringe First Award, 46
Ehn, Erik, 62, 199
Eisenberg, Jesse, 92
Elder Statesman, The (Eliot), 108
Eliot, T. S., 95, 106, 109, 111, 112, 121
Elizabeth I (queen), 172, 173
Enemy of the People, An (Ibsen), 74

England, Lynndie, 36
Enron (Prebble), 58, 60
Ensemble Studio Theatre, 9
Esterhazy, Peter, 81
Eurydice (Ruhl), 32, 181–2

Fabulation, or, the Re-Education of Undine (Nottage), 156–7
Factory Girl (Chang), 42
Falling Out of Time (Grossman), 132–3
Family Reunion, The (Eliot), 95, 106, 107, 114
farce, 125–7
fascism, 75
Fausto-Sterling, Anne, 177
feminism, 50
Fever Chart: Three Visions of the Middle East (Wallace), 210–13
Feydeau, Georges, 127
Fitzgerald, F. Scott, 97, 128
Five Star Billionaire (Tash Aw), 41
Flick, The (Baker), 6, 7, 20–4, 27
For a Song and a Hundred Songs (Liao Yiwu), 45
Foreman, Richard, 8
Fornes, Maria Irene, 9, 168, 170, 178
Foxconn, 42
Foxman, Abraham, 173
Frankenstein Must Be Destroyed, 93
Frayn, Michael, 188
Frederick Douglass Creative Arts Center, 52
Freedom Dreams: The Black Radical Imagination (Kelley), 217
Freud, Sigmund, 129
Friday Night Lights, 96
Friedkin, William, 101–2
Frogs (Aristophanes), 178
Frost, Robert, 7, 111
Fry, Stephen, 73
Fuddy Meers (Lindsay-Abaire), 121, 123–5
Fugard, Athol, 74
Fuller, Buckminster, 121

Garcia, Nicole, 85
Gardner, Lyn, 45
Garfield, John, 77
Gate Theatre (London), 105
Gates, Anita, 207
Generation Kill, 73
Gilman, Rebecca, 199
Giovanni's Room (Baldwin), 144
Glass Menagerie, The (Williams), 95, 148
Glengarry, Glen Ross (Mamet), 96, 184
Go On Living (Cowhig), 45
Golden, Thelma, 144
Good People (Lindsay-Abaire), 120, 134–8
Goodman Theatre (Chicago), 41, 45, 178, 188
Gourevitch, Philip, 63
Granted (Herzog), 75

Great God Pan, The (Herzog), 87–90
Great White Way, 120
Greenberg, Richard, 77
Greene, Alexis, 146
Greene, Graham, 6
Greenlaw, Lavinia, 6
Griffith, Trevor, 199
Grossman, David, 117, 132–3, 194
Guantánamo Bay, 36
Guantánamo: Honor Bound to Defend Freedom (Brittain and Slovo), 36
Guardian, The, 27, 41, 48, 59, 60, 187, 207
Guare, John, 1, 3, 75, 127
Guevara, Che, 75
Gullah-Geechee people, 69
Guys and Dolls, 8

Halesworth, Suffolk, England, 35
Hall, Katori, 2, 165
  Children of Killers, 62–5
  early life and influences, 48–50
  Hoodoo Love, 49–52
  Hurt Village, 49, 60–2
  Our Lady of Kibeho, 62, 65–8
  Pussy Valley, 68–9
  range of subjects and styles, 70
  Saturday Night/Sunday Morning, 49, 52–5
  The Blood Quilt, 69–70
  The Mountaintop, 49, 55–60
Hall, Peter, 199
Ham on Rye (Bukowski), 18
Hamilton (Miranda), 2
Hamlet, 8
Hammer and Hoe (Kelley), 209
Hansberry, Lorraine, 60, 199
Hard Weather Boating Party, The (Wallace), 213–15
Hare, David, 36, 197, 199, 205
Harper's Magazine, 102
Harris, Wilson, 147
Hay Fever (Coward), 188
Heart of Darkness (Conrad), 159
Hedley, Glenne, 95
Heideman Award, 146
Hellman, Lillian, 90, 142
Hellzapoppin, 122
Hersh, Seymour, 36
Herzog, Amy, 2
  4000 Miles, 76, 82–5
  After the Revolution, 76–7, 78–82
  Belleville, 85–7
  early life and family influences, 75–8
  family and politics, 77–83
  Great God Pan, The, 87–90
  political influences, 73–5
Herzog, Arthur, Jr., 77
Heston, Charlton, 168

High Fidelity, 120
Hiss, Alger, 74, 75
Hitler, Adolf, 172, 173
Hofstadter, Richard, 102
Hollow Men, The (Eliot), 106, 109
Holocaust, 172
Homecoming, The (Pinter), 95
Homicide: Life on the Street, 73
Honour Bound (Jamieson), 36
Hoodoo Love (Hall), 49–52
Hopper, Edward, 182, 183, 185
Hot Bed Theatre Festival (Cambridge), 210
House Un-American Activities Committee, 77
How We Talk in South Boston (Lindsay-Abaire),
      138
Howe, Tina, 1, 123
Huffpost Arts and Culture, 216
Huisman, Jacques, 15
Hungary (Herzog), 76
Hurston, Zora Neale, 51, 59
Hurt Village (Hall), 49, 60–2
Hurt, William (philanthropist), 60
Husky, Ferlin, 26
Hwang, Henry David, 30
Hytner, Nicholas, 199

Ibsen, Henrik, 74, 201
Iceman Cometh, The (O'Neill), 20
Ilibagiza, Immaculée, 63
In the Heart of America (Wallace), 200–3
In the Heights (Miranda), 2
In the Next Room or the Vibrator Play (Ruhl), 167,
      185–8
In Translation (Herzog), 75
Independent, The, 41, 45, 59
Inland Sea, The (Wallace), 207–8
Intimate Apparel (Nottage), 153–6
Ionesco, Eugène, 121, 123
Iowa Playwrights Workshop, 198
Iraq War, 175, 199
Isherwood, Charles, 20, 45, 63, 67, 82, 85, 87, 187,
      210, 214, 215, 218

Jackson, Glenda, 4
Jackson, Samuel L., 59
James A. Michener Center for Writers, University of
      Texas, Austin, 31
James, Henry, 9, 20
Jamieson, Nigel, 36
Jarrell, Randall, 202
Jenkin, Len, 75
Jerusalem (Butterworth), 58, 60
John (Baker), 7, 17, 24–7
Jones, Chris, 45, 59
Joseph, Julius, 77
Joseph, Lee, 77
Joseph, Rajiv, 74

Juilliard School, The, 49, 121, 123
Jules and Jim, 23
Jungle, The (Sinclair), 205

Kafka, Franz, 140
Kaufman, Moisés, 157
Keene Prize for Literature, 46
Kelley, Robin D. G., 216
Kennedy, Edward, 121
Kennedy, Robert, 55, 121
Kermode, Frank, 114
Killer Joe (Tracy Letts), 94, 95, 96–102
Killer Inside Me, The (Thompson), 99
Killers of Men, 66
Kimberly Akimbo (Lindsay-Abaire), 127–9
King Lear, 4, 134
King, Martin Luther, 48, 55–60
King, Stephen, 99
Kinney, Terry, 95
Kirkwood, Lucy, 41
Kizito, Maria, 199
Kristallnacht, 59
Kushner, Tony, 1, 3, 35, 49, 198–9, 201
Kwei-Armah, Kwame, 216

L'Adversaire (Garcia), 85
La Ronde (Schnitzer), 187
LaBute, Neil, 199
Lahr, John, 59, 62, 168, 169, 187
LaMaMa, 8
Lapine, James, 77
Las Meninas (Nottage), 152–3
Last Kiss, The (Ruhl), 167
Late: A Cowboy Song (Ruhl), 177–8
Law and Order, 49
Lazarus Laughed (O'Neill), 66
LCT3 (Lincoln Center), 85
Lehane, Dennis, 120, 121
Lehrer, Tom, 108
Letts, Tracy, 2, 3
      August: Osage County, 92, 93, 94, 96,
            108–13
      Bug, 94, 101–5
      early life and influences, 93–6
      influence of experience as an actor, 92–3
      Killer Joe, 94, 95, 96–102
      Man from Nebraska, 96, 105–8
      Mary Page Marlowe, 114–17
      Superior Donuts, 113–14
      Scavenger's Daughter, The, 114
Liao Yiwu, 41, 45
Licking Hitler (Hare), 205
Lidless (Cowhig), 35–41
Lindsay-Abaire, David, 2
      Devil Inside, A, 122–3
      Baby Food, 138
      Crazy Eights, 138

creative approach, 120, 139–40
early life and influences, 120–1
Fuddy Meers, 121, 123–5
Good People, 120, 134–8
How We Talk in South Boston, 138
Kimberly Akimbo, 127–9
Mario's House of Italian Cuisine, 121
Rabbit Hole, 120, 129–34
Ripcord, 139–40
Show of Hands, 121
That Other Person, 138–9
Wonder of the World, 125–7
Lion, the Witch and the Wardrobe, The, 48
Liquid Plain, The (Wallace), 216–18
Little Tigers Everywhere, 18
Lively, Penelope, 115, 116
Long Day's Journey into Night (O'Neill), 94, 111, 132, 199
Look Back in Anger (Osborne), 129
Lorraine, Claude, 208
Los Angeles Times, 164, 173
Love Is a Dog from Hell (Bukowski), 18
Love Song in Two Voices (Herzog), 76
Lovecraft, H. P., 24

Machete Season, 63
Macy, William H., 9
Madison Repertory Theatre (Wisconsin), 181
Magic Mountain, The, 9
Magritte, René, 180
Mahoney, Elizabeth, 207
Malkovich, John, 95, 113
Mamet, David, 9, 92, 96, 121, 184, 199
Man from Nebraska (Tracy Letts), 96, 105–8
Man Who Faked His Life, The, 85
Manhattan Theatre Club, 16, 41, 45, 123, 139
Mann, Emily, 157, 199
Mann, Thomas, 9
Mao Tse-tung, 75
Mario's House of Italian Cuisine (Lindsay-Abaire), 121
Martin, Steve, 95–6
Marx Brothers, 122, 123
Marx, Karl, 195
Marxism, 75
Mary Page Marlowe (Tracy Letts), 114–17
McCarter Theatre Center, Princeton, 178, 210
McConaughey, Matthew, 100
McCraney, Tarell Alvin, 199
McGrath, John, 210
McGrath, Thomas, 195
Melancholy Play (Ruhl), 168, 170–1
Merchant of Venice, The, 8
Metcalf, Laurie, 95
method acting, 15, 170
Midsummer Night's Dream, A, 168
Mildred Pierce, 148

Miller, Arthur, 1, 3, 4–5, 15, 42, 44, 45, 50, 59, 66, 67, 74, 78, 135, 142–3, 144, 165, 169, 172, 173, 184, 197, 201
Minetta Lane Theatre, Greenwich Village, 73
Minneapolis Mixed Blood Theatre, 68
Miranda, Lin-Manuel, 2, 142
Mishima, Yukio, 31
Mitchell, David, 24, 25, 180
Mitzi E Newhouse Theater, Lincoln Center, 85
Mnouchkine, Ariane, 31
Molière, 92
Montoya, Richard, 199
Morrison, Lucy, 215
Morrison, Toni, 145
Mother Courage (Brecht), 157
Mountaintop, The (Hall), 49, 55–60
Mr. Peters' Connections (Miller), 143
Mud, River, Stone (Nottage), 150–2
Mukangango, Marie Claire, 66
Mules and Men (Hurston), 52
Murder in the Cathedral, 173
Murdoch, Iris, 153
Murray, Bill, 168
My Name Is Rachel Corrie, 73

Nabokov, Vladimir, 116
National Theatre of Britain, 63, 199
National Theatre's The Shed, 41
Nature and Purpose of the Universe, The (Durang), 122
Nazis, 65
Nelson, Richard, 1, 3, 75
Neruda, Pablo, 107
New York Drama Critics' Circle Awards, 120
New York Magazine, 205
New York Post, 218
New York Theatre Guide, 218
New York Theatre Workshop, 73, 85, 206
New York Times, The, 41, 45, 59, 60, 63, 67, 73, 82, 85, 87, 94, 105, 127, 134, 138, 164, 187, 207, 210, 214, 215, 218
New York Times Outstanding Playwright Award, *The*, 77
New Yorker, The, 26, 36, 59, 62, 63, 90, 168, 187
Newman, John Henry, 26
Next Theatre Lab, 96
Nichols, Peter, 134
Night Is a Room (Wallace), 218–19
'night, Mother (Norman), 215
No Such Cold Thing, 212
No Time for Comedy (Behrman), 188
Nocturama (Baker), 16–17, 20
Noh Plays, 31
Noises Off, 173
Noonan, Polly, 168
Norman, Marsha, 1, 121, 129, 164
Norris, Bruce, 2, 3, 92

Nottage, Lynn, 2, 48, 50, 77
  By the Way, Meet Vera Stark, 161–4
  creative approach, 142–5
  Crumbs from the Table of Joy, 148–50
  Darker Side of Verona, The, 146
  early life and influences, 145–6
  Fabulation, or, the Re-Education of Undine, 156–7
  Intimate Apparel, 153–6
  Las Meninas, 152–3
  Mud, River, Stone, 150–2
  One More River to Cross: A Verbatim Fugue, 145
  Poof!, 146–7
  Por' Knockers, 147
  Ruined, 157–60, 164
  Sweat, 164–5
  Vera Stark, 160–4
Now and on Earth, 99

O'Connor, Flannery, 168
O'Neill, Eugene, 3, 9, 66, 92, 202
Obama, Barack, 40, 48, 56, 109, 144, 163, 165, 194
*Oberammergau: The Troubling Story of the World's
  Most Famous Passion Play* (Shapiro), 172
Obie Awards, 16, 200, 205
Observer, The, 199
Occupy Wall Street movement, 164
Odets, Clifford, 92, 142
Of Mice and Men, 99
Oldest Boy: A Play in Three Ceremonies, The (Ruhl),
  190–1
Olivier Awards, 58, 59
One Flea Spare (Wallace), 204–5
One More River to Cross: A Verbatim Fugue
  (Nottage), 145
One Short Sleepe (Wallace), 210, 212
O'Neill, Eugene, 20
Oprah Book Club, 93
Oregon Shakespeare Festival, Ashland, 216
Orlando (Woolf), 167
Orton, Joe, 122, 127
Osborne, John, 129
Our Lady of Kibeho (Hall), 54, 62, 65–8
*Our Lady of Kibeho: Mary Speaks to the World from
  the Heart of Africa* (Ilibagiza), 63
Our Man in Havana, 6
Our Town, 96, 112
Outer Critics Circle Awards, 120

Palin, Sarah, 109
Pape, Ralph, 95
Paris Review, 49
Parker, Alan, 203
Parks, Suzan-Lori, 49, 199
Passion Play (Ruhl), 167, 168, 169, 171–7
Pendleton, Austin, 95
Permanent Brain Damage, 8
Perry, Tyler, 92

Peter Pan on Her 70th Birthday (Ruhl), 167, 168
Peterloo Poets, 195
Philadelphia Theatre Co., 203
Piano Lesson, The (Wilson), 49
Picasso at the Lapine Agile, 95–6
Piepenbring, Dan, 49
Pinter, Harold, 16, 19, 73, 95, 101, 127, 200
Pirandello, Luigi, 123, 173
Pittsburg Public Theatre, 210
Piven Theatre Workshop, 168
Plain Dealer, The, 87
Playwrights Horizons, New York City, 12, 20, 77, 88,
  182, 188
Poof! (Nottage), 146–7
Por' Knockers (Nottage), 147
Portable Theatre, 36
post-blackness, 144
Prebble, Lucy, 58
Price, The (Miller), 135
Private Lives (Coward), 188
Pryor, Richard, 145
Public Theatre (New York), 31
Pulitzer Prize, 6, 20, 120, 134, 186
Pulp Fiction, 8, 21
Pussy Valley (Hall), 68–9

Quinn, Aidan, 168

Rabbit Hole (Lindsay-Abaire), 120, 129–34
Rabe, David, 1, 74, 199
Raisin in the Sun, A (Hansberry), 49, 61, 155
Ramona Quimby, 75
Rattlestick Playwrights Theater, 17
Ray, James Earl, 58
Reagan, Ronald, 94, 172, 176, 177
Real Presences (Steiner), 64
Rediker, Marcus, 216
Registry Five, 60
Revolutionary Worker, 194
Rice, Condoleeza, 156
Ripcord (Lindsay-Abaire), 139–40
Romand, Jean-Claude, 85
Romeo and Juliet, 168
Rosenberg, Julius, 74, 75
Ross, Herbert, 54
Roth, Philip, 104, 111
Royal Court Theatre (London), 69, 73
Royal Exchange Theatre (Manchester), 210
Royal National Theatre (London), 20
Royal Shakespeare Company, 205
Ruhl, Sarah, 2, 32, 93, 164, 165
  creative approach, 167–8, 191
  Dead Man's Cell Phone, 167, 182–5
  Dog Play, 169
  early life and influences, 168–70
  Eurydice, 181–2
  In the Next Room or the Vibrator Play, 167, 185–8

Late: A Cowboy Son, 177–8
Melancholy Play, 168, 170–1
Passion Play, 167, 168, 169, 171–7
Peter Pan on Her 70th Birthday, 167, 168
Stage Kiss, 185, 188–90
The Clean House, 178–81
The Last Kiss (Ruhl), 167
The Oldest Boy: A Play in Three Ceremonies, 190–1
Ruined (Nottage), 157–60, 164
Rwanda genocide, 62–5, 159

Sackville-West, Vita, 170
Salinger, J. D., 168
Sanders, Bernie, 81, 165, 204
Satie, Eric, 180
Saturday Night/Sunday Morning (Hall), 49, 52–5
Saved (Bond), 205
Say Goodnight Gracie (Pape), 95
Scary Movie, 129
Scavenger's Daughter, The (Tracy Letts), 114
Schomberg Center for Research in Black Culture, 52
Schopenhauer, Arthur, 65
Scream, 122
Second Stage Theatre (New York), 161
Serpico, 93
Sexing the Body: Gender Politics and the Construction of Sexuality (Fausto-Sterling), 178
Shakespeare, William, 92, 180
Shapiro, James, 172, 173, 175
Sharon, Ariel, 211
Shaw, Irwin, 74, 169
Shawn, Wallace, 92
Shelley, Percy Bysshe, 206
Shepard, Sam, 32, 92, 97, 199
Shinn, Christopher, 2, 73–4, 81, 199
Show of Hands, A (Lindsay-Abaire), 121
Shrek the Musical, 120
Shrine of Our Lady of Sorrows, Kibeho, 62
Signature Theatre, 60, 65, 218
Simakis, Andrea, 87
Simon, David, 50
Simon, John, 205
Simon, Neil, 188
Sinclair, Upton, 205
Sinise, Gary, 95
Slade House (Mitchell), 25
Slant Magazine, 138
Slaughter City (Wallace), 205–6
Slave Ship, The (Rediker), 216
Slovo, Gillian, 36, 73
Smith, Ali, 140
Smith, Anna Deavere, 92, 157
Smith, Zadie, 68
Socialist Worker, the, 194, 210
Socratic dialogue, 56
SoHo Rep Writer/Director Lab (New York), 85
Solid Gold Cadillac, The, 94

Soloski, Alexis, 27, 48, 73–4
Something Happened (Hare), 36
Sophocles, 95
Sopranos, The, 73
South Coast Repertory (Costa Mesa, California), 41, 153
Spencer, Charles, 45, 187
Spolin, Viola, 168
Stage Kiss (Ruhl), 185, 188–90
Stanley, Henry, 159
Starz network, 70
Steel Magnolias (Ross), 54
Steinbeck, John, 18
Steiner, George, 64, 65, 67
Steppenwolf Theatre Company (Chicago), 88, 95, 96, 113, 114, 182
Still, Jeff, 94
Stoppard, Tom, 75
Strasberg, Leo, 15
Streamers (Rabe), 74
Streetcar Named Desire, A (Williams), 94, 199
Strindberg, August, 49, 127
Studio Museum of Harlem, 144
Superior Donuts (Tracy Letts), 113–14
Susan Smith Blackburn Prize for women playwrights, 165
Sweat (Nottage), 164–5
Sydney, Philip, 214

Taking Orders, 8
Tale of Two Cities, A (Dickens), 182
Tash Aw, 41
Teachout, Terry, 54, 67, 70, 82, 138
Technology of Orgasm, The, 185
Tectonic Theater Project, 157
Terry, Megan, 168
That Other Person (Lindsay-Abaire), 138–9
theatre attendance figures, 3
Théâtre du Sol, 31
Things of Dry Hours (Wallace), 208–10
Thompson, Jim, 92, 98
Three Sisters, The (Chekhov), 49, 167
Three Tall Women (Albee), 114
Tiananmen Square protests, 29, 45
Time, 87
Time Out, 67, 218
Times, The, 41
Tiny Alice (Albee), 24
Tisch School, 8
Tishomingo Community Theatre, 93
Tony Awards, 120
Tooth of Crime, The (Shepard, Sam), 34
Touré, 144
Trafalgar Studios (London), 41, 58
Traverse Theatre (Edinburgh), 206
Treme, 50, 73
Trestle at Pope Lick Creek, The (Wallace), 206–7

Tricycle Theatre (London), 36, 212
Trilling, Lionel, 173
Tristan Bates Theatre (London), 177
Trump, Donald, 165
Tuskegee experiments, 104
Twain, Mark, 128
Twentieth Century Fox, 121
Two-Way Mirror (Miller), 143
Tyler, Anne, 8

Uncle Vanya, 9
U.S. National Poetry Competition, 195

Variety, 67, 138
Venona Project, 74, 75, 77
Vera Stark (Nottage), 160–4
Versailles, 152
Vidal, Gore, 201
Vietnam War, 58, 75, 175, 197
View from the Bridge, A (Miller), 3
Vineyard Theatre, Manhattan, 147
Visit, The (Durrenmatt), 127
Vogel, Paula, 1, 3, 34, 146, 168, 169, 171

Wagner, Richard, 65
Waiting for Lefty, 74
Wall Street Journal, the, 54, 67, 70, 82, 138
Wallace, George, 58
Wallace, Naomi, 2, 74, 165
    And I and Silence, 215–16
    Birdy adaptation, 203–4
    creative approach, 194–7
    early life and family influences, 197–8
    Fever Chart: Three Visions of the Middle East, 210–13
    In the Heart of America, 200–3
    Night is a Room, 218–19
    One Flea Spare, 204–5
    One Short Sleepe, 210, 212
    political influences, 194–7
    Slaughter City, 205–6
    The Hard Weather Boating Party, 213–15
    The Inland Sea, 207–8
    The Liquid Plain, 216–18
    Things of Dry Hours, 208–10
    Trestle at Pope Lick Creek, The, 206–7
    War Boys, The, 198–200
Wang Shuping, 45
Wantuch, Holly, 96
War Boys, The (Wallace), 198–200
Warren, Robert Penn, 111

Washington Times, The, 37
Wasserstein Prize, 45
Wasserstein, Wendy, 1
Watt (Beckett), 20
Watzfeld, Jean, 63
We Wish to Inform You That Tomorrow We Will Be Killed, 63
Weller, Michael, 74
Wellman, Mac, 9
Welty, Eudora, 168
Wendy Play, The (Herzog), 76
Wesker, Arnold, 78
Wharton, William, 203
WHATDABLOODCLOT!!!, 49
Where the Heart Is (Billie Letts), 93
Whiting Award, 77
Who's Afraid of Post Blackness? What It means to Be Black Now (Touré), 144
Who's Afraid of Virginia Woolf? (Albee), 1, 93, 94, 109, 110, 112, 132
Whorinsky, Kate, 157
Wiesel, Elie, 173
Wilde, Oscar, 7
Williams, Holly, 45
Williams, Tennessee, 3, 92, 142, 169
Williams, William Carlos, 218
Willing (Herzog), 76
Wilson, August, 1, 49, 50, 51, 56, 121, 142, 143, 144, 199
Wilson, Lanford, 1
Wire, The, 73, 121
Wittgenstein, Ludwig, 178
Wolfe, Tom, 50
Women's Project Theatre (New York), 203
Wonder of the World (Lindsay-Abaire), 125–7
Woolf, Virginia, 170
Woolly Mammoth Theatre Company (Washington, DC), 105, 182
Working Playground Inc, 138
World of Extreme Happiness, The (Cowhig), 41–5

Yale Cabaret, 76
Yale Drama Series Award, 45
Yale Repertory Theatre Workshop, 85
Yale School of Drama, 75
Yoruba culture, 69, 152, 156
Yugoslavia, 159

Zinn, Howard, 199
Zoglin, Richard, 87
Zoo Story, The (Albee), 1